Paper Recycling

Strategies, Economics, and Technology

EDITED BY KEN L. PATRICK

A **Pulp & Paper** Focus Book

 Miller Freeman
A MEMBER OF THE UNITED NEWSPAPERS GROUP

San Francisco, Atlanta, Boston, Chicago, Cupertino, New York, Brussels

Other *Pulp & Paper* Focus Books:

Modern Mechanical Pulping
in the Pulp and Paper Industry
edited by Ken L. Patrick

Process Control for Pulp and Paper Mills
edited by Kenneth E. Smith

Trends and Developments in Papermaking
edited by John C. W. Evans

Maintenance Practices in Today's Paper Industry
edited by Ken L. Patrick

Modern Paper Finishing
edited by John C. W. Evans

Also published by Miller Freeman for the pulp and paper industry:

Paper and Paperboard
Manufacturing & Converting Fundamentals
by James E. Kline

Pulp Technology and Treatment for Paper
by James d'A. Clark

Pulp and Paper Dictionary
by John R. Lavigne

An Introduction to Paper Industry Instrumentation
by John R. Lavigne

Instrumentation Applications
for the Pulp and Paper Industry
by John R. Lavigne

International Glossary of Technical Terms
for the Pulp and Paper Industry
edited by Paul D. Van Derveer and Leonard E. Haas

Mastering Management
by Roberta Bhasin

Pulp and Paper North American Factbook

Lockwood-Post's Directory

Pulp and Paper Mill Map

International Pulp & Paper Directory

Pulp & Paper International Factbook

PPI Map of the European Pulp and Paper Industry

PPI Map of the Asian Pacific Rim's Pulp & Paper Mills

Miller Freeman, Inc., 600 Harrison Street, San Francisco, CA 94107
Publishers of *Pulp & Paper* and *Pulp & Paper International* magazines

ISBN: 0-87930-231-3
Printed in the United States of America
Cover photo by Herb Nott & Co. Ltd.
91 92 93 94 95 96   5 4 3 2 1

Printed on recycled paper

CONTENTS

SECTION 5. Pulping, Screening, and Cleaning

SECTION 6. Deinking Technology

SECTION 7. Recycling Mill Expansions and Modernizations

FOREWORD

The recycling of paper and paperboard is not new to the pulp and paper industry. In 1969, for example, the wastepaper utilization rate at U.S. mills was about 23.5%, compared with only 27% in 1989. This approximate 3.5% increase is relatively modest for a 20-year period, particularly considering that public interest in recycling intensified dramatically in the mid-1980s.

Recycling, in fact, is about as old as the papermaking process itself. Paper and paperboard, along with used cloth fibers and other woven goods as well as almost anything that could be shredded into suitable fiber lengths, have been dumped into "pulping vats" since the dawn of modern papermaking technology.

Recycling prior to the 1980s was more or less a matter of economics, and the fact that the U.S. paper industry has been utilizing about a quarter of the available wastepaper for the past quarter century or so means that recycling is basically an economical process. This is especially true in Japan and Europe, where wastepaper recovery rates have traditionally been much higher than in the U.S., although the U.S. does produce and consume more wastepaper overall than any other country.

Denmark and The Netherlands, for instance, are recycling nearly 70% wastepaper into the total fiber furnishes of their paper and paperboard production. These countries are followed closely by Spain at about 62%, the United Kingdom at 58%, and Switzerland at around 50%. A key factor in the lower U.S. rates, some experts claim, has been the overuse of "throwaway" and "disposable" marketing adjectives in this country for at least the past half century. These factors are analyzed by several industry experts in articles throughout this book, especially in Section 3.

In 1990, wastepaper utilization in the U.S. increased significantly, vaulting 6% to a 33.4% recovery rate (or some 29 million tons). Most of this increase occurred in two grade sectors—old newspapers (ONP) and old corrugated containers (OCC). The ONP growth has been spurred by recent and pending legislation in some 25 states mandating that newspaper publishers use newsprint containing various levels (up to 90%) of recycled fiber. Additionally, several new federal laws now provide incentives for the manufacture of recycled newsprint.

The 1990 recovery rate for ONP in the U.S. was 45%, or 13.3 million tons. This easily collected and deinked fiber source is used not only for making recycled newsprint, but also in boxboards, tissue, and other paper and board grades, as well as in molded pulp products (paper plates, egg cartons), cellulostic insulation, packaging materials, etc.

Recovery rates for ONP are expected to exceed 50% by 1995. As rates increase beyond 50%, fiber supply tightens and eventually reaches a plateau. Some industry consultants believe that "recycling hysteria," in particular that brought on by new newsprint legislation of the late 1980s and early 1990s, is premature and may not result in the best use of ONP. For example, some observers feel that recycled newsprint could be more economically produced in certain metropolitan areas of the Northeast, Midwest, and West Coast, while virgin newsprint production remains best concentrated in Canada and perhaps the southeastern U.S., where fiber, water, labor, etc., are more conducive to its manufacture.

Such views, debated in several articles in this book, are at least partially supported by the fact that a high percentage of recent recycled newsprint capacity has been installed at virgin newsprint mills, including both chemical- and mechanical-pulp mills. This recycled capacity has been added primarily to meet recycled newsprint requirements in the 25 or more states with recently passed recycling legislation. Since, in most cases, the extra pulp capacity is not needed or cannot be fully utilized, it is seen by some as an unnecessary capital burden.

OCC recovery rates in 1990 went above 50%, and should continue rising through 1995. This grade will soon be at or near the ceiling of practical recovery (65%-70%), and some temporary spot shortages could begin occurring in the near future. The reason for such extensive recovery and reuse of OCC is that it is easily collected and sorted.

Most corrugated container use is in the business/industrial sector, which for many years has been segregating, bundling, and otherwise preparing OCC for collection by independent haulers and dealers. OCC is quickly and easily recognized for what it is, and even in the residential/public sector it can and is being effectively sorted at the source.

Another factor in the increased use of OCC as well as other wastepaper grades is the basic change in Rule 41 (railroad transportation) and Item 222 (truck cargo) away from bursting strength to compressive strength in corrugated shipping containers. This rule change generally eliminates mandatory basis weight requirements and permits the use of lighter weight boards containing higher percentages of recycled fiber, particularly OCC. Currently, the recycled fiber content for all U.S. containerboard is near 25%, which is expected to increase to at least 35% by 1995. The implications of these changes are detailed in several feature reports in this book.

Wastepaper utilization in tissue increased from 26% in 1970 to about 54% in 1990, a considerable increase over the past two decades. Likewise, utilization of recovered paper bags, old magazines (OMG), and several other paper and board grades have begun increasing in recent years as technical roadblocks have been slowly overcome. Some of the roadblocks for OMG, for example, have included various "stickies" (nonsoluble, difficult-to-disperse binders), ultraviolet cured inks on covers, metal ions in some inks, and an assortment of paper grades (including groundwood) often used together in a single publication.

The development and application of technology that has allowed increased utilization of these grades is examined in Sections 5 and 6, which cover pulping (including screening and cleaning) and deinking technology, respectively. The 10-article section on deinking includes reports on the very latest applied and developing technologies, including washing systems, flotation cells, and the cold dispersion techniques in use at some Japanese tissue mills.

But the greatest challenge, as far as collection, sorting, pulping, and deinking are concerned, is currently the mixed office waste area. Utilization of mixed papers actually declined significantly during the 20-year period (1969-89), from a utilization rate of about 22% to near 11%. This decline is due primarily to sorting and deinking difficulties.

Mixed office wastepapers represent a major potential fiber source for recycled fine papers, once significant processing hurdles are overcome. Currently, millions of tons of mixed papers generated monthly in large metropolitan business centers such as New York, Chicago, and Los Angeles, are being sent primarily to landfill or incineration. Relatively small amounts are being recycled into center plies of certain paperboard grades, and even smaller amounts go into cellulostic insulation and other non-paper and board applications.

Generally, mixed paper collecting and sorting problems begin in the workplace. First, most offices throughout North America generate and/or receive through the mail a wide variety of printing and writing grades containing a mixture of inks. Difficult-to-remove inks such as xerographic and laser-print inks represent perhaps the greatest deinking hurdle. As discussed in Section 6, these inks are thermally fused to electrically static-charged paper and cannot be effectively removed with the same deinking technology used with various offset printing inks, for example.

When a multitude of office wastepapers containing a wide variety of printing inks are collected together at the end of each workday in office buildings, the result is an instant sorting nightmare. Unlike with newspapers, corrugated containers, paper bags, or even old magazines, mixed office waste cannot be recognized specifically for what it is—photocopies, laser printed papers, offset printing, free sheets, groundwood-containing papers, coated papers, etc. Computer printout is perhaps the only easily recognized and sorted office wastepaper.

Unfortunately, most mixed office wastepapers, once in a wastebasket and particularly in large waste receptacles, all seem the same. Sorting is virtually impossible once they are mixed together. Some U.S. corporations have launched programs to sort office papers at the source—just ahead of each worker's wastebasket as well as wastebaskets at photocopiers, laser printers, printing shops, etc.

Some progress is being made in the mixed office wastepaper area as a result of such programs, and deinking technology is being slowly implemented that can efficiently remove toner inks along with other types of printing inks. The ultimate solution, however, may be the development and widespread utilization of inks that are more easily removed than any of those in current use.

Section 7 of this book contains 11 feature articles on recent recycling expansion/modernizations in North America. The recycled grades involved include newsprint, paperboard, tissue, linerboard, market pulp, and fine papers. The recycled fine paper mill is one of only a very few currently using some mixed office wastepapers in their furnishes. As more of the advanced technology and collection and sorting practices detailed in this book are implemented, this list will grow rapidly.

Kenneth L. Patrick
Editor in Chief, *PULP & PAPER*
May 1991

Recycling Capacity and Outlook

The U.S. pulp and paper industry has targeted a 40% wastepaper recovery rate by 1995. This amounts to some 40 million tons, or 50% more paper and paperboard than was collected in 1988. The industry seems to be on track to accomplish this goal, but with capital costs of new capacity continuing to increase rapidly, the 40% rate could become elusive.

This section examines recycling capacity plans on a grade-by-grade basis for the next several years. Deinking projects currently underway and on the drawing board are listed, along with data on specific capital spending and capacity additions by each company and mill. The proliferation of new federal and state laws has played and will continue to play a major role in the paper recycling race. Articles in this section explore developments and pending activities in this legislative arena.

Chapter 1

Recycling Capacity to Increase at Record Rates as Laws Proliferate

The paper industry will have to adjust over the next several years to major changes in markets and technology as public opinion shifts to a preference for recycled products

By DEBRA A. GARCIA, Senior News Editor

As recently as five years ago, wastepaper was considered to be primarily a lower-cost alternative to woodpulp. While it still retains this distinction, some other benefits have been added in recent years. Especially in the U.S., laws are being adopted to encourage consumers to buy more recycled paper and paperboard products. The paper industry has been responding to these market pressures with planned expansions in recycled fiber. In the 1990s, recycling is likely to be one of the most predominant concerns for this industry.

The North American paper industry is planning more than 60 projects involving secondary fiber processing plants, 50% more than a year earlier, according to an October 1989 *Project Report* (Table 1). Projects at paperboard mills remain the most common, but expansions in recycled tissue and newsprint have grown the fastest. Eighteen secondary fiber projects were listed in 1989 for newsprint mills, up from just six a year earlier; 15 projects were planned at tissue mills in 1989 compared with six in 1988.

This report was prepared with the assistance of Jaakko Pöyry Oy, which has recently completed a major multi-client study, "Recycled Fiber, An Underutilized Opportunity."

WASTEPAPER GROWTH. In a special wastepaper survey conducted in November 1988 by the American Paper Institute (API), U.S. papermakers told the U.S. trade association that their future plans would account for a consumption level by 1995 of 31.4 million short tons of wastepaper—mostly old corrugated containers (OCC) and old newspapers (ONP). This means a 50% increase in usage over the 20 million short tons reached in 1988.

API reported in its 1989 Capacity Survey that recycled fiber capacity would grow at twice the rate of woodpulp capacity over the next three years. Consumption of wastepaper in the manufacture of paper and paperboard will rise from an estimated 20.9 million short tons in 1989 to nearly 25 million short tons in 1992 (Tables 2 and 3). This rate of growth will average 6.2% annually through 1992, raising the percentage of wastepaper used by the industry to 27.2% by 1992 from 25.4% in 1989. Woodpulp consumption will drop to 72.8% of fiber supply from 74.6%.

During the first eight years of the 1980s, the paper and board industry's use of wastepaper worldwide grew by 50%, while its dependence on this recycled material source increased steadily, according to Jaakko Pöyry Oy. In its recently released study, "Recycled Fibre, An Underutilized Opportunity," the firm projects that worldwide use of recycled fiber will continue to grow. It expects global consumption of wastepaper to have passed the 100-mil-

Wastepaper processing projects at U.S. and Canadian mills.

Start date	Cost ($ million)	Company, mill site	Additional Information (capacity figures in metric tons)
U.S.			
1989	3.8	Atlas Tissue, Hialeah, Fla.	Tissue expansion with new deinking line sized to accommodate a future third paper machine
1990		Augusta Newsprint, Augusta, Ga.	Install new 90,000-tpy deinking plant
none	—	Bear Island, Ashland, Va.	Install deinking facilities once a pattern of recycling laws and market needs is established
1991	—	Bowater, Calhoun, Tenn.	Build new deinking facility at Bowater Southern newsprint mill
1991	11.0	Champion, Roanoke Rapids, N.C.	Install processing plant for old corrugated containers
1990	148.9	Chesapeake, Menasha, Wis.	New deinking line; part of 80,000-tpy tissue expansion which includes new paper machine
1990	20.0	Chesapeake, West Point, Va.	Replace high-density dispersion and screening equipment in secondary fiber plant to reduce contaminants and improve quality; adds 125,000 tpy to capacity
1989	—	Converters, Rockford, Mich.	Install Black Clawson Lo-density pulping system to upgrade wastepaper cleaning system
1989	4.3	Corrugated Services, Forney, Texas	Expand recycled medium capacity 50%; includes two 34-in. refiners, cleaning equipment
1992	200.0	Daishowa, Stockton, Calif.	Build new 350,000-tpy recycled containerboard mill with state-of-the-art secondary fiber technology; joint venture partner is Trans-Rim Ltd.
none	—	Daishowa, Port Angeles, Wash.	Considering production of directory paper as light as 20 lb with 30% recycled fiber
1988-90	—	Federal Paper Bd., Sprague, Conn.	Stock cleaning upgrade with seven Black Clawson Ultra screens to process ONP, OCC
1991	125.0	Fort Howard, Rincon, Ga.	Fourth recycled tissue machine installation includes fiber processing expansion
1989	62.0	FSC, Alsip, Ill.	New 80,000-tpy recycled tissue mill, with stock preparation system from Bird Escher Wyss
none	20.0	FSC, Alsip, Ill.	Supplement washing system at recycled newsprint mill with flotation to handle new wastepaper grades to be collected for adjacent new tissue mill
1989	0.6	Garden State, Garfield, N.J.	Replace washed news chest agitator; add pulper scavenger system
none	—	Garden State, Northeast U.S.	Studying construction of a greenfield recycled newsprint mill for U.S. northeast
1989	—	Gaylord Container, Antioch, Calif.	Black Clawson stock cleaning and screening system for mill upgrade
1989-91	35.0	Golden State, Pomona, Calif.	Two-year mill upgrade includes washing and screening improvements in deinking plant
none		Golden State, Pomona, Calif.	Studying addition of a new recycled newsprint machine, which would require additional deinking capacity; expanded mill would use up to 400,000 tpy of ONP
none		Great Northern, East Millinocket, Maine	Add 250,000-tpy deinking plant for recycled newsprint production
1989	25.0	Great Southern, Cedar Springs, Ga.	Modifications to boost recycled fiber usage in linerboard by 15,000 tpy
1989	—	Green Bay Pack., Green Bay, Wis.	Expand, modernize secondary fiber system for 350-tpd semichemical medium expansion
1990	—	Green Bay Pack., Morrilton, Ark.	Upgrade secondary fiber system for 350-tpd kraft linerboard expansion program
1989	—	Hyde Park Paper, Hyde Park, Mass.	Restarted idle mill to produce recycled fine papers on one machine
1990	35.0	Inland Container, Newport, Ind.	Recycled medium expansion; includes new pulper, refiners and cleaners for wastepaper
none	—	Intl. Paper, Riegelville, Pa.	Restart 375-tpd recycled containerboard mill; includes modernization of fiber system
1989	26	James River, Green Bay, Wis.	Build a secondary fiber plant to replace some sulfite capacity, adhere to discharge limits
none	—	James River, Halsey, Ore.	Studying a secondary fiber plant to supply tissue and communication paper mills in Halsey, Clatskanie, Ore., and Camas, Wash.
1991	—	Kenaf North Am., Muskogee, Okla.	Build new 750-tpd recycled linerboard mill
1989	150	Kimberly-Clark, Jenks, Okla.	Construct 68,000-tpy tissue mill; furnish will be combination of pulp and recycled fiber
1990	—	Kimberly-Clark, Loudon, Tenn.	Construct new tissue mill, about half the size of Jenks mill; furnish is pulp, recycled fiber
1989	12.5	Longview Fibre, Longview, Wash.	Construct new 300-tpd secondary fiber plant with pulping, screening and cleaning system for OCC from Black Clawson
1991	66.0	MacMillan Bloedel, Pine Hill, Ala.	Containerboard mill modernization includes changes to increase use of recycled fiber
1989	20	Macon Kraft, Macon, Ga.	Expand and modernize wastepaper pulping; part of quality program and liner expansion

Start date	Cost ($ million)	Company, mill site	Additional Information (capacity figures in metric tons)
U.S.			
1991	35.0	Menasha, Otsego, Mich.	Corrugating medium expansion; includes new wastepaper processing system to expand secondary fiber usage form 40% of total furnish to 50%
1990	66.0	Mi Ho Paper, St. Joseph, Mo.	Construct new fine paper mill furnish will be market pulp and recycled fiber
none	—	Mosinee, Cheboygan, Mich.	Install deinking facility at newly purchased mill for tissue expansion
none	480.0	Northampton Pbd, Northampton, Pa.	Proposed 300,000-tpy recycled linerboard mill
1991	300.0	North Pacific, Longview, Wash.	Newsprint expansion; new 180,000-tpy deinking plant will allow production of recycled news, supply 80% of additional fiber for new machine, and 25% of overall mill needs
1989	—	Putney Paper, Putney, Vt.	Install two new Voith Morden pulpers and Sulzer Escher Wyss deinking cells and screening equipment for tissue expansion
1990	14.0	Recycled Paper Board, Clifton, N.J.	Reopen mill to produce 200 to 300 tpd recycled board from up to 400 tpd of wastepaper
none	—	Smurfit, Fernandina Beach, Fla.	Expand secondary fiber facilities for 600-tpd recycled containerboard machine restart
1990	—	Smurfit Newsprint, Newberg, Ore.	Install flotation deinking system to enable use of magazine stock in recycled news furnish
none	—	Smurfit Newsprint, Northeast U.S.	Studying feasibility of building a new 255,000-metric-tpy recycled newsprint mill, to consume 300,000 tpy of wastepaper
1989	—	Smurfit Newsprint, Oregon City, Ore.	Flotation deinking system to enable mill to use magazine stock in recycled new furnish
1989	300.0	Southeast Paper, Dublin, Ga.	Newsprint expansion; includes Black Clawson 1,500-tpd Hydrapulper deinking system with 900 tpd cleaning and screening
1989	18	Stone Container, Uncasville, Conn.	Paper machine rebuild and recycled fiber system upgrade; adds 60,000 tpy medium
none	100	Trans Rim, Dunkirk, N.Y.	Proposed 200,000-tpy recycled containerboard mill, to process 220,000 tpy OCC
1989+	—	Virginia Fibre, Riverville, Va.	Install new 500-tpd Beloit Jones recycled fiber system at medium mill
1989	—	Visy Recycle, Hartford City, Id.	Restart shutdown 3M mill to produce 150 tpd of recycled medium
1991	30.0	Weston, Terre Haute, Ind.	Corrugating medium expansion; includes OCC recycling expansion with new refiners and repulper to improve stock cleaning and processing
Canada (C$ million)			
1989	—	Atlantic Packaging, Whitby, Ont.	New 185,000-tpy recycled newsprint and tissue mill; furnish will be 65,000 tpy of computer printout and ledger for tissue and 165,000 tpy of old newspapers for newsprint
1991	80.0	Balaclava Enterprises, Vancouver, B.C.	New 122,500-tpy market deinked pulp mill
1991	75.0	Canadian Pacific, Thunder Bay, Ont.	Install deinking plant to supply 237,500-tpy recycled newsprint output
1990	20.0	Cascades, East Angus, Que.	Install new 60-tpd deinking plant at boxboard mill to allow use of higher wastepaper grades
1989	30.0	Cascades, Kingsey Falls, Que.	Tissue expansion; includes new deinking line
none	100.0	Cascades/Steinbeis, East Angus, Que, or Niagara Falls, N.Y.	Joint venture to produce 100,000 tpy of recycled computer printout paper from 120,000 tpy of ONP; either location would require a new deinking plant
none	—	Daishowa, Quebec City, Que.	Considering use of recycled fiber in newsprint furnish
none	65.0	Donohue, unspecified location	Build 80,000-tpy deinking plant at Clermont, Que., or Montreal, Que.
none	75.0	Fletcher, undecided location, B.C.	Considering secondary fiber plant for Elk Falls or Crofton; both washing and flotation systems are under study
none	100.0	Fraser, Thorold, Ont.	Studying new 272-tpd deinking plant to boost secondary fiber use from current 23,000 tpy
none	53.0	Kruger, Bromptonville, Que.	Add deinking plant for recycled newsprint production
none	75.0	Mac. Bl., undecided location, B.C.	Build new 200- to 300-tpd deinking plant at Port Alberni or Powell River for recycled news
1991	45.0	Perkins Papers, Candiac, Que.	Tissue expansion with new paper machine, new deinking line
1991+	24.0	Quebec & Ontario, Thorold, Ont.	Convert washing deink plant to flotation and install post refining in flotation
1990	31.0	Scott, Crabtree, Que.	Build new 65-tpd secondary fiber line; boosts recycled fiber capacity to 165 tpd
none	—	Soucy, Riviere-du-Loup, Que.	Install deinking facilities once a pattern of recycling laws and market needs are established
1991	—	Stone-Consolidated, unspecified location	Add deinking at one of its Canadian mills

| Wastepaper grade | 1988 | | 1995 | |
	Actual demand	Recovery rate (%)	Projected demand	Recovery rate (%)
Old newspapers	4.8	34.8%	8.0	51.6%
Corrugated	12.4	51.6	18.8	66.0
Mixed	2.9	13.0	4.1	15.0
Pulp substitutes	3.6	100.0	4.0	100.0
High-grade deinking	2.5	37.0	4.4	50.0
Total	**26.2**	**30.6%**	**39.3**	**38.5%**

Source: Franklin Associates Ltd.

lion-metric-ton mark by 1996 and to reach 130 million metric tons by the end of 2001. the period its forecast covers.

Worldwide. close to 75 million metric tons of recycled fiber were used in paper and paperboard manufacture in 1988. accounting for almost one-third of the total papermaking fiber needs of the industry (Figure 1). In 1989. 27.6 million short tons of wastepaper were collected for recycling in the U.S. Of this, 21.3 million short tons were used by the U.S. paper industry and 6.3 million short tons were exported.

GRADES VARIED AND COMPLEX.

Wastepaper is also referred to as paperstock, secondary fiber, and recyclable paper. Mixed paper, ONP, OCC,

pulp substitutes, and deinking are the five official wastepaper grade categories used by the Dept. of Commerce and are generally accepted by the industry as the key benchmarks for numerous other grades. The Paper Stock Institute of America subdivides these five groups into more than 80 definitive grades with precise specifications that are periodically reviewed and updated.

The grade characteristics are as follows:

• Mixed paper: includes paper of varied quality, often office waste, as well as boxboard cuttings and mill wrappers.

• ONP: includes old newspapers, either collected from households or overissues at newsstands or inplant; also groundwood paper trim.

• OCC: includes used corrugated containers as well as container plant cuttings.

• Pulp substitutes: includes unprinted grades of brown and colored kraft, tabulating cards, white and semibleached sheets and cuttings, and shavings or trim of unprinted grades.

• Deinking: includes the deinking grades of white and colored ledger, computer printout (CPO) paper, coated book and groundwood paper, and bleached sulfate sheets and cuttings.

The demand for recycled fiber worldwide has grown fast—twice as fast as the demand for virgin fiber pulp (5.0% annually vs 2.5% annually during 1970-88), according to Jaakko Pöyry. In the U.S., results of API's 1989 Capacity Survey indicate that the U.S. industry's use of wastepaper will grow twice as fast as its consumption of woodpulp over the next three years, according to Richard E. Storat, API's vice president-economic and financial services.

Projected 1991 U.S. paper industry consumption of wastepaper will reach 23.7 million short tons, according to the latest API survey. Just a year earlier, the same survey results had reflected that consumption would be 23.0 million short tons—a

As more municipalities adopt waste-reduction laws, more households will be separating their recyclables before disposal. (Photo courtesy of Browning-Ferris Industries.)

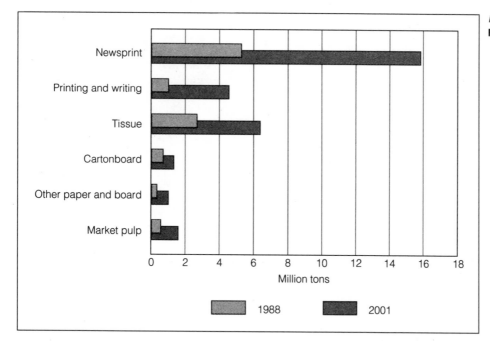

FIGURE 1: **World usage of deinked pulp, 1988 and 2001.**

boost of 714,000 short tons in projected expansions in surveys just one year apart. During the same period, planned 1991 woodpulp consumption is expected to drop by 2.3% to 65.1 million short tons.

LAWS SPUR DEMAND. Improvements in technology, scarcity of virgin fiber, and the incentive of a lower-cost fiber alternative have contributed to the growth in secondary fiber consumption. In recent years, however, environmental issues have been a significant catalyst. In the U.S., the landfill problem has caused lawmakers to look for alternatives, and recycling has proven to be the safest choice politically. The public is generally opposed to alternatives such as siting new landfills and incineration.

Laws preceding these, in the early 1980s, began to attack the solid waste problem by mandating municipal source-separation of recycled materials. A few years later, some of these public programs began to fail when more paper was generated than the market would accept. Now,

legislators have come back to the table with bills to enhance markets that could consume the increasing generation of wastepaper. Legislation on waste reduction has been enacted in about 20 U.S. states, in many municipalities, and is in the pipeline in many more.

Typically, the laws cover source separation, procurement preference, and recycled content in newsprint. These laws include the following: 1) laws requiring consumers of newsprint to use recycled-fiber newsprint for a certain portion of their total requirements (Table 4), 2) federal, state, and municipal procurement policies favoring recycled materials, and 3) mandated source-separation of newspapers by households. This

TABLE 3: **Total U.S. wastepaper consumption, 1988-92 (000 short tons).**

	1988	**1989[1]**	**1990[2]**	**1991[2]**	**1992[2]**
Total all grades	**19,886**	**20,878**	**22,570**	**23,740**	**24,982**
Total paper	**5,650**	**5,960**	**6,596**	**7,087**	**7,397**
Newsprint	1,431	1,498	1,754	1,831	1,965
Printing, writing, and related	1,416	1,447	1,517	1,608	1,635
Packaging and industrial converting	265	253	253	255	259
Tissue	2,538	2,762	3,072	3,393	3,538
Total paperboard	**13,371**	**14,034**	**15,021**	**15,671**	**16,594**
Kraft, bleached, and unbleached	2,042	2,311	2,694	2,830	3,035
Semichemical	1,845	1,935	2,063	2,093	2,294
Recycled corrugating	2,081	2,165	2,343	2,436	2,483
Other recycled	7,403	7,623	7,921	8,312	8,782
Construction paper and board	**885**	**884**	**953**	**982**	**991**

1. Estimated actual consumption.
2. Estimated consumption of full capacity operations.
Source: API Capacity Survey, 1989.

follows a goal set by the Environmental Protection Agency (EPA) for a 25% reduction in solid waste by 1992.

On June 22, 1988, EPA issued the "Guideline for Federal Procurement of Paper and Paper Products Containing Recovered Materials," as required under section 6002 of the Resource Conservation and Recovery Act (RCRA) in an effort to stimulate demand for products made from materials recovered from solid waste. One year later, all of the federal government agencies responsible for procuring paper were required to give preference to recycled products, and state and local governments that purchase $10,000 worth or more using appropriated federal funds must also follow the EPA guidelines (Table 5).

CANADIAN INVESTMENT RISKY.
In Canada, though, there is growing concern that recycled projects may be built more quickly than the supply of wastepaper can be generated. Canada recycles only about 10% of its wastepaper, compared with a U.S.

At the Candian Pulp & Paper Assn.'s (CPPA) annual meeting in January, Howard Hart, CPPA president, projected a shortage of ONP in Canada by the end of this year.

---

recycling rate of about 24%.

At the Canadian Pulp & Paper Assn.'s (CPPA) annual meeting in January, Howard Hart, CPPA president, projected a shortage of ONP in Canada by the end of this year. Hart noted that even if six out of ten old newspapers in Ontario—an estimated 340,000 metric tons—were to be collected for recycling, a short-

age would still exist. Canadian mills would be forced to import the rest—undoubtedly from the U.S. CPPA has moved recycling from its environmental agenda to its economic agenda, noted John Houghton, president of Quebec & Ontario Paper Co. Ltd., which is the only current producer of recycled-content newsprint in Canada.

Reportedly, the Ontario Forest Industries Assn. said the amount of newspapers collected for recycling in Ontario reached 234,000 metric tons in 1988, when Toronto began to recycle. About 190,000 metric tons of ONP are used by Q&O.

Companies in Canada are also more skeptical than those in the U.S. about the long-term benefits of investing in recycled fiber equipment. Besides concerns about possible secondary fiber shortages, they are also uncertain about whether it would be feasible for many Canadian mills to use wastepaper, as these mills tend to be remote from metropolitan areas. Canadian producers have begun asking local and federal agencies for assurances of their commit-

The 1990s will see a trend toward harvesting the urban forests of wastepaper, which are most productive in large metropolitan regions. (Photo courtesy of Jefferson Smurfit Corp.)

ment to recycling and for financial assistance.

Cascades Inc. and Kruger Inc. earlier this year separately postponed plans involving recycling projects, pressuring the government to provide some support. In the meantime, across the border in New York, state officials are offering economic incentives if Cascades decides to go ahead with its plans at Niagara Falls, N.Y.

Still, other Canadian companies are forging ahead with recycled-fiber projects. Canadian Pacific Forest Products Ltd. plans to add deinking at its mills in Gatineau, Que., and Thunder Bay., Ont., and Abitibi-Price Inc. has publicly stated it will build deinking facilities in Canada but has not selected any sites yet.

Kruger wants to build a C$53-million deinking plant adjacent to its newsprint mill in Bromptonville, Que., while Cascades has been looking at several locations for a joint venture with Steinbeis & Consortium GmbH (*P&P*, Nov. 1989, p. 39).

Using the Fed. Rep. Germany company's technology, a 100,000-metric-tpy recycled CPO and copier paper mill would use 100% ONP. Depending on where the mill is constructed, it could cost from C$40 to C$150 million.

Quebec reportedly is looking at a new program to encourage mills to use ONP and old magazines. This could include financial aid for new deinking plants. To qualify, deinking plants would have to draw at least 50% of their raw materials from

U.S. recycled newsprint legislation.

State laws	Fees or credits[2]	Consumption[2] Goal	Timetable	Status
California	Penalties not to exceed $1,000/violation	25% 50%	1/1/91 1/1/2000	Passed
Connecticut		20% 90%	12,31,93 12/31/98	Passed
Florida	10¢/ton tax until 10/92; 50¢/ton if goal not reached	50%	1992	Passed
Illinois				
H.B. 2912:	10¢/ton disposal fee		1991-93	Pending
H.B. 2458:	not to exceed $5,000		1/1/91	Pending
Kentucky		50% 75%	7/16/91 7/15/92	Pending
Louisiana	10¢/ton tax			Failed
Maine	Up to $1,000/violation	20% 90%	12/31/93 12/31/97	Pending
Maryland	$15/ton for every short of goal	12% 40%	1992[3] 1998	Pending
Massachusetts		20% 80%	12/31/93 12/31/97	Pending
Missouri				
H.B. 949:	10% of the cost/ton on virgin newsprint consumed	10% 50%	1992 1996	Pending
S.B. 513:		10% 50%	1993[4] 1997	Pending
Nebraska	$1/ton tax			Failed
New Jersey				
A. 627		45%	1990[4]	Pending
A.B. 4703		45% 90%	12/31/89 1991	Pending
New York				
S.B. 4504:	Paper not meeting requirement not to be sold in state		1991[4]	Pending
S. 6779:	$500 to $1,000/violation	11% 40%	1/1/92 1/1/2000	Pending
N. Carolina	10¢/ton tax			Failed
Oregon	$1/ton tax			Failed
Pennsylvania	2% reduction in state income tax if goal is reached	50%		Pending[4]
Rhode Island				
H.B. 7923:	Restraining order issued	20% 90%	1993 1998	Pending
S.B. 2053:	$20,000/day	10%	1/1/91	Pending
H.B. 8411:		50%	1/1/96	

Quebec. The province's Forestry Act may also be amended to require greater use of not only wastepaper but also woodchips in order to conserve forests.

In Alberta, the provincial Liberal environmental critic Grant Mitchell criticized the provincial government for attracting kraft pulp mills to the province while the North American trend is toward recycling.

In Canada, as in other areas of the world, future growth in recovery rates for wastepaper may not be as promising as it is in the U.S. (Recovery rate is the ratio of recovered fiber collected to paper and board consumed.) Much of what will be needed to meet future growth in world demand for secondary fiber will come from the U.S.

Jaakko Pöyry projects the world-wide recycled fiber utilization rate will increase to 41.0% in 2001 from 32.8% in 1988, assuming global consumption and production of paper and paperboard will grow an average of 2.6% (to 317 million metric tons from 226 million metric tons in 1988). The U.S. utilization rate will grow to 31.3% from 22.8% currently during this period (Table 6). (Utilization rate is the ratio of recycled fiber consumed to paper and board produced.)

WORLD GROWTH TIED TO U.S.

While both Western Europe and Japan will be self-sufficient to a high degree (importing some better qualities mainly to reinforce the strength of the secondary fiber stream), the

State laws	Fees or credits[2]	Consumption[2]		Status
		Goal	Timetable	
S. Dakota	10%/ton cost of virgin newsprint used short	10%	1992	Pending
	of goal	50%	1996	
Vermont				
S.B. 326:		25%	7/1/91	Pending
		90%	7/1/95	
H. 766:	10% of annual newsprint cost or formula based on	25%	7/1/93	Pending
	"consumers recycling index"	10%	1/1/98	Pending
Virginia	10¢/ton tax			Failed
Washington				
S.B. 6338:	Up to $1,000/violation	25%	1/1/92	Pending
		50%	1/1/2000	
H. 2562		10%	1/1/92	Pending
		30%	1/1/2000	
Wisconsin				
S.B. 300:	10% of total annual newsprint cost multiplied by	10%	1991	Pending
	recycling status	50%	1995	
Amendments:	Voluntary compliance	5%	1991[5]	Pending
		20%	2001	
W. Virginia		25%	1/1/93	Pending
		80%	1/1/96	
Federal laws:				
S.B. 1763:	Credits for excess recycled newsprint made	10%	1990	Pending
	are transferable	30%	2000	
S.B. 1764:	Credits for excess recycled newsprint made	10%	1990	Pending
	are transferable	40%	2000	
H.B. ????:	(Esteban Torres, D-Calif.)	2% increase each year		

Note: Does not include preference purchasing provisions for government agencies. Includes states where legislation is most advanced.

1. Fees are generally taxes or penalties on virgin-fiber newsprint consumed. Credits generally apply to recycled-fiber newsprint used, and are usually used to offset taxes/penalties.
2. Applies to amount of total consumption that must be recycled-fiber based, unless otherwise noted. Ranges imply goals to be phased-in between these dates.
3. Goals are aggregate of recycled fiber consumed in proportion to total newsprint consumed by individual publisher.
4. State task force has proposed voluntary guidelines. (New York's proposal is to increase recycled fiber consumption gradually from 7% in 1990 to 40% by 2000. Pennsylvania publishers have agreed to use at least 50% recycled newsprint by 1995.
5. Goals are an aggregate of statewide recycled fiber consumed in proportion to total newsprint consumed. Compromise reached late in 1989 proposes to make all consumption goals voluntary and only applicable when recycled-fiber newsprint is available in the quantity, at the quality, and of competitive price to virgin-fiber newsprint.

Sources: American Newspaper Publishers Assn., American Paper Institute.

Far East, Canada, and Mexico will be major importers of wastepaper—and only the U.S. will have the potential to meet their needs as well as its own growing requirements.

The U.S. is by far the largest exporter of wastepaper, with shipments reaching a record 6.3 million short tons in 1989. Canada, meanwhile, gets most of its paperstock from the U.S., importing approximately 257,000 short tons last year.

API is projecting continued robust growth in U.S. exports of wastepaper for three main reasons. First, the recovery rates in many prime overseas markets are already reaching their limits, such as in Japan, where the collection rate has actually slipped; second, recycled fiber capacity is expanding worldwide; and, finally, U.S. long-fiber wastepaper is actively sought.

Demand for U.S. wastepaper exports could reach 11.0 to 14.2 million short tons by 1995, according to API estimates. This is based on moderate growth in paper and paperboard consumption outside the U.S. through the mid-1990s and the expectation that the weighted average wastepaper recovery rate for all countries except the U.S. edges up only slightly (Table 7).

Jaakko Pöyry expects that activity in U.S. wastepaper exports will include the following: 1) cross-Pa-

TABLE 5: **EPA minimum-content standards on major grades.**

Grade	Recovered materials (%)	Postconsumer recovered materials (%)	Wastepaper (%)
Newsprint	—	40	—
Printing/writing			
Offset printing	—	—	50
Mimeo and duplicator	—	—	50
Stationery	—	—	50
Office paper	—	—	50
Copier paper	—	—	—¹
Envelopes	—	—	50
Form bond	—	—	—¹
Book paper	—	—	50
Bond paper	—	—	50
Ledger	—	—	50
Cover stock	—	—	50
Cotton-fiber paper	25	—	—
Tissue			
Toilet tissue	—	20	—
Toweling	—	40	—
Napkin	—	30	—
Facial tissue	—	5	—
Doilies	—	40	—
Industrial wipes	—	0	—
Unbleached packaging			
Corrugated boxes	—	35	—
Fiber boxes	—	35	—
Kraft bags	—	5	—
Recycled paperboard			
Folding cartons and other	—	80	—
Pad backing	—	90	—

1. EPA found insufficient production of these papers with recycled content to assure adequate competition.
Source: E.H. Pechan & Associates Inc.

cific trade from the U.S., 2) export of ONP (and also, possibly, magazines) from the U.S. to Canada, 3) export of high-quality OCC and deinking grades from the U.S. to Western Europe, and 4) trade within Western Europe and, later, from Western Europe to Eastern Europe.

"To meet total demand, both domestic and export new collection records will be set and the collection system will continue to expand," noted J. Rodney Edwards, vice president of API's paperboard group. API estimates world demand for U.S. wastepaper alone will reach about 40 million short tons by 1995, including the estimated 31.4 million short tons of U.S. consumption and 11 million short tons or more that will be exported from the U.S.

Postconsumer grades will constitute nearly 90% of the incremental tonnage required between 1988 and 1995, according to Franklin Associates Ltd. In a study done for API, the firm estimated that by 1995, the collection limits for ONP and OCC will be close to their maximum limits.

U.S. RECYCLING GOAL: 40%. API announced earlier this year that the U.S. paper industry had set a goal to collect and reuse 40% of total domestic production of paper and paperboard by 1995. Currently, the collection rate is 30%. API projects that the U.S. recovery rate in 1995 will be between 38.5% and 41.7% of new supply, which will generate material approximately in balance with projected demand.

EPA has established a procurement guidelines hotline to answer questions from government agencies, paper mills, merchants, and the public. Copies of the guidelines as well as lists of manufacturers and vendors of recycled paper products that meet EPA recommended standards can be obtained. The number is 703-941-4452.

A report recently released by the New York State Newspaper Recycling Task Force found that a 65% newspaper recycling rate is possible in the U.S. by the year 2000. By that time, New York State publishers say that they will voluntarily use recycled fiber for at least 40% of their total newsprint requirements. This would have a significant effect on Canadian producers, who now supply much of that consumption.

The report, which resulted from several months of study by the state government, newsprint industry representatives, the New York Newspaper Publishers Assn., and Andover International Associates (AIA), was done to find "realistically attainable" levels of recycled newsprint manufacturing capacity and to investigate steps to encourage investment in new or expanded recycled newsprint facilities.

By 1992, under expansion plans announced through late 1989, North American recycled newsprint capacity will increase by approximately 375,000 short tons, which is just 18% of the total newsprint capacity expansions planned at that time. However, several more projects have been announced since the study was released, including those mentioned earlier (Table 8).

The growth in deinking capacity in the coming decade is expected to increase to 40% by 2000 from roughly 7% in 1988 (Table 9). According to figures from New York State's Dept. of Economic Development and AIA, a 65% ONP recycling rate in 2000 would mean that 10.2 million short tons of ONP will be diverted from the solid waste stream. This assumes a U.S. newsprint consumption figure of 15.8 million short tons.

No growth is expected to occur in newsprint consumption between 1988 and 1990. This, combined with the expansion of primarily virgin-fiber newsprint manufacturing capacity through 1992, could have a dampening effect on recycled newsprint expansions through 1995. Depending on the extent to which currently weak newsprint market con-

TABLE 6: **Wastepaper utilization in North America, 1988-2001.**

Grade	Paper and board production 1988	2001	Recycled fiber consumption 1988	2001	Utilization rate (%) 1988	2001
	(million metric tons)					
Newsprint	15.4	19.2	1.5	7.3	9.5	38.0 %
Printing and writing paper	22.7	35.8	1.3	3.4	5.8	9.5
Tissue	5.5	7.0	2.3	3.8	41.6	55.0
Liner and fluting	25.3	33.9	6.2	12.7	24.5	37.5
Cartonboards	7.8	9.3	3.0	3.3	38.4	35.0
Other paper and board	10.0	10.1	5.5	5.5	55.0	55.0
Total	**86.7**	**115.2**	**19.8**	**36.0**	**22.8**	**31.3**

Note: A further 16 million tons of wastepaper will be used in North America by 2001. Liners and fluting medium will use an additional 6.5 million tons and the utilization rate in the corrugating material industry will rise significantly, from 24.5% at present to 37.5%. The use of wastepaper and board will increase in the production of testliner, kraft linerboard and fluting medium. Source: Jaakko Pöyry Oy.

TABLE 7: **U.S. wastepaper exports (million short tons).**

	World paper/board consumption (except U.S.)	World recovery rate (%) (except U.S.)	World wastepaper recovery (except U.S.)	World wastepaper utilization rate (%) (except U.S.)	Potential U.S. exports
Actual					
1986	145.1	33.7%	48.9	53.0	4.1
1988	162.8	35.3	57.5	63.5	6.0
Projected					
1995					
(low)	193.5	36.0	69.7	80.7	11.0
(high)	207.1	36.0	74.6	88.8	14.2
Average growth					
1986-88	5.9		8.4	9.5	21.0
1988-95					
(low)	2.5		2.8	3.5	9.0
(high)	3.5		3.8	4.9	13.1

Source: *Pulp & Paper International*, with projections from American Paper Institute.

TABLE 8: **North American recycled newsprint projects, 1989-91.**

Announced Company	Mill/location	Capacity[1] (metric tons)	Startup	Recycled content (%)
Southeast Paper Mfg. Co.	Dublin, Ga.	215,000[2]	1989	95 to 100
Atlantic Packaging Corp.	Whitby, Ont.	136,100[2]	1990	100
Augusta Newsprint Co.	Augusta, Ga.	90,000[3]	1990	25 to 40+
North Pacific Paper Corp.	Longview, Wash.	230,000[2]	1991	25 to 40+
Canadian Pacific	Thunder Bay, Ont.	100,000[3]	1991	40+
Forest Products Ltd.	Gatineau, Que.	182,500[3]	1991	40+
Bowater Inc.	Calhoun, Tenn.	109,500[3]	1991	40
Stone-Consolidated Inc.	n.a.	n.a.[3]	1991	n.a.
Proposed				
MacMillan Bloedel Inc.	Port Alberni, B.C.	n.a.[3]	n.a.	n.a.
	Powell River, B.C.	n.a.[3]	n.a.	n.a.
Fletcher Challenge Ltd.	Crofton, B.C.	n.a.[3]	n.a.	n.a.
	Elk Falls, B.C.	n.a.[3]	n.a.	n.a.
Kruger Inc.	Bromptonville, Que.	n.a.[3]	n.a.	n.a.
Garden State Paper Co.	Northeast U.S.	n.a.[2]	n.a.	100
Smurfit Newsprint Corp.	Northeast U.S.	255,000[2]	n.a.	50+
	Newberg, Ore.	275,000[2]	n.a.	50+
Balaclava Enterprises	Vancouver, B.C.	122,500[3]	1991	n.a.
Great Northern Paper Co.	East Millinocket, Maine	250,000[3]	n.a.	40
Donahue Inc.	Clermont, Que.	n.a.[3]	n.a.	n.a.
Bear Island Paper Co.	Ashland, Va.	n.a.[3]	n.a.	n.a.
Atlantic Packaging Corp.	Whitby, Ont.	n.a.[2]	n.a.	100

1. Adding deinking capacity does not necessarily mean an increase in papermaking capacity.
2. New paper machines.
3. Deinking to be added to existing mills.

Source: *Pulp & Paper Week.*

ditions will affect growth in ONP use, demand could rise by 39% to 66% during 1988-95 and by 71% to 116% during 1988-2000, according to New York State's report.

PRICE INSTABILITY. Wastepaper prices are determined by a combination of demand and the ease with which supplies can be obtained. The actual relationship is hard to quantify, and it varies with the grade of wastepaper. There are also some important differences between countries. But in principal, the buyers, through their actions, set the price level. Mills are prepared to pay more to generate additional supplies but expect to pay less as their requirements are slowing down.

The main characteristic of wastepaper prices in all countries is their instability. Prices are highly cyclical, and their cycles follow the general paper and board industry; but the important divergence is in terms of price peaks and valleys, with wastepaper prices moving up and down long before paper and board produc-

TABLE 9: **North American newsprint and deinking capacity 1988-2000 (000 short tons).**

	1988 Newsprint	1988 Deinking	1992 Newsprint	1992 Deinking	1995 Newsprint	1995 Deinking	1997 Deinking	2000 Deinking
U.S. (23 mills—1992)								
Northeast	546	220	600	350	828	630		
North Central	180	180	350	250	425	340		
South Atlantic	1,057	220	1,310	450	1,562	785		
Sout Central	2,439	0	3,040	200	3,012	640		
Mountain/Pacific	1,881	592	2,500	750	2,568	820		
Total	**6,102**	**1,212**	**7,800**	**2,000**	**8,395**	**3,215**	**—**	**—**
Deinked as % of total		19.9%		26%		38%		
Canada (40 mills—1992)								
Maritimes	1,894	0	2,100	—	2,100	295		
Quebec	5,140	0	5,860	400	5,900	970		
Ontario	2,080	210	2,480	400	2,405	600		
Western	1,980	0	3,360	200	3,200	420		
Total	**11,094**	**210**	**13,800**	**1,000**	**13,605**	**2,285**	**—**	**—**
Deinked as % of total		1.9%		2%		17%		
Total North America	**17,196**	**1,422**	**21,600**	**3,000**	**22,000**	**5,500**	**6,800**	**9,200**
Deinked as % of total		8.3%		16%[1]		25%	31%	40%

1. Assumes that those mills with deinking facilities are operating at 100% capacity, while the overall industry operating rate will be 87%.
Source: New York State Newspaper Recycling Task Force, Projections from Andover International Associates.

tion takes the same turns. Thus, maintaining supplies of wastepaper is a matter of making prices an incentive to spur collections.

Long term, though, wastepaper prices have been downward in real terms, as has also been the case with market pulp. The highest-quality grades, though, are the exception to this rule in the U.S. Jaakko Pöyry expects that prices for grades such as OCC and high-grade deinking will strengthen relative to other grades and will probably rise in real terms. And prices of ONP and magazines—which will be in abundant supply—will remain depressed, leading more mills to find ways to utilize these grades to a greater degree than they are now.

Overall, though, there is some evidence that prices will be more stable in the future, Jaakko Pöyry notes in its study. Mills will become more involved with the collection of wastepaper through their interests in wastepaper merchants, and new storage systems may reduce price fluctuations.

Throughout the world, wastepaper has common sources and collection systems are largely similar. Basic sources of preconsumer wastepaper are printers and converters. And prime sources of postconsumer wastepaper are retailers, offices, industry, and households.

Preconsumer waste is normally the most valuable, as it is of a largely consistent and often clean quality and is available on a regular basis. Virtually all preconsumer waste is already collected and recycled in the industrialized countries.

Postconsumer waste accounts for the great bulk of all wastepaper collected in every region. The recovery of waste from retailers (principally OCC) is normally quite high, as is the recovery of wastepaper from industry whenever it is suitable for recycling. However, the recovery of office waste is often still low, as is the recovery of household wastepa-

per—despite current progress with source-separation of ONP and magazines in many countries.

How will this growth affect the wastepaper business itself? Its structure is certain to change, projects Jaakko Pöyry. The merchant/packer sector will be rationalized. There will be further integration between mills and merchants. In addition, foreign importers will become more involved in the U.S. market. "But the business will be more attractive than in the past and, hopefully, more stable," its study indicates.

Throughout the world, the wastepaper merchants are at the center of the business—collecting, sorting, packing, and marketing wastepaper. They are supported by many small collectors feeding wastepaper in-

TABLE 10: **Wastepaper prices—major grades ($/short ton, f.o.b. seller's dock, New York).**

	Old newspapers (6)	Corrugated containers (11)	Hard white shavings (30)	Colored ledger (39)
1989				
4Q	$−16.00	$17.50	$355.00	$112.50
3Q	−5.00	20.83	358.33	115.66
2Q	9.16	29.16	358.33	125.00
1Q	17.50	35.00	327.50	127.50
1988				
4Q	35.00	43.33	335.00	119.16
3Q	45.83	55.83	343.33	125.00
2Q	50.00	51.66	323.33	125.00
1Q	58.30	52.50	320.00	122.50
1987				
4Q	55.00	54.17	296.66	112.50
3Q	44.16	70.00	276.66	90.83
2Q	47.50	42.50	276.66	85.83
1Q	40.00	40.00	285.83	78.33
1986				
4Q	25.00	22.50	180.00	79.16
3Q	31.67	45.83	248.33	88.33
2Q	35.00	33.33	210.00	72.50
1Q	30.00	25.00	187.50	72.50
Year-end				
1985	25.00	22.50	180.00	72.50
1984	42.50	37.50	245.00	115.00
1983	42.50	47.50	212.50	112.50
1982	30.00	30.00	200.00	67.50
1981	27.50	27.50	252.50	110.00
1980	45.00	33.00	251.50	127.50

Note: Prices reflect paper and board mill purchase prices, exclusive of delivery charges, and contract rather than premium spot sales. Numbers after each grade correspond to definitions in the current Paper Stock Institute of America Standards & Practices Circular.

Source: *Pulp & Paper Week.*

Overall, though, there is some evidence that prices will be more stable in the future, Jaakko Pöyry notes in its study.

to merchants' yards and by brokers involved in trading wastepaper rather than collecting and packing.

MILL INVOLVEMENT. Paper and board mills, however, are becoming increasingly involved in the wastepaper business through the acquisition of merchants and specific support of independent merchants. The mills are keen to ensure long-term stability of their wastepaper supplies due to increasing competition, especially in better qualities—hence their interest in acquiring merchant operations. At the same time, stronger financial backing for merchants will improve their ability to invest in new storage and sorting facilities in the future, and with greater control by mills, the demand/supply and price aspects of the wastepaper business may stabilize.

Jaakko Pöyry has forecast the following trends in the structure of wastepaper merchanting in North America:

• A limited increase in direct mill ownership of big brokers or merchants in the foreseeable future

• Greater mill involvement with packers—outright control in some cases and special arrangements in other cases

• More foreign buyers will have offices in the U.S., and some could acquire U.S. packers to safeguard their supplies.

• Both municipalities and nontraditional organizations will become more involved with the handling of wastepaper from households.

• Generally, medium-size packers will find life hard and will disappear or be absorbed into bigger groups.

TECHNOLOGY AIDS EXPANSION. Improving technology in the fields of cleaning, deinking, and handling of wastepaper has played an important role in the continuing expansion of wastepaper processing plants and, conversely, can be seen as a major bottleneck for recycled fiber

usage as well. But present development work with fiber fractionation and separation handling of those fiber fractions will, in the long term, bring about economically feasible solutions, according to Jaakko Pöyry.

Up-cycling (use of lower-quality wastepaper for production of high-value-added products) has been the major subject of numerous recent technological research efforts. However, to date it has not advanced far enough to be considered economical compared with uses in applications other than primarily industrial.

Hartwig Geginat, president of the European Paper Institute (EPI) and chairman of the executive board of Feldmühle AG, points out, though, that advances in deinking technology alone should enable wastepaper to be upgraded to qualities that were not available just a few years ago. "This should open up completely new fields of application—in the area of superior hygienic paper, for example," Dr. Geginat noted.

FIGURE 2: **Production costs on a new newsprint mill.**

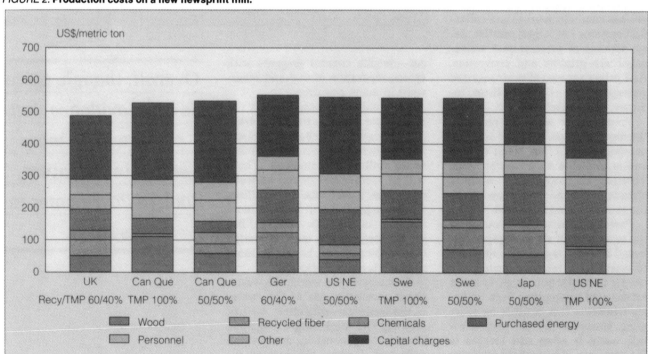

Some key developments in improved secondary fiber processing technology, noted by Jaakko Pöyry, include the following:

• Improvements in stock preparation technology, including deinking, bleaching and fractionation. This is yielding a more homogeneous raw material stock with less impurities and other detrimental particles.

• More technology-driven know how of paper and board mills, enabling them to use specific recycled fiber grades for getting certain properties in end products

• The development of multilayering technology, leading to a more effective use of recycled fiber in different layers of the product, particularly in the manufacture of board and tissue

• Improved runability of the paper machine with a recycled fiber furnish due to modern paper machine technology with closed draws and highly automated process control and measurement, as well as

TABLE 12: **U.S. recycled newsprint mills.**

Company	Mill	Capacity (metric tpy)	Recycled content (%)	Publisher equity (%)
U.S.				
F.S.C. Paper Co.	Alsip, Ill.	121,500	100	—
Garden State Paper Co.	Garfield, N.J.	199,500	100	Media General Inc. (100%)
Golden State Newsprint Co.	Pomona, Calif.	122,500	100	—
Manistique Papers Inc.	Manistique, Mich.	56,000	100	—
North Pacific Paper Corp.	Longview, Wash.	704,000[1]	25[2]	—
Jefferson Smurfit Corp.	Newberg, Ore.	350,000	50	The Times Mirror Co. (20%)
	Oregon City, Ore.	217,000	50	The Times Mirror Co. (20%)
Southeast Paper Manufacturing Co.	Dublin, Ga.	415,000[3]	95	Cox Enterprises Inc. (33⅓%) Knight-Rider Inc. (33⅓%) Media General Inc. (33⅓%)
Stone Container Corp.	Snowflake, Ariz.	264,100	60	—
Canada				
Atlantic Packaging Corp.	Whitby, Ont.	136,100[4]	100	—
Quebec & Ontario Paper Co.	Thorold, Ont.	310,000	55	Tribune Co. (100%)

Sources: Newsprint Information Committee, *Pulp & Paper Week.*

1. Includes new 230,000-tpy machine starting up in late 1991.
2. Estimated net recycled content among mill's three paper machines.
3. Includes new 215,000-tpy machine started September 1989.
4. New 136,100-tpy machine starting up mid-1990.

FIGURE 3: **Production costs and delivery to U.K.**

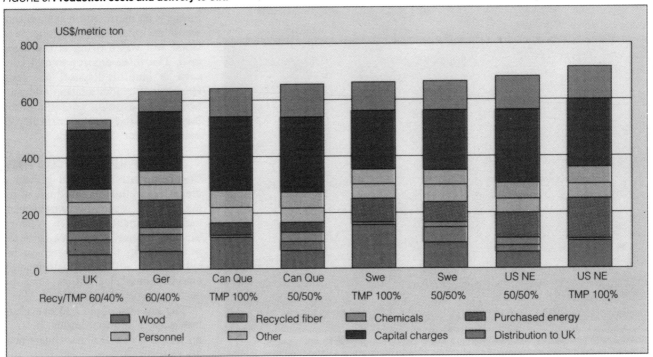

cleaning equipment

• Advances in coating technology and use of pigments. These developments, together with the improved smoothness and surface properties of a recycled-fiber basesheet, will contribute to the increased use of coating, especially in the manufacture of cartonboard.

• Soft-calendering to improve surface properties, especially with a deinked pulp furnish in newsprint manufacture.

Present papermaking technology allows increased use of recycled fiber in standard newsprint (up to 70% without problems in product quality), linerboard and fluting, tissue, and also some cartonboard and packaging paper grades. To a limited extent, the present technology also allows for the use of secondary fiber in uncoated free-sheet grades, coated free-sheet, lightweight coated and supercalendered paper, liquid packaging board, and foodboards.

At Atlantic Packaging Products Ltd.'s Whitby, Ont., mill, a 134,500-metric-tpy newsprint machine that is scheduled to start up late in 1990 is using both washing and flotation in its deinking system. The two-process system is rare in North America (although popular in Europe and Japan) but is becoming the new trend in deinking, as it can process both ONP and coated magazine paper and produce fiber with some beneficial characteristics.

Flotation technology is being used at Smurfit Newsprint Co.'s Oregon City, Ore., mill, Atlantic Packaging's Scarborough, Ont., tissue mill, and Stone Container Corp.'s Snowflake, Ariz., newsprint mill.

HURDLES REMAIN. The primary technical bottlenecks limiting the use of recycled fiber, as specified by Jaakko Pöyry, include the following:

• The high-brightness requirements in printing paper, which make bleaching costs for recycled grades cost-prohibitive. Consumers may have to accept a gray shade.

• The lower-strength properties found in recycled grades. As recycling grows, this will be a problem as stronger fibers will be scarcer.

• The aging and yellowing of recycled grades due to high mechanical pulp content. This will cause more problems in maintaining archives for libraries, etc.

• The higher prevalence of stickies, resulting in greater incidence of mechanical problems on the paper machine. This will, potentially, lower operating efficiencies and raise operating costs.

• Environmental concerns caused by the effluents from deinking, including heavy metals, etc. Costs associated with pollution abatement at these mills can be high.

Wastepaper use and processing has a sound environmental basis. It helps to minimize the amount of solid waste by recycling a portion of it. Some of this can be sorted and handled in such a way as to save forests, water, and energy. However, it also generates environmental problems.

The heavy metals in ink waste, one environmental problem, come from certain printing colors. One solution is to substitute organic colors. A second problem is disposing of deinking waste and other wastepaper processing rejects. A possible solution is an incineration system that would optimize the heat economy of wood and waste firing at the same mill. The third environmental concern is landfill disposal of waste from ash after incineration and possible ground-water contamination. Some deinking waste currently is being used for composting.

WOODPULP VS RECYCLED FIBER. Cost-competitiveness has played a major role in the increased use of recycled fiber, especially in newsprint and tissue manufacture in Western Europe. In North America, though, newsprint production based on recycled fiber will be driven more by environmental legislation than by cost-competitiveness.

The low cost of old and overissue newspapers and magazines, however, would give a U.S. Northeast producer using 50% recycled fiber and

Advances in technology will continue to sustain the strong growth in wastepaper demand in paper and paperboard production. (Photo courtesy of Inland Container Corp.)

Recycling Capacity to Increase

50% thermomechanical pulp (TMP) a production cost advantage of roughly $40/metric ton compared with a 100% TMP-based newsprint producer in the same region, according to Jaakko Pöyry's estimates (Figure 2).

A Canadian producer in Quebec with a very low energy price and reasonable wood costs would have approximately the same production costs with 100% TMP compared with 50% TMP and 50% recycled fiber (imported from the U.S. Northeast) in the newsprint furnish. However, the Quebec producer would be cost-competitive both in the U.S. Northeast markets (against U.S. producers) and in deliveries to the U.K. (against the Swedish producers) with current exchange rates (Figure 3).

The implications of the increased utilization of recycled fiber for paper and board producers throughout the world are many and involve both opportunities and threats. In general terms, the growing use and acceptability of recycled fiber will allow mills to reduce production costs but will involve significant investment in wastepaper handling, cleaning, deinking, and bleaching equipment, which will often be an additional cost. Jaakko Pöyry expects that there will also be an important marketing opportunity in explaining and capitalizing on the environmental benefits of using recycled-fiber-based grades.

With strong growth in demand and a greater interest on the part of its customers in securing supplies of the correct grades, the wastepaper business has a very bright future. The major threat to the business is that of oversupply of certain grades generated by mandatory separation and collection in North America and potentially in Western Europe. If the market becomes oversupply driven, there is a danger of price and structural breakdown.

Growth in wastepaper demand will spur demand for wastepaper processing equipment and chemicals also. Demand for deinking lines will be particularly strong, noted Jaakko Pöyry. By 2001, 31 million metric tons of wastepaper will be deinked globally, up from about 11 million metric tons currently. Improvements in cleaning and fiber upgrading equipment will show strong growth. Equipment manufacturers increasingly will be looking at the consequences of using recycled fiber on paper machines. ■

Chapter 2

Wastepaper Market on Rocky Road: Unusual Conditions Impede Recovery

U.S. wastepaper markets have never experienced the changes and challenges they are presently, while long-term prospects are even more uncertain

By DEBRA A. GARCIA, Senior News Editor

Pick almost any facet of the wastepaper market today, and it will have changed remarkably in the space of just a couple of years. Since the latter part of the 1980s, the business of collecting, sorting, baling, shipping, selling, and consuming wastepaper has undergone drastic adjustments. This has caused an upheaval the industry has never before experienced—and the transition has just begun. In the next decade, the industry will face even more challenges. How it will fare is anyone's guess.

Since 1987, when public recycling programs began to grow in leaps and bounds, the wastepaper business has gone downhill. It was most noticeable in old newspapers (ONP), the grade that municipal curbside recycling programs have been most successful at generating. The price mills pay for No. 6 newsprint, the lowest ONP grade and the one identified with curbside collections, peaked at $60.00/short ton, f.o.b. seller's dock, in New York, N.Y., in late 1987. Since then prices have fallen steadily to their current level of $0.

Recovery of ONP shot up 86% between 1983 and 1990,

according to the American Paper Institute (API). Figures released by API in early 1991 indicated that ONP collections were up about 500,000 short tons in 1990 to a record level of 5.9 million tons. This represents a recovery rate of 45% of the 13.3 million tons of newsprint used in the U.S. in 1990. API expects the recovery rate of ONP to exceed 50% by 1995, when the industry plans to recover 40% of all paper and paperboard it produces. This will mean that total collections will have to increase from the 28.9 million tons reported for 1990 to approximately 40 million tons in 1995.

IS 40% RECOVERY ATTAINABLE BY 1995? Achieving this goal will take not only a 5% annual growth in domestic consumption but also a 10% annual growth in exports, according to Bradley N. Currey, president of Rock-Tenn Corp. "Whether this happens is not all under our control, especially exports," he said.

There's no doubt that domestic consumption is on the rise, particularly for such grades as ONP and old corrugated containers (OCC), but export growth will likely hinge on a number of factors that are not entirely predictable. Presently, for instance, the Persian Gulf war has caused a shortage of steamship containers that has put a significant dent in wastepaper exports this year. Rebuilding Kuwait will continue to put a strain on container availability in the foreseeable future. A drop in exports in 1991, after more than a decade of growth (Figure 1), would not be inconceivable given the container situation, and this could cause a glut of paperstock on the domestic market. Given this scenario, prices would continue to fall, and a number of smaller operators in the wastepaper collection business would fail—possibly impeding progress in raising recovery rates.

For mills gearing up to use increasing quantities of wastepaper, future success depends on securing adequate and reliable sources of good-quality wastepaper. In the past two years, many mills have either acquired firms in the wastepaper collection business; signed agreements with recyclers, such as Laidlaw Inc., to handle paperstock procurement; entered into joint ventures with collection companies; or created their own internal procurement divisions.

FIGURE 1: **U.S. wastepaper recovery, consumption, and exports, 1970-90 (000 short tons).**

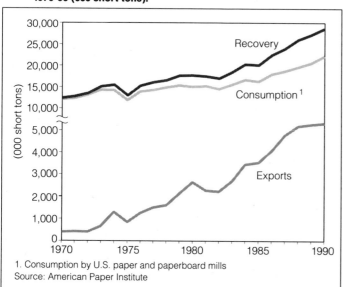

1. Consumption by U.S. paper and paperboard mills
Source: American Paper Institute

OCC SHORTAGES ARE BIG CONCERN. One sector of the paper industry that is most worried about future paperstock shortages appears to be containerboard producers. Shortages of OCC, which is used in producing boxboard, corrugating medium, and linerboard, are likely by the mid-1990s. OCC supplies are tight already even at the current 50%-plus recovery rate, and more capacity to consumer OCC is coming onstream. This situation could change, however, if exports of OCC drop. However, both domestic consumption and exports of OCC are expected to grow in 1991. Future growth in OCC collection, though, could be impeded by contaminants such as hot-melt glues, tar tape, and coated, wax, and film laminates, according to Currey.

The tightness in OCC markets has kept prices relatively firm during the current down cycle for wastepaper. Prices in the New York City region, for instance, have declined only about 50% since they peaked in late 1987 at $70 to $80/ton. This compares with a 100% drop in No. 6 newsprint prices during the same period (Table 1). The amount of OCC consumed by domestic paper and paperboard mills in 1990 reached 10.447 million tons, 46.7% of the total wastepaper consumed. Consumption of other grades within the industry was considerably lower, with ONP being the highest at 4.679 million tons, or 20.9% of the total.

During the period 1990-93, total wastepaper consumption is expected to increase at a pace averaging 7.2%/year, more than twice the growth rate of any other fiber source, according to API. By 1993, wastepaper will comprise 29.3% of all fiber consumed by U.S. mills. According to API's 1990 "Paper, Paperboard, Woodpulp Capacity Survey," wastepaper use by the U.S. paper industry will rise from 20.442 million tons in 1989 to 27.148 million tons in 1993.

Consumption growth will be greatest among the lowest grades of wastepaper. OCC consumption is expected to increase at the rate of 6.3%/year for the period 1989-92, reaching 13.298 million tons in 1993. According to API, capacity for recycled linerboard made exclusively from wastepaper or with a high wastepaper content is expected to increase at a high annual rate of just over 39% to reach 1.453 million tons in 1993. Capacity to produce recycled newsprint, meanwhile, will boost ONP consumption almost 50% between 1990 and 1993. During this period, ONP use will rise 9.4%/year to 5.353 million tons.

MIXED PAPER PROVIDES GREATEST CHALLENGE. Perhaps the grade with the greatest potential but the biggest challenge is mixed paper. This category has always contained grades that were too costly to presort and were therefore sold to mills where bulk rather than appearance was a priority, such as in construction grades, setup boxboard, and the underside of clay-coated folding carton. The growth in office presort programs is helping to unmix mixed papers and allow them to be reclassified as higher grades (ledgers, hard whites, etc.). But quality will remain a problem until better programs can be implemented in offices and other collection centers. This would boost demand for these grades from such users as tissue and printing/writing paper producers. API expects mixed paper use in the paper industry to rise from 2.356 million tons in 1989 to 3.007 million tons in 1993.

Growth trends in the remaining two major categories of wastepaper, high-grade deinking and pulp substitutes, will depend largely on how the issue of postconsumer waste is settled.

Consumer groups are advocating that only paper consumed by the end user and tossed out for disposal should be considered as recycled fiber in recycled-content standards being drafted by local, state, and federal legislators. The paper industry, however, argues that preconsumer waste, which includes discards from industry prior to use by the end user, will end up in the solid waste stream if not reused, making the issue of preconsumer vs postconsumer moot.

API projects that mill use of pulp substitutes will grow from 2.889 million tons in 1989 to 3.318 million tons by 1992, while consumption of high-grade deinking will rise from 1.691 million tons to 2.307 million tons during the same three-year period.

The future of the wastepaper business will depend on the regulations being adopted to govern recycled-content standards and other requirements, technology improvements that will have an impact on the amount and types of wastepaper grades that can be used to produce various grades of paper and paperboard, customers' buying habits dealing with their preference for either recycled or nonrecycled grades of paper and paperboard, the results of the restructuring currently under way as producers and related industries establish their positions in the marketplace, and uncertain factors such as steamship container availability. ■

TABLE 1: **U.S. wastepaper prices for selected grades ($/short ton, f.o.b. seller's dock, New York, N.Y.).**

		No. 6 old newspapers	Old corrugated containers	Hard white shavings	Computer printout (with laser)
1991					
	1Q	$0	$35.00	$248.33	$172.50
1990					
	4Q	−1.33	23.33	266.67	175.83
	3Q	−4.67	20.00	270.00	185.83
	2Q	−1.66	16.66	273.33	211.66
	1Q	−5.00	12.50	308.75	235.00
1989					
	4Q	−16.00	17.50	327.50	255.00
	3Q	−5.00	20.83	358.33	260.83
	2Q	9.16	29.16	358.00	230.83
	1Q	17.50	35.00	355.00	210.00
1988					
	4Q	35.00	43.33	335.00	213.33
	3Q	45.83	55.83	343.33	236.66
	2Q	50.00	51.66	323.33	230.00
	1Q	58.30	52.50	320.00	221.66

Prices are quarterly averages of paper and board mill purchase prices, f.o.b. seller's dock, exclusive of delivery charges, and they represent contract rather than spot or premium sales.

Source: *Pulp & Paper Week, Paper Recycler.*

Chapter 3

New Deinking Projects Proliferate as Industry Meets Recycling Demand

Despite industry downturn and capital spending cuts, North American pulp and paper companies continue to invest in deinking plants

By MARY CORBETT, News Editor

The North American paper industry continues to demonstrate its commitment to using increased amounts of recycled fiber by the abundance of deinking projects planned or proposed to start up in the next couple of years. At least 45 deinking projects will start up in 1991 at new or existing mills, adding 2,879,825 mtpy recycled fiber capacity.

Although many paper companies have cut back on capital spending plans for 1991, they are continuing to invest in secondary fiber projects. This is largely due to legislation requiring increased recycled fiber content in newsprint but also because using secondary fiber is becoming more economically viable and more customers are demanding it in tissue and fine paper as well as newsprint and packaging grades.

Commenting on the American Paper Institute's (API) recent capacity survey, president Red Cavaney said, "The steeper rise in paper and paperboard capacity relative to that of total woodpulp reflects the industry's commitment to the increased use of recovered wastepaper as a papermaking fiber."

DEINKING WASTEPAPER SUPPLY. Demand for old magazines (OMG) for use in deinking is increasing, as improved technology removes processing obstacles, such as dealing with difficult-to-disperse stickies and inks that adhere to paper coating. OMG does have benefits in the deinking process for some grades. Clay in OMG stabilizes the bubbles in the flotation process, long fibers in OMG add strength to the next generation of paper, and brightness is generally higher.

OMG is most commonly used in containerboard, combination folding boxboard, and industrial packaging but is finding increased use in newsprint, tissue, and some fine writing paper. ONP will show the greatest percentage gain in consumption of all the grades through 1992 due to the rapid growth in recycled newsprint production slated to come onstream through 1992.

The strong economic advantages in using recycled fiber for tissue, containerboard, and newsprint are not yet clear for printing and writing paper, although environmental motivations may create markets for these grades. To secure a source for what may become a required raw material in the future, mills must establish a good working relationship with local collection services or offices.

Projects listed in Table 1 are definite or very likely to move ahead, pending approval. Many more companies have indefinite plans to install deinking facilities, or they have put projects on hold because of capital limitations at this time. Addition or expansion of deinking capability is often tied to papermaking capacity expansion. Thus, a few companies have postponed deinking facilities along with new paper machines.

Jefferson Smurfit Corp. has put on hold a second recycled newsprint machine along with deinking equipment and a new cogeneration facility at its Pomona, Calif., mill, acquired from Golden State Newsprint in 1990. The mill is currently in the middle of a two-year, $35-million capital spending program aimed at improving newsprint quality and raising output 10% to 15% but has put any further expansion on indefinite hold.

Smurfit is also in the final round of site selection for a New York State recycled newsprint mill with a deinking plant to start up in 1994. Canadian companies that have postponed projects or kept them on hold include Boise Cascade Canada Ltd., Stone-Consolidated Inc., F.F. Soucy Inc., and Stora Forest Industries Ltd.

Most of the deinking projects to come online in 1991 continue to be in newsprint or market deinked pulp mills that sell to newsprint manufacturers, but projects for other grades, particularly tissue, are increasing.

NEWSPRINT. Recycled newsprint capacity is projected to increase by 150% by the end of 1991; 30% of that capacity will contain at least 40% recycled fiber by the end of 1992, and 85% will be at existing mills that have added deinking capacity to replace virgin-fiber pulping capacity. The remaining 15% will come from greenfield newsprint mills now under construction.

Ten new deinking facilities will start up in 1991, adding 1,009,825 tpy of recycled fiber capacity. Eight will start up in 1992, adding another 784,350 tpy. Four of these are market deinked pulp mills that would sell

TABLE 1: **U.S. and Canadian deinking projects.**

Company/mill/site	Startup	Deinking capacity (mtpy)	Recycled fiber content (%)	Recycled furnish requirements (mtpy)	Grades
Newsprint					
Abitibi-Price, Thunder Bay, Ont.	May '92	55,000	40	76,550	70% ONP, 30% OMG
Alabama River Newsprint, Claiborne, Ala.	spring '92	100,000	45	140,000	70% ONP, 30% OMG
Atlantic Newsprint, Whitby, Ont.	Jan. '91[1]	146,000	100	73,000	70% ONP, 30% OMG
Augusta Newsprint, Augusta, Ga.	Mar. '91[2]	86,750	variable	115,000	70% ONP, 30% OMG
Bear Island, Ashland, Va.	late '92[3]	43,500	20	60,000	ONP, OMG
Boise Cascade, W. Tacoma, Wash.	1992	70,000	40	109,500	ONP, OMG
Bowater, Calhoun, Tenn.	Sept. '91	109,500	variable	138,700	70% ONP, 30% OMG
Canadian Pacific Forest Products, Gatineau, Que.	late '91	182,500	variable	182,500	70% ONP, 30% OMG
Canadian Pacific Forest Products, Thunder Bay, Ont.	late '91	100,375	variable	100,375	70% ONP, 30% OMG
Cascades/Donohue/Maclaren, Cap de la Madeleine, Que.	early '92	90,000	20	112,900	70% ONP, 30% OMG
Champion International, Sheldon, Texas	1992	138,800	n.a.	208,200	ONP, OMG
Daishowa Forest, Quebec City, Que.[4]	Feb. '92	110,000	variable	120,000	80% ONP, 20% OMG
Daishowa Forest, Port Angeles, Wash.[4]	spring '92	65,000	variable	75,000	50% ONP, 10% OMG, 40% old directories
Inland Empire, Millwood, Wash.	late '91	37,000	40	42,000	ONP
Kruger, Bromptonville, Que.	1992	41,640[5]	variable	52,050	ONP, OMG
Newstech Recycling, Vancouver, B.C.	Nov. '91	122,300	variable	140,000	70% ONP, 30% OMG
North Pacific Paper, Longview, Wash.	Apr. '91	156,000	variable	225,550	ONP
Smurfit Newsprint, N.Y. State (site not chosen)	1994	n.a.	n.a.	n.a.	n.a.
Stone-Consolidated, Shawinigan, Que. (under study)	n.a.	70,000	variable	83,000	70% ONP, 30% OMG
(Indefinite)					
Alberta Newsprint, Whitecourt, Alta.	n.a.	n.a.	n.a.	n.a.	n.a.
Fletcher Challenge, Elk Falls and Crofton, B.C.	n.a.	n.a.	n.a.	n.a.	n.a.
Georgia-Pacific, E. Millinocket, Maine	n.a.	86,750	variable	120,000	ONP, OMG
Manistique (Kruger)[7], Manistique, Mich.	proposed	34,700	100	n.a.	OMG, books, inserts, catalogues
Kenaf Paper, Raymondville, Texas	n.a.	n.a.	n.a.	n.a.	n.a.
Tissue					
Scott, Owensboro, Ky.	proposed	n.a.	n.a.	n.a.	n.a.
Perkins Papers, Candiac, Que.	Aug. '91	48,500	100	100,000	ledger (woodfree)
Atlas Paper, Hialeah, Fla.	June '91	21,000	100	29,200	white leger coated book
Putney Paper, Putney, Vt.	Feb. '91	15,000	100	9,100	white ledger coated book
Marcal Paper, Elmwood, N.J.	n.a.	n.a.	n.a.	n.a.	n.a.
Bay West (Mosinee), Middletown, Ohio	1991	79,810	100	120,000	postconsumer
Fort Howard, Rincon, Ga.	1991	n.a.	100	n.a.	n.a.
American Power, Bala Cynwyd, Pa.	1993	138,800	n.a.	173,500	postconsumer
Orford Recycling, Drummondville, Que.	n.a.	120,000	n.a.	n.a.	n.a.
Fox River Fiber, De Pere, Wis.	July '91	69,400	n.a.	109,500	ledger grades
Mississippi River Corp., Natchez, Miss.	Jan. '91	n.a.	n.a.	n.a.	n.a.
Caithness King, Pejepscot, Maine	1993	190,850	n.a.	273,750	50% ONP, 50% OMG
Caithness King, Midland, Mich.	1992	190,850	n.a.	273,750	50% ONP, 50% OMG
Ponderosa, New York, N.Y.	n.a.	n.a.	n.a.	n.a.	n.a.
Ponderosa, Augusta, Ga.	1992	34,700	n.a.	n.a.	n.a.
Ponderosa, Oshkosh, Wis.	1992	34,700	n.a.	n.a.	n.a.
Ponderosa, Memphis, Tenn.	1992	34,700	n.a.	n.a.	n.a.
Printing/Writing					
Noranda Inc., Thorold, Ont.	proposed	120,000	50 to 100	144,000	ledger, office waste
Noranda Forest Recycled Papers, Thorold, Ont.	1991	32,965	variable	36,500	postconsumer
Patriot Paper, Boston, Mass.[6]	Aug. '91	34,700	100	40,150	white office waste
Riverside Paper, De Pere, Wis.	n.a.	n.a.	n.a.	n.a.	n.a.

1. Will reach full capacity by September '91.
2. Date it will reach full capacity.
3. An additional 410,000 tpy capacity using 200,000 tpy of wastepaper (40%) will come online by 1995 or '96.
4. Produces newsprint and directory paper.
5. An additional 100,000 tpy will come online by 1995.
6. Expansion of existing facilities.
7. Also produces groundwood specialty grades.

their output to existing newsprint mills.

In the U.S. Southeast, Augusta Newsprint Co.'s deinking line at its Augusta, Ga., mill is nearly up to its full capacity of 250 tpd (see article, p. 76). The deinked pulp will enable either of the mill's two paper machines to make up to 40% recycled-content newsprint and can be varied according to a customer's specifications. The $27-million deinking line was purchased from Black Clawson and uses a flotation system with some washing. It will use a mix of 70% ONP and 30% OMG, totaling about 115,000 tpy of wastepaper, which will be obtained from both municipal and private sources.

Alabama River Newsprint Co. in Claiborne, Ala., plans a second-quarter 1992 startup for its $56-million deinking facility. The plant will produce 100,000 tpy of deinked pulp to supply its 220,000 tpy of newsprint with a 45% recycled fiber furnish. The combination flotation and washing system will make use of about 140,000 tpy of ONP and OMG sourced partly from wastepaper brokers and partly from municipal reclamation systems. Parsons & Whittemore and H.A. Simons are currently doing the engineering, and suppliers are being chosen.

Bowater Southern's Calhoun, Tenn., deinking plant is under construction and will start up in September 1991. The plant will make 109,500 tpy of deinked pulp, using 138,700 tpy of ONP and OMG that is sourced from wastepaper brokers. The $74.5-million facility includes a dual flotation and washing system on alkaline, then on acid, by Black Clawson and a pulping drum by Ahlstrom. The engineering was done by CRS Sirrine. The sludge and ash generated by the facility will be landfilled, although boiler capacity may be increased in the future so the waste can be burned.

In the Northwest, Inland Empire Paper Co. is installing a new deinking plant at its 66,000-tpy newsprint mill in Millwood, Wash. It will use 42,000 tpy of ONP to produce 37,000 tpy of deinked pulp. The company may have to go a considerable distance to find sources of ONP because North Pacific Paper Co. planned to start up a 156,000-tpy deinked pulp facility in Longview, Wash., in April. North Pacific, a joint venture of Weyerhaeuser Co. and Jujo Paper Co. Ltd., will source its 225,550 tpy of ONP through Weyerhaeuser. The deinking line is tied to a third paper machine, which will bring total capacity to 2,000 tpd of variable recycled-fiber content newsprint.

Daishowa America Co. Ltd. is starting up a $40-million, 65,000-tpy deinked pulp facility at Port Angeles, Wash., in spring 1992. The facility will use 50% ONP, 40% old directories, and 10% OMG for its newsprint/directory mill. Daishowa has developed its own top secret deinking technology, which will enable it to use old directory paper. A spokesperson for the company did say it is a combination flotation and washing system. Daishowa is also building a deinking facility at its Quebec City, Que., newsprint/directory paper mill. This facility will use 120,000 tpy of wastepaper from Canada and the U.S. (80% ONP and 20% OMG) to produce 110,000 tpy of deinked pulp. The recycled fiber content can be varied according to a customer's needs.

Atlantic Packaging Products Ltd. in Whitby, Ont., is starting up its 146,000-tpy deinked pulp line. It uses 73,000 tpy of ONP and OMG sourced from community recycling programs. Voith provided the engineering and supplied the combination flotation and washing system. The company is not yet up to full capacity on its 400-tpd paper machine, which produces 100% recycled newsprint.

DEINKED PULP. Legislation is driving newsprint makers to include high recycled-fiber content, but those who cannot afford to build their own deinking facilities may come to depend on market deinked pulp manufacturers. Paul Stern, Caithness King Co.'s environmental scientist, said, "A lot of publishers are under pressure from their readers to come up with recycled-fiber content paper. We believe companies will be to an advantage to begin now proactively including a percentage of recycled fiber. These companies will be in a much better position than if they sit and wait until the legislation comes along and says include 60% recycled fiber."

Market deinked pulp manufacturers are confident there will be a continued demand for recycled content and that the most efficient and economical way to provide it, for mills that don't have a tremendous need, is with deinked market pulp. Stern said, "It's either a make or buy decision. At our economy of scale we can sell them the pulp for a lot cheaper than if they had to make it themselves."

Caithness King is building two nearly identical market deinked pulp facilities—one in Midland, Mich., and the other in Pejepscot, Maine. Both projects will produce 550 tpd of deinked pulp, using 750 tpd of wastepaper—50% ONP and 50% OMG. Construction will begin in Michigan in July, and the plant will start up 1992. The Maine mill will start up in 1993. Bechtel is doing the engineering and suppliers are currently being chosen. Customers are being sought in production of value-added grades, such as directory, SCA, SCD, and coated Nos. 4 and 5, but no contracts are finalized. The process is a

> *"These companies [that include a percentage of recycled fiber] will be in a much better position than if they sit and wait until the legislation comes along and says include 60% recycled fiber."*

multi-stage washing and flotation system using hydrogen peroxide and sodium hydrosulfite for brightness.

Ponderosa Fibres of America Inc., North America's largest market deinked pulp producer, is planning 100-tpd expansions at three mills (Augusta, Ga., Oshkosh, Wis., and Memphis, Tenn.) and has proposed a new mill for the New York City area. The company is experiencing increasing demand for its product from printing/writing, tissue, and other specialty grade manufacturers. It considers itself at an advantage since anticipated legislation is prompting papermakers to use more recycled fiber, but many cannot afford to build deinking facilities. The company currently makes 700 tpd of deinked market pulp at four mills using primarily colored ledger, white ledger, and poly-coated board.

PRINTING/WRITING. A lack of federal guidelines and the problems with a clean source of secondary fiber in printing/writing paper have caused these grades to lag behind tissue and newsprint in secondary fiber usage. Before these manufacturers make the investment in deinking facilities they must be assured that a dependable source of quality wastepaper, such as office waste, is available.

Recyclable paper products account for approximately two-thirds of all office waste, yet improper sorting may cause contaminants (glues, tape) or paper of unacceptable quality to enter the deinking process. The situation is improving as offices and commercial buildings are jumping on the recycling bandwagon. Source separation is the key factor in the effective utilization of office waste. Pickup is often supplied free by waste collection groups, and companies may save on waste disposal costs. Also, office workers are demanding that recycling bins be made available.

Noranda Forest Inc. has created a new division called Noranda Forest Recycled Papers to handle its recycling efforts at its integrated Thorold, Ont., mill, which includes three paper machines and a deinking facility. The company is currently implementing process changes to bring the capacity up to about 95 tpd from 25 tpd last year and will use about 150 tpd of wastepaper by the end of 1991.

Don Duncan, vice president-operations at the mill, said that until last year the company had not been selling the paper as recycled. "By making the move to become an Eco-Logo qualified producer with 50% deinked fiber, it has allowed us to put far more through that deinked plant and maintain quality. It's interesting that the dirt specks that used to be a problem in the past are no longer a problem now that we're selling it as recycled paper."

The company had announced plans more than a year ago to construct a 120,000-tpy greenfield wet-lap deinking facility in Thorold, but that project will now be considered separately, falling under Noranda Inc. Duncan said the company is not prepared to make such a large investment at this time, and it wants to try introducing new products through the integrated facility first. The proposed new facility would consume approximately 144,000 tpy of ledger and sorted office waste to produce a sheet with 50% to 100% recycled fiber content and would also sell market pulp. Duncan said since the product produced by the new greenfield facility will compete on the pulp market, that investment will involve a long-term look.

TISSUE. More than half of the tissue supply coming onstream from 1990 to 1993 will make use of deinked wastepaper, as more tissue makers turn to 100% recycled in response to environmental pressures, procurement guidelines, and customer demand. According to API's 1990 capacity survey, eight new tissue machines will come onstream between 1990 and 1993, raising capacity from 5.976 million short tons to 6.349 million short tons. Four of these machines will use deinked wastepaper to make tissue.

Three-quarters of the recycled fiber furnish used in tissue production is supplied from pulp substitutes and high-grade deinking grades; mixed paper, ONP, and OCC provide the rest. Fort Howard Corp., Chesapeake Corp., Pope & Talbot Inc., and FSC Paper Co. make only 100% recycled tissue, while Scott Paper Co., James River Corp., Procter & Gamble Paper Products Co., and Georgia-Pacific Corp. include an average of 20% wastepaper in their tissue.

Construction began in spring 1990 on a 48,500-tpy deinking facility at Perkins Paper Ltd.'s Candiac, Que., tissue mill. The facility starts up August 1991 in conjunction with a new Valmet twin-wire, 6,500-fpm tissue machine. The combination flotation and washing system includes equipment from Hymac, Black Clawson, Fiberprep, and Escher Wyss and was engineered by Joseph Miller Consultants of Montreal. The facility will make use of 100,000 tpy of woodfree wastepaper sourced from Montreal and Toronto as well as the northeastern U.S. Perkins has been making 100% recycled tissue since 1971.

Mosinee Paper Corp. is expanding its Bay West subsidiary in Middletown, Ohio, including a $17-million deinking plant, due to be completed in third-quarter 1991. When added to the existing 100-tpd plant, the combined operation will produce 330 tpd of recycled pulp for the mill's towel and tissue machines. The mill will use 450 tpd of varying grades of postconsumer waste.

A couple of small tissue manufacturers are expanding deinking capability. Putney Paper Co. in Putney, Vt., raised its capacity 40% in 1990 to about 50 tpd with a machine rebuild. The expanded deinking system will produce about 44 tpd of deinked pulp for its 100% recycled tissue. Escher Wyss supplied the flotation system. Atlas Tissue Mills in Hialeah, Fla., is in the startup phase of a new flotation deinking line from Black Clawson. It will use 80 tpd of ledger and coated book wastepaper to produce 100% recycled tissue. ■

Wastepaper Supply and Demand

New markets for recycled paper and paperboard products have sprung up almost overnight in recent years. Popular recycled commodities have included newsprint, paperboard, linerboard, paper bags, and most recently fine papers. These increased markets are already taxing wastepaper supplies in some sectors, notably old newspapers (ONP) and old corrugated containers (OCC).

In the mid to late 1990s, tightening supplies of ONP and OCC could drive prices for these grades considerably higher in the world marketplace, detrimentally affecting their competitiveness with virgin fibers. This section analyzes developing wastepaper supply, demand, and pricing trends into the foreseeable future for several grades, including printing and writing papers.

Also included in this section are several articles on the paper industry's role in helping reduce municipal solid waste loads. Existing and potential wastepaper supplies from various state and municipal programs and drives are assessed for five years into the future.

Chapter 4

New Markets Open as Public Demand Grows for Recycled Paper Products

Legislators and major corporations drive paper industry to develop new grades containing more postconsumer wastepaper

By SUSAN KINSELLA

In the 1990s, Americans are facing a solid waste disposal crisis, hazardous waste and toxic industrial processes, water and energy shortages, pollution, and depletion of natural resources. Industries that conformed well to the turn-of-the-century goals of development and expansion are now being pressured to reform their products and processes to meet these new national needs. With paper as one of the most pervasive products in American society, the paper industry finds itself squarely in the environmental spotlight.

Recycling is hardly new. The first paper mill in the U.S. was a recycled mill that manufactured from rags. Recycling rates have long been high among the board, tissue, and domestic newsprint industries. Even in high-grade printing and writing paper, several mills discovered long ago that deinking can be very economical. Miami Paper Corp., now owned by Cross Pointe Paper (Pentair), installed deinking equipment as early as 1915. More than 20 years ago, Simpson Paper Co. located a mill at San Gabriel, Calif., near the Los Angeles asphalt jungle instead of in cool green forests, and turned to deinking.

A MARKET OF ITS OWN. It wasn't until the first Earth Day in 1970 that recycled paper began to take on a life and a market of its own. At the time, recycled meant brown paper full of specks and blotches, and its market was small and unstable. In the mid-1970s, mills were leery of publicly acknowledging that they produced paper from deinked wastepaper because the product had an image of inferiority. They were afraid they would lose their markets. Conservatree's argument, in fact, was just the opposite.

"I went to Bergstrom [now P.H. Glatfelter] and River-

Ms. Kinsella is director of communications and research, Conservatree Inc., San Francisco, Calif.

side [Paper Co.] and other mills with the proposal that I could gain them customers they had never had simply because their paper contained recycled fiber," said Alan Davis, founder and president of Conservatree. Since its founding in 1976, Conservatree has played a unique role in the paper industry. For most of its history, the company has been the only one in the country dedicated to the wholesale distribution of recycled paper. In fact, the company has always pursued two goals simultaneously.

"We knew that the production of recycled paper offered many environmental advantages that would become increasingly important," Davis explained. "We focused on high-grade papers because that is where the least recycling was going on, even though it is the fastest-growing segment of the industry. Since the paper industry would need to know there was a vital market for the paper before investing in deinking, we set out to show that a market was there and to enlarge it to the point that the switch to recycled paper would become the obvious thing to do."

Now recycled means high-quality paper in whites, colors, and designer styles, and it includes almost every grade. The market extends to federal, state, and local governments; major corporations, and the printers that supply them; as well as publishers, organizations, and the public at large. Most significantly, these customers indicate that this is only the beginning.

GOVERNMENT MARKETS AND DEFINITIONS. Confidence in the market was supported by passage in 1976 and 1977 of laws in California, Oregon, and Maryland giving procurement price preferences to recycled paper. For many years it was state governments that provided the major markets for recycled paper.

In 1983, Conservatree brought California's 5% recycled procurement preference together with Simpson Paper's expertise in xerographic papermaking to produce the first high-speed copier paper with 50% recycled content, including 10% postconsumer fiber. Currently, state and local governments across the country are clamoring for recycled copier paper, and more mills, including Great Northern Nekoosa Corp. and Hammermill Papers, are now producing top-notch paper to meet the need. In fact, Noranda Forest Inc.'s Fraser mill in Thorold, Ont., has recently introduced the first copier paper to carry the explicit blessings of Xerox (Canada), with 50% recycled content and 5% postconsumer fiber to meet Canada's national Ecologo program requirements.

While state preference laws kept recycled paper markets afloat for many years, they also fractured the market with widely differing definitions of what constitutes recycled paper. When the Environmental Protection Agency (EPA) was finally forced to produce government-wide recycled paper procurement guidelines in 1988 to fulfill the requirements of the 1976 Resource Conservation & Recovery Act (RCRA), everyone hoped it would provide a national definition to settle the dilemma. Instead, it increased the volatility.

"We were simply trying to set minimum standards for federal agencies implementing recycled paper procurement programs," according to Richard Braddock, who manages EPA's procurement-guideline-implementation program. "We never intended to provide leadership outside our own agencies."

Nevertheless, the fact that the federal government has defined recycled paper differently from the states has clouded rather than clarified the requirements for recycled high-grade fiber content. By allowing some mill broke to be counted as recycled content, EPA guidelines have encouraged many mills to introduce new recycled sheets, which has increased the success rate for procurement officers buying recycled paper. However, not rewarding the use of postconsumer waste has decreased the incentive for mills to invest in deinking. It is no longer possible to talk about recycled paper markets without talking about which definition to use.

People in the paper industry frequently ask, "What difference does it make if it's pre- or postconsumer? It all needs to be reused anyway." It is to the industry's credit that noninked, preconsumer wastepaper has always been reused, even in the production of virgin paper. But customers are buying recycled paper because they believe it alleviates the municipal solid waste crisis. Postconsumer waste is ending up in landfills, not mill broke, sawdust, or pulp substitutes. It also makes more taxpayer sense for government's price preferences to be used in stimulating the use of materials that do not have alternative markets rather than simply rewarding what already has sufficient free-market stimulus.

Government and corporate policy-makers have been disturbed to learn that much of the paper they have been buying does not achieve their solid waste management goals. "Anyone who has had a landfill closed in their district would be disappointed to learn that the federal definition of recycled paper does not promote the diversion of used paper from entering our landfills," said Congressman John Porter (R-Ill.). "We need to clarify the necessity for postconsumer waste content."

Because of the confusion about fiber contents, Conservatree has introduced a ranking system that labels paper according to the source of its recycled content. This ranking system, which labels paper from C1 (the highest ranking, containing postconsumer waste) to C4 (the lowest ranking, reserved for paper which meets only the minimum EPA guidelines), is based on California, New York, and Oregon procurement definitions, all of which have successfully stimulated the development of recycled paper for years.

"I think it helps immensely," said Jim Seeberg, senior vice president of Chicago's LaSalle Messinger Paper Co., a Paper Corp. of America company. "Many of our customers want to pin down whether the paper they are buying contains postconsumer waste."

Members of Congress are dismayed at the result of EPA guidelines for high-grade paper. Senator Al Gore (D-Tenn.) concluded after a Congressional hearing on recycling, "I'm glad to see that paper mills already use virtually all the wastepaper produced in their manufacturing processes. This shows what economic incentives can do to ensure demand for specific materials. Now I believe that it is Congress's tack to produce incentives for the wastepaper that is not being used, and that means postconsumer waste."

Some officials are concerned that mills will make paper to meet the looser federal guidelines at the expense of stricter state and local procurement policies. John Rarig, in Pennsylvania's Commonwealth Agency Recycling Office, said, "The federal government is such a big consumer that their failure to set a substantial postconsumer standard for high-grade paper means that the states are left to try to move a national market on their own. We would like support and reinforcement from the national guidelines. We want to empty the national waste stream as much as possible. The federal guidelines don't do that. They are missing the point—to put it politely."

TABLE 1: **Conservatree recycled paper ranking.**

Conservatree recycled rank		Type of recycled content						
		Postconsumer fiber % by fiber / % by weight		Deinked fiber % by fiber / % by weight		Secondary postmill % by fiber / % by weight		EPA wastepaper % by fiber / % by weight
C1+		20 or 15	and/or	100 or 80				
C1	(Calif.)	15 or 10		and		60 or 50		
C2	(N.Y.)			50 or 40				
C3						60 or 50		
C4	(EPA)							50 or 40

Conservatree products are labeled with content by percent of fiber/recycled rank.

MAJOR CORPORATIONS JOIN IN. It is on the local level that government faces the starkest reality: What to do with their residents' trash? They are taking solutions to the corporations. "I tell corporate offices that collecting their paper is important, but it's not enough," said Amy Perlmutter, recycling coordinator for San Francisco's Recycling Program. "They have to buy recycled paper as well if they really want to make a difference."

Governments are not alone in pressing for a corporate switch to recycled. According to Susan Swanson, print production manager for Tandem Computers, "Employees notice if you don't use recycled products. Everyone is very happy that Tandem has gone recycled. We're a company interested in taking a leadership role, in terms of the environment and responsibility to the community. Everyone recognizes what a problem the nation is in environmentally—it is a disaster ready to happen. With corporations being part of 'the evil empire,' recycled paper makes you look like a good guy and makes our employees feel better. Our designers are learning to design for the paper instead of the other way around, and they're coming up with new choices," she explained.

Paper merchants are seeing the same phenomenon. "We supply some of the largest printers in the world, and they want recycled," said LaSalle Messinger's Seeberg. "The nuances of fiber content are sinking in. They're understanding that unless you've got postconsumer waste, you're not going to solve any problems."

At Minneapolis Inter-City Paper Co., another PCA division, Bob Dowler makes a similar report. "We got interested in recycled paper first of all because we are concerned about the environment and the effect that paper disposal has on it. Initially, state agencies were asking about recycled paper, then it spread to smaller governments and large environmentally concerned corporations. Now it's down to quick-print shops and individuals who want it for their own use. It is virtually universal now. The education of the print purchasers in the past 18 months surpasses all the education in the past 18 years. Currently, it is large printers and state agencies that are asking for postconsumer waste content. I think that sophistication will spread the same way."

Because selling recycled paper still frequently calls for selling the concept along with high-quality paper, it sometimes takes more time and effort. For this reason, Conservatree has recently introduced Conservatree Consultants to assist major corporate paper buyers in making the switch to recycled. "Even when a company decides to switch, implementation can be difficult because there is still so much misinformation," said Alan Davis. "We can help them through the process because we have so much experience with it ourselves."

POSTCONSUMER PAPER. The customer has the last word. Tandem's Swanson said, "We try to go with papers that have more postconsumer waste in them. We're even willing to pay a little bit more to get them."

David Assmann, publisher of *Mother Jones* magazine,

Alan Davis, founder and president of Conservatree.

added, "As far as I'm concerned, recycled paper with no postconsumer content is not recycled paper."

Some in the paper industry argue that making high-grade sheets is not possible from deinked and postconsumer content. But too many high-quality sheets are already on the market to support that argument. A number of mills see the future of recycled paper and already are perfecting sheets with postconsumer contents. Nekoosa's xerographic sheet has 10% postconsumer fiber, and Hammermill added postconsumer to its sheet recently. Fox River Paper Corp. goes even further. Although EPA guidelines have required no wastepaper content for rag bond paper, Fox River produces rag bond with 100% deinked fiber, in addition to 25% rag, resulting in a high-quality, 89 brightness sheet, with approximately 15% postconsumer content.

In text and cover, most of the new recycled sheets meet only minimum EPA guidelines. Some, however, such as Conservatree's new Four Seasons from its Howard mill, contain 50% deinked fiber as well as 10% postconsumer content.

Some mill managers argue that making recycled paper means the industry has to develop whole new grades of paper. But don't tell that to book publishers, who have been printing many of the nation's bestsellers, including *Roots* and *Iacocca*, on recycled paper for years, simply because some of the best archival-quality paper in the country also happens to have recycled content.

And Simpson wasn't making a new grade of paper when it produced the first recycled xerographic paper. It was simply making xerographic with a different fiber source. Fox River wasn't producing a new grade of paper when it came out with the first deinked wastepaper content rag bond. It was simply producing the same high-quality paper using a different source for fiber.

Jobe Morrison, president of Cross Pointe's Miami Paper mill, said the deinking mill was upgraded because "we believe our industry has to develop the ability to use postconsumer waste in printing and writing paper to have an impact on the solid waste crisis our nation is facing. The marketplace is going to demand that the printing and writing industry use postconsumer waste as part of the recycled fiber content in high-grade papers. What's going to happen in the office collection programs is the same thing that happened in newsprint. All the collection programs are kicking in right now, but there is no market currently for the waste being collected."

A number of nonintegrated paper mills have been creatively testing the market for postconsumer content fibers by buying deinked fiber from Ponderosa Fibres' pulp mills or from tissue mills. The strong demand for these sheets has led at least two companies to plan their own deinking pulp mills. Fox River Fiber is ready to break ground on a new mill, and James River Corp. is ordering equipment for a new deinking mill in Halsey, Ore.

NEW RECYCLED SHEETS NEEDED. However, while manufacturers respond to customer demand, in some grades of recycled paper this response has been exceedingly slow. "Even though I've compiled a list of publications using more than 100,000 tons of coated Nos. 4 and 5 papers per year, no mill has shown a serious interest in supplying this kind of recycled paper," said Assmann of *Mother Jones.* "Obviously a massive demand is not being met." Niagara Paper Co. Inc. has just introduced a small quantity of high-end No. 4 but not enough even to dent the market. Ironically, Watervliet Paper Co., the only mill making a truly recycled No. 3 coated sheet, including postconsumer content, just suspended its operations.

However, major catalogs, such as Esprit and Patagonia, haven't waited. Peggy Bernard, Patagonia's catalog director, explained, "We've been looking for a recycled sheet for a long time. Finally we decided that even if the 'right' paper wasn't yet being made, we were willing to take the risk. And the quality of even the film-coated that we used was a positive surprise."

WHAT'S AHEAD? Distributors across the nation are learning recycled paper and expanding their lines. Conservatree has formed "comerchant" agreements with top paper distributors across the country that make its brand-name paper available at the local level. But more has to be done to expand the market.

Conservatree has become a bridge between paper mills and customers, providing cutting edge information on markets and manufacturing capabilities to manufacturers, customers, governments, and paper merchants. "We realize that it's not simple for a mill to switch to deinking," Davis explained.

"There are many pieces to the puzzle—adequate and uncontaminated wastepaper supply, support for recycling capital investments, clear messages about the future solidity of the recycled paper market, further deinking technology research, and a level playing field, which all have to fall into place at the same time. We work with legislatures and governments to put those pieces into place. We work with customers to increase the demand. And the more mills work with us on developing new paper and increasing supply, the more accurately we can reflect true problems that need to be resolved."

Clearly, the industry has been thrust, willing or not, into leading the country into an environmentally sound future. The question is no longer whether the paper industry will get into recycling. It is now more a question of how gracefully and boldly the industry will lead. ■

This article is given out as part of a Greenline Membership program by Conservatree Information Services. For complete details on this educational program, write CIS, 10 Lombard Street, Suite 250, San Francisco, CA 94111.

Chapter 5

Demand Increases for Recycled Printing and Writing Paper

Improved quality and the issue of solid waste disposal has increased demand from both the public and private sectors

By ROBERT B. GALIN, News Editor

Mills, merchants, and customers are beginning to realize that recycling is an issue that won't go away. As the paper industry fights tough mandatory recycling legislation, customers are increasing their requests for access to quality recycled paper, particularly in the printing and writing grades.

"Merchants know that there's a demand out there on the part of customers for more recycled products," says John J. Buckley Jr., president of the National Paper Trade Assn. (NPTA). "This is no longer an issue of just the maniacs and the radicals—it's becoming more and more of an issue for mainline customers [such as printers]," Buckley says.

"Merchants are finding the biggest demand for recycled printing and writing paper right now is in big business [and] the government contract business," he adds.

What's leading this realization is the very visible problem of what to do with the accumulation of solid waste, about 41% of which is composed of paper and paperboard, according to the National Solid Waste Management Assn. That's about 65 million tons of garbage in 1986 alone.

"The issue of disposal of solid waste is at an absolute critical point. The paper industry is going to have to address that," says Jobe B. Morrison, president of Miami Paper Corp., a unit of Cross Pointe Paper Corp., a Pentair Inc. company. Cross Pointe sells a variety of recycled paper from its Miami mill in West Carrollton, Ohio, and Flambeau Paper in Park Falls, Wis.

Morrison says there are correlative issues, such as dioxins resulting from the bleaching of recycled fiber. He wonders if the public is prepared to accept less bright or off-color paper.

These recycled grades—as opposed to those using clean, preconsumer or precommercial waste—are not what many customers are used to seeing, explains Bill Litviak, a sales representative for Wilcox-Walter-Furlong Paper Co. WWF Paper represents Cross Pointe, P.H. Glatfelter Co., and French Paper Co.

Shelley Hamel, marketing coordinator at Earth Care Paper Co., a mail order retailer of recycled paper products, thinks the public is indeed ready for such paper. In fact, she says, the company's most popular business paper is called Minimum Impact, an unbleached, 100% recycled paper from Glatfelter. Minimum Impact has "kind of" a beige color.

The biggest problem, Hamel says, is the price differential between recycled-fiber paper and virgin-fiber paper. Currently, recycled grades cost about 10% more than their virgin fiber counterparts. The price differential has increased recently because of strong discounts in virgin-fiber uncoated free-sheet paper while demand for recycled papers has increased.

NPTA's Buckley agrees but says there's a gap between what customers say they want and what they're actually willing to pay for. "There is a strong feeling out there that no one is willing to pay more to get a recycled fiber [paper]." They may say they're willing to accept slightly lower quality and performance, but when it comes to spending more, they back off and choose the virgin fiber, Buckley says.

Still, Hamel says her company is experiencing rapid growth. "Customers want to buy recycled paper," she says. Earth Care sells copy and forms paper, stationery, note cards, and other products directly to consumers, retail stores, and other customers.

Litviak says some customers, particularly printers, had bad experiences with 100% recycled paper in the 1970s. That paper had problems with stability and runability. Now, however, improved quality has pushed demand for recycled printing and writing paper beyond the fad stage.

Currently, about 34 mills in North America are producing at least a small amount of printing/writing paper they classify as recycled (Table 1). However, many of these mills use primarily preconsumer or precommercial waste, which means they are often such "waste" as envelope clippings and other high-grade, clean white pulp substitutes.

Mills such as Hammermill Papers and Westvaco Corp. have introduced recycled grades with at least 50% wastepaper, although it is preconsumer. Nekoosa

Papers Inc. has introduced a lower-brightness copy paper made with some deinked fiber.

MERCHANTS GET INVOLVED. There are essentially three issues in the solid waste problem, says Buckley of NPTA. One is stemming the reduction of resources. The second is incineration/energy generation. The third is recycling.

NPTA has formed a Solid Waste Action Network, which so far has about 100 volunteers from member locations. When the network becomes mobilized, these

TABLE 1: **Recycled printing/writing paper mills.**

Company	Mill	Capacity*	Wastepaper content (%)	Grades
Appleton Papers Inc.	West Carrollton, Ohio	122,000 tpy	50	Carbonless
C.P.M. Inc.	Claremont, N.H.	11,440 tpy[1]	50 to 100	Kraft/white envelope, school construction
	East Ryegate, Vt.	17,160 tpy[1]	50 to 100	Envelope, other
Cross Pointe Paper Corp.[2]				
Miami Paper	West Carrollton, Ohio	110,000 tpy	50	Book, text and cover, 25% cotton, opaque
Flambeau Paper	Park Falls, Wis.	133,500 tpy	50	Cover and text
Domtar Inc.	St. Catharines, Ont.	250 tpd	100	Writing, envelope stock
Eastern Fine Paper Inc.	Brewer, Maine	64,000 tpy	50	25% cotton, offset, mimeo, copy
Exton Paper Manufacturers	Modena, Pa.	60 tpd	n.a.	Kraft for envelope, wrapping, etc.
Fox River Paper Corp.	Appleton, Wis.	35,570 tpy	100[3]	Cotton, cover, opaque, typewriter
French Paper Co.	Niles, Mich.	18,000 tpy	50+	Cover and text
Georgia-Pacific Corp.	Gilman, Vt.	71,000 tpy	50	Copy
	Kalamazoo, Mich.	140,000 tpy	50	Copy
P.H. Glatfelter Co.	Neenah, Wis.	135,000 tpy	50	Book, writing, envelope, film-coated offset
IP/Hammermill Papers	Oswego, N.Y.	74,760 tpy	50	Copy
Hopper Paper[4]	Taylorville, Ill.	37,000 tpy	50	Cover and text, writing
	Reading, Pa.	20,000 tpy	50	Cover and text, writing
James River Corp.	Ypsilanti, Mich.	17,800 tpy	50+	Text and cover
JR-Fitchburg	Fitchburg, Mass.	52 tpd	50+	Cover
Kerwin/Riverside	Appleton, Wis.	42,600 tpy	50/92	Writing band, school construction
Lyons Falls Pulp & Paper Inc.	Lyons Falls, N.Y.	76,000 tpy	50	Book, reply card, tablet, forms, specialties
Manistique Papers Inc.	Manistique, Mich.	35,500 tpy	100	Groundwood specialties
Nekoosa Papers Inc.	Nekoosa/Port Edwards, Wis.	160,200 tpy[5]	50**	Copy
Noranda Forest Inc.	Thorold, Ont.	102,000 mtpy	50[6]	Book, forms, copy, envelope, tablet
Potsdam Paper Mills	Potsdam, N.Y.	65,000 tpy	40+	Opaque offset, writing, book
Putney Paper Co.	Putney, Vt.	25,000 tpy	up to 100	MG/MF printing, coated book, ledger, thin
Simpson Paper Co.	Pomona, Calif.	120,000 tpy	25 to 60[7]	Copy
	Ripon, Calif.	39,000 tpy	25 to 60[7]	Copy
	Vicksburg, Mich.	35,000 tpy	25 to 60[7]	Copy
Sorg Paper Co.[8]	Middletown, Ohio	74,750 tpy	50 to 100[9]	Bond, offset, book
Valentine Paper Co.	Lockport, La.	49,840 tpy	50	Offset, tablet, reply card
Ward Paper Co.	Merrill, Wis.	35,000 tpy	100	Watermarked bond, mimeo, duplicator
Watervliet Paper Co.	Watervliet, Mich.	40,000 tpy	50 to 85	Coated and uncoated book offset
Westvaco Corp.	Tyrone, Pa.	87,220 tpy	50	Envelope paper
Geo. A. Whiting Paper Co.	Menasha, Wis.	9,000 tpy	80 average	Cover and text
Cascades/Steinbeis	East Angus, Que.		Under study	
	Niagara Falls, N.Y.			
Champion International Corp.	Hamilton, Ohio		Under study	
Daishowa Forest Products	Port Angeles, Wash., Quebec City, Que.		Under study	
Hyde Park Paper Inc.[10]	Boston, Mass.	55,000 tpy	Closed	Copy, book, offset, cover
Mi Ho Paper	St. Joseph, Mo.		Under study	
Performance Papers Inc.	Kalamazoo, Mich.	250 to 300 tpd	Closed	Book, other

*Tonnage is total mill capacity, except as noted.
**Postcommercial and/or postconsumer wastepaper.
1. Estimated average: Claremont produces 40 tpd and East Ryegate 60 tpd operating five to six days/week.
2. Subsidiary of Pentair Inc.
3. 100% recycled 10 to 15% postconsumer waste.
4. Separate operating company of Georgia-Pacific Corp. Will be using 50% postconsumer in 1990.
5. Less than 50,000 tpy recycled.
6. 5% postconsumer, 45% postcommercial.
7. 25%, 50% and 50% plus 10% postconsumer.
8. Subsidiary of Mosinee Paper Corp.
9. 50 to 100% with 10% postconsumer.
10. Leased from James River; new buyer possible.
Sources: E.H. Pechan & Associates Inc., *Pulp & Paper Week*, *Pulp & Paper Forecaster*.

and other volunteers will become educated on resource issues and will take an active interest in local issues related to recycling and waste management.

The purpose of the network is to help educate the industry while the industry helps educate the public. It is an effort to influence legislation on a local level. Already, many states and municipalities have implemented or are considering strict legislation on recycling and the content of recycled paper.

NPTA's effort is separate from the approximately $4-million program being implemented by the American Paper Institute this year, though the NPTA also works with API, Buckley says. ■

TABLE 2: **North American recycled newsprint producers.**

Company	Mill	Capacity (metric tpy)	Recycled content (%)	Publisher equity (%)
U.S.				
F.S.C. Paper Co.	Alsip, Ill.	121,500	100	—
Garden State Paper Co.	Garfield, N.J.	199,500	100	Media General Inc. (100%)
Golden State Newsprint Co.	Pomona, Calif.	122,500	100	—
Manistique Papers Inc.	Manistique, Mich.	56,000	100	—
North Pacific Paper Corp.	Longview, Wash.	704,000[1]	25[2]	—
Jefferson Smurfit Corp.	Newberg, Ore.	350,000	50	The Times Mirror Co. (20%)
	Oregon City, Ore.	217,000	50	The Times Mirror Co. (20%)
Southeast Paper Manufacturing Co.	Dublin, Ga.	415,000[3]	95	Cox Enterprises Inc. (33⅓%) Knight-Rider Inc. (33⅓%) Media General Inc. (33⅓%)
Stone Container Corp.	Snowflake, Ariz.	264,100	60	—
Canada				
Atlantic Packaging Corp.	Whitby, Ont.	136,100[4]	100	—
Quebec & Ontario Paper Co.	Thorold, Ont.	310,000	55	Tribune Co. (100%)

Sources: Newsprint Information Committee, *Pulp & Paper Week.*
1. Includes new 230,000-tpy machine starting up in late 1991.
2. Estimated net recycled content among mill's three paper machines.
3. Includes new 215,000-tpy machine started September 1989.
4. New 136,100-tpy machine starting up mid-1990.

Chapter 6

U.S. Leads the World in Production and Consumption of Wastepaper

Increasing recovery and reuse is expected to continue, but it will depend on many factors in addition to environmental pressures

By MATTI OLKINUORA

It probably does not surprise anyone that the U.S. is the world's largest source of wastepaper (recovery in 1986 was 20 million tons), followed by Japan (10 million tons) and Fed. Rep. Germany (4 to 5 million tons). These three countries are the leading consumers of paper, paperboard, and wastepaper in the world. In terms of recovery rate, included among the most efficient wastepaper collectors are countries such as Hong Kong (54%), Kuwait (53%), Japan (50%), and Taiwan (48%). In Europe, the Netherlands has a long tradition in wastepaper collection, with a high recovery rate of 46% (Table 1). Recycled fiber usage is driven by the following forces:

- Technical status, market requirements, and scale of the regional or local paper industry
- Trends in the levels of consumption of paper and paperboard

Mr. Olkinuora is vice president-marketing research, Jaakko Pöyry Oy, Helsinki, Finland. This article originally appeared in the company's "Know-How Wire" publication.

- Development trends in wastepaper collection, trade flows, and processing technologies and their impact on the availability of suitable recycled fiber in various markets
- Cost of recycled fiber compared with competing virgin fiber raw materials
- To some extent, growing ecological and environmental pressures.

CONSUMPTION AND UTILIZATION. Considerable regional differences exist in recycled fiber usage. The three leading consumers are the U.S. (16 million tons), Japan (11 million tons), and Fed. Rep. Germany (4 million tons), accounting for almost half of the world's total consumption (Table 2).

Recycled fiber's relative importance as a raw material of the paper industry is quite pronounced in the Asian and Latin American countries, which utilize an average of 40% to 46% of waste-based materials in their fiber furnish compared with, for example, North America's fairly modest 25%. In Western Europe, the average wastepaper proportions have traditionally been at an extremely low level (for example, Sweden at 11% and Finland at 4% [Figure 3]).

TABLE 1: **Wastepaper consumption vs paper and paperboard consumption, 1986.**

	Paper and paperboard consumption	Wastepaper recovery (million tons)	Wastepaper recovery rate (%)
U.S.	71.6	19.6	27.4
Japan	21.0	10.5	50.0
Fed. Rep. Germany	10.5	4.5	42.9
People's Rep. China	10.9	2.1	19.3
U.S.S.R.	9.8	1.9	19.4
U.K.	8.4	2.4	28.6
France	7.2	2.1	29.2
Canada	5.6	1.1	19.6
Italy	5.2	1.1	26.9
Brazil	4.1	1.3	31.7
Others	49.3	16.0	32.5
World total	**203.6**	**62.9**	**30.9**

TABLE 2: **Wastepaper consumption vs paper and paperboard production, 1986.**

	Paper and paperboard consumption	Wastepaper recovery (million tons)	Wastepaper utilization rate (%)
U.S.	65.0	16.3	25.1
Japan	21.1	10.7	50.7
Canada	15.1	1.5	9.9
U.S.S.R.	10.4	1.7	16.3
People's Rep. China	10.0	2.1	21.0
Fed. Rep. Germany	9.4	4.1	43.6
Finland	7.5	0.3	4.0
Sweden	7.4	0.8	10.8
France	6.5	2.0	35.7
Italy	4.6	2.0	43.5
Others	47.7	22.2	46.5
World total	**203.8**	**63.7**	**31.3**

Wastepaper suitable for recycling consist of various grades, excluding "disposable" grades, such as tissue paper, wallpaper, and cigarette paper. Books and documents tend to have a long life and rarely find their way to recycling. The best grades for recycling are mainly telephone directories, newspapers, magazines, printed advertising material, carton boards, and corrugated containers. Paper should be free of extras (envelope windows, samples attached, heavy gluing, etc.).

The most desirable raw materials are acquired from printing waste. Almost 100% of these products are recy-

FIGURE 1: **Total fiber consumption in paper and board production, 1986 (total fiber = 210 million tons).**

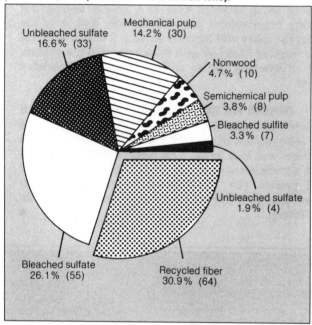

FIGURE 2: **Changes in world paper and paperboard furnish components, 1973-2000.**

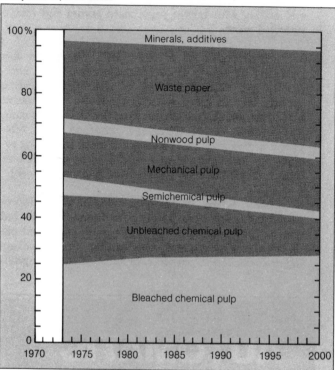

FIGURE 3: **Usage and recovery of recycled fiber.**

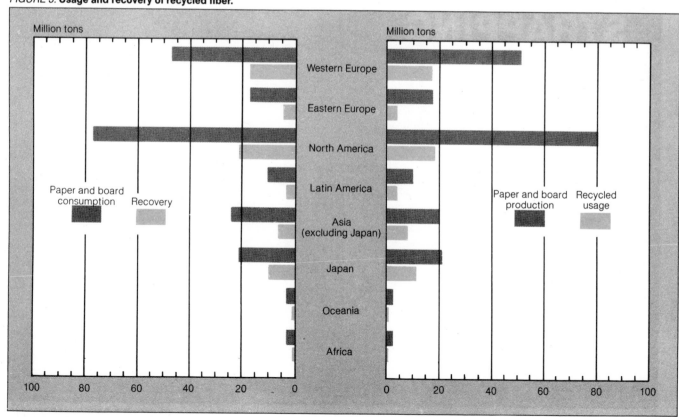

clable, contrary to, for example, household waste, of which over 15% is normally unusable. Other important sources of wastepaper supply are department stores, supermarkets and other enterprises, industrial units, converting plants, and offices. Wastepaper is generally classified and priced according to quality, starting with higher quality (white clippings, newspapers, magazines) and ending with brown paperboard grades and mixed unsorted waste.

WASTEPAPER AS A COMMODITY. Wastepaper has gradually become a marked international trade commodity too. Overall tonnage of wastepaper crossing country borders today exceeds 8 million tons. Almost half of this tonnage originates from the U.S. and is comprised mostly of old corrugated containers (OCC), telephone directories, etc. The world's main importing regions are Asia (more than 3 million tons) and Western Europe (3 million tons, mainly from regional sources).

WIDE RANGE OF END-USE APPLICATIONS. Unprocessed wastepaper has traditionally found its main end uses in the manufacture of lower-grade paper and paperboard products, mainly intended for various packaging or construction purposes. In addition to these products, sorted or deinked waste is currently used for many demanding end products, such as newsprint, printing and writing paper, tissue, packaging paper, various corrugated board raw materials, and carton boards.

The term "wastepaper" may give one the impression of something with inferior quality, but this is not the case with several recycled-fiber-based products meeting high international quality standards. Some newsprint mills are reportedly producing 100%-wastepaper-based newsprint. Printing and writing paper producers could also be using recycled fiber to a greater degree, but quality requirements are still so high that it is unlikely the share will increase notably. It is also doubtful that recycled fiber will gain more ground in the production of specialty grades such as security and telefax paper.

DEMAND FOR RECYCLED-FIBER-BASED PRODUCTS. It is safe to predict that the rapid average growth rate for consumption of recycled fiber will continue in the medium and long terms. This forecast is based on both past developments and increasing activity in product and process R&D. Therefore, the term "wastepaper-based product" may become even more misleading in the future. ∎

Chapter 7

Municipal Solid Waste and the Paper Industry: The Next Five Years

Municipal collection programs are depressing the cost of old newspapers at the same time that consumers are clamoring for recycled fiber

By FRED D. IANNAZZI and RICHARD STRAUSS

The problems associated with disposal of municipal solid waste (MSW)—diminishing landfill capacity, resistance to siting new incinerator capacity, skyrocketing disposal costs—are well known to everyone in the paper industry because the paper industry is always singled out whenever a governmental authority decides that we should "do something" about MSW. The only politically acceptable method of dealing with MSW is source reduction, to be achieved principally by increased recycling. As a result of these public perceptions, a host of laws and directives intended to increase recycling of paper products has been proposed or instituted in the past year, and apparently the flood of legislation is accelerating.

The legislative approaches to reducing MSW incorporate a wide range of incentives and penalties, including targeted percent recycle fiber in specified paper products, mandated reductions in solid waste load, mandated source segregation and collection programs, tax penalty for use of nonrecyclable packaging materials, government-agency purchasing directives requiring a minimum level of recycle fiber in certain paper products, and tax incentives for wastepaper processing facilities and equipment. While some of these initiatives have repeatedly proven to be ineffective or counterproductive, for example, mandating a source segregation

Mr. Iannazzi is president, and Mr. Strauss is senior consultant, Andover International Associates, Danvers, Mass.

program for old newspapers (ONP) without finding a market for the collected product, there is no doubt the legislative activity has captured the attention of the paper industry and prompted some very useful and statesman-like actions on the part of the industry. This article reviews the current status of recycling of paper products and projects what is likely to happen to wastepaper recovery and recycling in the next five years.

HOW BIG IS THE WASTEPAPER PROBLEM? The logical place to start an analysis of the present and future state of paper recycling, in the context of the MSW problem, is to present statistics on the magnitude of MSW and the relative fraction that paper products contribute to it. Unfortunately, good statistics on MSW and its composition are remarkably hard to come by. For example, the report "Facing America's Trash: What Next for Municipal Solid Waste?" produced by the U.S. Office of Technology Assessment (October 1989), cites per capita generation of MSW in selected cities ranging from 1.9 lb/day (Yakima, Wash.) to 9.4 lb/day (Chattanooga, Tenn.), a *five fold* variation. Similarly, in 49 studies of the composition of MSW, the estimated percentage of total paper in MSW ranged from 29.9% to 54.7%.

The figures most often quoted, apparently "consensus" figures, are 3.6 lb/day per capita for total MSW generation, with a paper content of 40%. Using these figures, the annual U.S. totals are then about 160 million tons of MSW, containing about 63 million tons of paper. To illustrate the uncertainty in these estimates—even if we hold the total MSW figure at 160 million tons—a difference of 30% to 50% in the paper content would pro-

TABLE 1: **Disposition of paper products in U.S. (million tons).**

Potentially recyclable paper products	U.S. consumption	Recovery for reuse and export	% recovery	Disposed in MSW
Newsprint (ONP)	13.7	4.5	33	9.2
Magazines and inserts/supplements (OMG)	6.4	Negative	Negative	6.4
Printing and writing (P & W), less OMG	17.5	8.5	49	7.0[1]
Old corrugated containers (OCC)	22.9	11.8	52	11.1
Other packaging	7.4	Negative	Negative	7.4
All other disposable paper and board[2]	11.9	Negative	Negative	11.9
Totals	**79.8**	**24.8**	**31.1**	**53.0**

1. About 2.0 disappears in permanent records.
2. Not including tissue.
Source: A.I.A.

duce a paper loading in MSW ranging from 48 million tons to 80 million tons. With much variability inherent in these numbers, it would be impractical to use them as either a basis for setting target reductions or a means for monitoring achievements of targets.

A better method of determining the paper contribution to the MSW load is to build up the figures from the statistics for the major grades of paper. Based on data from the American Paper Institute (API) and the U.S. Dept. of Commerce, Andover International Associates (AIA) has compiled the totals (Table 1). We can now examine the major grades individually and project what is likely to happen in the next five years to the quantity of each of the grades in MSW.

OLD CORRUGATED CONTAINERS (OCC).

OCC, in common with some other wastepaper grades, is peculiar in that its rate of demand (consumption in medium and liner) is dependent on its rate of supply (production of corrugated containers). This cyclic situation is best illustrated by Figure 1, a format develped by AIA. Of the U.S. consumption of 22.9 million tons, 11.8 million tons (51%) were recovered for recycling or export and 11.1 million tons ended up in the MSW stream. Because some of the recovered OCC is used for products other than liner and medium and because some OCC and linerboard are exported, the recycle fiber content in U.S. corrugated containers was only about 25%, even though the recovery of OCC was 51%. Too often in discussions of possible legislative action to alleviate MSW load, the percent recycle fiber and percent recovery are considered to be synonymous.

What should be done to stimulate increased recovery of OCC? The short answer: nothing. OCC is in rather short supply at present, and we project it will become even tighter in the future. Even though the consumption of corrugated containers is expected to increase by 4.3 million tons (19%) from 1988 to 1995, the OCC load in MSW is projected to decrease by 2.3 million tons over that same period because of the forecast increase in OCC pulping capacity (Table 2). At the projected 1995 recovery rate of 68%, OCC will be in short supply indeed. Although the recovery rate will not have reached the practical limit, which we estimate to be about 75% to 80%, it will be close enough for the OCC market to be a sellers' market. There is no reason to impose incentives or penalties on OCC recovery or reuse to reduce its presence in the MSW stream. Existing market forces will do the job nicely.

ONP AND OLD MAGAZINES.

On the face of it, the picture for increased recycling of ONP looks rather bleak (Figure 2). For more than ten years, the recovery rate has held at 30% to 33%, and since the newsprint industry is currently overbuilt, there seems to be no compelling reason for producers to install new deinking capacity. Moreover, despite continuing research efforts, there is no present or potential application for ONP other than newsprint that offers any significant opportunity for growth. The fallout from the MSW crisis, however, has completely changed the operating parameters of the newsprint industry. Now there is good evidence for the view that the demand for ONP will rise dramatically in the next few years so that by the end of the decade the demand will be challenging the limits of supply.

The newsprint industry has felt the impact of the MSW problem in two areas of its business:

1. New laws in Connecticut, California, and other states have set progressively increasing targets for recycle fiber in newsprint. Although the existing state laws are inconsistent and some are probably unworkable, it is clear to many newsprint producers that some set of minimum recycle fiber standards will be adopted and that it will be necessary in the future to have ONP deinking capacity in order to be able to sell newsprint.

2. The good news of the MSW crisis is that it has had, and will continue to have, a depressing effect on the cost of ONP to the newsprint producers. The disappearance of

FIGURE 1: **U.S. supply and disposal of corrugated containers.**

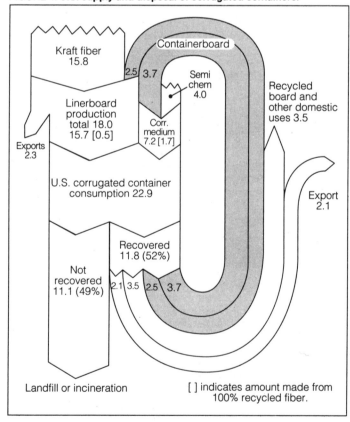

TABLE 2: **The OCC load in MSW is expected to decrease by 2.3 million tons from 1988 to 1995.**

OCC (mm tons)	U.S. consumption	Recovery for reuse and export	% recovery	Disposed in MSW
1983	18.4	8.4	46	10.0
1988	22.9	11.8	52	11.1
1995	27.2	18.4	68	8.8

landfill capacity has driven the price of MSW disposal to an average of about $60/ton in the Northeast, and the prospect is for continued escalation of disposal costs in all areas of the country. Many municipalities have instituted segregation and curbside collection of ONP simply to avoid having to pay to dispose of it, and they are willing to pay anything less than the prevailing tipping fee to have it removed. In effect, the tipping fee (avoided cost) is subtracted from the collection/sorting/baling/transport costs (incurred costs) to arrive at the price for ONP delivered to the deinking facility. When priced on this basis, ONP becomes an economically attractive alternative to virgin pulp, in many cases even if a new deinking facility displaces an existing thermomechanical pulp facility.

To determine quantitatively what effect the new market conditions will have on ONP recovery, we must select for analysis one set of recycle fiber targets from among the many that have been legislated or proposed. We will use the recently announced New York State standards because New York standards will necessarily be influential in the industry. AIA worked with New York to assist in developing these standards. The New York standards for percent recycle fiber content in newsprint and the corresponding recovery rates calculated by AIA are shown in Table 3.

The limit on the rate of increase in recycle fiber content is the rate at which new deinking capacity can be built. Our estimate is that the deinking capacity will, in fact, be in place slightly faster than the New York schedule requires. Although at present the potential ONP supply far exceeds demand, when 65% recovery is required the demand will press the limit of practical recovery. We conclude that the mechanism is already in place to achieve the maximum possible reduction of the ONP load in MSW. What is now required is to standardize recycle fiber targets in newsprint and to maintain consistent legislative policies for the next several years.

It is interesting to note that the newer ONP deinking processes not only permit but also benefit from an admixture of about 1:2 old magazines (OMG) to ONP. By the year 2000, if the 65% recovery of ONP is achieved, about 5.5 million tons of OMG will be required in ONP deinking, over half the OMG potentially available at that time. Thus, the new conditions imposed on the ONP market will greatly reduce the OMG load in MSW.

PRINTING AND WRITING PAPER. Used printing and writing (P&W) paper, a major contributor to the MSW load, if properly segregated, is a valuable product for which ample profitable markets exist. Paradoxically, this is the one major wastepaper stream for which no organized program in hand will significantly reduce the load in MSW. Problems inhibit recovery of this potentially valuable resource:

1. In contrast with ONP, for example, the P&W paper feedstock is extremely varied in composition. The major grade classifications that comprise P&W include uncoated free-sheet, coated free-sheet, bleached bristol, coated groundwood, and uncoated groundwood. Within these major categories are many subcategories that must be monitored during storing and segregation to obtain the highest-value recycle paper.

2. For maximum utilization, the wastepaper must be collected and segregated into relatively uniform feedstocks. The paper is presently classified in three major wastepaper grades: pulp substitutes, high-grade deinking, and mixed. Within each of these major grades are multiple subdivisions recognized by the wastepaper industry. For example, API has four grades within the pulp substitutes and high-grade deinking categories, and the Paper Stock Institute of America further subdivides these four grades into 23 codes.

3. Compared with ONP and OCC, wastepaper originating from P&W grades is generated in low concentrations

FIGURE 2: **North American supply and disposition of newsprint—1988.**

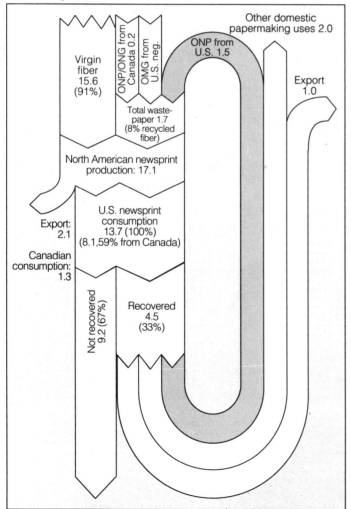

TABLE 3: **New York State targets for recycle fiber content in newsprint.**

Year	N.Y. target recycle fiber content	ONP recovery rate calculated by A.I.A.
1992	11%	35%
1995	23%	43%
1997	31% .	54%
2000	40%	65%

at scattered sites, many of which would be too small to justify pickup by wastepaper processors.

As a result of these multiple difficulties, the wastepaper industry has traditionally concentrated on recovery and reuse of the most accessible of the waste P&W paper: the preconsumer converter waste. This paper is usually found in high concentrations from identifiable sources and is clean and well segregated. Little postconsumer office waste is recovered at present, and postconsumer P&W household waste is essentially unrecovered.

There are now signs that the MSW crisis will begin to affect the recovery of P&W paper just as it has affected recovery of ONP. However, because of the fragmented nature of the supply, generation, and utilization of P&W paper, no single action could be taken by government or industry that would significantly increase utilization of this wastepaper. Rather, a series of actions by both government and industry will be required to alleviate the load of used P&W paper in MSW, and we believe that we will begin to see significant progress in the next few years in achieving this objective.

We see ahead developments that will lead to evolutionary—not revolutionary—progress in reducing the P&W load in MSW:

1. Much more prevalent office waste segregation programs, impelled both by the wish to avoid escalating disposal fees and the genuine desire on the part of the environmentalists (that is to say, everyone) to conserve scarce landfill capacity.

2. Implementation by municipalities and/or wastepaper dealers of systems for collecting small quantities of segregated office waste from scattered sites and concentrating them in central dropoff points.

3. Implementation by municipalities and/or wastepaper dealers of systems for collecting small quantities of segregated household fine paper waste, in conjunction with established programs for curbside collection.

4. Improved programs by wastepaper dealers to collect segregated fine paper from dropoff points, leading to more efficient and economical collection and processing of multiple grades.

5. Improved sorting and contaminant-removal processes at wastepaper handling sites.

6. Improved deinking/pulping processes that would be more tolerant of mixed feedstocks (like the newer ONP deinking process that permit high OMG content).

7. Increasing imposition of purchasing specifications by government agencies and others requiring a minimum recycle fiber content in specified products.

8. Increasing attention by government authorities and industry participants to reducing or eliminating fiber mixtures or converting additives that inhibit fiber reuse.

9. Increasing recognition by the paper industry that the market will actually favor a product with significant recycle content, even if qualities such as brightness or contaminant content are not equivalent to paper made from virgin pulp. ∎

Chapter 8

States, Municipalities Change Course in Dealing with Wastepaper Handling

Development agencies help educate consumers, assist in setting up recycling programs to reuse collected postconsumer wastepaper

By WILLIAM M. FERRETTI

Because of solid waste pressures, recycling markets, particularly recycled fiber markets, are undergoing important changes that will significantly alter their character. By now the litany of the U.S. solid waste management crisis should be familiar to most paper mill managers and their corporate executives. Landfills are filling up faster than they are being replaced. Incineration, despite the fact that most state and federal officials acknowledge it as an acceptable waste management option, will be limited by economic, environmental, and public-acceptance constraints.

As a consequence, recycling will continue to play a growing role in most state and local solid waste management efforts. And paper, given its sizable contribution to the waste stream and its inherent recyclability, will be targeted by government officials for diversion from the landfill and incinerator waste streams.

CHANGING MARKET. Along with markets for other materials, such as glass, plastics, and metals, supply and demand for recycled fiber is being redefined by a growing shortfall in solid waste disposal capacity. Public policy is now moving toward a goal of eliminating certain classes of products (including paper products) as waste, creating pressures for those products to be "source reduced" (i.e., to have lower material utilization and toxic content) and redesigned to be reusable or recyclable.

In the case of wastepaper—specifically postconsumer grades of wastepaper (e.g., old newspaper [ONP], office paper), these pressures have caused an unlinking of traditional supply and demand. Supply once responded to demand. Now, demand is responding to the promise and inevitability of supply.

Mr. Ferretti is director, Office of Recycling Market Development, New York State Dept. of Economic Development.

An executive of a well-known U.S. manufacturer of recycled paper recently related that the company once based its pricing strategy on the need to create supply for its mills (i.e., the higher the price offered, the more wastepaper delivered). Now, however, the company uses pricing to manage the supply of ONP available to it, rewarding quality and discouraging contaminated, unusable material.

SHORT-TERM IMPLICATIONS. The 1989 ONP "crisis" was the most obvious disruption that resulted from this unlinking. ONP supply grew faster than the pace of demand. In fact, demand growth, largely because of a drop in exports, stagnated, while supply continued to surge. The bottom line was that mill prices fell. For municipalities that relied on intermediaries to process and move their ONP to market, the weak mill price translated into a charge, the so-called "negative" price that still prevails in many areas.

In New York State, the crisis was handled by turning to the biggest opportunity sector, newspaper publishers. In May 1989, Governor Mario Cuomo invited the state's newspaper publishers to join with the state in crafting a voluntary action plan to bolster the ONP market. Around the same time, similar efforts were initiated in other northeastern states, including Pennsylvania and Massachusetts. Connecticut, in responding to the problem, took a different course by mandating that publishers make use of specified quantities of recycled newsprint.

The significant outcome of these initiatives has been a commitment by newspaper publishers in the region to adopt "buy recycled" purchasing goals. In New York, this commitment involves meeting an annual recycled-fiber consumption level of 40% by the year 2000.

In turn, newsprint manufacturers have responded. In eastern North America alone, nearly 1 million tons of new deinking capacity have been announced (for start-up in 1992). In addition, Smurfit Newsprint Corp. announced its intention to build a recycled newsprint mill in the Northeast, a move that would more than double the region's recycled newsprint production capacity and add considerably to its ONP consumption capacity.

Municipal recycling officials are now beginning to realize the benefits of this increased capacity. Across the Northeast, mills have offered to buy municipal ONP on the table. Significantly, these offers include positive prices, a signal that the market turnaround for ONP has begun.

ONP CRISIS REPEATED? Concerns have been raised by both skeptics and optimists about the likelihood of the ONP crisis repeating for other materials or other wastepaper grades (e.g., printing and writing paper). Whether a crisis is repeated elsewhere will largely depend on the actions taken by state and local governments, businesses, and industry.

At least two conditions should be fulfilled to prevent future crises: Municipal suppliers of recyclables should exchange their "garbage-collector's ethic" for a "market ethic," and major consumer sectors must assert their preference for recycled products and enforce that preference through purchase/contract practices.

Under the garbage-collector's ethic, the approach to municipal recycling is simply to get rid of the waste in the most expedient fashion. This approach treats recycling just like garbage management. The garbage collector/recycler collects the materials comingled (glass, paper, plastics, and metals mixed together) in a packer truck—the same truck used to haul garbage the other four days of the week. This approach also assumes that homeowners cannot handle complexity and perform some sorting at the source. The result is a low-grade, low-value, or worthless product that, just like garbage, costs the municipality to eliminate.

By contrast, the market-ethic recycler seeks to capture the intrinsic value of the materials collected. The market recycler treats recycling as a business activity, recyclables as products, and recycling industries as customers. The market recycler collects and prepares the material in a way that enables the locality to meet (and possibly exceed) the customers' expectations. The result under this approach is a quality product, an earned reputation as a preferred supplier, long-term stability and reliability of market outlets, and a lower cost than dumping the material or, possibly, a net revenue.

To help municipal officials make the transition in New York State, the Office of Recycling Market Development (ORMD) has awarded grants to communities that organize into regional cooperatives for marketing recyclables. Such cooperatives can be a cost-effective means for participating communities to focus on the market-driven aspects of recycling. In addition, ORMD serves as a public service consultant to municipalities, providing advice on collection and marketing strategies and sponsoring market opportunities workshops. The bottom-line message of these consulting efforts is that recycling success is dependent on a community's ability to generate a product that will fulfill the end user's (i.e.,

paper mill's) requirements.

The second way to prevent another materials recycling crisis focuses on the consumers of a paper mill's products. Any mill's use of recycled fiber is largely driven by the customer's willingness (assuming no difference in price) to buy a product with recycled content or, more importantly, the consumer's indifference to a product's content (virgin or recycled), where performance is indistinguishable. As such, the demand for municipal wastepaper is derived from the demand for the products that are or could be made from that paper.

Consumers have reached a point of indifference regarding the virgin or recycled content of many well-established paper and paperboard products. For other products, such as newsprint, however, consumers only recently had the option of purchasing a recycled product that delivers the same utility as its virgin counterpart. Despite that availability, many newspaper publishers continued to assert that recycled newsprint was inferior to its virgin counterpart.

Only by providing evidence that such an assertion was based on past experience and is no longer relevant were more than 90% of New York's daily newspaper publishers persuaded to purchase recycled newsprint. Market developers for recycling, in order to make consumers commit to buying recycled, must face the constant challenge of correcting consumers' misperceptions regarding recycled paper's performance.

LONG-TERM IMPLICATIONS. The market for recycled fiber is undergoing what economists call a fundamental structural change, implying that the factors guiding supply, demand, and price have changed. For example, in this market, which has traditionally been characterized by price volatility, there is an impetus toward stability and predictability. This is largely due to the new players that have entered the scene—municipalities on the supply side and manufacturers that traditionally relied on virgin resources for their raw materials on the demand side.

The virgin-based manufacturers that are now converting to recycling depended on forests that produced

Recycling markets are evolving to a point that matches the long-term objectives of both the new supply-side (municipalities) and demand-side (manufacturers) players.

Supply once responded to demand. Today the company uses its pricing to manage the supply of ONP available to it, rewarding quality and discouraging contaminated, unusable material.

predictable quantities of fiber at predictable levels of quality. That predictability reduced those companies' exposure to risk. They still pursue risk minimization in the recycling market by demanding predictability of supply as well as consistency of quality from new fiber sources, namely municipalities and/or brokers. Municipalities have a similar desire to minimize risk by seeking predictability and reliability of demand for their recyclables. By sharing the same objectives, these new (and major) players are having a leveling effect on the market.

DISTINGUISHING FEATURES. These changes coming into view present a picture of the possible recycled fiber market of the 1990s. To begin, there will be expanded demand for postconsumer wastepaper grades—those generated by households, offices, and commercial establishments. This demand will come as a result of the paper industry's major customers (e.g., publishers, printers, converters, institutions) asserting their intentions to help close the recycling loop for their products by not only buying recycled but working with paper companies to ensure that the finished products (e.g., newspapers, directories, boxes, office paper), once discarded, are used in the manufacture of new paper and paperboard. As a result, the "urban forest" will be the next major fiber resource for the paper industry to harvest.

Secondly, the major players in the recycled fiber market will be risk managers seeking to maintain stability and predictability. Therefore, little price volatility can be expected for the wastepaper grades traded by these players.

Until recently, municipal participation in the recycling market was largely passive, conducted through third-party agents, such as brokers and wastepaper dealers. Under these arrangements, localities were left free to continue the garbage-collector's approach to recycling, leaving the brokers to figure out how to move the municipally collected wastepaper. Also, municipalities,

understandably, pay to have the material processed and marketed and, as a result, capture none of the value-added benefit from upgrading and marketing themselves. Municipalities are expected to take a more active role in the future. Specifically, direct contracts will be made between mills and municipalities. In many cases, these contracts will also include backhaul arrangements, where manufacturers arrange to carry wastepaper back to the mill using the same vehicles that deliver the finished product.

Another feature of the active role played by municipalities will be their pursuit of diversified supply strategies. Specifically, local recycling officials will seek to avoid the risk inherent in contracting with a single buyer. Rather, they will negotiate multiple supply contracts—some with mills directly, some through brokers—to prevent a halt in the flow of their wastepaper.

Cooperative marketing by municipalities will be another feature of the 1990s' fiber market. Localities will join together to increase their attractiveness as supply sources and improve their bargaining leverage in negotiating deals. In New York State, three such cooperatives were recently formed with startup grants provided by the ORMD.

While municipalities are expected to play a more active role in determining the fate of their fiber supplies, the role of the traditional packers and brokers—providing support services to a more sophisticated municipal client—will remain. These services include contract baling and/or marketing that portion of a municipality's (or co-op's) wastepaper that has not been committed to mill-direct contracts.

Finally, manufacturers will be directly involved in developing the municipal supply of wastepaper to meet the mill's specifications. This will involve company outreach to municipal recycling officials, advising those officials not only of the mill specifications but also of alternative means for setting up local collection programs to generate the required fiber quality. ∎

Chapter 9

Legislation Pushing Paper Industry Despite Limited Recycling Know How

Industry may be developing "recycling hysteria" because forced demand for recycled products has occurred too quickly without proper planning

By KEN L. PATRICK, Editor in Chief

Recycling, along with many other environmental issues, is receiving increased attention worldwide. Paper recycling, already well established in Europe, is generally considered to be in its infancy in North America. However, U.S. mandatory recycling legislation goes into effect in the 1990s, requiring certain grades of paper to be made with as much as 25% recycled fiber.

Industry experts agree that recycling is one of the pulp and paper industry's toughest environmental challenges. Although companies have responded with a myriad of approaches, most have boiled down to defensive measures designed to minimize vulnerability. The result is methods dictated by public policy.

Unfortunately, this has created legislation prepared without constructive dialogue, and most industry leaders agree that many of the realities of recycling have not been adequately addressed. One of these realities, according to many paper companies, is the technology—or lack of it—to process wastepaper and turn it into a quality, marketable product.

To discuss the aspects of recycling technology—specifically, the problems involved in separation of wastepaper and the continuous repulping of fibers—*Pulp & Paper* interviewed Roland Fjallstrom, president of Celleco Hedemora Inc. Fjallstrom is a native of Sweden who arrived in Canada in 1974 as a market and product research scientist. In 1979, he moved to Atlanta, Ga., to establish the North American headquarters for Celleco. Since 1985, Fjallstrom has been president of Celleco Hedemora, which in 1989 moved its new North American headquarters to the Atlanta area.

P&P: *Specifically, what problems, or realities, is the paper industry facing as it begins to use more wastepaper for furnish?*

Fjallstrom: There are two areas—the characteristics of secondary fiber as a fiber source and the effects of fiber supply exceeding demand. Recycling in the U.S. is currently a small but open market for both buyer and seller. Wastepaper recycling companies [can] pick and choose their sources, plus they handle a small volume of wastepaper that is relatively easy to process. The U.S. has mostly recycled wastepaper that has been carefully prepared and segregated, such as newspapers, magazines, ledger grades, clippings (both brown and white), etc.

This secondary fiber is more similar to the virgin source it will be blended with. By recycling secondary fiber produced from the same process for which it will be reused—newsprint being recycled into newsprint, for example—a significant process advantage is achieved. At this time, pulp and paper mills using wastepaper can pick and choose from "quality" wastepaper and the suppliers that provide it.

But the realities of collection under recycling legislation will be very different. The segregation of wastepaper grades will be limited due to sheer volume. The mixed waste fiber source will increase dramatically and will contain fibers that have been recycled more than one time. Mixed waste of this type will have a dramatic difference in optimum fiber characteristics, resulting in operating as well as quality problems. At this time, the U.S. paper industry is not prepared for the effect of a mandatory recycling program.

Currently, most wastepaper comes from small recycling programs that are essentially experimental, where citizens voluntarily separate, for example, newspapers from the rest of their trash. To expect widespread voluntary compliance from the public and expect them to separate all paper into different paper grades is not very realistic, at least not before laws go into effect. In other words, the supply of nicely segregated paper will not increase automatically to meet new legislative requirements.

P&P: *Numerous wastepaper dealers are operating in North America and have been for some time. Why can't these companies continue to do what they have been doing and simply expand as needed?*

Fjallstrom: Some of those wastepaper dealers probably will stay in business, but their operations will not be as profitable in the future. As pulp mills demand a larger volume of wastepaper, dealers will exceed their supply of voluntarily segregated paper, and they will have to separate it themselves straight from the "trash."

There will definitely be a difference in the quality of wastepaper the industry is using now and what it will be able to get if current legislation is used to drive the industry. For example, the board stock inside a cereal box is a low-grade gray pulp similar to what the industry will eventually recycle into several paper grades. The U.S. paper industry is simply not prepared for that.

Europe has developed a workable system during a long period of time. In the U.S., there is only what I call "surface legislation" (and it is quite unacceptable) rather than realistic and strategically implemented legislation. With such mandatory recycling programs, the industry will be forced to accept a lower-grade fiber source.

P&P: *How and why is the European situation functionally different from that in North America? Why can't our mills simply do what European mills do?*

Fjallstrom: The U.S. paper industry does not have the proven technology and methods necessary to use vast amounts of wastepaper. The characteristics of fibers used in Europe are very different, so simply copying their systems isn't possible. But more importantly, the North American industry is not organized to recycle on a widespread basis, even to recycle fiber once.

In reviewing the progress of recycling programs in Europe, the same fiber is being recycled five to eight times. One reason they are able to do this is their recycling programs keep paper much more segregated, so they do not have as much mixed waste as we probably will. Until the industry has experience in using recycled fiber as a supplementary source, including recycling fiber several times, there is actually very little data to use as comparison.

P&P: *What happens to fiber as it is progressively recycled? Is there a limit to the number of times it can be recycled?*

Fjallstrom: Any time a fiber is recycled or reprocessed, a degradation of its original structure occurs, resulting in a loss of key characteristics (Figure 1). Methods to restructure the fiber chemically or mechanically have shown relatively good results the first time around. But eventually, depending on the number of times the fiber is processed, it will lose its most important characteristics.

P&P: *Why is mixed wastepaper more difficult to process? Is it important that mills know the origin and process used with the original fibers?*

Fjallstrom: The retreatment or reprocessing necessary to enhance the remaining key fiber characteristics is easier if the mill knows the type of fiber and the original process used to pulp it. Also, the differences between hardwood and softwood fibers and which geographical region this hardwood/softwood comes from are important factors. The difficulty comes in dealing with mixed waste having an unknown mixture of these variables.

P&P: *Recycling is being touted as a solution to North America's growing landfill problem. But aren't there some environmental drawbacks to recycling?*

Fjallstrom: Recycling is not "all good," even though it is widely thought of as 100% environmentally friendly. The results of recycling and the attempt to establish good fiber characteristics will generate fiber material that cannot be used, such as undesirable fines, due to poor characteristics.

If various nonfiber material is considered—such as inks, fillers, etc.—there is a discharge from the process that will increase in volume. To maintain the runability of paper made with recycled fibers, an increase in chemical use is also expected, which could have a negative impact on the environment.

With current technology, the yield loss, or "yield shrinkage," is about 20% to 30%. That means only about 70 to 80 tons out of 100 tons of mixed wastepaper can be used for recycled paper, sending 20 to 30 tons of that to landfills, unless efficient incineration technology can be developed. However, even incineration is not a complete solution because some materials, such as filler, are not affected by incineration, which means that an increase in solids going to the landfill is inevitable.

P&P: *You mentioned another aspect of recycling—fiber supply exceeding demand. In addition to reducing prices, what will be the effects of this?*

Fjallstrom: The industry currently has a relatively good balance between worldwide paper demand and committed pulp/fiber production. The addition of wastepaper at current projected levels will exceed pulp/fiber demand by 10% to 15%.

This is an effect of recycling that is crucial for the in-

FIGURE 1: **As fibers are continually recycled, they gradually lose strength and bonding capabilities.**

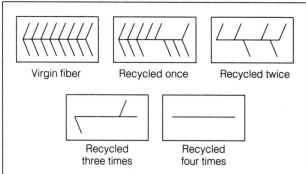

Virgin fiber   Recycled once   Recycled twice

Recycled three times   Recycled four times

dustry and lawmakers to understand, and it is a very delicate balance. The paper industry's growth is based on meeting continuously increasing demands for quality. And growth is what enables the industry to invest in research and development, not only to keep the cycle going by meeting quality demands but to adjust to issues like recycling—they go hand in hand. Meeting recycling demands does not help the industry grow because it does not help meet quality demands; in fact, it works against it.

So when mills see an overabundance of fiber—fiber that actually works against quality increases—they do not want to invest money now in technology that may be useless to them because it is probably not designed to work with recycled fiber. This creates a vicious cycle—the distance between demand for quality and ability to meet that demand grows wider and wider. This is already happening. Everyone wants to play it safe and take a "wait and see" attitude.

While that may be playing it safe for the individual mill or company, it is bad news for the pulp and paper industry in general. The industry should be charging ahead to meet the future but instead is stalled, or if measured by the quality demand/supply difference, may actually be going backwards (Figure 2).

P&P: *How can recycling laws be altered to prevent this cycle?*

Fjallstrom: Regrettably, industry's attitude is no different than what has existed for years. The industry lacks professional communication between producers and legislators. As a result, the industry is suffering from "recycle hysteria." The pulp and paper industry is as interested in the environment as anyone, but to change this situation, a team approach must be taken by producers and legislators, not allowing lawmakers to forget many of the other issues that affect the public.

There must be an organized legislative plan that sets a realistic proportion for secondary fiber—one that meshes with future growth instead of today's committed and invested production. That will keep the "recycle hysteria" in check.

The industry must at least give this alternative a try. As far as I know, it is one of the few practical ways, maybe the only way, to maintain industry profitability and make sure everyone understands and accepts wastepaper as a fiber source.

P&P: *As recycling continues, fiber will be recycled over and over again until it is useless to anyone. How can the industry control the number of times fiber is reused?*

Fjallstrom: One possible solution might be to establish a proper proportion of recycled fiber for prime paper grades. This would minimize the degradation of the overall pulp furnish and still maximize utilization. Currently, this is far from reality, but in the future it needs to be routine.

Roland Fjallstrom, president, Celleco Hedemora, Atlanta, Ga.

P&P: *In your opinion, what should the industry as a whole be doing to respond to recycling? Should programs be modeled after those in Europe?*

Fjallstrom: Through trade organizations, the industry should establish communication with legislators, set realistic targets for the future, and not dwell on existing conditions, which are impossible to change instantly.

Europe does not have the ultimate answer to recycling either, but many European companies do have experience in dealing with secondary fiber use. The industry leaders in the U.S. certainly should listen to and use experiences of other countries to improve the speed at which these programs can progress.

P&P: *How is Celleco Hedemora responding to U.S. recycling issues?*

Fjallstrom: First, we have taken a very careful look at what has happened in Europe over the last 20 years and what will be happening in this country in the future. We have also studied the effects that recycling has had and will have on the end users of paper products that have high recycled fiber content. Frankly, I think we have an obligation to the industry to be both realistic and thorough. We must continuously improve our view of how this changing market condition will affect the pulp and paper industry and how we can best provide the technological advances and leadership in our area of expertise—separation technology. New methods will be necessary for the industry to successfully meet the recycling challenge—and that is exactly what we are working on today. ∎

FIGURE 2: **With an ever-increasing demand for a quality product, and an outcry for more paper recycling, a gap may begin to form in which the demand for quality cannot be met.**

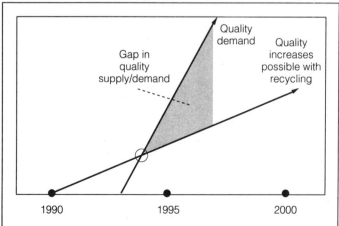

Chapter 10

Trash Crunch Drives Demand for Recycled Printing/Writing Papers

Small market may get a boost from Los Angeles's plan to send city's office wastepaper to People's Rep. China for recycling

By ROB GALIN, News Editor

Recycled printing and writing papers are becoming more readily accepted and may come way out from under the tons of trash generated by Americans each year. This trend is exemplified by a recent announcement that the city of Los Angeles, Calif., People's Rep. China (PRC), and Conservatree Paper Co. have begun a pilot project that could lead to shipping up to one-quarter of the city's office wastepaper to the PRC. Once there, it will be recycled into printing and writing grades. Los Angeles produces about 4,000 tpd of office wastepapers.

China Paper Partners (CPP), which is an affiliate of Conservatree, a San Francisco, Calif.-based distributor specializing in recycled printing/writing papers, is handling the project. CPP has already signed an agreement to construct a wastepaper sorting facility that will process 400 tpd of trash, including a 200 tpd deinking pulp mill in Tianjin Province, PRC. The mill was scheduled to come online in late 1990. Negotiations are under way for additional mills at three other locations in the PRC, according to a Conservatree official. "This is probably the biggest thing that's been done in the wastepaper business," says Alan Davis, president of Conservatree and chairman of CPP.

Once the deinking mill is online, the pulp will be sold to paper mills in the province and, possibly in the future, to a paper mill where Conservatree will serve as a principle, Davis said. Conservatree will also be looking at prospects for similar programs in the U.S. The firm was one of the bidders for James River Corp.'s former Hyde Park, Mass. mill. James River eventually awarded a five-year lease to Nolichucky Industries Corp., which has yet to reopen the idled mill.

Under the Los Angeles pilot program, which began Feb. 1, all dry paper (including newsprint) is being collected from desks at City Hall and three private office buildings and then analyzed for its export value, though none is actually being shipped to the PRC. Instead, the current haulers will continue to sort and resell the paper on the open market.

The project ultimately will assess the feasibility of a full-scale program to ship up to 1,000 tpd of wastepaper to the PRC for sorting, cleaning, and processing. However, the initial collections are more likely to be around 10 to 20 tpd. Los Angeles, like most cities, is running out of landfill space; the city's landfills are expected to reach capacity by 1993.

The PRC is experiencing a severe shortage of paper, including printing papers, stationery, and computer stock. The country is feeling the effects of rapid modernization combined with a lack of forest reserves, a spokesperson said. As a result, several paper mills, including some in Tianjin Province, have been shut down due to a lack of pulp, says Davis.

Davis believes this project is the first of its kind in the U.S. and says it is designed as a model for public-private partnerships dealing with the mounting trash disposal crisis faced by many municipalities. "There's an enormous amount of pressure for cities to recycle, and there's an enormous amount of pressure for China to find some pulp sources," Davis says. "I think the two things come together for everyone's benefit."

A decision by the Chinese on whether to go forward with the deinking mill is expected after preliminary results from the pilot project become available, says Davis. Once Conservatree's mill is online, newsprint could be pulped into the rest of the waste fiber, but most will be sorted out and sold.

BARRIERS TO RECYCLING STILL EXIST. Growth in recycled printing and writing papers is likely to remain moderate because mills still face limits on removing contaminants and other factors that affect both production and consumption. Demand could increase substantially if the federal and more state governments implement recycling regulations. Still, moderate growth is better than no growth, and many involved in the area believe the market for recycled printing and writing papers will prosper, even without additional government intervention.

Demand for recycled printing/writing papers "definitely seems to be increasing," says Susan Kinsella, Davis's assistant at Conservatree. "It's almost as though everyone put [buying recycled paper] on their fall calendars." Most of the paper Conservatree sells is from 40% to 60% recycled, with no mill broke in the furnish.

Tad Kline, a customer service representative with French Paper Co., Niles, Mich., says demand for recycled grades from his mill has "really taken off," although part of the recent growth may be due to the strong paper market in general.

"I think there's a kind of renaissance in recycling," agrees Ed Gillis, vice president-sales, P.H. Glatfelter Co. "The potential for demand is much more real today than it was five or ten years ago," he adds.

Glatfelter makes, among others, a 50%-recycled textbook grade often used for encyclopedias, various blends, and a 100%-recycled sheet that varies in shade within a roll and from roll to roll. These grades are made in Neenah, Wis. French produces some stationery papers, including a designer sheet, plus text and cover grades.

Still, Davis decries the slow expansion of recycled paper capacity. The only project due online in the near future is a mill in St. Joseph, Mo., to be built by Korean businessman Hwa-Jin Yu under the name Mi Ho Paper Co. Davis believes that, especially in the U.S. paper industry, "there's a natural bias against recycling and, secondly, the conglomeration and competition is . . . intense and, therefore, doesn't allow for the investment in the deinking technology and process for other mills to compete."

HIGH-GRADE WASTEPAPER USE UP. The U.S. government said that for printing and writing papers to be considered recycled, they must have a minimum of 40% recycled fiber, says James Hutchison, vice president-printing/writing papers division at the American Paper Institute. Most states require 50%.

Statistics on the size of the U.S. recycled printing/writing paper market were not available. However, the last API capacity survey shows that in 1987, about 351,000 tons of high-grade deinking stock were used in printing/writing and related grades, and this was ex-

---

Government procurement laws lift demand for recycled papers

Conservatree Paper Co., San Francisco, Calif., was founded in 1976 by attorney Alan Davis and now distributes over 280 grades of recycled printing and writing papers, most of which contain 50% recycled fiber. A few papers are 100% recycled fiber, and a couple are 30% to 40% recycled fiber. Conservatree sells a small amount of 100% virgin paper to fill in the line of paper that printers want but for which there isn't any recycled paper.

The company said it is the only distributor that stocks a complete line of recycled printing and fine papers in the U.S. In 1987, Conservatree sold 3 million lb of its Premium High Speed Xerographic paper, which has a 50% recycled content. It calculates that this saved 12,750 trees, 3 million kWh of energy, and 6.25 million gallons of water and reduced air pollution by 22.5 tons and solid waste by 2,250 yd³.

RCRA may step up federal procurement. The Resource Conservation & Recovery Act (RCRA) passed in 1976 required the Environmental Protection Agency to issue guidelines for government procurement of recycled paper. A lawsuit brought against EPA because of its failure to meet deadlines for complying with the act ended in 1988 when a federal judge signed a consent decree that obligated EPA to issue guidelines for procurement.

In the absence of federal regulation, 23 states had enacted government procurement laws for recycled products as of early 1988. The laws are not uniform, which means papermakers may have to fulfill different qualifications in different states. For example, for paper to qualify as recycled for purposes of government procurement in California, it must contain 50% recycled fiber, 10% of which must be postconsumer waste. If recycled paper meets these qualifications, then the state will give a 5% purchasing preference to the supplier in bidding for state contracts. (A bill pending in the Assembly would lift the preference to 10%.) Most procurement bills in the east consider a recycled sheet to be 50% recycled fiber, with no specifications made for postconsumer waste.

In 1988, Sen. Max Baucus, D-Mont., chairman of the Hazardous Waste & Toxic Substance Control Sub-

committee, held two hearings on the reauthorization of RCRA at which he submitted a mandatory recycling and procurement bill. Debate on this bill will heat up now that the transition to a new administration is over. Baucus's bill would require any federal agency to use recycled material in contracts worth $1 million or more, unless the contractor certifies that recycled material is not available or is not available at a cost of 10% more than virgin materials. It would also impose a fee on virgin materials used for packaging at a rate of $7/ton or 0.7¢/rigid container. Packaging made from recycled materials would be made exempt.

The bill sets a national goal of 25% municipal solid waste recycling within four years and 50% in ten years, where recycling constitutes least-cost disposal. While industry sources do not expect the bill to pass as is, the pressure to keep paper out of landfills is mounting and recycled paper and board mills stand to gain if the bill goes into effect.

—*Regina McGrath, News Editor*

Conservatree's price book offers over 280 grades of recycled printing and writing papers to businesses, nonprofit groups, and government agencies.

pected to climb by about 14% to 400,000 tons in 1990. In addition, about 1.014 million tons of pulp substitutes were used in printing/writing papers in 1988.

Major contaminants are ink, adhesives, fillers, and plastics, such as those on window envelopes, according to Hutchison. Paper used with computer laser printers is not recyclable for printing and writing grades because the heat bonds the ink to the cellulose fibers, he says. However, used laser paper can be recovered for use in tissue. In fact, says Hutchison, 60% of the scheduled new tissue capacity is wastepaper-based. "Most of the material suitable for printing/writing papers is now being used," he added.

Davis said the deinking pulp mill that the company may build in the PRC will take all papers, regardless of inks and coatings.

But Al Strickman, who is in charge of government relations and resource recovery, western region, Garden State Paper Co. Inc., agreed that quality of wastepaper is an issue. Strickman, who is also chairman of the recently formed California Coalition of Recycled Paper Mills, said it is not enough to simply pull fiber out of the solid-waste stream. "If it's mixed with a lot of contaminants . . . we can't use it."

Strickman adds that he would like to see the private collection industry that is now in place be supported rather than supplanted by government agencies. The existing paperstock industry works well, is capable of change, and can deliver quality, he noted.

MEETING CUSTOMERS' NEEDS. The recycled printing/writing paper market is still evolving, and mills and merchants will have to identify customers' needs. But suppliers will also have to educate buyers and the public at large about recycled papers "to make sure we all understand what recycling means and that we understand the value of recycling," one source says.

For mills, recycling doesn't necessarily mean large cost savings. In fact, Kline says, there is not much difference between the cost of materials for recycled or virgin fiber grades. And equivalent products sell for essentially the same price in the market.

Strickman and others suggested that incentives for customers, if not also for mills, should be implemented to increase demand for recycled printing/writing papers. Rod Miller, legislative coordinator for Californians Against Waste, says possible incentives include tax credits for mills and procurement preferences instituted by area governments.

API has opposed procurement preferences for 17 years, although the group is reevaluating the paper industry's positions on all questions relating to solid waste, Hutchison says. Procurement programs will not result in significant reductions in solid waste, he says. API does have in place various promotional programs to encourage recycling. Hutchison notes that roughly 90% of all recycling is being done by the paper industry. ■

Economics of Recycling

Paper recycling has been practiced for centuries simply because it is economical. Depending on the paper being recycled and the resulting grades being produced, very little capital equipment—mainly just for defibering (pulper tubs), screening, and cleaning—is required, unless, of course, extensive deinking is involved. But even in some deinking operations, such as for newsprint or tissue, the economics still can favor recycling.

As discussed in several articles in this section, the per-ton production cost of virgin pulp for newsprint will tend to exceed the cost for a 100% ONP furnish by as much as $70, obviously depending on the size and pulping process used at the virgin mill. Although raw material costs are currently higher for ONP, other process costs, and particularly costs for power, are significantly lower.

For other grades, especially printing and writing papers, the picture is mixed, for both capital costs and production costs. This section makes a thorough comparative analysis of production costs for most grades, considering expenditures for raw materials, chemicals, and personnel, as well as capital outlays.

Chapter 11

Economics Favor Increased Use of Recycled Fiber in Most Furnishes

Grade-by-grade cost analysis shows various advantages, but savings depend on geographics, fiber availability, and desired product quality

By ARTHUR C. VEVERKA

Worldwide, nearly 75 million tons of recycled fiber were consumed by the paper industry in 1988, accounting for almost one-third of the total papermaking fiber needs of the industry. North America and Western Europe (as a whole) each consumed some 20 million tons of wastepaper in 1988, followed by Japan with a consumption of 12.5 million tons. These three regions accounted for about 70% of the total worldwide use of recycled fiber.

During the period 1970 to 1988, the demand for recycled fiber grew twice as fast as the demand for virgin pulp on a worldwide basis (Figure 1). This growth amounted to 5%/year for recycled fiber vs 2.5%/year for virgin fiber. It appears the use of recycled fiber will continue to grow even more rapidly in the future.

By 1996, consumption of wastepaper is expected to have passed the 100-million-ton mark and to reach 130 million tons by 2001. With the assumption of an average growth rate of 2.6%/year in global consumption and production of paper and board products, the worldwide recycled fiber utilization rate is expected to increase from 32.8% in 1988 to 41% in 2001.

Current demand, however, has not been even across all countries. In Western Europe, the use of recycled fiber has grown nearly four times as fast as the demand for virgin fiber. By contrast, North American recycled fiber use has grown at only 3.4%/year, or slightly more than the increase in virgin fiber use for the same period. Clearly this would seem to indicate a significant potential to use more recycled fiber in North America.

By grade, the packaging board industry, particularly linerboard and fluting producers, has been and will con-

Mr. Veverka is president and CEO of Jaakko Pöyry Consulting Inc., Briarcliff Manor, N.Y. All figures, data, and results cited in this article are based on the multi-client study recently completed by Jaakko Pöyry Oy.

tinue to be the main user of recycled fiber. However, on a percentage basis, the most remarkable increases are expected in newsprint, printing and writing paper, and tissue products.

Growth in the importance of deinking grades will be one of the key trends in the wastepaper business. Currently, some 11 million tons, or approximately 14% of the recycled fiber used, are deinking grades. Approximately half of this is used for newsprint, with another quarter going to tissue products. Thus, the great bulk of wastepaper—64 million tons, or close to 85% of the total—is used without deinking, mainly in packaging grades. By 2001, the deinking grades are expected to have increased to about 31 million tons, or 24% of the total consumption of recycled fiber. In a strengthening of the past usage pattern, more than half of the deinked pulp will be used for newsprint.

A major improvement in the recovery rates of wastepaper will be necessary to meet the forecast demands for secondary fiber. An increase is expected in the recovery rates in virtually every area of the world (Table 1). The increases in Western and Eastern Europe will be particularly noteworthy. However, it is in North America, and particularly in the U.S., where the most dramatic

FIGURE 1: **Recycled fiber demand worldwide grew almost twice as fast as virgin fiber demand from 1971 to 1988, and that margin is expected to widen even more, doubling again by 2001.**

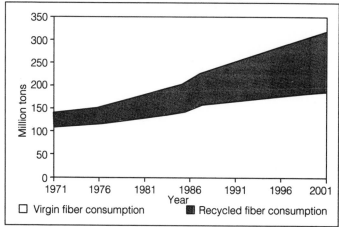

increases in wastepaper recovery will take place. In the case of the U.S., the recovery rate is forecast to go from 30.2% in 1988 to more than 44% just after 2000.

Recovery rates, however, are only part of the equation. Some areas of the world not only will use all of the wastepaper they recover but also must import secondary fiber to satisfy their total needs for raw materials. When considering the trade flows of recycled fiber, wastepaper utilization rates achieved by these areas of the world must be analyzed and compared with recovery rates.

Table 2 shows expected utilization rates. Countries where recovery rates (from Table 1) exceed utilization rates are net exporters of fiber. Countries with recovery below the utilization rates are net importers. Thus, Japan, with a recovery rate of 48% in 1988 and a utilization rate near 51%, is a net importer. North America is by far the largest source of wastepaper exports in the world, with an export surplus of 4.6 million tons in 1988, expected to increase to 10.8 million tons by 2001.

Wastepaper trade flows throughout the world show the importance of the U.S. as a major exporter of secondary fiber. The U.S. sends 3.18 million tons of wastepaper to Pacific Rim countries and 1.12 million tons to Central America. The recovery of wastepaper and board in North America is forecast to expand and continue to outstrip demand, allowing for a growing export surplus. A recovery rate increase from 29.4% to 42.9% for North America as a whole (Table 1), combined with a utilization rate increase of about 8.5% for the forecast period (22.8% to 31.3% in Table 2), allows for a doubling of offshore exports by 2001. The U.S. will be the most dominant source for all wastepaper, exporting between 4 million and 5 million tons to Canada, in addition to more than 10 million tons to offshore users.

NEW DRIVING FORCES. The key driving force for the use of wastepaper has traditionally been economics. Wastepaper enabled mills and countries without abundant forest resources to compete effectively on bulk grades with integrated producers using virgin fiber. This was the case in large paper- and board-consuming regions, such as Japan and Western Europe, where it has been relatively easy to collect and process large volumes of wastepaper. In the Far East, it is doubtful if local industries could have progressed without the cost economies of wastepaper. In North America, on the other hand, abundant forest resources have not historically encouraged the use of recycled fiber.

Technology has also played a role in the traditional use of recycled fiber. Improved technologies in the fields of cleaning, deinking, and handling of wastepaper have allowed production of acceptable end products using secondary fiber as the raw material source.

This situation is now changing. There are new forces scarcely mentioned in previous times—problems associated with disposal of solid waste and the environmental factor. The paper industry is now being told to use wastepaper not because it is good for the paper industry but rather because it is good for the environment. The introduction of these considerations into the industry's thinking and growing reinforcement by mandatory legislative measures are creating strong pressures to recover and recycle more wastepaper in North America.

Despite the emergence of environmental forces for the use of wastepaper, economic reasons will continue to be important and, in many respects, a necessary ingredient for promoting recycled fiber use in the paper and board industry. Furthermore, technical developments in recycled fiber handling, such as fiber fractionation, bleaching, in addition to the other separate handling techniques, will, in the long-term, bring

TABLE 1: **To meet increasing demand for secondary fiber, wastepaper recovery rates are expected to increase in almost every area of the world, with North America experiencing the greatest percentage increase (13.5%) by 2001.**

Region	1988	2001
	%	
North America	29.4	42.9
U.S.	30.2	44.4
Western Europe	35.8	41.5
E.F.T.A. countries	40.9	47.8
European Community	35.1	40.7
Eastern Europe and U.S.S.R	29.0	38.7
Oceania	24.8	31.3
Latin America	33.6	36.8
Japan	48.0	52.0
China	20.4	24.5
Rest of Asia	34.2	40.9
Africa	16.5	19.0
World total	**32.7**	**41.0**

TABLE 2: **A comparison of recovery rates (Table 1) with utilization rates shows North America could possibly double wastepaper exports by 2001.**

	Total paper and board production		Wastepaper consumption		Wastepaper utilization (%)	
	1988	2001	1988	2001	1988	2001
North America	86,737	115,198	19,778	36,030	22.8	31.3
Western Europe	57,633	78,844	19,811	31,228	34.4	39.6
E.F.T.A. countries	22,350	30,400	2,967	5,198	13.3	17.1
European Community	35,283	48,444	16,844	26,031	47.7	53.7
Eastern Europe	17,988	22,193	4,868	8,746	27.1	39.4
Oceania	2,487	3,864	702	1,271	28.2	32.9
Latin America	10,506	15,909	4,757	7,801	45.3	49.0
Japan	24,624	34,892	12,538	19,415	50.9	55.6
China	12,645	19,760	3,084	8,305	24.4	42.0
Rest of Asia	12,218	22,431	8,369	15,877	68.5	70.8
Africa	2,524	679	679	1,092	26.9	30.5
World total	**227,362**	**316,669**	**74,586**	**129,766**	**32.8**	**41.0**

additional economically feasible solutions to increased secondary fiber use.

COST COMPETITIVENESS. With these varied forces in mind, a change exists in the current economic situation for use of recycled vs virgin fiber for five specific grades—newsprint, printing and writing paper, tissue, linerboard, and corrugating medium. For comparison purposes, cost estimates were prepared for the production of the five products for various locations worldwide using both recycled and virgin fiber.

The basis for the cost estimates is a computerized cost-estimating model developed by Jaakko Pöyry. This model uses technical and economic mill data within a simulation framework and is typically used to examine the relative differences in production costs between existing pulp and paper mills. However, for this study, hypothetical new greenfield mills were simulated rather than using existing ones. This was done to present a more generic picture and to make the results as uniformly applicable as possible.

The new mills represent the most modern technology in typical mill/machine sizes for each of the paper and board grades examined. For technical and wastepaper procurement reasons, the average size of a mill using recycled fiber as the main raw material may be smaller than that of a virgin fiber-based mill. Costs are calculated for reels only, without regard to possible sheeting or converting operations. Capital costs, which have been included, represent a return on investment of 17%.

The unit prices and cost of raw materials, chemicals, energy, labor, and other production factors represent regional averages. Recycled fiber prices are average prices of the recycled fiber mix used in each grade. The cost level used for each recycled grade is that of third-quarter 1989. The units are U.S. dollars (US$)/metric ton. In the case of purchased chemical pulp, pulp substitutes, and high-grade deinking waste, long-term trend prices have been used instead of the actual third-quarter 1989 prices to get a more realistic picture of the cost competitiveness between virgin and recycled fiber-based products. Therefore, the price used for northern bleached softwood kraft (NBSK) pulp represents a long-term trend level of $650/metric ton.

For each of the cost-competitive comparisons, the specifications for the grade and mills are presented, followed by the production costs of the grade in question.

NEWSPRINT. Capacity of the simulated newsprint mill is the same for both recycled fiber or virgin fiber mills, at 220,000 metric tpy (Figure 2). The finished product is standard newsprint at a basis weight of 45 g/m². The furnish ranges from 100% thermomechanical pulp (TMP) to 100% deinked recycled fiber.

The recycled fiber component for newsprint was a mixture of highest-quality old newspapers (ONP) and sorted newspaper and magazine waste collected from households. Typically this mixed newspaper and magazine waste contains approximately 70% ONP and 30% magazines, pamphlets, inserts, and other advertising

FIGURE 2: **Production costs for new 220,000-metric-tpy newsprint mills, in selected areas and with typical fiber furnishes, show that recycled fiber use can be a competitive alternative to a 100% virgin fiber mill, especially in the northeastern U.S., where savings could be $110/ton.**

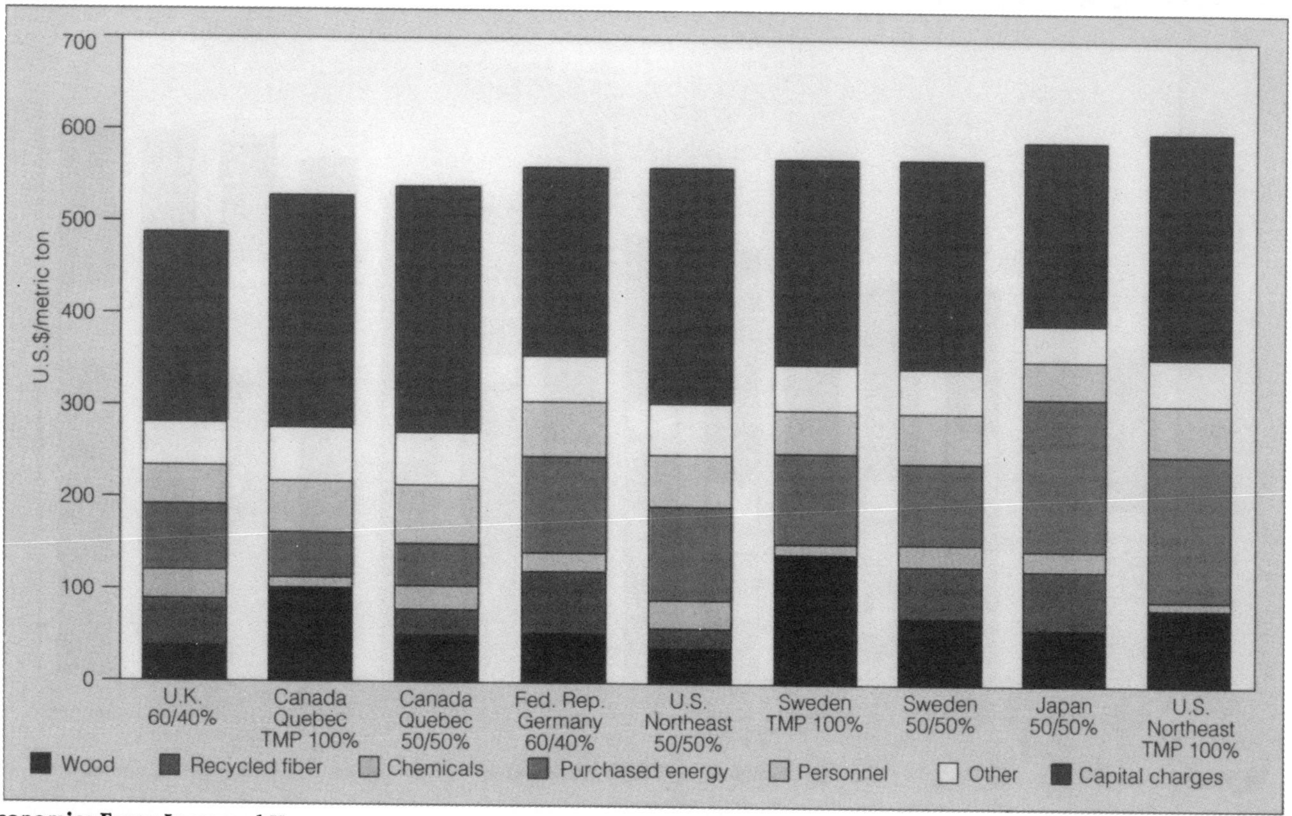

materials. The yield when processing the furnish into deinked pulp was assumed to be 86%.

Production cost estimates of new newsprint mills in selected regions, with typical fiber furnishes for the region, are shown in Figure 2. The most competitive regions are the U.K. and Quebec. In Canada, there is no advantage from use of a partial-recycled furnish because of the low wood cost and, in particular, the low power prices. In Sweden, a 100% TMP-based newsprint mill would be as competitive as a 50% recycled fiber-based operation since the high price of recycled fiber (approximately three times the northeastern U.S. price) and the somewhat higher personnel and capital requirements associated with two fiber lines effectively counterbalance the savings in wood and energy costs.

In general, the same problem of having two relatively small fiber lines instead of one line of economical size affects all 50:50 concept mills. Adding a second paper machine at the mill site would improve, to a considerable extent, the total mill economy of using a 50% recycled fiber furnish. Nevertheless, the savings in a northeastern U.S. mill (at a 50% recycled fiber content) are close to $50/ton.

Production of newsprint with a 100% recycled furnish would, however, look attractive in all regions studied. Savings in production costs range from $25/ton in Sweden to $110/ton in the northeastern U.S. It should be remembered that production of 100% recycled fiber-based newsprint requires procuring a very clean, homogeneous, and virgin fiber-containing newsprint stock on a continuous basis. With higher rates of utilization being forecast throughout the world, this may become increasingly difficult to do and could, in the long term, put a limit on the amount of recycled fiber used in a typical newsprint furnish.

PRINTING AND WRITING PAPER. For printing and writing grades, the production cost estimates were calculated assuming the finished product is a typical printing paper used by offices, namely an uncoated offset paper suitable for copy paper or computer printouts. Basis weights of these grades would typically be in the 60 to 80 g/m² range. For this grade, the capacities of the virgin fiber and recycled fiber-based mills would be considerably different. Capacity of the virgin fiber mill was taken to be 280,000 metric tpy, while the recycled fiber mill, due to the considerations originally mentioned, would typically be in the range of 150,000 metric tpy (Figure 3). The other major difference with this grade was the brightness, with the virgin fiber product being the brighter of the two (86% ISO vs 80% ISO).

An additional variable in the equation is that two types of recycled fiber were considered. The first was white ledger computer printouts and other printed wood-free waste. In the second case, a 50:50 mixture of magazines and ONP was used. The assumed deinked pulp yields varied between 86% and 82%. In addition to all of the above, the virgin fiber-based mill (except for Fed. Rep. Germany) was assumed to be integrated with a 400,000-metric-tpy kraft pulp mill.

FIGURE 3: **Comparison of production costs for a 280,000-metric-tpy virgin fiber mill and a 150,000-metric-tpy recycled mill show a mixed competitive picture. Mills using higher-grade wastes (Rec 1) generally have slightly higher costs than virgin fiber mills. However, if lower-quality waste can be used, secondary fiber can provide cost savings.**

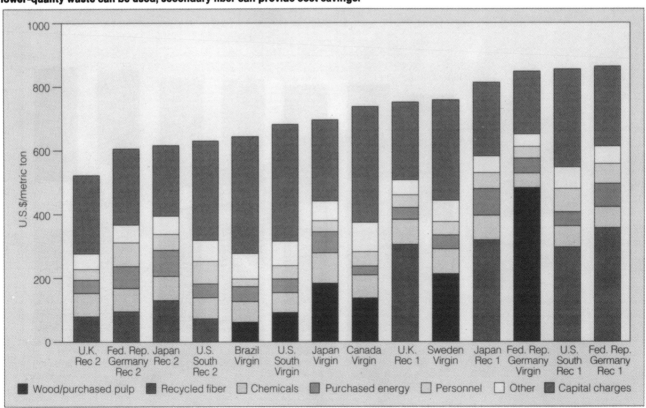

The uncoated wood-free product presents a somewhat mixed cost-competitive picture (Figure 3). A printing paper mill using pulp substitutes and high-grade deinked wastepaper has no advantage in total raw material and energy costs compared with an integrated kraft mill. Actually, the raw material and energy costs for a southern U.S. mill are less than half those of a high-grade recycled paper mill. For total production costs (including capital costs), the virgin fiber-based mill has a cost advantage over a high-grade wood-free waste-based mill, amounting to some $170/ton in the southern U.S. and almost $115/ton in Japan. In Fed. Rep. Germany, the production costs of a nonintegrated virgin fiber-based mill and a recycled mill using high-grade waste are approximately at the same level.

If allowance is made for a lower product quality (including brightness), considerable cost savings can be achieved in all regions, if the lesser-quality recycled fiber furnish (blend 2) is used. Total production cost savings range from $235/ton in the case of the nonintegrated virgin fiber mills in Fed. Rep. Germany to about $70/ton in Japan and $55/ton in the southern U.S. (comparison is to integrated virgin fiber mills).

The lower-quality printing paper seems interesting in areas where the competitors are unintegrated producers—for example, the U.K. and Fed. Rep. Germany. However, it is, quality-wise, a totally different product. When using lower-quality raw material, the resulting product quality difference is reflected in the price structure of the products. This can clearly be seen in the price of recycled fiber-based continuous stationery, which is priced up to 30% to 40% lower than the virgin wood-free continuous stationery.

In most cases, the main advantage of the use of lower-quality waste has been the ability to offer the buyers a differentiated and less-expensive product, often with a clear gray shade for color. In addition, this has often been the only possibility for small unintegrated mills to continue operation since they are not competitive with the production of virgin fiber-based products.

TISSUE. For tissue production, a 70,000-metric-tpy machine was chosen as the representative mill size for both the recycled and virgin fiber-based products (Figure 4). The additional assumptions are that the virgin fiber mill would not be integrated with a chemical pulp mill and also that the purchased hardwood/purchased softwood mixture would be roughly 50:50.

The deinked pulp for the recycled fiber-based mill was based on a newspaper and magazine mix. While this may be typical for a European or Japanese mill, it is not necessarily a recycled fiber furnish favored by U.S. mills, where there is a tendency to use a somewhat higher grade of recycled fiber because of consumer desire for a higher-quality end product. The deinked pulp yield for the mixed newspaper/magazine input was assumed to be 80%.

The product specifications chosen were that of a toweling grade produced in jumbo rolls. The cost of any conversion of the jumbo rolls to consumer-size rolls was not figured in.

A considerable cost savings is attainable due to the use of recycled fiber in this grade (Figure 4). The savings in raw material and energy costs are approximately $500/ton and total productions costs between $350 and $400/ton when pure virgin fiber and pure recycled-based products are compared. Although not shown on the diagram, estimates show that production based on the use of a 50:50 recycled fiber/virgin fiber mix would result in a savings of about $200/ton in total production costs.

Obviously, the cost comparisons can be affected greatly by the use of a higher-quality recycled fiber to improve end product quality or by the use of bleached chemi-thermomechanical pulp (BCTMP) in the place of chemical pulp. Nevertheless, the recycled fiber product consistently shows a production cost advantage over a virgin fiber-based tissue product.

It should be noted that despite lower production costs associated with the recycled product, this cannot automatically be translated to increased profit since prices of the finished product react substantially to quality levels. However, to date, the price differential between recy-

FIGURE 4: **Production comparison costs for a 70,000-metric-tpy tissue mill producing jumbo rolls show considerable savings are possible using secondary fiber—up to $400/ton when pure virgin fiber production is compared with pure recycled fiber production.**

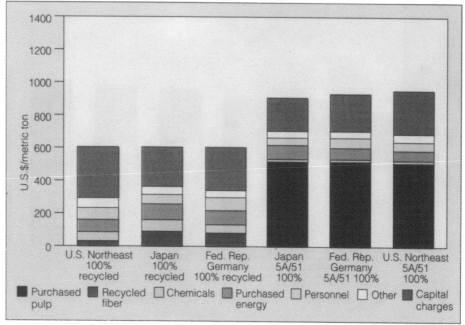

cled fiber-based and virgin fiber-based jumbo reels has been somewhat smaller than the 35% difference in the production costs shown. Typically, this has been in the 15% to 25% range in Western Europe. Through environmental concern and product branding, it has been possible in many cases to set the prices of recycled fiber-based end products even nearer those of virgin fiber-based products. In some cases, the differential has been reduced to the 10% to 15% range.

LINERBOARD. For comparison of linerboard costs, the mill models differed in size between the virgin (kraft liner mills) and the recycled (test liner mills) (Figure 5). The typical kraft liner mill capacity was assumed to be 400,000 metric tpy, while the test liner facility was based on a 250,000-metric-tpy capacity. In both cases, production costs were calculated for a 150 g/m² product.

In principle, no technical reason exists for the recycled linerboard machine to be smaller than the kraft liner machine. In practice, however, recycled liner machines tend to be smaller for raw material procurement reasons, and the 250,000-metric-tpy machine size chosen is actually very large in comparison with existing test liner machines.

Two furnishes for kraft liner were investigated: a 100% unbleached kraft pulp and a mix of 80% unbleached kraft pulp and 20% old corrugated containers (OCC). Integration with an unbleached chemical pulp mill is assumed. For the test liner mill, the furnish chosen was 90% OCC and 10% double lined kraft (DLK) clippings. The average yield when processing corrugated waste to cleaned recycled pulp is assumed to be 92%.

The cost comparative data in Figure 5 clearly show that the attainable savings in raw material and energy costs will vary with the recycled fiber content. In a case of 100% recycled linerboard, the energy costs are clearly higher because no energy-generating pulp mill is nearby. The chemical costs are likewise higher because of the surface sizing requirement of test liner.

In areas with high wood costs, such as Sweden, a test liner mill can have $75 to $80/ton savings in total raw material and energy costs over a kraft liner mill. However, in the southern U.S., where wood costs are low, only a minor advantage can be achieved with an increasing use of recycled fiber ($4/ton when using OCC and $5/ton when 100% OCC/DLK is used).

When total production costs are examined, the capital intensity of the virgin fiber mill, with its integrated pulp mill, clearly translates into a higher capital cost. Among virgin fiber-based producers, the southern U.S. and Brazilian (eucaliner) producers have a clear advantage. All the recycled fiber-based producers however, are competitive in their own local markets, including Japan.

According to calculations, in a new mill the production costs of test liner are about 13% to 27% lower than those of kraft liner in Western Europe. This also corresponds roughly to the price difference. In the southern U.S., the total cost difference is smaller due to lower wood costs and amounts to only about 15% to 20%.

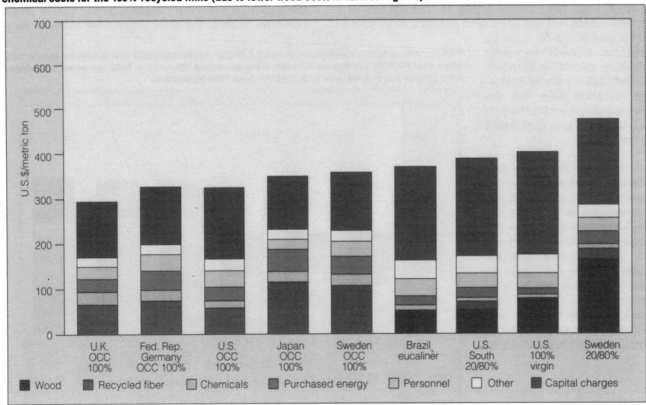

FIGURE 5: **Comparison of production costs for a 400,000-metric-tpy kraft linerboard mill with a 250,000-metric-tpy test linerboard mill shows that the major cost difference is in capital costs for a virgin fiber mill (due to an integrated pulp mill) and raw materials and chemical costs for the 100% recycled mills (due to lower wood costs in various regions).**

Economics of Recycling

CORRUGATING MEDIUM. For production of corrugating medium (fluting), the choice between virgin and recycled fiber is not a very important consideration in most areas of the world, except in the U.S., since this grade is already predominantly based on the use of recycled fiber. The typical mill size studied, at 250,000 metric tpy, was the same regardless of the fiber input (Figure 6). The basis weight of the product chosen for comparison was 150 g/m². In the case of the virgin fiber product, the furnish was assumed to be 100% NSSC pulp. For the recycled mill, the furnish was assumed to be 75% OCC and 25% mixed waste. Fiber yield on this furnish was assumed at 92%.

In fluting, the NSSC-based product can, in the southern U.S., reach similar or even slightly lower manufacturing costs than a waste-based product (Figure 6). However, this is possible only in the U.S., where wood prices are low. When considering the heavy capital cost of a new NSSC pulp mill, the cost comparison changes in favor of the recycled fiber-based product in the southern U.S. This advantage is approximately $50/ton. A northern U.S. location would be even more favorable for recycled fluting.

Given the relatively modest differences in production costs of recycled-based corrugated medium in various regions of the world, it is easy to understand why there is a relatively limited international trade in this product.

IMPLICATIONS TO BUSINESS. This cost-competitive analysis focused on the differences between new greenfield recycled fiber mills vs virgin fiber facilities. When considering the total spectrum of cost competitiveness, several other scenarios have to be considered:

• The cost implications of replacing an aging kraft mill at an integrated facility with a secondary fiber processing plant

• The potential of gaining incremental papermaking capacity and satisfying that increment with the use of recycled fiber.

Each of these alternatives would, given the proper circumstances, probably be very cost-competitive and cost-effective uses for recycled fiber. On the other hand, some conclusions relative to cost competitiveness and its impact on the increased use of recycled fiber can be made from the comparative study.

In newsprint production, using recycled fiber currently yields a definite cost advantage. In North America, this will probably mean that, in the long run, there will be a transition of newsprint production from areas having abundant wood resources toward areas having abundant recycled fiber resources.

In printing and writing grades, there would appear to be minimal economic incentive for including recycled fiber in finished products. However, it is likely that recycled fiber-based products will be produced and sold, not because of any potential economic advantage but because of a public concern for the environment and a desire to purchase "environmentally friendly" products.

For tissue products, recycled fiber use can definitely lower the cost of production, but some quality differences exist in the products. Current indicators show that consumers in North America will be willing to accept slightly lower product quality and, hence, will favor recycled tissue products over virgin fiber-based products.

Linerboard production in the U.S. currently already contains, for the most part, a substantial recycled fiber quantity (20% OCC). The economics, though, would indicate that there is a potential for increasing the amount of recycled fiber used by existing mills and that there is also the possibility for producing an economically viable test liner mill. Despite apparent cost advantages, the increased use of recycled fiber in linerboard will probably depend on changes in applicable shipping rules, e.g., Rule 41.

For most of the world, no competitive activity exists between recycled fiber-based and virgin fiber-based corrugating medium. The clear economic advantage is toward the waste-based product. In North America, it is probably fair to say that the future should favor the introduction of more recycled fiber medium. However, in areas with low hardwood costs, NSSC medium can still be a very cost-competitive product. ∎

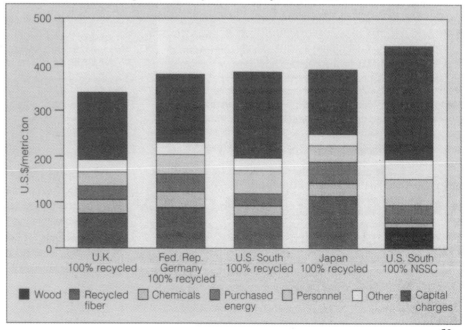

FIGURE 6: **Production costs for a new 250,000-metric-tpy corrugating medium mill show that recycled fiber mills clearly have an advantage over a virgin-based NSSC mill, which mirrors the fact that production of this grade is already based on recycled fiber use.**

Chapter 12

The Economics Are Right for U.S. Mills to Recycle Old Newspapers

More states are enacting mandatory collection and procurement laws to ease landfill crises, but they are ignoring market forces

By FRED D. IANNAZZI

Of the total U.S. solid-waste stream of 145 million metric tpy, paper and paperboard products comprise 64 million tons, or 40% of the total. By far, the two largest components of paper and board waste are old corrugated containers (OCC) and old newspapers (ONP). OCC, which is used to make the corrugating medium layer of corrugated containers, is actually in short supply. The recovery of OCC has risen from 44% to 50% over the past five years and is projected to rise even further in the next few years. Market forces alone will ensure that OCC will become a lessening burden in the waste stream.

ONP, however, is a different story. Only 32% of ONP is reused. That percentage has remained essentially unchanged for the past five years and shows no sign of increasing. Unrecovered ONP alone accounts for 15% of the paper and paperboard waste, or 6% of total U.S. solid waste. Since the recovery of ONP is not increasing as a result of market forces and since ONP is relatively easy to segregate at source (not in a mixed-solid-waste stream), many states and municipalities are enacting legislation that encourages or mandates greater recycling and reuse of ONP.

ONP GENERATION AND REUSE. The U.S. is by far the largest single consumer of newsprint, accounting for almost 41% of world consumption—about four times the usage of Japan, which is the second largest consumer. The U.S. is the only country in the world whose consumption of newsprint greatly exceeds its production. Only about 42% of the U.S. requirement is produced domestically.

Obviously, the U.S., as the world's largest consumer of newsprint, is also by far the largest generator of ONP and the largest potential market for ONP. The problem of

Mr. Iannazzi is president, Andover International Associates, Danvers, Mass. This article is based upon information contained in a multi-client study published by AIA. All tons in this article are metric.

ONP in the solid-waste stream on the scale encountered in the U.S. is unique to the U.S. Because of this vast tonnage, other countries' experiences in ONP recovery cannot necessarily serve as a model for the U.S.

Figure 1 shows the overall supply and disposition balance for newsprint in the U.S. in 1987. Starting in the center of the chart, we see that total U.S. consumption of newsprint was 12.3 million metric tons. Only 32% of this newsprint was recovered, and the remainder—about 8.4 million metric tons—ended up in the solid-waste stream.

The three markets for recovered ONP are newsprint manufacture, fiber furnish for other paper and board products, and export. We can assume that essentially all the export ONP is used to make newsprint, and, therefore, about half of the recovered ONP is recycled to newsprint.

There is little opportunity for increasing the reuse of ONP for nonnewsprint paper and board products; an ample supply of other grades of wastepaper better satisfies these applications. To increase the reuse of ONP significantly, we should encourage its increased use by newsprint mills in the U.S., keeping a few things in mind:

1. Only 24% of the fiber used in newsprint manufacture in the U.S. is recycled, and 76% is virgin fiber.

2. U.S. mills produce more than three times as much newsprint from virgin fiber as from ONP.

3. Fully 58% of total U.S. newsprint requirement is imported (almost all from Canada), despite the fact that a valuable low-cost resource—ONP—is burdening the U.S. with waste disposal problems and costs.

BARRIERS TO REUSE OF ONP. The supply of ONP is not a barrier to increased use. Existing supply channels could easily collect far more ONP than is presently collected if a viable market for it exists. In market terms, the volume of ONP recovered and recycled is *demand* limited, not *supply* limited. Legislation that mandates increased collection of ONP merely increases the supply; it does nothing to increase the demand. Unless demand is increased, any supply of segregated ONP will inevitably end up exactly where the unsegregated ONP does now—in landfills or incinerators.

COMPARATIVE COSTS: ONP VS PULP. If it can be demonstrated that newsprint manufacture from ONP is economically attractive compared with virgin fiber and if the newsprint mills install the capacity to increase the demand for ONP, the supply of ONP could easily be increased 50%.

In the virgin fiber process, pulpwood is delivered to the mill as logs, the logs are debarked and chipped, and the chips are converted to pulp by cooking and mechanical defiberizing. Most integrated paper mills are, of necessity, closer to wood supplies than to urban areas.

Making newsprint out of clean and segregated ONP requires only deinking to produce slush pulp; the remainder of the process is similar to papermaking that starts directly from logs. It should be noted that in both processes, the product of the pulping stage is a very dilute slurry of pulp in water. It is uneconomic to dry and ship the pulp, so all U.S. newsprint mills are integrated. The virgin fiber process has a lower raw material cost but higher operating costs (particularly for power), and the process based on 100% ONP has a clear cost advantage (Table 1). However, the quality of newsprint made from 100% ONP is somewhat inferior to that produced using virgin fiber. This quality difference can be avoided by using ONP as a partial substitution rather than a 100% replacement for virgin fiber. Similar to the use of OCC as a blending fiber in manufacturing linerboard, ONP can be used to expand pulping facilities incrementally, without the costly burden of expanding wood handling and virgin fiber pulping capacity.

SUPPLY, DEMAND. Even with its cost advantages, the additional ONP pulp capacity that is slated to come online by 1991 in Dublin, Ga., totals only some 200,000 metric tpy. This is not even enough to

compensate for the expected growth of about 1 million metric tpy in additional ONP that will be available by 1991. What is the problem?

The problem is that projected U.S. and Canadian installed pulping capacity for newsprint will exceed the projected demand by about 2 million metric tons, enough to preclude building significant new newsprint pulping capacity before 1992-93 at the earliest. Despite the fact that a new mill based on ONP would, under current conditions, be more economical than a virgin-fiber

FIGURE 1: **U.S. supply and disposition of newsprint.**

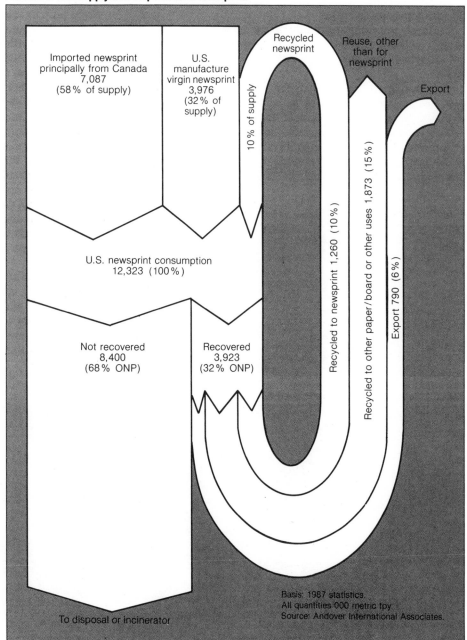

mill, it is decidedly uneconomic to shut down an existing virgin mill and replace it with a new ONP-based mill.

This situation will continue until more newsprint pulping capacity is needed, at which time the lower operating cost should tip the balance in the incremental capacity toward ONP-based mills. As with all generalizations, the above has numerous exceptions, particularly when we consider regional supply/demand balances (Table 2).

HOW TO INCREASE ONP USE. These are some suggestions on what will not work and what might be successful for increasing ONP use:

1. Simply imposing regulations to increase the supply of ONP without increasing the demand for ONP will not alleviate the burden of ONP in the solid-waste stream.

2. Imposing arbitrary targets for percent recovery of ONP and arbitrary timetables for achieving the targets will not create additional demand for ONP.

3. Setting up wastepaper collection and distribution systems in parallel or competition with the existing wastepaper dealers will not create any more demand for ONP and will cause confusion in the existing industry

and market. The existing system will supply ONP to keep pace with any increase in demand, without the need for outside initiatives.

4. When establishing segregation and recycling ordinances, the advice of the potential user who must handle and market the product should be solicited to ensure that the regulations produce the highest possible quality of ONP for the newsprint mills.

5. Setting a minimum overall recycled content in the newsprint that is purchased for government use could be quite helpful in tilting new pulp lines toward ONP.

Although the current economics appear to favor ONP over virgin pulp as the fiber stock for newsprint, industry history, investment philosophy, and mill locations favor continuing with the traditional pulpwood feedstock. Legislative initiatives regarding investment, such as rapid depreciation or tax incentives for ONP pulping facilities, could be helpful.

Also, because of vast differences in the regional ONP supply/demand balances and in companies' ONP pulping capacities, flexible nationwide targets for ONP use would probably be more effective than regional targets or company targets. With national targets, it may be possible to permit intercompany bartering of "ONP utilization credits," i.e., a company that was using more than the target fraction of ONP in its newsprint could sell the excess credits to a company that was not in a position to use more ONP. In this way, the market would determine how the industry as a whole could best comply with the national target.

Building ONP pulping facilities requires about two years from project approval, but, in any case, there will be no need for additional newsprint pulping capacity in the U.S. before 1991. Any timetables for increased recovery/reuse of newsprint should be established with industry input so that they can be supported by the industry. ■

TABLE 1: **Operating cost comparison for newsprint manufacture.**

	Cost ($/metric ton)[1]	
	Virgin Pulp	100% ONP
Raw material	66	91
Power	157	66
Other process costs	164	158
Total cost newsprint	387	315

1. Not including investment-related costs.
Source: Andover International Associates.

TABLE 2: **Supply/demand of ONP in the U.S. (1987).**

Region	Newsprint consumption	ONP domestic use[1]		Net ONP exports	Total ONP recovered	Recovery rate (%)
		Total	Newsprint manufacturing			
New England	746	139	0	0.3	139	19
Mid-Atlantic	2,414	634	241	83	717	30
East north central	1,908	669	122	0.8	670	35
West north central	678	54	0	0.8	54	8
South Atlantic	2,185	439	220	18	457	21[2]
East south central	409	76	0	0	76	18
West south central	1,216	128	0	204	332	27
Mountain and Pacific	2,761	810	592	457	1,267	46
Total U.S.	**12,323**	**3,220**[3]	**1,260**	**764**	**3,984**[3]	**32**[3]

1. Includes newsprint manufacture plus others (e.g., recycled board and tissue).
2. Garden State Paper Co. Inc. (Southeast Paper Manufacturing Co.) is installing a second newsprint machine at Dublin, Ga. The additional ONP demand (220,000 tpy) will increase the recovery rate to about 32%.
3. Includes 270,000 tpy used for insulation manufacture. This additional amount is not distributed on a regional basis by API.
Source: Andover International Associates.

Chapter 13

Environmental Concerns, Economics Drive Paper Recycling Technology

Paper industry will focus efforts on new methods of repulping, contaminant removal, deinking, and bleaching of wastepaper

By DON SORENSON

Recycled fiber is playing an increasingly important role in papermaking for a variety of reasons. In parts of the world with limited wood resources, the strategy is to maximize its use or value. Figure 1 shows the expected higher recycled fiber utilization rates in countries having limited wood resources.

In other parts of the world, including the U.S., the traditional driving forces are quality and economics. In many of the higher grades of paper, a point has been reached where further quality increases cannot be measured by the consumer. For producers of these grades, the challenge is to maintain quality at a reduced production cost.

With lower-value paper, the driving force is to increase product quality while holding production costs constant. At both ends of the spectrum, papermakers are looking to recycled fiber to help meet these industry challenges.

ENVIRONMENT DRIVES CHANGE. Perhaps the main reason for interest in recycled fiber is the lack of landfill space. As a nation of sophisticated consumers, the U.S.

Mr. Sorenson, formerly with CRS Sirrine Inc., is now with Simons-Eastern Consultants, Inc., Greenville, S.C.

FIGURE 1: **The U.S. trails Japan, Fed. Rep. Germany, Italy, and France in its utilization rate of recycled fiber.**

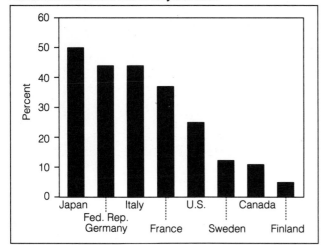

discards 160 million tons of garbage each year. Only 17% of this waste is recovered and recycled. Since 41% of municipal solid waste is paper or paperboard, the paper industry is a likely target for legislative solutions to the solid waste disposal problem.

While the federal government has implemented procurement practices favoring recycling of many paper grades, the states are generally targeting newsprint. Each year in the U.S., 12.3 million tons of newsprint are consumed. Only 3.9 million tons are recovered, and only 1.3 million tons (10%) are recycled as newsprint.

In the early 1990s, legislation in several states will likely require newsprint to have a 25% to 50% recycled fiber content. At the same time, newspaper publishers and readers are demanding higher-quality newsprint, and the furnish is changing to a grade often viewed as inferior. While it is natural to resist change, opportunities do arise:

• Quality newsprint can be manufactured from recycled fiber, provided the deinking plant design is well thought out and provided operational personnel understand the unique operational parameters of the system.

• Recycled newsprint can be profitable. A recent study prepared for the American Newspaper Publishers Assn. shows that mills near an old newsprint supply can achieve an economic advantage in using discarded newsprint.

Many papermakers have considered recycled fiber as a cost-prohibitive and sometimes inferior furnish compared with virgin pulp. For all of the reasons already examined, it is encouraging today to see developments in process technology, which leads to better quality and greater opportunity for use.

Recycling is a series of simple functions. While these are interrelated, it is helpful to review each as a separate unit. A good design will tie them together to form an efficient system. Important functions to consider include the following:

• Wastepaper supply
• Defibering
• Contaminant removal
• Ink/ash removal
• Bleaching.

WASTEPAPER SUPPLY. Deinking mills that are run effectively recognize the importance of understanding and controlling wastepaper supply, including procurement, receiving and storage, and pulping. Industry grade definitions define both types of paper and acceptable levels of extraneous contaminants. But frequent checks should be made to ensure that the quality purchased is the quality delivered.

Curbside recycling programs add a new dimension to wastepaper management. The price may be right; however, quality and uniformity may suffer.

DEFIBERING. Traditionally, low-consistency (5% to 8%), attrition-style pulpers have been the mainstay for defibering. Today, the advantages of higher-consistency, nonattrition-style units should be considered. The tub-style unit operates at 12% to 15% consistency, and the large helical rotor promotes top-to-bottom circulation with high-shear, fiber-to-fiber interaction.

With high-consistency pulping, the ink can be too finely dispersed and perhaps redeposited on the fiber, leading to brightness loss. However, this can be avoided if pulping is continued only to the point of defibering.

A second style of high-consistency unit—the drum pulper—features an inclined rotating drum that operates at 20% consistency and also promotes defibering through a tumbling action in the presence of water and chemicals. Pulp discharges through the drum's screening section, while contaminants discharge from the drum's open end.

This system provides excellent contaminant removal. But wet strength furnishes may be a problem. Gentle defibering action may leave flakes in the pulp.

CONTAMINANT REMOVAL. One of the biggest challenges in today's recycling systems is the removal of plastics, styrenes, hotmelts, and contact adhesives from the pulp. These contaminants should be removed quickly from the system while they are in large pieces.

Progress has been made in both fine-slotted screening and reverse cleaning technology. The fluidization achieved with contoured plate design allows the use of slot sizes of 0.010-in. on old corrugated containers (OCC) grades and 0.006-in. to 0.008-in. on ONP grades.

Debate continues on the merits of cascade vs feedforward screening systems. The vibrating tailings screening position can now be accomplished with a closed, nonvibrating device.

Heavy contaminant removal is accomplished with forward flow cleaners. Also, cleaners provide much lower energy requirements for lightweight contaminant removal, and a mechanically driven, centrifuge-type device removes lightweight contaminant in a single stage.

INK REMOVAL. Ink is removed from the fiber by the combination of mechanical and chemical action in the pulper. In North America, washing systems remove the ink once it is in suspension. With ink particle size below ten microns and/or with high ash content furnishes, washing offers the highest efficiency.

Due to the evolution in printing—xerography, laser printing, UV cured inks—the benefits of flotation must be considered. Water-based flexographic inks are even causing problems for flotation. Where the need exists for both ink and ash removal, a combination washing and flotation system should be considered.

Careful attention must be paid to the chemistry in these systems—washing requires a dispersion approach and flotation a collector approach. Dispersion and collector chemistries are quite different. Fortunately, chemical suppliers have developed chemical formulas balancing the needs of both, and suppliers continue to improve methods of washing and flotation. Much of the flotation development includes better bubble-size control and mixing and a more closed, compact cell. Mechanical aeration/mixing has been replaced by hydraulic shear through static devices.

Dispersion devices have been developed that, with a combination of thermal and mechanical energy, break residual ink or stickie contaminants down to ultrafine particle size. The particle size of the stickies is sufficiently small to reduce greatly the tendency for plugging machine forming fabrics. Wet end chemistry helps to prevent agglomeration of these particles.

BLEACHING. For lower-brightness systems generally involving mechanical pulps, a low-consistency sodium hydrosulfite bleach stage is often sufficient. Where additional brightness is required, a high-consistency peroxide bleaching stage is added.

The peroxide stage, followed by a sodium hydrosulfite stage, provides high brightness along with the color stripping capabilities of the hydrosulfite. Another reductive bleaching agent showing promise is thioureadioxide. According to published reports, one tissue mill in Austria is using thioureadioxide under production conditions. For wood-free grades (i.e., ledger), occasional use of chlorine or hypochlorite is employed. ∎

FIGURE 2: **Many papermakers have considered recycled fiber use cost-effective.**

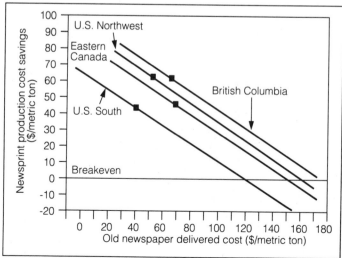

Chapter 14

New Technology, Economic Benefits Give Boost to Secondary Fiber Use

While the U.S. lags behind other countries, environmental concerns and legislation are helping increase both wastepaper recovery and use

By LAWRENCE A. BROEREN

The use of secondary fiber for pulp and paper products can lower costs significantly, preserve forest reserves, and assist in reducing the mounting solid waste problem. With an increasing emphasis on recovering wastepaper, secondary fiber use is growing rapidly, and both fiber recovery and use are expected to continue increasing.

Recovery rate is the amount of wastepaper recovered for reuse compared with paper consumed. Utilization rate is the amount of secondary fiber (recovered fiber) used compared with total fiber used. The two rates will differ depending on the amount of imports and exports of paper and wastepaper and inventory changes.

WASTEPAPER RECOVERY. In the U.S., the recovery rate of wastepaper for recycling is about 27%. Japan and Taiwan have recovery rates approaching 50%, and Europe currently has a recovery rate of about 30%, with Germany at about 35% and Holland between 45% and 50%. The practical recovery rate limit may be about 50%. In terms of imports and exports, the U.S. imports a very small amount of wastepaper, while more than 20% of the wastepaper collected is exported. Several major factors affect the recovery of wastepaper:

Standard of living. Higher standards of living are correlated with increased use of cultural paper, such as newspapers, magazines, and books, and with commercial-industrial activities generating office paper, reports, and computer printouts.

Population concentration. The collection of wastepaper from both commercial-industrial generators and households is easier and more economical with a high population concentration.

Alternate fiber uses. The major alternate fiber use is fuel. Using fiber as fuel can be discretionary or legislated. Fiber used as fuel, however, obviously is not available for papermaking.

Mr. Broeren is corporate consultant, Simons-Eastern Consultants Inc., Decatur, Ga.

Social conscience. Some wastepaper is recovered as a matter of social conscience. Recycling wastepaper reduces the number of trees harvested and helps preserve forest reserves.

Price of wastepaper. Larger volumes of wastepaper are recovered from commercial-industrial operations and households when wastepaper prices are high. There is also a minimum price below which the recovery of wastepaper falls drastically.

Price of competitive fiber. Wastepaper prices are influenced by the price of market pulp. One wastepaper classification—pulp substitutes—tracks market pulp prices.

Legislation. Some communities have laws requiring households to separate recyclable waste products (paper, glass, metal) from other refuse for separate collection and recycling.

The sum total of all the factors affecting the recovery of wastepaper indicates that total recovery and the recovery rate will both continue to increase.

SECONDARY FIBER UTILIZATION. Secondary fiber utilization in the U.S. is about 25%. In Japan, it is about 50%. Europe has a rate of about 48%, with Germany at about 45% and Holland at almost 70%. Five major factors affect secondary fiber utilization:

Quality. Historically, low-quality products were made from secondary fiber. Currently, high- and low-quality products are, or can be, made from secondary fiber.

Technology. Contaminant removal technology, including equipment, chemicals, and process control, has been improving rapidly. The technology must link the wastepaper to the finished product.

Contaminants. New contaminants are continuously developing. New contaminants not only increase the concentration of contaminants and change the combination of contaminants but also require improved contaminant removal technology.

Economics. The primary business reason for using secondary fiber is reduced costs. Reduction can be in both operating and capital costs.

Legislation. Legislation requires the use of secondary fiber in some products. The use of postconsumer waste secondary fiber also has been legislated.

WASTEPAPER GRADES, CATEGORIES. Wastepaper is graded according to Circular PS-83, "Paper Stock Standards and Practices," published by the Paper Stock Institute of America, a division of the National Assn. of Recycling Industries Inc. PS-83 also defines conditions of sale. There are 49 standard wastepaper grades, with nine grade numbers not currently in use and 32 specialty grade numbers.

Wastepaper is commonly grouped into five categories:
• Deinking
• Mixed paper
• Pulp substitutes
• Newspaper
• Corrugated.

The 1988 use for each category is shown in Table 1.

TABLE 1: Of the five major categories, wastepaper use in 1988 was highest for corrugated, with 49% usage.

Category	Usage (× 1,000 tons)	%
Deinking	1,714	9
Mixed paper	2,180	11
Pulp substitutes	2,901	15
Newspaper	3,227	16
Corrugated	9,747	49
Total	**19,770**	**100**

Source: API.

Figure 1 shows the growth in use for each category from 1986 and projected to 1991. Secondary fiber use as a percent of total fiber is shown in Table 2. The use of secondary fiber in each of the eight U.S. regions is shown in Figure 2, along with the percent of total fiber. Wastepaper categories have been associated with specific processes and finished products (Table 3).

CONTAMINANTS. Contaminants include everything that must be removed from wastepaper to make the fibers usable. Common contaminants include ink, staples, paper clips, rocks, sand, chemicals, and stickies. Stickies include all rubber-like substances that retain their tackiness.

The amount of some contaminants, such as ink, determine the wastepaper grade. For example, hard, white shavings (Grade 30) must be free of printing, and sorted white ledger (Grade 40) must be free of heavily printed stock.

TABLE 2: As a percentage of total fiber, secondary fiber is expected to increase slowly and possibly even dip slightly in 1991.

	1986	1987	1988	1989	1990	1991
Secondary fiber (%)	24.5	24.4	24.7	25.2	25.9	25.6

Source: API.

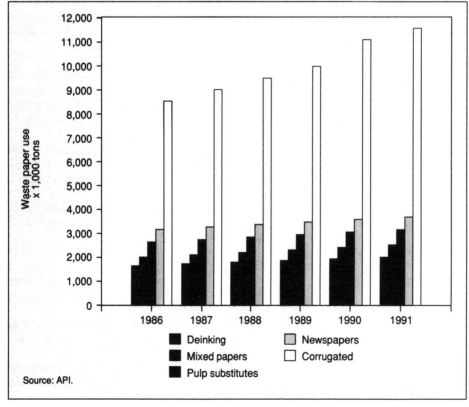

FIGURE 1: **Wastepaper use is expected to continue increasing, with the most use remaining in the corrugated grade.**

Source: API.

Any material that renders wastepaper unusable as the grade specified is classified as a prohibited material and is not permitted in most grades. A small amount (less than 2%) of prohibited material is permitted in a few "low" grades of wastepaper.

Out-throws are materials unsuitable for the wastepaper grade. Out-throws include permitted prohibited materials. Allowable out-throws range from 0% to 10%, with most grades limiting out-throws to 1% or 2%.

A specific material may be classified as an outthrow in one wastepaper grade and a prohibited material in another. Carbon paper is a prohibited material in sorted white ledger (Grade 40), which does not permit prohibited materials. The same carbon paper is an out-throw in mixed paper (Grade 1), which allows up to 10% outthrows.

Within the limits of the grading system, the type and amount of contaminants can vary significantly. During wastepaper and fiber shortages, the tendency is to reduce wastepaper quality in a grade and to increase the wastepaper grade.

New contaminants are constantly being developed. For example, *National Geographic* recently had a holographic cover and insert. Those holographs will be included in some wastepaper for recycling.

Some contaminants, such as nonimpact inks, are significantly increasing in volume. Nonimpact inks are difficult to remove, especially with a washing deinking system. When the volume of nonimpact inks was small, the nonimpact ink dirt count was also small. Now that the volume of nonimpact inks is increasing, the dirt count is also increasing. Steps are being taken to deal

TABLE 3: **Wastepaper categories are associated with specific processes and finished products.**

Wastepaper category	Process	Finished products
Pulp substitutes	Pulping	Fine paper Tissue
Deinking	Pulping Screening Cleaning Deinking	Tissue Fine paper
Newspaper	Pulping Screening Cleaning Deinking	Newsprint Folding cartons
Mixed papers	Pulping Screening Cleaning	Packing Packaging Molded products
Corrugated	Pulping Screening Cleaning Asphalt dispersion	Corrugating medium Linerboard Kraft towels

FIGURE 2: **Of the eight major U.S. regions, secondary-fiber use in 1988 was highest in the east north central and mid-Atlantic regions.**

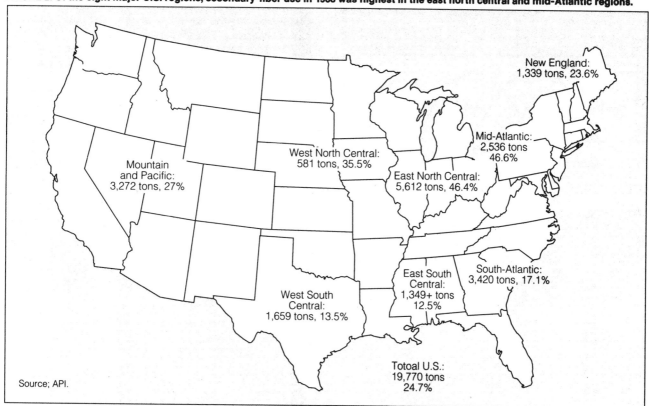

New England: 1,339 tons, 23.6%

Mid-Atlantic: 2,536 tons 46.6%

Mountain and Pacific: 3,272 tons, 27%

West North Central: 581 tons, 35.5%

East North Central: 5,612 tons, 46.4%

East South Central: 1,349+ tons 12.5%

South-Atlantic: 3,420 tons, 17.1%

West South Central: 1,659 tons, 13.5%

Totoal U.S.: 19,770 tons 24.7%

Source; API.

with the increasing amounts of nonimpact inks. The white ledger grade now has a higher-priced subgrade with minimum nonimpact inks. New processing techniques are being developed and used to remove non-impact inks.

Coordination and cooperation between all wastepaper participants—buyer, user, broker, packer, sorter, and seller—are essential. With significant differences in finished product specifications, wastepaper grades and contaminants, process, and the variability in wastepaper grades and contaminants, matching wastepaper to an existing process and finished process specifications is an ongoing, time-consuming task.

PROCESSING. As mentioned, the process must link the wastepaper to the finished product. The process must be able to remove enough contaminants so that the secondary fiber can be used to make the finished product within specifications. The major process steps for each of the five secondary fiber categories are shown in Table 4.

Pulp substitutes should require only pulping. To provide paper machine protection, the slushed fiber is usually screened and cleaned, often with the paper machine screens and cleaners. Pulp substitute systems often are stretched by adding small amounts of lightly contaminated wastepaper. Removing these small amounts of contaminants may require using screens, cleaners, and washers.

Corrugated systems require pulping, screening, and cleaning, often in multiple stages. Traditionally, asphalt dispersion systems have been used to disperse contaminants, resulting in a "clean" finished product. New corrugated systems do not include asphalt dispersion.

In the past, processing newspaper for newsprint has been done with a multistage washing deinking process. Current newspaper processing technology uses flotation as the primary ink removal technique. Washing is also used, and dispersion after processing is being evaluated. Dispersion breaks up most of the particles remaining after processing. The dispersed particles are below visual size and, thus, are not visual dirt. These finely dispersed particles can be left in, washed out, or agglomerated and floated out.

Although the major process steps are similar, newsprint deinking is usually considered unique and separate from deinking other wastepaper. This is due to the specific processing requirements for removing oily newsprint ink. In addition, the high percentage of mechanical pulp and the low brightness make this deinked fiber uniquely suited for newsprint and little else.

FIGURE 3: **Particle-size removal by flotation deinking.**

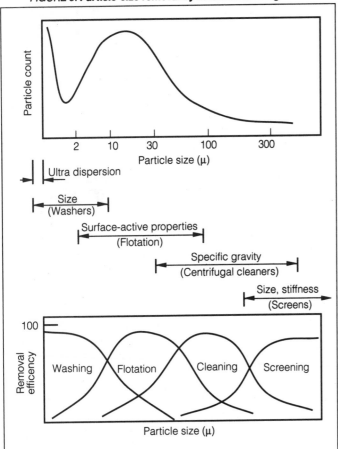

TABLE 4: **Major process steps for each of the five secondary fiber categories.**

Process	Pulping	Screening	Cleaning	Asphalt dispersion	Washing	Deinking flotation	Dispersion
Wastepaper category							
Pulp substitutes	1						
Mixed paper	1	1	1				
Corrugated	1	1	1	2			
Newspaper	1	1	1		1	3	4
Deinking	1	1	1		1	3	4

1 = Always.
2 = Many in use.
3 = Most new facilities.
4 = Future.

In the past, the U.S. has used the washing process for removing ink, while Europe has used the flotation process. New deinking facilities usually use flotation with washing. Many washing systems are being retrofitted for flotation, and dispersion is also being considered and tried. Flotation deinking particle-size removal is shown in Figure 3.

In washing deinking systems, wastepaper is pulped longer and at a higher pH to end up with more small particles (less than ten microns) and fewer medium-size particles (ten to 25 microns). Washing will remove a high percentage of small particles but only a low percentage of medium-size particles.

Water reuse and clarification is an integral part of deinking. It is especially important in washing deinking systems where there is a return loop from the pulper to the washer to the clarifier and back to the pulper. This loop saves heat, chemicals, and water. The clarifier removes contaminants, specifically ink and clay, so that they are not recycled back into the pulper. Some amount of wastewater must be discharged from the system. This wastewater can be treated by conventional wastewater treatment methods.

The deinking fiber yield ranges from 65% to 85%. The shrinkage, or loss, is from 15% to 35%. The loss from a 200-tpd deinking facility can be from 30 to 70 tpd. This solid waste loss must be dealt with in an environmentally approved manner. The major portion of this solid waste can be burned, spread, or landfilled. A small portion must go to landfill.

EQUIPMENT FOR FLOTATION DEINKING. Major pieces of equipment in a flotation deinking system with washing include the following:
• Pulper: a high-consistency (15%) batch pulper with a separate dump screening system
• High-density cleaner: a high-density (3%) cleaner with automatic dump
• Coarse screens: a system including several stages. The coarse screen baskets can have holes with diameters as small as 0.040 in. Feedforward screening also should be considered.
• Fine screens: a system consisting of several stages. The fine-screen baskets can have slots with diameters as small as 0.006 in. Feedforward screening should be considered as an option.
• Washers: a system that might include sidedhill screens, screw extractors, gravity deckers, or new high-speed (3,000 fpm) washers
• Flotation cells: flotation done in multiple (up to eight) cells in series. A second stage of flotation may be used for fiber recovery.
• Forward cleaner system
• Reverse cleaners: follow the forward cleaners. The flowthrough reverse cleaners have high reverse cleaning efficiency and low reject rates. A mechanical reverse cleaner is being used in Europe.

• Disperger: a recent development, the disperger is similar to a refiner but without cutting plates. The stock feeding the disperger is hot (195°F) and at a high consistency (30%). The hot, thick stock is worked mechanically by the disperger, which breaks up many of the remaining contaminants, including both ink particles and stickies. After dispersion, the ink particles are below visual size.
• Water clarifier: because of a high level of water use, contaminants must be removed so that they are not reinjected into the stock. A dissolved air flotation (DAF) clarifier is used to remove contaminants from the water. A filter can be used ahead of the clarifier to reduce stock losses.
• Solid waste thickener: because most solid waste is removed from the system at a low consistency, it must be dewatered to the appropriate consistency for final disposition. The consistency could be 20% to 30% for landfill and more than 50% for incineration. The solid waste is typically thickened by a belt press for landfill and a screw press for incineration. The filtrate is recycled back to the process.

CHEMICAL PROCESS. In wastepaper deinking, especially flotation deinking, the chemistry is of paramount importance. Pulper chemicals include the following:
• Caustic for defibering
• Sodium silicate for a stabilizer
• Deinking chemicals:
  1. Dispersants for washing
  2. Collectors for flotation
  3. Displectors for washing and flotation
• Calcium chloride for water conditioning
• Hydrogen peroxide for bleaching and preventing yellowing of groundwood.
Process chemicals include defoamers and acid for pH adjustments. Water clarification and sludge thickening require individual polymers. Bleaching can range from none to minimal to extensive. Examples of minimal bleaching would include peroxide added to the pulper or hydrosulfite introduced at the end of the deinking process.

Extensive bleaching would be done in a multistage bleach plant. Typically, this would be CH or CEH. Because of the generation of dioxin in chlorine bleaching,

TABLE 5: **Capital cost range comparison for two wood-based facilities and two wastepaper facilities.**

Facility	Size (tpd)	Cost (× $1,000)
Wood-based facility		
Bleached kraft pulp	800 to 1,200	$600 to $450
Bleached CTMP	300 to 600	$400 to $330
Wastepaper facility		
Deink	200	$175 to $125
Pulp substitutes	200	$100 to $50

new bleaching sequences using chlorine dioxide, oxygen, and other chemicals are in the process of being developed. Black ink cannot be bleached, so it must be removed.

QUALITY CONTROL. Major factors affecting secondary fiber quality are the wastepaper and the capability of the process. Most processing equipment will remove a percentage of certain contaminants. Altogether, most contaminants will be removed, but some will still remain. Some contaminants will be removed in the papermaking process. The contaminants remaining in the paper must be within finished product specifications. Processed fiber specifications typically include the following:

- Brightness
- Dirt count
- Stickies count
- Ash
- Groundwood content.

Samples are taken from each pulper and visually inspected prior to discharging stock from the pulper. If the pulper sample is not satisfactory, steps, such as adding additional chemicals and extending pulping time, may be taken. If the pulper stock is not satisfactory for processing with these additional steps, then it is put in the bad-batch chest and blended with other upgraded stock.

Other possible actions are reprocessing off-quality stock through the system or increasing contaminant reject rates. Some process samples are taken at selected process locations to verify operating conditions. Bleach plant chemical addition rates are varied so that brightness can be controlled.

ECONOMICS. The capital cost ranges for an economy-of-scale (cost-effective) bleached wastepaper processing facility are lower than those for an economy-of-scale bleached wood-based fiber facility. Table 5 shows capital cost ranges.

An economy-of-scale wastepaper facility is smaller than an economy-of-scale wood-based facility. A wastepaper facility may be uniquely sized for a production level that is not appropriate for an economy-of-scale wood-based facility.

Bleached kraft pulp manufacturing costs vary widely. The deinking manufacturing cost range is within the bleached kraft pulp range. The pulp substitute manufacturing cost range is higher than the deink range. Fiber manufacturing cost ranges (given in dollars/ton) are as follows:

- Bleached kraft pulp: $236 to $445

> *Unit disposal costs at approved public landfills are high . . . Approved private landfills have proven to be not only expensive to construct but also costly to operate.*

- Bleached chemi-thermomechanical pulp: $225 to $275
- Deink: $325 to $375
- Pulp substitutes: $425 to $475.

One of the elements in deink manufacturing cost, solid waste disposal, is currently in transition. Traditionally, deink solid waste disposal has been in public or private landfills at a low unit cost in the order of $10/ton. However, only a few landfills are approved. Unapproved landfills must shut down. Unit disposal costs at approved public landfills are high, at approximately $50/ton. Approved private landfills have proven to be not only expensive to construct but also costly to operate.

A typical 200-tpd deinking facility for tissue products would cost about $30 million. This cost includes wastepaper storage, flotation deinking with internal water clarification, and solid waste sludge thickening. In addition, mill services, such as steam and electric power, would necessarily be required to service the deinking facility.

The deinked fiber manufacturing cost would be about $350/ton. This is near the average manufacturing cost for bleached kraft pulp but with one-quarter of the capital cost. A nonintegrated tissue manufacturer not using deinked fiber would be using market pulp or pulp substitutes. Market pulp is currently selling at $700/ton and pulp substitutes at $450/ton.

Using deinked fiber instead of market pulp at a usage level of 200 tpd would result in savings of $350/ton or $70,000/day. This $24.5-million annual savings, with a 40% tax rate, would have a simple payout of two years on a $30-million deinking facility.

Using deinked fiber instead of pulp substitutes would result in $100/ton savings, or $20,000/day. The $7-million annual savings would result in a seven-year payout. Some pulp substitute equipment and buildings could be used in deinking, which would reduce the capital cost and the payout.

There are five major factors for success in secondary fiber:

- Commit to secondary fiber, even though it is different from virgin pulp
- Research the process and equipment
- Develop operating techniques that will optimize performance
- Investigate the causes of low-quality pulp and make the required changes
- Make sure the facility is appropriate to process the selected wastepaper into the quality of stock required to meet the finished product specifications. ∎

Chapter 15

OCC Consumption Expected to Grow as Cost of Virgin Fiber Increases

New technology, equipment can reduce OCC quality variations while new opportunities for building recycled mills increase

By RICHARD A. REESE

Recovery and consumption of recycled corrugated containers is growing at a rapid rate. Table 1 shows changes in consumption that have occurred since 1977. Growth in domestic consumption averaged 1.8% from 1977 to 1982 and 7.5% from 1982 to 1987. Most of the change in consumption has been increased use of old corrugated containers (OCC) in kraft linerboard and semichemical corrugating medium. OCC now comprises about 10% of kraft linerboard and 30% of semichemical medium furnishes. Recycled fiber is the "fortifying fiber" on most semichemical medium machines.

Export tonnage has grown at an even faster rate. The average annual change in export tonnage was 10% between 1977 and 1982 and 23.3% between 1982 and 1987. Collections grew by 2.5%/year between 1977 and 1982 and 9.3%/year between 1982 and 1987. Collections were 40.2% of domestic consumption in 1977, 44.3% in 1982, and 48.8% in 1987. The practical limit for OCC recovery is now likely between 60% and 70%.

ECONOMICS OF OCC CONSUMPTION. Table 2 shows corrugated waste consumption by region. The large consumption in the East north central, Mountain, and Pacific regions is primarily by mills using 100% recycled fiber. The high consumption in the South Atlantic region is mostly by kraft linerboard and semichemical corrugating medium mills. It is obvious that some areas, such

Mr. Reese is OPTEC technical manager, Rust International Corp., Birmingham, Ala. This article is based on a paper presented at the Third International Unbleached Kraft Conference held in Atlanta, Ga., in November 1988.

as New England, where OCC is available but consumption is low, could be locations for recycled mills.

Figure 1 shows year-end OCC prices in different areas since 1980. The same trends have occurred in all regions. In 1985, relative prices increased significantly on the West Coast due to high demand for export. This change has made it attractive for West Coast consumers to buy OCC from as far away as Chicago, Ill. Figure 2 shows linerboard production for domestic use between 1940 and 1987. Recycled linerboard was 40% of total production in 1940 vs 3% in 1987. Recycled linerboard tonnage fell from 800,000 tons in 1940 to 475,000 tons in 1987. Figure 3 shows corrugating medium production for the same period. This grade was 32% of domestic production in 1940 and 23% in 1987. Corresponding recycled corrugating medium tonnages were 290,000 in 1940 and 1.64 million in 1987.

RECYCLED VS VIRGIN PULP MILLS. Recycled containerboard mills can be competitive with kraft mills as long as OCC prices are reasonable. Two of the largest recycled linerboard mills have cogeneration systems that improve their economic positions.

Capital cost per daily ton is lower for a recycled mill than for a comparable mill using virgin pulp. Cost ranges are from $150,000 to $250,000 for a recycled mill and from $300,000 to $400,000 for a greenfield mill.

Why isn't everyone building recycled containerboard capacity? Containerboard prices have not been high enough until recently to justify new greenfield capacity.

TABLE 1: **Recycled corrugated consumption in short tons (000).**

	1977	1982	1987
Consumption at U.S. mills	6,025	6,770	9,299
Exports	592	887	1,922
Total collected	**6,797**	**7,657**	**11,221**

TABLE 2: **Corrugated waste consumption by region—1987.**

	000 tons	% total
New England	360	3.9
Mid-Atlantic	681	7.4
East north central	2,426	26.3
West north central	330	3.6
South Atlantic	1,986	21.6
East south central	776	8.4
West south central	815	8.8
Mountain and Pacific	1,840	20.0

OCC Consumption Expected to Grow

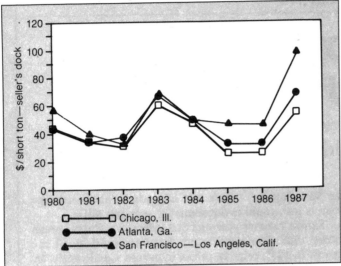

FIGURE 1: **Old corrugated prices.**

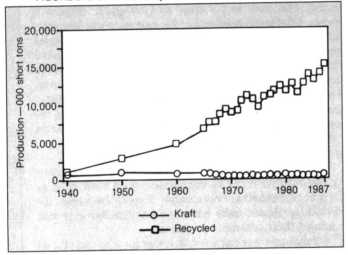

FIGURE 2: **U.S. linerboard production, 1940 to 1987.**

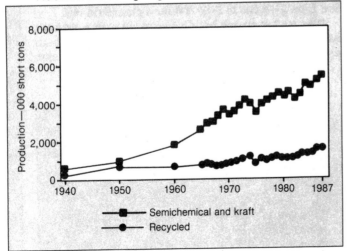

FIGURE 3: **U.S. corrugating medium production, 1940 to 1987.**

The only new greenfield capacity for containerboard in the last ten years has been at International Paper Co., Mansfield, La., and the Inland Container Corp. 100% recycled mill at Ontario, Calif.

New papermaking technology in the forming and pressing areas has made paper machine rebuilds attractive. The high cost of capital equipment encourages optimization and upgrade of existing facilities. Fiber used in many kraft linerboard and semichemical corrugating medium expansions has been recycled fiber.

QUALITY DIFFERENCES. Compared with virgin kraft containerboard, recycled containerboard has inherently lower strength, appearance, and printability/surface characteristics. The differences have greater significance on linerboard than on corrugating medium. Since the latter is sandwiched between linerboard sheets, appearance and printability differences are not really important. Accordingly, recycled corrugating medium has had a much greater acceptance in box plants.

Strength differences can be compensated by wet end additives and/or running a size press. In fact, some recycled mills achieve better compression strength than mills using virgin fiber. Recycled linerboard has a "dull" look rather than the "sheen" look of kraft linerboard. Most recycled mills add dye to the wet end or size press to match the color of kraft linerboard sheets.

Recycled sheets generally do not look as clean as virgin kraft sheets and are characterized by spots of different sizes, color, and shape, depending on the effectiveness of the stock preparation cleaning and screening systems. Some box plants prefer to use recycled linerboard on the inside of corrugated boxes, where sheet appearance is less obvious to users.

Printing ink soaks into recycled linerboard sheets more than into kraft sheets. This leaves printing voids on the surface, which can be objectionable depending on box application. Some manufacturers feel that the greater penetration is related to more short fibers on the surface. Smoothness can also affect print quality.

The presence of stickies in the sheet can cause separate layers of paper in rolls to stick together, in addition to causing appearance problems. Contaminants can restrict calendering as web consolidation tends to flatten the stickies and make them cover a larger area.

The presence of wax and other slippery materials can result in a lower coefficient of friction in finished sheets. This can cause slippage of boxes from stacks and other problems. Some mills apply a silica antiskid material that can cause problems in corrugating plants by coming off on printing plates and reducing cutter blade life. One mill reported a coefficient of friction of 16 to 18 without an antiskid material and 25 to 27 with its application. Effective removal of waxes and other slippery materials can eliminate the need to apply antiskid materials. Some U.S. mills spray silica solution on the web at the dry end of the paper machine.

Economics of Recycling

Recycled containerboard often runs differently on corrugators than do virgin sheets. Corrugating plant operators must adjust operating conditions to achieve good performance. For example, test liner can warp, so more heat must be applied to dry the web. Test liner also will not stand as much abuse on the pressure roll as kraft linerboard. Pressure roll loadings that are 20% to 25% lower must be used when running test liner.

SECONDARY FIBER SYSTEMS. The key to successful production of test liner is delivery of good-quality recycled fiber to the paper machine. Recycled fiber contains several different types of contaminants that must be removed to avoid paper appearance problems. Technology exists to remove virtually all contaminants from recycled fiber. No existing 100% recycled mills have state-of-the-art secondary fiber systems. The challenge is to install and operate a cost-effective system that will provide satisfactory fiber quality.

The major raw material used in recycled containerboard is OCC. Types and levels of contaminants vary depending on the source and end use of OCC. For example, moving boxes are relatively clean and free of contaminants, while boxes used for fruit and produce often have heavy wax treatment to provide a water barrier. Contaminants can include the following:
- Heavyweight materials—metal, grit, wire, sand, ceramics, and rocks
- Lightweight materials—plastics, polystyrene foam, wax, hotmelt
- Adhesives and latex-based stickies
- Other materials—asphalt, shives, chop, bark, and ink.

Average yield of good fiber is 85% on an oven-dry basis. OCC in the U.S. is normally about one-third corrugating medium and two-thirds kraft linerboard. Strength is somewhat lower than kraft pulp since corrugating medium is produced from semichemical hardwood pulp.

European OCC has lower strength and different contaminants than OCC in the U.S. The lower strength is related to the fact that European OCC normally has been recycled four to five times. European OCC generally has less waxes and hotmelts than OCC in North America but higher gross contaminant levels due to plastic bags and other materials. Asphalt is used as a moisture barrier. European mills also use some other grades of wastepaper in test liner, including wastepaper that is both bleached and unbleached, and chemical and mechanical fibers.

Nearly all stock preparation systems include the following:
- Pulpers to break up the bales of waste fiber and put paper fibers and contaminants in a water slurry
- Baggers and junk towers on the pulpers to collect wire, staples, rags, stones, and other large contaminants
- High-density cleaners to assist in the removal of heavyweight contaminants

- Coarse screens (0.078-in. holes) to assist in the removal of relatively large contaminants
- Fine screens (0.014-in. slots) to remove smaller contaminants
- Secondary and tertiary equipment to treat rejects removed from the primary fiber line
- Thickeners to increase stock consistency for storage.

STATE-OF-THE-ART FOR U.S. OCC. A schematic of a basic state-of-the-art secondary fiber system is shown in Figure 4. The system shown is a "removal system" in which each unit operation is accomplished at optimum consistency for efficient removal of contaminants. The system shown in Figure 4 does not include fractionation by fiber length or dispersion. The following are major components and their primary functions:
- Material handling—delivers recycled fiber bales to pulper
- Pulper—separates individual fibers by water dilution and agitation and removes large contaminants, such as wires, staples, rocks, and soda cans
- Pulper detrasher—removes large lightweight contaminants and returns good fiber to pulper
- High-density cleaners—remove smaller heavyweight contaminants, such as stones, short pieces of wire, and coarse grit
- Coarse hole screens—remove relatively large light and heavyweight contaminants
- Medium-density cleaners—remove finer heavyweight contaminants, such as sand and grit
- Fine-slotted screens—remove smaller-scale materials, primarily lightweights
- Through-flow cleaners—remove most lightweight contaminants not removed previously, such as waxes
- Dewatering unit—thickens stock to approximately 12% consistency for efficient storage
- High-density storage—surge capacity between stock preparation system and paper machine
- Reject handling—equipment to remove water from rejected material to minimize landfill hauling costs
- Clarification system—system to remove some contaminants from water to permit recirculation.

KEY GUIDELINES. Proper consistencies for efficient contaminant removal in each operation are as follows:
- Pulper—4% to 5%
- High-density cleaning and coarse screening—3% to 3.5%
- Medium-density cleaning and fine screening—1.5% to 1.8%
- Through-flow cleaners—1%
Recommended barrier opening sizes are as follows:
- Pulper extraction plate—0.5 to 0.7 in.
- Pulper detrashing unit—0.25 to 0.50 in.
- Coarse screens—0.055- to 0.079-in. holes (bar-type cylinders)
- Fine screens—0.010- to 0.014-in. contour slots.

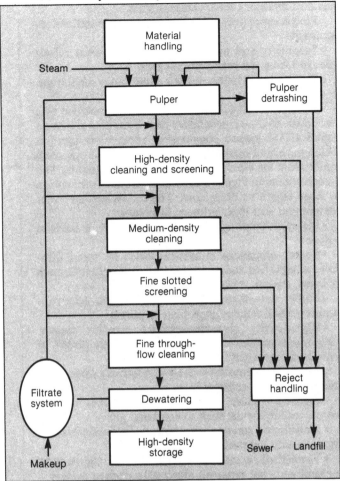

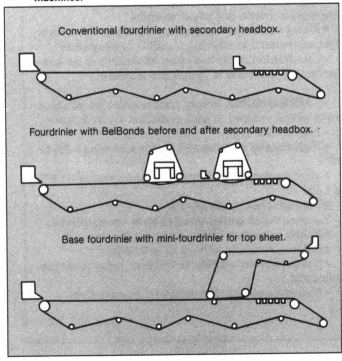

FIGURE 5: **Fourdrinier arrangements on recycled linerboard machines.**

Conventional fourdrinier with secondary headbox.

Fourdrinier with BelBonds before and after secondary headbox.

Base fourdrinier with mini-fourdrinier for top sheet.

Secondary and tertiary screens to process rejects from each stage should have the same opening sizes as primary screens. Medium-density cleaners must be installed ahead of the fine-slotted screens to achieve satisfactory basket life. Medium-density cleaners remove sand and other abrasive materials that cause rapid wear of contour fine-screen plates.

Some suppliers recommend installation of fine forward-flow cleaners ahead of the through-flow cleaners. Others feel that fine forward-flow cleaners should be installed on the paper machine. Machine cleaners would also remove contaminants that enter the system from the paper machine broke system and also from other sources.

Few mills in Europe use reverse or through-flow cleaners. Reverse and through-flow cleaners require close control of operating pressures and consistency to achieve good separation. It is likely that fewer lightweight contaminants in European OCC also contribute to the lack of through-flow cleaner application.

Secondary fiber equipment suppliers say that good test liner appearance can be achieved without a dispersion unit. However, no major test liner mills in North America are operating without dispersion systems. Some kraft linerboard mills claim to be achieving good recycled stock cleanliness with reverse or through-flow cleaners, but they are running relatively low percentages of OCC.

It is difficult to project sheet cleanliness based on laboratory trials since rejects are treated differently in laboratories than in commercial installations. However, a test liner mill is currently installing through-flow cleaners and will shut down its dispersion system.

EUROPEAN VS U.S. SYSTEMS. Most European OCC stock preparation systems are significantly different from that depicted in Figure 4. Most systems operate at consistencies of more than 3% and include fractionation and dispersion systems. High-consistency operation reduces the amount of contaminants that can be removed. Fractionation permits separation of long and short fibers for use in top- and basesheet test liner or use of short fiber on corrugating medium machines.

European systems seem to be based on taking out coarse contaminants at the pulper and detrashing units, high-density cleaning and screening, fractionation, and dispersion of long fiber fraction. These systems generally do not include removal of fine contaminants in cleaners and screens.

A basic system such as that shown in Figure 4, with provisions for stock fractionation at 3% to 3.5% consistency after fine through-flow cleaning and inclusion of a dispersion system between the dewatering unit and high-density storage, appears to have the best potential for U.S. recycled mills. Commercial experience with state-of-the-art systems will determine if dispersion systems can be eliminated.

PAPER MACHINE. Three different forming section configurations are currently used on recycled linerboard machines (Figure 5). Current machines in the U.S. use conventional fourdriniers with secondary headboxes. The fourdriniers are long to compensate for the low freeness and slow drainage rates of secondary fiber furnishes. Slow drainage rates can result in a concentration of short fibers on the top of the basesheet. Low tear and cracking/score problems can be experienced on heavy-weight grades, such as 69-lb linerboard. Major U.S. test liner producers are evaluating changes to improve forming section performance.

Top-wire units with vacuum dewatering are installed on some machines in Europe running 100% recycled fiber. Performance is good, and one mill reported concerns with dewatering capacity with top-wire units.

Mini-top fourdriniers are installed on several European test liner machines. This concept includes forming top- and basesheets separately and joining them at a moisture content of about 10%. Overall sheet strength is increased by forming separate lighter-weight plies. One potential problem is low ply bond between the top- and basesheets. Some mills spray starch between the two sheets to improve ply bonding. Good ply bond can be achieved by closely monitoring moisture content of the top- and basesheets at the joining point.

There is some concern that paper machine efficiency will be lower using a top fourdrinier rather than a conventional fourdrinier or a fourdrinier with top-wire units. Some top fourdrinier machines installed in the U.S. have not performed well. Some of the problems experienced have been unique applications and lack of expertise.

A mini-top fourdrinier may be the best choice for a recycled test liner machine. The major reason is better drainage capacity by producing lighter-weight sheets and higher sheet strength. Higher strength will reduce the amount of refining necessary to achieve acceptable strength tests. A conventional fourdrinier with top-wire units would be an alternative selection.

PRESSING. A good press section can consolidate the web and increase mullen and ring crush tests. Recycled stock generally dewaters more easily in the press section than virgin kraft furnishes. Sheet dryness of 3% to 4% higher is typical at comparable press loads. Most paper machine suppliers recommend a double-felted first press followed by a long-nip or wide-nip second press. There are two basic options for good test performance on the last press nip on linerboard machines:

• Long-nip press (LNP). This is a large-diameter-roll, double-felted press with a maximum nip pressure of 2,000 pli. Nip width is 2.5 to 3.5 in.

• Wide-nip press. These presses have nip pressures of 5,500 to 6,000 pli at a nip width of approximately 10 in. The Beloit Extended Nip Press (ENP) has a ceramic shoe with a rubber blanket running between the shoe and the top roll. The Voith Flexonip has a rotating flexible cover on the bottom press roll. The Sulzer Escher Wyss Intensa S design has a concave Nipco shoe inside a flexible roll shell in the bottom position and a standard Nipco roll in the top position.

Wide-nip presses achieve sheet dryness of 3% to 4% higher than long-nip presses. Expected sheet dresses would be about 45% to 47% with an LNP and about 50% to 51% with a wide-nip press using a typical U.S. test liner furnish. The greater dewatering provided by a wide-nip press would permit installation of fewer dryers. This would partially offset the higher capital cost of these units.

SIZE PRESS. One of the key questions from a technology standpoint is whether or not a size press is necessary on a recycled linerboard machine. Most machines producing recycled linerboard have size presses, while machines producing kraft linerboard generally do not have size presses. Size presses generally increase mullen tests 3 to 5 points and enhance ring crush.

One U.S. test liner mill does run a size press. It previously ran a size press and conducted trials a few years ago with and without the size press. Its box plants could not see a difference, so the mill eliminated the size press, allowing higher machine speeds since the sheet was not rewet in the middle of the machine. The mill runs internal cationic starch, which it feels is more cost-effective than operating a size press.

All European test liner machines use size presses, operating with sheet moisture content of 10% to 20% entering the size press. High sheet moisture content improves starch penetration in the sheet, which is necessary to achieve good sheet runability and glueability on corrugators. Some European mills indicated that they could probably run without size presses if they had U.S. quality OCC.

A size press should be included on a new test liner machine installation in the U.S. Size presses enhance ring crush tests, and the growing emphasis on ring crush adds credence to inclusion of a size press.

SUPPORT SYSTEMS. Use of recycled fiber can create some special problems on paper machines. The key parameter is the effectiveness of contaminant removal in the stock preparation system. Most paper machines running recycled fiber have problems with filling on forming fabrics, press felts, and dryer fabrics. Some mills have developed procedures and special equipment to minimize the effects of contaminants on the paper machine.

Recycled fiber is more difficult to dewater on the forming section than virgin kraft. Some mills are running double- or triple-layer forming fabrics to increase dewatering capacity. Special-design press and dryer fabrics are not necessary, but designs that are easy to keep clean should be considered. ∎

Wastepaper Collection Practices

The collection and sorting of wastepapers, regardless of the flurry of recycling activities of the past few years, remains basically unchanged from 50 years ago. Some new equipment is now being used to speed up and improve the sorting process, but basically it's still a laborious manual process, particularly for mixed office wastepapers.

However, some major advances have been made in organizing the collecting process and in sorting at the source by both municipalities and paper companies. This section takes a close look at collection operations recently established by several paper companies, and examines the techniques and equipment they use to sort by grade and to remove first-level contaminants. The changing role of wastepaper dealers is also explored.

Chapter 16

Wastepaper Dealer Sees Boom Ahead as Industry Ups Recycling Efforts

Florida-based recycler employs strict quality measures to ensure product consistency from collecting and sorting to baling and shipping

Flores Paper Recycling, Miami, Fla., is typical of many U.S. companies currently involved in a national effort to reduce solid waste disposal problems by returning valuable raw materials to the primary manufacturing process. The company's success as a high-grade wastepaper collector has progressed rapidly in concert with an increased environmental awareness in the U.S. and the consumption of record quantities of recycled fiber by the paper industry worldwide.

Recycling efforts today include a variety of collection techniques, with everything from household curbside collection programs to organized collection and sorting operations inside companies. These activities have helped Flores steadily increase its "supplier companies" (known as loose paper accounts) as more and more corporations join the recycling movement.

COMMUNITY INVOLVEMENT. "We began our company as active participants in the Dade County metro recycling program, aimed at addressing solid waste management problems in south Florida," explained CEO

Eddie Flores. "That involvement led to our commercial success today, but the return of used raw materials to the manufacturing process is not always as simple as it sounds. A lot of education needs to take place, particularly on the local levels."

For Flores that meant getting involved in local recycling programs early in the process to help educate and involve the whole community. He continued, "On the whole, corporations have better resources to educate people and implement recycling programs. That's why we, in addition to our primary business of office and printer waste collection, decided to get involved to help the local government in its recycling efforts."

On the commercial side, Flores provides instructive seminars for new suppliers' employees to verse them in separation techniques. "We teach a variety of topics to help supplier company employees understand what the recycling program is all about. That includes the importance of the separation of various grades to facilitate their reuse in the manufacturing process. Few people know much about that, but we're making progress."

HIGH-GRADE FIBER COLLECTION. Flores collects a variety of high-grade fiber, including white ledger, computer printout, coated book stock, colored ledger, hard and soft white shavings, printed and unprinted bleached board, and file stock. The company's suppliers include banks, attorneys, hospitals, printers and other converters, and commercial businesses.

Most of the fiber recycled by the company is used in tissue and toweling manufacture, with the balance used in printing and writing grades. However, Flores sees the fine grades playing a more prominent role in recycled fiber use in the future. "The demand in this area is increasing and will become considerably higher," he predicted, "because more and more mills, outside of tissue and newsprint, are taking steps to include recycled fiber in their furnish, particularly in view of current laws and pending legislation."

Of the fiber Flores supplies to paper producers, ap-

Each bin of incoming paper is hand sorted before being baled for shipment.

proximately 60% goes to U.S. mills, while the other 40% is shipped to various locations in Central and South America and Europe. Among the countries currently using Flores' products are Bolivia, Brazil, Venezuela, and Spain.

QUALITY KEY TO SUCCESS. "We have become the sole supplier to several mills, I believe, primarily because of our commitment to consistent quality," Flores emphasized. "Papermakers do not like surprises. They want and need raw materials that are as consistent as possible. You'll probably find that wastepaper dealers in general tend to have a less than favorable reputation. With the emphasis being put on recycling today, that's got to change. We—dealers, brokers, and recyclers—have to control quality."

Flores pointed out that quality control, hands-on supervision in his case, must begin with the collection and sorting process and continue through the baling process and even to the loading of containers for shipment. While approximately 30% of the recycled fiber received at the plants is presorted by the company providing the paper, Flores has implemented several in-house measures to ensure his quality goals are met. For example, all incoming paper is hand sorted and checked by a supervisor before being sent to the baling operations. A second supervisor then checks all bins dumped into the baler.

A third person is then responsible for making sure bales are properly loaded in shipping containers before they leave the dock. "Fortunately, our new baler has been outstanding," Flores stated. The new C&M unit is capable of processing 50 bales (1,700 lb each)/hour and includes a state-of-the-art conditioning chamber that has significantly improved the physical integrity of Flores' bales. "You don't want a bale falling apart halfway to a customer," he emphasized.

PAPERMAKING BACKGROUND. Working in the paper industry is nothing new for Flores, who at age 12 began

Flores has over 60 trucks serving the Miami and Orlando areas.

Jose Rivera Sr. (right), loose accounts director, discusses an order with CEO Eddie Flores.

working for his father at a local paper mill sweeping broke. From there, he worked in a variety of manufacturing positions in the mill and later at his father's wastepaper brokerage firm. A little more than four years ago he teamed with Luis Ziegenhirt, Flores president, to form Flores Paper Trades (a wastepaper brokerage), which shortly thereafter became Flores Paper Recycling when the company began a dedicated effort to recycle high-grade wastepaper in Dade and Broward counties.

Since the first days of operation in 1987, Flores has experienced phenomenal growth. "That year," recalls Flores, "we processed about 300 tons/month." In 1988 the company had ballooned to an average of 1,000 tons/month, and it grew another 300% to 3,000/month during 1989. In 1990, the company recycled between 4,200 and 4,500 tons/month and is still expanding.

Also in that period of time, Flores has grown to include three processing plants (two in Miami, one in Orlando), 63 employees, 60 trucks, four balers, more than 8,000 portable bins, and a complex computer network that includes order tracking, loose account monitoring, and supplier and customer profiles. The company recently opened its third plant in Orlando with a base of 72 customers supplying 500 tons/month to a base of 72 customers, a market developed in less than a year.

FUTURE PLANS. Flores says he is expecting the recycled fiber business in Florida to slightly outpace growth throughout the U.S. "I see the Florida market growing at least 30% for the next five years, while the overall wastepaper market will probably grow at about 20%." As for the company itself, Flores also sees continued growth. "My goal is to be processing 10,000 tons/month by the end of 1991. We also eventually want to look into the Tampa and Jacksonville markets for future expansion." ∎

Chapter 17

More Recycled Capacity Will Affect Wastepaper Supply Quality, Quantity

Analysis of various collection methods and companies must be made to ensure a constant wastepaper stream comes into mills

By KELLY H. FERGUSON, Projects Editor

Legislation and public concern have expanded the markets for recycled paper products, causing numerous North American mills to plan for recycled production. According to the June 1990 *Pulp & Paper Project Report*, approximately 54 new recycled mill projects are planned, including greenfield mills, restarts of idle mills, or additions of separate or new recycled lines. Another 22 mills are studying or planning upgrades to improve the quality and production of their recycling systems. Those new projects do not include mills already in operation.

Such increases in recycled capacity, possibly within the next two years, mean these mills must have a constant stream of wastepaper. While certainly there is enough wastepaper in North America for this supply, there is concern among established mills that this sudden demand, without a strong collection network in place, will mean a lessening of quality wastepaper as a furnish.

This same concern was shared by such companies as Garden State Paper Co. and Southeast Paper Manufacturing Co. when they started up mills, prompting those companies to set up their own procurement arms. Recently, Stone Container announced a joint venture with Waste Management Inc.—called Paper Recycling International—to supply Stone's mills with wastepaper. Many companies are developing contracts with wastepaper dealers, long a source of fiber for paper mills. Others are working with local municipalities and paper drives.

To discuss some of these concerns, *Pulp & Paper* interviewed experts from Fluor Daniel, an engineering company that is currently involved in various pulp and paper industry recycling projects. Those interviewed were Don Buck, vice president, pulp and paper business unit; Chuck Morrow, director of pulp and paper engineering; Jim Thornton, process engineer; and Tom Cheves, vice president of business development.

P&P: Many mills are considering adding recycled fiber to their furnish, especially in light of recent legislation. Where will these mills get a constant supply of wastepaper?

Buck: During the past ten to 12 years, mills have procured wastepaper mainly from dealers. It has only been a matter of getting the best price for the wastepaper and buying it from that particular dealer.

Cheves: At times, when the wastepaper market has been soft, some mills have continued to buy wastepaper—storing it wherever possible because they knew they would need it. It is estimated that the U.S. currently has a 30% recovery rate of wastepaper, which means there is much more that can be recovered. In fact, some municipalities have a surplus of wastepaper.

Morrow: An important issue is probably how far these dealers will have to ship the wastepaper to mills. I recently attended a wastepaper seminar attended by three of the major railroads, which indicates there are areas where there may not be large enough supplies of wastepaper. Demand is going to push manufacturers to find al-

Don Buck, vice president, pulp and paper business unit.

Chuck Morrow, director of pulp and paper engineering.

ternate wastepaper sources farther from their mills. Brokers will also be supplying paper from locations farther from the mill, and that could have an effect on price and supply.

P&P: *How far will mills go to get that constant supply?*
Thornton: I believe mills will shift their collection networks to limited areas. Newsprint mills, for example, will probably backhaul wastepaper from the same areas they ship product. Some mills already operate this way. A mill in the Midwest supplies newsprint to publishers in Denver, Los Angeles, and San Diego. It backhauls ONP [old newspapers], in its own rail cars, to use in the mill.
Cheves: The mills we are siting that plan to recycle are looking for areas within a certain radius of municipal-

ities, where they know there will be a wastepaper stream. For recycled greenfield operations, mills will be built closer to the people than trees.

P&P: *Companies such as Southeast Paper Manufacturing and Garden State Paper have set up their own procurement agencies. Also, Stone Container recently formed a joint venture with Waste Management. Do you think these types of arrangements will continue?*
Thornton: Brokers will continue to be the leading suppliers of wastepaper to mills, but some of the larger paper companies will probably set up such arrangements with major end users. For example, a mill I recently visited had an arrangement with Safeway grocery stores. The mill took all of Safeway's corrugated containers to

---

Wastepaper backhauling boom

Backhauling, long a method for transport companies to cut hauling costs, has found increased interest from recycled paper mills looking for a way to bring in wastepaper at low cost. Trucking companies have practiced backhauling in the paper industry for years, negotiating a cheaper rate to haul wastepaper into the small number of recycled mills for which they delivered a finished product.

According to Terry Conklin, a consultant with Simons-Eastern Consultants, Decatur, Ga., "Transport companies will normally negotiate a lesser rate for the backhaul because they probably wouldn't have a haul on the return trip. These companies can't make money if they don't find a load for the return trip."

But the boom in recycling has caused rail lines to step into the competition to meet the needs of numerous new recyclers. "The railroads are becoming much more aggressive in backhauling," Conklin said. "Truckers have had most of that business because it hasn't been on a large scale.

"With newsprint and magazine recycling exploding, rail companies see it as a natural fit because they're delivering large amounts of newsprint out of the North to the South

and returning with a number of empty cars. For example, the two main Canadian lines have about 15,000 to 20,000 cars a year returning empty. Since many of those cars are dedicated to newsprint, wastepaper backhauling is perfect.

"Trucking rates are pretty well defined right now, but rail lines are working hard to compete with those rates," Conklin added. "One nontraditional way they are competing is by setting contracts based on a price per highway mile. That makes them more competitive with the truck lines. And when a company takes a load of wastepaper into a mill, they are a candidate for an outbound load."

A MATTER OF COST. Cost savings of backhauling depend on mileage. In transportation, there are two component costs: the waiting time of loading and unloading and the distance traveled. The costs for distance traveled can also be analyzed for primary haul and backhaul.

Conklin uses a trucking company as an example. "Generally, a trucker's rate for the backhaul portion of the distance traveled would be about two-thirds that of the primary haul. If a truck has a 40,000-lb load (about as much paper as you can get in a truck), it will cost about $12/ton for a 100-mile primary haul. On a backhaul, the cost would be about $10/ton for the same distance.

"However, that is a very short trip. For a haul in the 400-mile range, the cost difference would be about $30 for primary vs $22 for backhaul (Figure 1). If the mill is in an urban area, there will probably be an average distance of about 250 to 300 miles for a haul, so a company could save about $5/ton. That can mean significant savings for a mill in transportation costs."

While companies are always looking for a backhauling arrangement, Conklin said the practice becomes cost prohibitive at less than 100 miles for truck (150 to 200 miles for rail) unless a specific load is waiting to be backhauled. By having wastepaper for pickup, mills create a desirable situation for transporters.

"Many mills operate their own fleets this way, but I don't know of any setting up circuits for outside fleets on a regular basis," Conklin said. "But more mills may contract to set up circuits for outside fleets, especially if transporters are delivering into major metropolitan areas, where large amounts of wastepaper are waiting to be hauled out."

FIGURE 1: **Based on a truck carrying a 20-ton load, the cost/ton of a backhaul can be significantly less depending on the distance of the primary haul.**

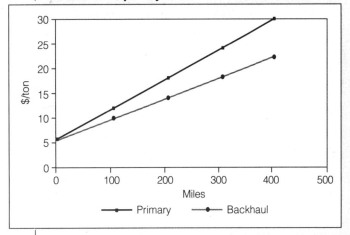

produce 100% recycled corrugating medium and test linerboard. Such arrangements will be made as more mills invest in recycling, but they will be set up gradually.

Buck: More waste management companies will also be setting up dealer-type arrangements. For example, the company that collects garbage used to take everything it picked up straight to the landfill. Now it supplies containers, so households sort out their newspapers. This will probably develop into a completely separate business.

Cheves: I think collection is much more sophisticated now than most people understand. At one time, people went to grocery stores or package stores to find boxes for moving. But if you go to those stores now, there normally aren't any. Those boxes are going into compactors, enabling dealers to procure OCC [old corrugated containers]. In doing that, companies are almost assured of getting a pure supply without having to sort.

P&P: Do you think there will be legislation or ordinances to mandate separation of materials at the household level?

Thornton: I think there will be legislation on percentages of wastepaper that must be recycled; certain states have begun enacting such legislation, especially states that have a real crisis at landfills. But so far, that is the only area where legislation has been enacted or is pending.

I think there will be more interest directed towards individual grades of paper. There are certain grades that can be recycled 100%, even though the industry isn't recycling at that level. There are also certain paper grades that possibly can't be recycled—for instance, contaminated papers or papers containing certain additives.

Cheves: Source separation has so many advantages. First, the person doing it will probably have a high accuracy rate. Second, when that sorted material is picked up, it's checked again. That's two checks before the material is sent to a collection center where it might be sorted and checked again.

Buck: There are volunteer programs right now. Municipalities give containers for plastic, aluminum, glass, and newsprint. As I drive around, I see more and more of these recycling bins. So there are entrepreneurs who are getting a free supply of recyclable materials.

And if a municipality provides the bins and gets a dealer to collect it, the municipality doesn't have to collect the real garbage as often. That can mean monetary savings for citizens.

Morrow: I'm not sure municipalities will have to pass ordinances or fine homeowners to make them separate waste, as long as those municipalities ask for reasonable separation. If you ask people to separate their newspapers, they'll probably do it. Voluntary separation and collection of wastepaper was going very well in the late 1970s and early 1980s. There was even a surplus of wastepaper at one time. But because the industry did

Jim Thornton, process engineer.

Tom Cheves, vice president, business development.

not use that wastepaper, the voluntary effort collapsed. Now that effort must be resurrected.

P&P: A large volume of high-quality wastepaper comes from offices. Is there a market for that wastepaper, and what will it take to get offices to separate their wastes?

Buck: From the experience at our office, it will take the initiative of key individuals within each company to get offices to separate waste. Fluor Daniel has a separation system within our buildings, and it has been a huge success. All responsible companies will want to do something like this.

Morrow: Before offices began sorting, that type of wastepaper was considered mixed papers. Now it is actually a number of higher grades of wastepaper, and that probably could replace many of the ledger grades as a furnish. These grades of wastepaper will be much less expensive than mixed ledger but come very close to the quality.

Cheves: Recycled fine papers have not received the attention that tissue, newsprint, and OCC markets have. But as more end users demand fine papers with a recycled fiber mix and as more legislation is enacted, the fine paper sector will be driven to use secondary fiber.

P&P: Will mills be able to procure a constant, high-quality supply of wastepaper, especially for grades where more mills are adding deinking lines, such as newsprint?

Thornton: Based on my experience, there are a number of newsprint mills that have arrangements with brokers. However, quality will probably deteriorate as demand increases. There will always be a supply. But one thing that could hurt the supply of ONP is the use in producing other paper grades, such as tissue. ONP is primarily used in newsprint now, but that could possibly change.

Another consideration of supply to newsprint mills is that more mills will be using magazine stock to enhance the flotation deinking operation. Even if the industry uses some ONP for other segments, there should be a balance with increased use of magazine stock. ∎

Chapter 18

Southeast Recycling Corp. Expands to Ensure Ample ONP Supply at Mill

Southeast Paper's fiber procurement arm more than doubled its number of facilities to supply an expanded Dublin, Ga., mill

By KELLY H. FERGUSON, Projects Editor

As state legislators have begun pushing publishers to use more recycled newsprint, newsprint mills have begun considering recycled lines and searching for a quality source of secondary fiber. Most recycled grade mills have used wastepaper dealers and brokers in the past and continue to use those sources. More recently, mills have turned to legislatively mandated municipal recycling programs, which involve home sorting of recyclables and curbside collection.

Southeast Paper Manufacturing Co.'s, Dublin, Ga., mill wanted to ensure the availability of quality secondary fiber after startup in 1979. Mill management didn't want to depend exclusively on dealers and brokers but wanted to ensure a constant flow of old newspapers (ONP) to the mill. The decision was made to set up a network of procurement and processing facilities, working through a subsidiary company, Southeast Recycling Corp., to provide that supply.

"We wanted to make sure we had a secure and constant flow of the paper to the mill," said E. James Fletcher, executive vice president of Southeast Recy-

Besides collecting ONP, Southeast Recycling's centers collect office, computer, and kraft paper, which it then sells to dealers.

cling. "We also wanted to make sure the supply quality met the mill's standards, which is a special deink grade-8 quality."

To begin this network of procurement facilities, Southeast Recycling set up offices in Atlanta, Ga., and purchased an Atlanta collection facility from Rock-Tenn Co. From the base in Atlanta, other facilities were started up in Marietta, Ga., Savannah, Ga., Montgomery, Ala., New Orleans, La., Orlando, Fla., Polk County, Fla., and Volusia County, Fla.

When the decision was made in 1987 to expand the Dublin mill, including adding a second newsprint machine, Southeast Recycling added ten more facilities (Figure 1). Three of the facilities were bought from Garden State Paper Co. Inc.—Richmond, Va., Tyson's Corner, Va., and Silver Spring, Md. The other facilities were expansions—Gwinnett County, Ga., Baton Rouge, La., Ft. Myers, Fla., Ft. Pierce, Fla., Jacksonville, Fla., Brevard, Fla., and Seminole County, Fla.

Southeast's focus on Florida for eight of its facilities is due to the state's "high availability of newspapers and reasonable freight rates to our plant in Dublin," Fletcher said. "Florida has an unusually large amount of old

FIGURE 1: **With the expansion of the Dublin, Ga., mill, Southeast Recycling Corp. added ten new collection centers, bringing its total to 18.**

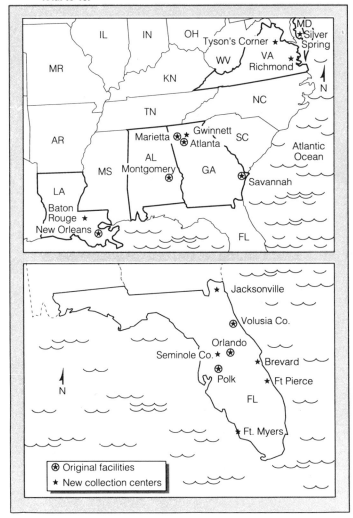

newspapers available, as well as growth well above the national average."

PROCUREMENT AND PROCESSING. When Southeast Recycling began operation, approximately 200,000 tpy was being sent to the Dublin mill. Tonnage per year increased as machine production was increased. At No. 1 machine's peak, Fletcher estimated Southeast Recycling provided about 250,000 tpy.

With the new No. 2 machine, about 550,000 tpy will be needed to meet the needs of both machines running at peak production. The paper is bought by the ton or over the scale by pounds, and the price varies, depending on whether the facility picks it up or it is delivered, or whether it is sorted or nonsorted. The average, over-the-scale price is between $5 and $10/ton.

Southeast Recycling procures wastepaper in several different ways. Churches and other nonprofit groups hold collection drives, and the paper is either delivered to a Southeast facility by those groups or is collected at a central site for pickup by trucks from those facilities.

Wastepaper brokers and dealers, normally a source for quality wastepaper, provide presorted loads. Those dealers and brokers that Southeast deems dependable can ship direct to the mill, bypassing the processing centers.

Municipal programs have recently become a source of wastepaper for Southeast. In Silver Spring, Southeast took over the Montgomery County collection program—the first time Southeast has had responsibility for maintaining curbside collection of newspapers. However, these programs generally mean more work for Southeast's facilities because less sorting is done before a load is received.

Southeast has also worked with a few corporations in setting up collection programs to procure office and computer paper and ONP. However, in setting up such programs, Southeast researches how much paper is generated, how much processing will be required, and how much time will be needed to operate the program.

For example, Southeast buys all the paper generated by Conoco Inc., a New Orleans-based oil company. Southeast provided it with an extra container to collect the newspapers, computer paper, and office paper. The company is responsible for separating the paper and loading the container. Southeast's New Orleans facility then collects from the large container.

Once the wastepaper is delivered to a Southeast facility, it is sorted by facility employees to remove contaminants, such as telephone books, junk mail, and plastic bags. Then, depending on the specific facility, the paper is sent by truck or rail to the mill in Dublin.

Staffing depends on the type of facility. A baling facility may have 20 to 30 employees. Some of the smaller operations may have five or six employees. Southeast operates five facilities that bale the newspapers and deliver by rail or truck. The other operations are termed "loose" facilities, where the paper is sorted and loaded loose into trucks for delivery to the mill.

ASSURING QUALITY FIBER. When the loads are received at the Dublin mill, no further sorting is done. Therefore, quality of ONP is left to the individual facilities or the dealers and brokers delivering the loads.

The loads are inspected, and if a certain amount of outthrows or contaminants are found, the load is rejected. Once rejected, the load goes back to the shipper at cost to the shipper. Southeast's facilities are included in that process and have had loads rejected.

Some of Southeast's highest-quality ONP supply is provided by nonprofit groups, because the amount they are paid depends on how well the paper is sorted. But recent legislation in some states mandating community recycling has forced some nonprofit groups out of collecting newspapers. In these areas, facility procurement costs have been driven up, and municipalities are normally paid less per ton because more work is required to sort loads.

Southeast's facilities will not, however, accept any loads mixed with garbage, a requirement some communities attempt to bypass. In municipal programs, Southeast requires separation of newspapers from other recyclables at the original source—the home. However, residents still believe they can put in junk mail, phone books, or magazines.

EXPORTING AND BROKERING? While the Dublin mill normally uses all the ONP procured by Southeast Recycling, part of Southeast Recycling's supply was exported to England and Mexico during a 1989 market glut. The only other alternative would have been to turn away some of the collection programs, including the nonprofit drives.

"Exporting is not our business," Fletcher said. "We did try to maintain the flow by continuing to buy because the second machine hadn't started up."

Besides ONP, Southeast Recycling's facilities accept other grades—office paper, computer paper, and corrugated grades—depending on the ability to sell the paper and the facility's ability to handle other grades. Most of the other grades comes from municipal and corporate collection programs. That paper is processed at the facilities and brokered to other dealers or sold to other companies.

Southeast also encourages collectors to put newspapers in grocery bags. The bags are then baled and sold for recycled kraft pulp. Some facilities even accept glass and aluminum, especially if the facility is involved in a community-run program. As a service, Southeast will accept the glass and aluminum, process it, and sell it to dealers.

"With some municipal programs coming online with multi-material collections, we may have to get into more recyclables. People like to bring their recyclables

Once a shipment is received at a collection center, employees sort out plastics, direct mail fliers, etc. to ensure the quality of ONP shipped to the Dublin mill.

Southeast Recycling Corp.'s Atlanta facility has its own trucks to collect ONP.

to one place," Fletcher said. "As our operations mature and the mill's fiber needs are met, we might supplement our business by procuring other grades, but only as a sideline operation."

With such extensive facilities, Southeast is set up possibly to move into brokering. Fletcher says, however, that is far in the future. Currently, a feasibility study is being done for a new mill in the Northeast, South, or Southwest. With that expansion, more procurement and processing facilities would probably be added.

"Our primary objective would be just to supply our mill, but I guess there is the possibility that if we get excess tonnage, we could supply other users of ONP," Fletcher said. "I would think we would not supply a company putting in a greenfield mill but rather a mill adding deinked capacity—a situation that would require less ONP tonnage." ∎

Chapter 19

Contaminant Removal, Timely Use Vital to Quality ONP Fiber Yield

Brightness and strength decline as supply ages in storage; sorting household collections at processing centers beneficial for clean supply

By WILLIAM C. ANDREWS

For many paper grades, recycled products can be and should be as good as their virgin counterparts. With recycled newsprint some individual characteristics will differ, but for the end use, performance must be comparable to virgin newsprint in terms of quality of the finished product and operating efficiency. Characteristics of wastepaper that affect quality and efficiency are contamination, age, and moisture.

Contaminants are a problem in the manufacture of any recycled paper product, and the worst of these substances are pressure-sensitive adhesives and hotmelt materials, collectively known as "stickies." Stickies adhere to machine parts and to adjacent layers of paper in wound rolls, causing breaks on the paper machine and in the pressroom.

Sophisticated screening and cleaning equipment has been developed to effectively remove contaminants, including stickies, but no approach is perfect, and removal efficiency is currently at about 90%.

CLEAN SUPPLY A MUST. It is important that collected old newspapers (ONP) be clean, containing only what is delivered with the newspaper, free of prohibitive materials, and having less than 1% of out-throws. Prohibitives include metal or glass of any type, plastics, laminated products, garbage, and non-water-soluble adhesives and tapes from book binding or pressroom waste. Out-throws include grades of paper such as brown bags, magazines, junk mail, and heavily inked pressroom waste, all of which could be used but would cause quality and appearance problems.

The best way to improve markets for waste newspapers—or for that matter any recyclable material—is to concentrate on source separation before the material is mixed with the general solid waste stream.

Age of the ONP is important because the principal fiber component of newsprint is mechanical pulp, which degrades both in color and strength when exposed to ultraviolet light and heat (Figure 1). Newspapers will yellow in a matter of hours when exposed to bright sunlight, as compared with business paper grades, which are made from chemical pulp and change very little.

Normally newspapers are not subjected to extreme light or heat and can be used even up to a month with little degradation, but they definitely will show brightness and strength deterioration after six months regardless of storage conditions, and inventories should be rotated on a short-range basis.

Wet paper causes mildew, mold, and accelerated deterioration, particularly when stored, and has a negative economic effect in terms of lower fiber content. Moisture should not exceed 10% of total weight.

WASHING AND FLOTATION CRITERIA. The Garden State deinking process is a washing method using only ONP. Coated and supercalendered grades, such as magazines and advertising material, are undesirable because nonfibrous components comprising up to 30% of the weight would represent a loss and an added load in effluent treatment.

All of the different types of inks that are used in printing newspapers can be satisfactorily deinked by the Garden State washing process, including oil-base inks used for offset and letterpress printing and water-base inks used for flexographic printing. Many publishers in the U.S. are converting to flexography, particularly medium-size, and the total could reach 10% to 25% of printed newspapers.

Flotation is very common in Europe and Asia, and newsprint mills in North America are also committing to this approach. Essentially, these mills use a combination of newspapers and magazines because the mineral filler or clay content of the magazines benefits the ink removal efficiency of the flotation cells.

Mr. Andrews is corporate lab supervisor, Garden State Paper Co., Garfield, N.J.

Magazines generally constitute about 30% of the deinked pulp content and can be either coated or filled supercalendered grades, which would also include advertising flyers. Currently many of the magazines being recycled come from preconsumer sources that are low in contaminants, such as overruns, returns, and pressroom waste.

Postconsumer sources are largely untapped, but expansion of flotation deinking would represent a significant outlet for these grades. The fiber content of magazines, which like newsprint is a mixture of mechanical and chemical pulps, has a higher percentage of chemical pulp, which is stronger and brighter than mechanical pulp.

Flexographic-printed newspapers have caused more of a problem in flotation compared with washing deinking because flotation requires a larger ink particle size for effective removal. The water-based flexo inks are highly dispersed and have small particle sizes.

SEPARATION TECHNOLOGY.

Sorting of ONP is essentially a hand operation. In the processing of highly contaminated wastepaper, devices such as magnets for metal removal and trommels for separation of glass, metal, and other heavy objects can be effective. But for the sorting of different grades of paper and plastic, no mechanical methods so far have approached the efficiency of hand separation.

The best approach by far is to educate households in segregating newspapers at the source and avoid contamination with other disposable items from the start. Newspapers are easy to handle when stacked and wrapped separately, and clean grades of ONP from well-run collection programs frequently command a higher price. At Garden State Paper, these grades also go "mill direct," meaning that they can bypass the processing centers.

Unfortunately, quality of paper from some municipal programs is often far from desirable, particularly when the programs are hastily organized and mandated by law, such as happened in New Jersey two years ago.

GARDEN STATE'S SORTING PROCESS.

To facilitate the sorting of household collections, Bruno & D'Elia, a subsidiary of Garden State Paper involved in procuring ONP, has installed a new processing center at Port Carteret, N.J. The sorting relies on hand separation, but this is accommodated by moving the paper along belts at waist level on an elevated platform. The out-throws are dropped to the floor below, where they are placed on a separate conveyor.

The system was designed by Baling Service using a Mayfran sorting system and a Harris 1OAS HRB baler. Using 12 employees—ten sorters, one truck operator for loading, and one baler operator—250 bales weighing 1,500 lb each can be processed in an eight-hour shift.

The paper from a single loading conveyor is split between two lines, each with two level sorting conveyors in series and a hump in between for flipping the paper. The first conveyor is run at 30 fpm and the second at 45 fpm. Each line has stations for 14 sorters, although normally four are used, and two more sorters at the loading conveyor cut and remove twine.

The out-throws on the floor under the sorting conveyor are periodically pushed by truck onto a separate conveyor at floor level that feeds the baler directly, and these are baled when the sorting conveyors are shut down. Since most of the out-throws are slick inserts delivered with the newspapers, these bales are sold as magazine grades.

Other contaminants, such as twine and plastic, are not dropped on the floor but instead are placed in separate containers at the sorting level for discard. Corrugated and other brown grades are initially dropped with the slick out-throws and later separated at the baling conveyor and processed separately.

In the Garden State Paper approach, the philosophy in sorting is to remove the contamination and have the good material (ONP) remain on the conveyor. With higher grades of wastepaper, the role may be reversed, with white ledger being removed at one station, color ledger at another, computer paper at a third, and the undesirable grades remaining on the conveyor. ∎

FIGURE 1: **Age of ONP is very important when considering storage. According to an ONP waste study, characteristics such as brightness, breaking length, and burst factor decline fairly rapidly as ONP ages.**

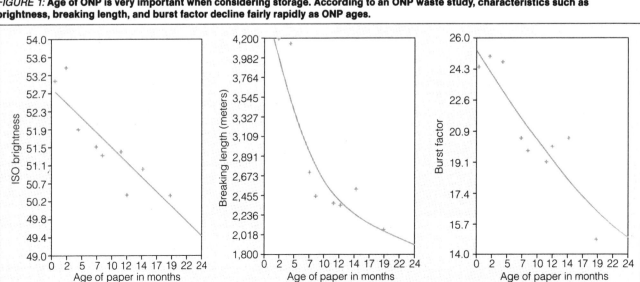

Chapter 20

Noranda Meets New Fine Paper Postconsumer Waste Standards

Noranda Forest Recycled Papers' increased collection program
and Thorold mill expansion keep pace with doubled requirement

By JIM YOUNG, Technical Editor

Noranda Forest Recycled Papers (NFRP) is a new entity backed by a long recycling tradition. Established in November 1989, it is centered at the former Fraser Inc. mill in Thorold, Ont., where recycled fine paper has been produced for 50 years. The mill was the first one licensed by the Canadian Standards Assn. (CSA) to use its EcoLogo (Figure 1), guaranteeing that the sheet contains a minimum of 50% postcommercial recycled paper by weight, including 5% from postconsumer sources.

The 50% recycled requirement is the easy part, at least comparatively. Postcommercial wastepaper has traditionally been collected from converting facilities and print shops and sorted without too much difficulty. Postconsumer waste is something else again. Coming mainly from offices, the wood-free computer and xerographic paper used by Noranda is separated from mechanical pulp-containing newspapers and magazines, often at the office source. Further sorting by collectors/dealers separates papers with acceptable inks from those with difficult-to-deink laser and xerographic imprints.

The current North American recovery rate of postcommercial wastepaper is already about 85% so additional supplies for recycled fine paper will have to come from office waste. According to Gordon Sisler, NFRP's manager, product development, the demand for recycled fine paper exceeds supply. In fact, some customers are now more concerned with how the product is made than they are with its appearance.

COLLECTION. Initially concerned about the quality of postconsumer deinking wastepaper supplies, NFRP considered establishing its own collection and sorting program for office wastepaper, then opted to use its commercial wastepaper broker and dealer network to supply all of the 37,000 tpy of combined postcommercial and postconsumer stock to the Thorold facility. (Figures are in metric tons and Canadian dollars.)

Vic Baltrusaitis, NFRP's director of sales, says that office collection in the southern Ontario area jumped from virtually none to 90,000 tons in about 12 months, a figure he estimates to be more than 35% of the available supply. "I think this is fertile ground," he observes. "The Ontario populace is environmentally sophisticated and responsive. They are keen to recycle." Provincial and municipal governments have sponsored programs on collection and equipment. Voluntary response to recycling is aided in no small measure by rapidly rising dumping fees that will reach $150/ton in May.

A company analysis states that, in general, office wastepaper contains the following:
- 55% laser- and xerographic-printed paper
- 35% white and colored paper
- 5% groundwood paper and old newspapers
- 3% brown kraft paper
- 2% contaminated paper, plastic, adhesives, glass, metals, etc.

FIGURE 1: **The Thorold mill was the first one to receive the Canadian Standards Assn.'s Environmental Choice logo.**

Over 50% recycled paper

Including 5% postconsumer fiber

Office wastepaper is valued at $0 to $25/ton when it arrives at one of several collector/dealer facilities in the Toronto area. A crew of up to ten persons hand sorts an estimated 1½ tpd/person. With mechanization limited mostly to conveyors moving the graded paper, labor costs are high at about $60/ton. Baltrusaitis has figured that as of the end of 1990, mills were paying close to $240/ton for computer printout paper and about $130/ton to $160/ton for white xerographic paper from wastepaper dealers and brokers. Figure 2 illustrates "full circle" fine paper recycling dynamics. Sisler predicts that as the circle becomes more fully closed, the true cost of waste disposal will be shouldered by the generators of wastepaper.

DOUBLING RECYCLING CAPACITY AT THOROLD. The Thorold mill expanded its recycled pulp capacity last year from 21,000 tpy to a current 37,000 tpy and is heading toward a 42,000-tpy goal. This July, the CSA's 5% postconsumer requirement will double to 10%. Sisler explains that 10% of a 50%-recycled sheet means 20% of the fiber line will be handling postconsumer waste. "To the guy on the street, 10% postconsumer waste is nothing, but that's 20% of the 120 tpd that we cook, so we will have to bring in more than 24 tpd of postconsumer waste," he says. "It's tough to get that quantity in the quality that we need." The average office worker generates 0.5 lb of high-grade deinkable wastepaper each day, based on the experience of established office waste collection programs. That translates to 300,000 participating employees to meet the requirements of the Thorold mill alone.

Still, few mills are as geographically well situated to take advantage of wastepaper as Thorold. Drawing from southern Ontario, western New York, the Eastern Seaboard, and reaching into the Midwest, there are 5 million people within a 100-mile radius of the mill, 125 million within a day's hauling distance.

From working with a long-established broker and dealer network, through deinking secondary fiber that has to be competitive in quality to virgin fiber, and on to sheet formation, Sisler notes that there is no substitute for the mill's 50-year experience. This is particularly true in tracking the performance of the blend of both suppliers and their paper grades, month after month, as an important aspect of process control.

The recycling capacity was increased by a series of small changes, led by replacing a rotor in one of the four Hydrapulpers to raise consistency from 8% to 12%. A second Finckh primary screen with 0.01-in. slots was added while the secondary and tertiary screens had sufficient capacity to keep up with the expansion. Process optimization steps included the installation of a wastepaper scale for bale-weight verification and proper pulper loading, the addition of a warm water system, and twinning the deinking fiber supply system to the paper machines, allowing each machine the option of two qualities of deinked pulp. In the area of environmental treatment, the additional load remained within design limits with the help of such optimization as reducing flow variations to the activated sludge effluent treatment plant and improving the operating efficiency of the sludge thickener.

AGRICULTURAL SLUDGE APPLICATION. The mill's deinking sludge is recycled in agricultural applications, acting as a soil conditioning agent. Its high cellulose content is beneficial to high-clay soils that are deficient in organic matter. At the same time, the fiber opens the structure of high-clay soils, reducing compaction and helping to create conditions allowing for better nutrient uptake by plants. As the cellulose breaks down, it takes nitrogen out of the soil so it becomes necessary to add supplementary nitrogen to the sludge in the form of ammonium nitrate. Added at a level of about 1.0% on dry sludge it prevents the depletion of soil nitrogen.

Clays and fillers, representing about half of the sludge weight, are not par-

FIGURE 2: **Fine paper recycling dynamics.**

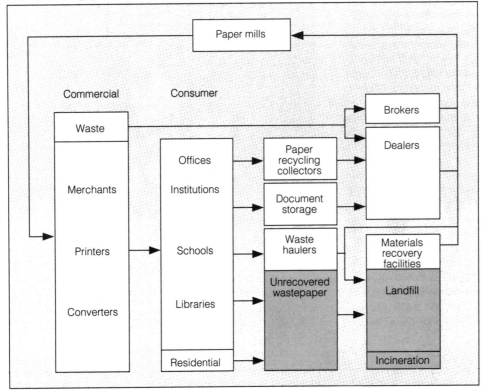

ticularly beneficial except in the case of sandy soils, where clay will improve soil water retention. Other ink particles and paper-making additives are present only in insignificant amounts and are unlikely to provide any measurable advantage.

Pilot tests were run on corn crops to determine the benefit of sludge addition. Yields improved 10% to 15% with the addition of 12 tons/acre and 20 lb of ammonium nitrate/ton of sludge. Some other parameters of plant growth, cob length and weight, leaf color, and leaf area showed additional improvement.

George Kubanek, right, discusses new recycled fiber application technology with S.F. Ali at Noranda's Forest Technologies Laboratory.

The land application rate is usually 12 tons/acre on a wet sludge basis (32% dry). The mill's annual disposal requirements can be met by approximately 2,000 acres of land. Sludge is taken to landfill only when weather prevents delivery to farm sites or if sludge is excessively wet and can't be handled by farm spreading equipment.

FUTURE 115,000-TPY EXPANSION. The doubling of the Thorold mill's recycling capacity was the first objective of NFRP when it was formed in late '89. At the same time, preparations for a 115,000-tpy mill expansion were initiated. Don Duncan, vice president, operations, says the process design and preliminary engineering have been completed, an environmental impact study has been made, and some pilot plant work on proposed effluent treatment systems has been accomplished. A 95-acre site is being prepared for easements, and the purchase of additional land to bring power and gas to the mill site and water to and from the site is under way. While the property will soon be ready for future building, none is planned for the immediate future. "Because of the current economic climate, Noranda will not proceed with construction in the short term," Duncan explains; however, data from the pilot plant will be used to update the permit application with Ontario's Ministry of the Environment.

NORANDA TECHNOLOGY CENTRE. Like NFRP, the Forest Technologies Laboratory at the Noranda Technology Centre in Pointe Claire, Que., is a recent development building on a long tradition. The Centre was established in 1963, primarily serving corporate metallurgical processing operations. Its forest products facility was established two years ago as part of a $19-million building expansion and is now staffed with 16 scientists and engineers working in pulp and paper, environmental, and wood products areas.

The person in charge of the laboratory, George Kubanek, explains that he and his staff are at work developing both new and improved technology, including recycled fiber applications at the Thorold mill and at the Maclaren newsprint mill in Masson, Que. The Centre is working closely with mill personnel to optimize sheet quality, papermaking furnishes, and paper machine operation. Research is also being conducted with the Thorold and Masson mills on improving the recovery of fiber from sludge. The Centre joined in the development of Thorold's effluent treatment program, with pilot plant testing at the mill.

Other research areas include optimizing chemical recovery and recausticizing in kraft mills and improving corrosion abatement. In addition, programs are under way to enhance lumber, panelboard, and other wood products. "We've made a good start and have a strong program under way with some very good people, but we are still pretty new," Kubanek says.

'90s PROJECTIONS. Don Reid, vice president, marketing, says a major thrust carrying well in the '90s will expand on the mill's book and offset paper business in Canada and the U.S. Pulp from high-grade deinked wastepaper has a number of advantages in these grades, including improved bulk and opacity as well as flexible fibers from the alkaline deinking conditions. Future markets for nonpermanent publications may incorporate a groundwood blend.

In addition to its 75,000-tpy capacity to produce Eco-Logo 50% recycled content printing and writing paper—specifically book and commercial printing paper, computer paper, photocopy paper, forms, and stationery—Thorold can produce 25,000 tpy with a range of recycled content by direct entry: wallpaper substrate with minimal recycled content; coated-one-side packaging paper with 20% to 60% recycled content; and its new "Renaissance" reply-card, envelope, and tablet stock with 75% recycled content, including 30% postconsumer waste.

Also looking into the '90s, Sisler says, "It is almost inevitable that governments will legislate material such as office waste out of dumps. I don't see much choice there—certainly not in an area like Toronto, which I am most familiar with. We have to focus on grades where deinked pulp makes sense for fine paper, with other office waste placed in other grades before legislators determine recycled content in every fine paper. That makes it difficult for everybody." ∎

Pulping, Screening, and Cleaning

Considerable improvements have been made in the basic recycled pulping operation in recent years, although no major breakthroughs have occurred. Most gains have been in increased efficiency, especially in the removal of contaminants. The trend toward higher consistencies has lowered overall costs while improving recycled pulp quality.

This section reports the latest engineering approaches to high-efficiency pulping of secondary fibers. Several mill installations are examined in terms of equipment used and specific process designs. Screening equipment in particular is compared for different grades being produced at several recycled paper mills.

Chapter 21

Increased Use of Wastepaper Spurs Improvements in Pulper Efficiency

Design changes now allow mills to customize selection, depending on types of wastepaper, amount of contaminants, and space availability

By GREG SLEEPER

Repulping of wastepaper has traditionally been performed either in continuous or in batch pulpers, with consistencies that normally range from 2.5% to 4% for continuous operation and 6% to 8% for batch. In the past, batch pulping of material has been limited to a maximum production rate of about 200 tpd. Above that tonnage, continuous operation is dominant.

However, changes in design and efficiency have allowed mills to customize pulper systems to fit their needs. This means pulper selection should be given as much consideration as the remaining equipment of a

Mr. Sleeper is senior product engineer, Beloit Corp.—Jones Div., Dalton, Mass.

system. Wastepaper types, amount of contaminants, type of contamination, space constraints, and end product should be considered when making the decision to install a pulper. Rejects removal in the beginning module of a system is equally important because of its influence on subsequent modules. Adequate information and cooperation between the supplier and mill will result in selection of the best alternative for the application.

TRADITIONAL OPERATION. Operating in batch mode has always provided repetitive results and complete defibering. Installed costs have typically been greater due to the larger size of the pulper, pumps, piping, and dump chest. And decontamination has been accomplished by operators manually cleaning the tank after a number of cycles, depending on the degree of contamination.

Continuous pulper operation has been used not only

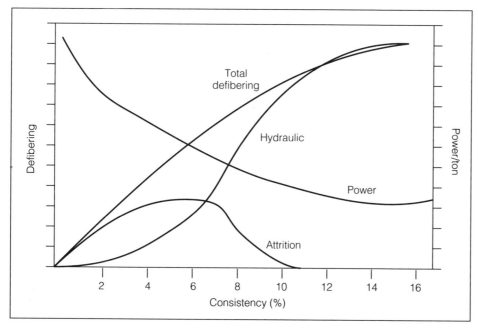

FIGURE 1: **The effect of consistency on hydraulic vs attrition defibering.**

for larger production rates but also where complete defibering is not required. Decontamination has been accomplished by continuous bucket-style junkers as well as junk towers that have clam-bucket hoists.[1] Small holes (0.125 in. to 0.375 in.) were initially used in the extraction grate to hold back contaminants and to provide good defibering (90% to 97%).

As the amount of plastics increased in grades such as old corrugated containers (OCC) and mixed waste, the small holes would plug, resulting in loss of capacity. Larger perforations were installed in the extraction grates to maintain production rates, and the increased hole size necessitated use of satellite pulping units and/or coarse screening modules to handle the rise in fiber flakes and contamination downstream.

NEW PULPER DESIGNS. Improvements in pulper design and decontamination equipment during the past decade have allowed a more customized selection for mills. Depending on the type of wastepaper and end product, mills can select from low-consistency (4% to 6%), medium-consistency (10% to 12%), or high-consistency (more than 12%) repulping. Economic factors for operations, such as deinking, favor medium- to high-consistency pulping. Reducing water requirements by one-half to one-third provides a significant savings in steam and chemical use.[2] Ink dispersion also improves

> *Depending on the type of wastepaper and end product, mills can select from low-consistency . . . , medium-consistency . . . , or high-consistency (more than 12%) repulping.*

at higher consistencies.

As consistencies increase beyond 6%, mechanical attrition action decreases and hydraulic shear action increases (Figure 1). This is a result of increased fiber-to-fiber rubbing as well as the conveying vs pumping action that is needed to circulate this mixture, which has a higher viscosity. Also, specific energy requirements are reduced by the more efficient defibering action. Hydraulic shear defibering benefits contaminant removal by less degradation of plastics, allowing for easier separation by cleaning or screening modules.

Pulper selection for a particular application should include consideration of such factors as production rates, available space, and the type of production process. Higher-consistency pulpers will allow increases in batch production rates to approximately 300 tpd, depending on the furnish. Above 300 tpd, consideration should be given to continuous operation or multiple pulpers. Available space for the installation may also limit the type or number of units that can be installed.

Medium- to high-consistency pulpers are recommended for a deinking operation, depending on the type of wastepaper used. Deinked furnishes fall into two categories—easily dispersible inks (e.g., newsprint) and inks set by drying (e.g., ledger, magazine, and packaging grades).[3]

Inks that are easily dispersed should be run at medi-

FIGURE 2: **The Tri-Dyne continuous pulper with Sigma tank has a twin-fold effect that allows for fast bale submergence and increased differential velocities.**

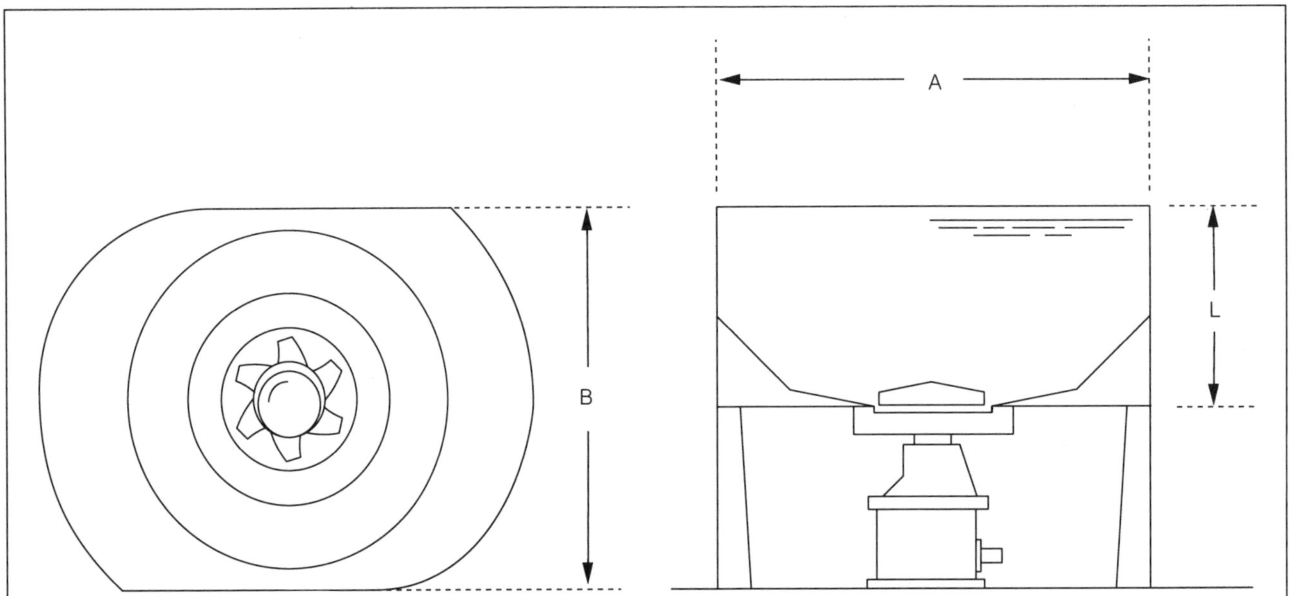

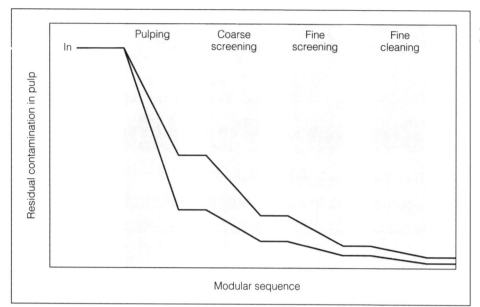

FIGURE 3: **Effect of early decontamination of total system efficiency.**

um consistency (8% to 12% maximum) to prevent over-dispersion, which could allow the particles to enter the lumen of the fiber. When that occurs, the ink is virtually impossible to separate by washing or flotation deinking.

Ledger, magazine, and packaging paper are usually printed with inks that do not disperse readily, resulting in specks in the sheet.[3] Wastepaper containing these inks requires high-consistency pulping. A mill can then take advantage of the improved defibering and dispersion action of the high-consistency pulper.

Recycled board grades, such as OCC, should still be repulped at low consistency to ensure operation of the ragger and other decontamination units. Improved tank and impeller designs have reduced the specific energy requirements for repulping such grades to less than 1 hp-day/ton because of lower power demands needed to circulate the tank and provide submergence of bales.

Most continuous pulpers operate at 200 hp/1,000 ft³ to 400 hp/1,000 ft³ of operating volume. Improved designs have lowered that to 125 to 250 hp/1,000 ft³. Figure 2 shows the Beloit Jones Tri-Dyne with a Sigma tank, which incorporates the new design. No baffles are required in the tank. Submergence is improved by the two sharp breaks at the tank ends, which causes the circulation to fold back on flow, submerging the material.

DECONTAMINATION IMPROVEMENTS. Regardless of the type of pulper process, early removal of rejects is important to the entire system. Figure 3 shows that early reject removal yields a better end-product quality, regardless of the number of stages of cleaning in each subsequent module. Early decontamination is influenced by extraction perforation size, pulper purging, and temperature.

While bucket junkers and junk towers are still used in waste pulpers, they are passive in the nature of removal. Material has to find its way into these units by gravity or the pumping action of the impeller. Improved pulper purging units, such as the Bel-Purge, provide better cleaning by inducing a flow directly from the pulper tank, thus conveying the rejects to the unit. Rejects are collected in the chamber for a preset period of time and then sluiced to recover any usable fiber. The rejects are emptied from the unit to the reject handling system.

FIELD RESULTS. The Beloit Jones OCC system, installed at a southern mill, has been equipped with a continuous design 62-in. Tri-Dyne pulping unit and Sigma tank, operating at 4% to 5% consistency. Decontamination of the pulper includes a Bel-Purge (heavy and light rejects removal), junk tower (additional heavy rejects removal), and ragger operation (baling wire removal). Original design was for 500 tpd, but rates of more than 600 tpd have been achieved. The pulper was installed with a 500-hp motor, which yields 160 hp/1,000 ft³ and 0.83 hp-day/ton (at 600 tpd).

The Tri-Dyne, a multifunctional impeller, is equally suitable for medium-consistency applications, such as ledger pulping at 12% and poly-coated milk carton pulping at 8% to 12%. Medium-consistency pulping of the milk carton stock allows separation of the poly coating from the usable fiber with little breakdown of the polyethylene, allowing for easier removal. During a triple extraction process, the coating is isolated in the pulper tank and then dumped to the rejects handling system. ∎

REFERENCES
1. Norm Hoch, *Pulper Requirements for Reclaimed Papers*, September 1971, *Paper Trade Journal*.
2. Steve Paraskevas, *Repulping Stock at High Consistency Cuts Power, Energy Requirements*, Beloit Jones Performance Report.
3. Luigi Silveri, "Beloit Technological Update—Secondary Fiber," 1989 CPPA Beloit Technical Seminar.

Chapter 22

Alkali Soaking Ups Quality, Yield of OCC Used in Boxboard Furnishes

Installed in the reject treatment line, technique eliminates deflakers and minimizes contaminant attrition throughout the process

By ED HEALEY

When treating old corrugated containers (OCC) for the manufacture of folding boxboards or linerboard, the principle objective is to produce a very clean, strong product in a system that is both economical in installed cost and low in power consumption. One method of accomplishing this has been the use of soaking tower technology developed in Japanese mills through the work of Aikawa, parent company of Fiberprep. Test results with soaking tower systems have shown improved stock yield, lower power consumption, and improved quality of pulp.

In treating OCC, the most important consideration from the standpoint of quality is to minimize attrition throughout the process to keep contaminants as large as

Mr. Healey is president of Fiberprep, Taunton, Mass.

possible for easy removal. If this can be accomplished, a significant gain in the overall yield can be achieved.

ALKALI SOAKING. During the past few years, certain data have been published relative to alkali soaking, which basically involves the use of a soaking tower following the continuous pulper and dewatering press. The pulped stock is dewatered to a consistency of approximately 30% and then diluted with caustic solution to 18% for soaking. This approach is particularly effective for stock deflaking.

Alkali soaking in the main stock preparation line also increases drainage and strength. But it is best used in the reject treatment line, applied for defibering at as low a shear force as possible to minimize degradation of impurities responsible for oil spot problems.

Oil spot problems can be determined with the Oil Spot Procedure, described as follows:

FIGURE 1: **NaOH soaking: soaking time vs defibering efficiency.**

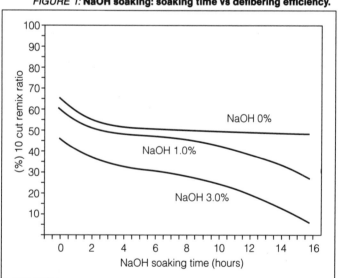

FIGURE 2: **NaOH soaking: NaOH content vs defibering efficiency.**

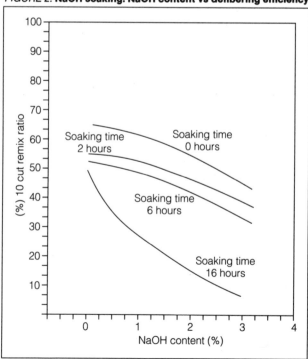

TABLE 1: Retained stock on 0.010-in. slotted flat screen.

	Without soaking	With soaking
Pulper dump chest	33.90%	33.90%
Chest afer soaking	—	10.50%
First ADS inlet	27.30%	6.10%
First ADS outlet	0.74%	0.33%
First ADS light reject	32.00%	3.40%
First ADS second reject	21.70%	6.10%
Second ADS inlet	21.70%	6.10%
Second ADS outlet	0.84%	0.37%
Second ADS light reject	13.90%	4.10%
Second ADS reject	13.30%	7.60%
CVA inlet	13.30%	7.60%
CVA outlet	1.60%	0.72%
CVA reject	50.00%	67.10%

- Make ten to 20 handsheets based on TAPPI (Technical Assn. of the Pulp & Paper Industry) standards.
- Heat and furnace at 140°C for 20 min.
- Count oil spots for the individual sizes.
- Calculate total area.
- Convert to mm²/100 grams of stock.

In alkali soaking, the injection rate of caustic soda and the soaking time are the most important factors. Figures 1 and 2 show the effect of these factors on stock defiberability. As can be seen, alkali soaking time must be longer than 16 hours to obtain the sufficient effect, and 2 to 6 hours of soaking is of no practical value.

SOAKING TESTS. Tests were conducted to determine the results of soaking with the four systems depicted in Figure 3. The four systems each include a piece of equipment developed by Aikawa of Japan called the ADS, which is a primary screening element. The ADS is the newest technology in the screening of OCC, providing high-quality pulp at relatively low energy levels. Principally, this machine allows for both coarse screening and fine screening within the same machine. It also allows the selective removal of lightweight contaminants through the core in the primary section and further provides a gentle deflaking action within the same unit.

The four separate systems piped together and depicted in Figure 3 are as follows:

Test 0—OCC was defibered in the pulper and rejects from the primary ADS were used as sample stock for the reject soaking treatment system (T-3).

Test 1—Rejects from the ADS on Test 0 and the final reject sample from the coarse and final screening processes were combined and dewatered in the screw press and processed without soaking treatment.

Test 2—This system shows a conventional system, in which a deflaker is used to improve yield and provide defibering as opposed to soaking.

Test 3—As described under Test 0, stock was dewatered in the screw press and caustic was added. Stock was soaked for 16 hours and processed in a typical ADS-type system without deflaking. The stock consistency was 30% at the screw press and 18% at the soaking tower. Soaking was accomplished at room temperature.

TEST CONCLUSIONS. When the stock was processed by the ADS after soaking, the yield was 15% higher than without soaking. In Test 3, the yield was 7% higher after soaking than in Test 2, where the deflaker was installed in the tailings line without soaking. This shows that in this type of system, deflakers are unnecessary and the removal of the deflaker eliminates the shredding of contaminants.

Alkali soaking in the reject system contributes to an improvement in stock yield, increase in screen capacity, and elimination of deflakers. The freeness of the waste material is approximately 65 cc CSf lower with soaking than without soaking in the reject line. When this material is remixed with the primary stock, the mainstream accepts are 20 to 25 cc CSf lower than stock not mixed with reject soaking. This affects power. For example, if a final freeness of 400 cc is required and the production rate is 300 tpd, the required power for refining is 688 kW without soaking and 543 with soaking (a 20% to 25% reduction).

The quality of stock after soaking is remarkably improved at the accepts of the ADS. As can be noted in Table 1, the accepts as measured on a 0.010-in. flat screen improved from 0.74% to 0.33% retention with soaking. ∎

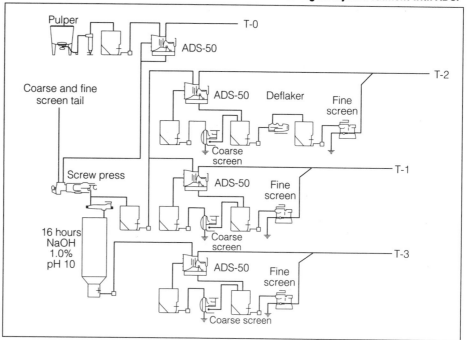

FIGURE 3: Experiment flow to research the effect of alkali soaking on reject treatment with ADS.

Chapter 23

Separate Pulping of Magazines, ONP Yields Cost, Consistency Benefits

A split pulping-deinking system can take your mill past the year 2000, delivering improved control while coping with varying furnishes and inks

By DON McBRIDE

A deinking system is primarily a separation process. Contaminants from old newspapers (ONP) and magazines are separated into the rejects stream and usable fiber into the accepts stream. In a deinking system, quality is defined as maximum removal of ink particles and other contaminants with minimum fiber loss.

Deinking of secondary fiber involves repulping and defibering, and the ink is separated from the cellulose fibers by cleaning, washing, and screening. Removal of the ink begins in the pulper and is basically a laundering operation. The objective is to produce a pulp of high quality from recycled paper.

Equipment is now available to remove not only the most troublesome contaminants but also well over 90% of the ink. Deinking engineers can utilize this modern technology, which involves a combination of flotation and washing systems, to make possible the production of very high-quality recycled paper.

In designing a system, careful matching of the latest equipment and chemicals is essential because this will ultimately determine the success of the system. The deinking system we will be discussing is designed to support 100% of the furnish for a high-speed paper machine to produce high-quality newsprint. As a combination flotation and washing deinking system with both a kneading and dispersion stage, it will effectively remove a wide variety of ink and contaminant combinations in the wastepaper stream.

SPLIT PULPING. If you are considering bringing a deinking system into your mill, you need to realize that all wastepaper stock is not created equal. Baled wastepaper stock comes in several varieties, two of which we will be discussing: ONP and waste magazine. When con-

Mr. McBride is deinking process engineer, Rust International Corp., Birmingham, Ala.

sidering deinking and pulping processes, take into account the kind of waste stock that you will be processing first.

If you are dealing with a mix of newspaper and magazine stocks you might want to consider "split" pulping as an alternative to pulping them together.

If 100% ONP is pulped at high consistency (above 12%) the possibility of smearing of dispersed ink particles back onto the fiber can result in irreversible brightness reversion. Low- or medium-consistency (4% to 8%) pulping of 100% ONP at a moderate pH (9.2 to 9.8) will prevent the rubbing of the easily dispersed, soft, greasy inks back into the fiber.

A kneader, unlike a deflaker or a refiner-type dispersion unit, does not chop nor disintegrate ink particles.

Waste magazines, however, which are heavily coated, can contain hard-set inks that are difficult to disperse. This type of furnish requires a high-consistency pulping environment at a higher pH (10.0 to 10.8). This type of deinking system will also deliver better control of the pulping and deinking process.

The advantages of split pulping are as follows:
- Reduced chemical costs because the chemical application is optimized
- Controlled blending of the newspaper and magazine pulp
- Optimization of pulping consistency.

In a split pulping-deinking system, baled postconsumer waste (newspaper and magazine) will be received by railcars or trucks and unloaded directly to the pulper feed conveyor or stored in the bale storage warehouse. Loose waste can also be received by truck.

If only one pulper can be used to pulp ONP and magazines, the best alternative to split pulping is a continuous drum pulper. Because there is no rotor nor cutting device on a drum pulper, contaminant attrition is much lower.

PULPING. The pulping operation begins with loading bales of reclaimed waste newspaper and magazine onto two separate conveyors. The wires around the bales are cut and the bales spaced evenly on the conveyors, permitting a uniform flow of bales into the pulpers.

The rate of addition of the chemicals, e.g., caustic, silicate, a chelating agent, hydrogen peroxide, and a surfactant (displacter) suitable for the flotation/washing process, is variable depending on the furnish quality and quantity. These chemicals help saponify the ink binder and therefore remove the ink from the fibers and render it hydrophobic for easier removal. (See sidebox for more information on deinking chemicals).

The chemistry of a combination flotation and washing deinking system differs from an all-flotation or all-washing deinking system. Successful flotation depends on rendering larger 30- to 200-micron ink particles hydrophobic with the aid of the clay in the magazine furnish. In a combination flotation and washing deinking system, the standard fatty acid/calcium chloride chemistry removes little ink in the washing stage. The small ink particles of less than 30 microns that are removed by washing, however, are the ones most detrimental to brightness. Nonionic displacter chemistry will remove ink particles in both flotation and washing stages, resulting in a wider range of ink particle sizes removed and a brighter pulp.

Stock is pumped from the pulper to the pulper dump retention chest. This chest is sized to give sufficient retention time for the deinking chemicals to fully react.

CENTRIFUGAL CLEANING AND SCREENING. The stock is pumped from the pulper dump chest at approximately 3% consistency to the high-density cyclone cleaners. Heavy rejects, such as staples, wire, and tramp metal,

are separated by centrifugal action, collected in a trap, and periodically dumped into a dumpster that is hauled to a landfill. The accepted stock is then processed through three stages of coarse screens equipped with screen baskets having 0.051-in. holes and three stages of screens equipped with screen baskets having 0.012-in. slots.

Accepted stock from the primary screens discharges to the disc filter feed chest and is then pumped to the disc filters for thickening. The effluent from the disc filters is pumped to the clarifier and, after clarification, recycled for system dilution.

The stock is now blended in the pulp blend chest and pumped to twin-wire presses, where it is dewatered from 8% to 30% consistency.

KNEADING. After the primary presses, the stock is discharged at 30% consistency into the high-consistency

---

Deinking chemicals

Sodium hydroxide (caustic) creates alkalinity, swells the fiber, releasing ink into the suspension, and induces saponification to hydrolize the ink vehicles and binders.

Sodium silicate acts as a wetting agent and a mild dispersant to release the ink and also stabilizes the alkalinity.

Hydrogen peroxide gives a higher brightness to pulp. It suppresses the yellowing action caused by alkali on mechanical or groundwood pulp.

Chelant/sequestrant stabilizes the hydrogen peroxide by the complex binding of heavy metal ions and aluminum ions. A chelating agent is used to aid in the bleaching efficiency by deactivating metallic ion contaminants, including aluminum (alum). Metal ions in the deinked pulp cause rapid decomposition of hydrogen peroxide.

Diethylene diamine pentamethylene phosphonic acid (DTPMPA) is the phosphonic derivative of diethylene diamine pentamethylene (DTPA). DTPMPA is more efficient in reducing hydrogen peroxide breakdown than DTPA. Based on recent trials, some of the benefits of using DTPMPA are as follows:
- Higher residual H_2O_2
- Less silicate use (up to 50% less)
- Higher brightness (up to 2 points)
- Improved retention of fines and fillers on the paper machine because of the reduction of silicate usage
- Improved runability and higher drying rates on the paper machine
- Less scale formation and filling of felts.

Surfactant is a combination dispersant/collector or "displacter." Surfactant benefits include the following:
- Providing 100% active liquid
- Requiring no makedown system
- Requiring no added calcium chloride
- Combining both of the properties of a dispersant and a fatty acid soap collector.

kneaders for a gentle fiber-to-fiber rubbing action that enhances ink separation.[1] The treatment of fibers by a "kneader" is unlike treatment by a deflaker or a refiner-type dispersion unit. A kneader does not chop nor disintegrate ink particles, plastic contaminants, or fibers.

At 30% consistency, intensive activity takes place between the two counter-rotating screws of the kneader. Little or no relative movement occurs between the pulp and the screws; all of the movement goes on between the fibers themselves with a lot of shearing and twisting forces. This fiber-to-fiber rubbing action effectively detaches the ink from the fiber. The best location for a kneader is just before the flotation stage.

HIGH-DENSITY EXTRACTION OR SOAK TOWER. Recent advances in deinking technology focus on a high-consistency soak tower that produces high-quality pulp.[2] Stock of low freeness tends to adhere to the inner walls of a conventional high-consistency tower. If wastepaper stock is deposited in a dead zone of the tower, it ferments and can decompose, compromising quality and brightness.

The features of the soak tower include agitation devices that comprise four to six rakes mounted on the bottom part of a shaft suspended from the center of the tower. Dilution water, which contains residual deinking and bleaching chemicals, is fed from the center of the bottom and the side walls of the soak tower. The diluted stock is scraped off by rake arms and falls to the bottom of the tower to be discharged by a suction pump. Stock is pumped out uniformly, aided by continuous dilution.

SEPARATION BY FLOTATION. The stock is pumped to the flotation feed chest, diluted to 1% consistency, and pumped to the primary flotation cells.

In a flotation cell, high-pressure aeration produces a

FIGURE 1: **A split pulping-deinking system pulps, cleans, and screens ONP separate from magazines.**

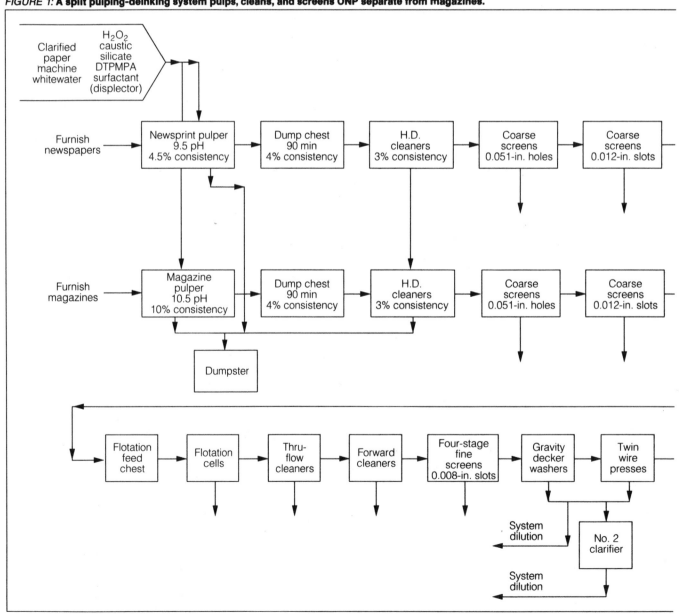

wide spectrum of air bubbles, maximizing both the collision frequency and attachments of the ink particles to the air bubbles.

Hydrophobic particles—in particular the printing ink particles detached from the fiber—are deposited on the air bubbles and rise to the surface, creating a foam suspension. The foam is separated and drawn off by the reject system, dewatered to a consistency of 40% to 50%, discharged to a dumpster, and then taken to a landfill or to an incinerator.

CLEANING. The accepted stock from the flotation cells discharges to the through-flow cleaner feed chest at 1% consistency. The stock is then pumped to through-flow cleaners to remove the lightweight contaminants remaining after the stock has passed through the flotation modules. Typical lightweight contaminants removed are polystyrene, hotmelts, waxes, plastic, and stickies.

Stock discharges from three stages of through-flow cleaners to the forward cleaner feed chest. From there the stock is pumped to the forward cleaners to remove heavyweight contaminants, such as sand, metal, glass, and ink specks.

FINE SCREENING. Fine screening begins as stock discharges from the forward cleaners into the fine screen feed chest. The stock is then pumped to four stages of the fine screens equipped with 0.008-in. slots to remove glass, metal, shives, stickies, hotmelts, plastic, styrofoam, etc. Accepted stock from the fine screens discharges to the decker/washer feed chest. The rejects from the fine screens discharge into the reject system.

GRAVITY DECKER/WASHERS. Stock coming from the decker/washer feed chest is pumped to the decker/washers for fine-ink-particle removal, washing, and thickening. Decker/washer effluent is rich in suspend-

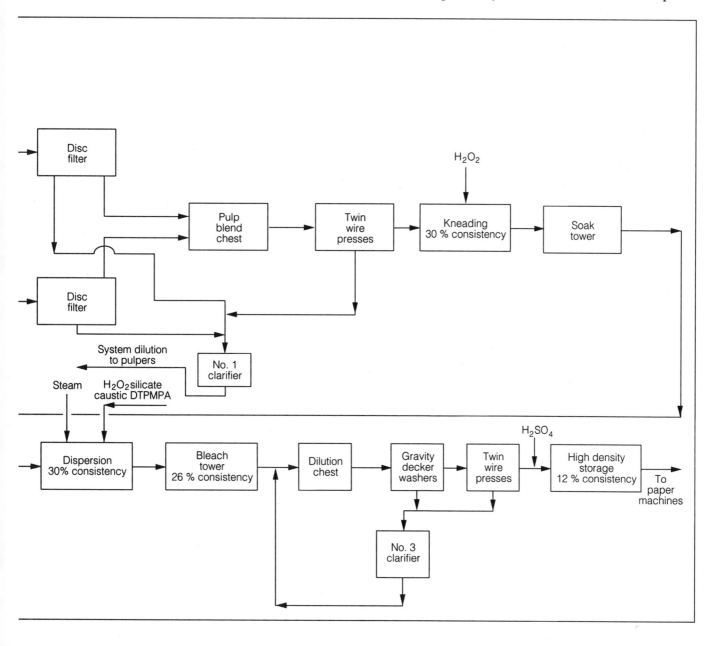

ed solids (ink and ash) and will be clarified before being used for system dilution. The decker/washers thicken the stock to a consistency of 4% to 6%.

Following a washing stage, all of the washer filtrate is sent through spray filters or scalpers to recover the reusable fiber. The filtrate is sent to a clarifier where the ink and lightweight contaminants are removed by dissolved air flotation, aided by polymers and flocculants.

DISPERSION. The dispersion stage begins with a twin-wire press. Here the stock is thickened from 4% to 30% consistency. The stock mat is then shredded by a breaker screw and transported by conveyor to a heating screw, where it is heated to approximately 200° F by direct steam.

Plastic, glue, and wax particles become soft and lend themselves to dispersion. Large ink specks in the furnish are reduced to 30- to 40-micron size by the disper-

sion unit. The majority of these specks, after both the kneading and dispersion stages, will be too small to attach themselves to an air bubble for secondary flotation. Therefore, a postdispersion washing stage is more appropriate for fine-ink-particle removal.

A dispersion unit will disintegrate any remaining contaminants into ultrafine particles smaller than can be detected by the human eye. Also, any remaining ink particles will be separated from the fiber for secondary washing.

Bleach liquor, e.g., hydrogen peroxide, sodium hydroxide (caustic), sodium silicate and DTPMPA[3] are added into the dispersion unit, which is followed by a bleach tower, producing a pulp of higher brightness. Dispersion is necessary for a high-quality pulp, but removal of ink and contaminants is the only true way to assure high quality.

CLARIFICATION. The filtrate from the presses will discharge to the clarifier where contaminants and ink will be separated. The clarified filtrate will discharge to the clarified water chest. This clarified water will be used for dilution in the system. The sludge from the clarifier will discharge to the rejects processing system.

The rapid adoption of the flexographic printing ink formulation has caused problems for many deinking plants. Flotation deinking is not capable of removing flexo ink, which is water-base and does not contain the standard mineral oil formula of regular printing inks.

Flexo inks are rapidly dispersed in the washing and deinking process and must be removed from the filtrate by clarification, with some additional polymer cost. The dispersed ink must now be reagglomerated with the aid of polymers and removed from the recycled water.

CLARIFY THE PAPER MACHINE WHITEWATER. A paper machine, besides producing paper, is in essence a giant washer. Retention aids, alum, defoamers, rosin size, felt cleaning chemicals, residual ink particles, and stickies all end up in the paper machine whitewater.

Introducing this water as dilution into a deinking system, without first being clarified, directly interferes with the deinking and bleaching process. Also, the cost of the chemicals used in the deinking process goes up considerably to compensate for the various chemicals, metal ions, and ink introduced into the system.

Unclarified paper machine whitewater at 4.0 pH can actually set the ink into the fiber, making it very difficult to deink. By simply clarifying the paper machine whitewater, you can prevent the contamination of the pulp that you are trying hard to deink. ∎

Thinking before deinking: some important considerations

• If the wastepaper is allowed to be stored outside—exposed to sun and wind—the solvents and binders in the ink will evaporate, setting the dried ink onto the fiber and making the wastepaper difficult to deink. Sand and dirt carried by the wind will only add to the contamination problem and cause wear of expensive screen baskets and cleaners. Wastepaper bales more than six months old, whether stored inside or outside, will have the same problem to a certain degree.

The wastepaper procurement person who thought he or she was getting a bargain on a large lot of older wastepaper because the price was low probably did not inquire or consider that such wastepaper is better suited as furnish for recycled folding boxboard than for deinking.

Fresh wastepaper, stored inside a warehouse for less than six months, will cause fewer problems with brightness reversion in the deinking process. The bales should be rotated on a regular basis to assure a high-quality deinked pulp.

• The surface of the wastepaper storage area is also an important consideration. Many deinking operations have learned a hard lesson by storing wastepaper bales on an asphalt surface simply because asphalt is less expensive than concrete. On an asphalt surface, each time the fork truck operator picks up a stack of bales or the front-end loader operator pushes loose paper onto the conveyor, a small amount of asphalt inevitably ends up on the conveyor and in the deinking process, contaminating the entire system.

• The right combination of equipment, chemistry, and employee training will make deinking a lot easier.

• Keep in mind that the design of the rejects handling and sludge systems as well as the whitewater systems are as important as the design of the main deinking system.

REFERENCES
1. F. Togashi and E. Okada, 1989 TAPPI Pulping Conference Proceedings, TAPPI PRESS, Seattle, Wash. p. 343.
2. Pollcon Engineering Co., *Japan Pulp & Paper*, Vol. 22, No. 1, May 1984.
3. G. Galland, E. Bernard, Y. Verac, *Paper Technology* Vol. 30, No. 12, Dec. 1989.

Chapter 24

Cleaning of Secondary Fiber Stickies May Necessitate Monitoring for VOCs

Felt cleaning solvents can contain volatile organic compounds, making paper machine exhaust stacks a possible emission source

By FREDERICK H. INYARD

Faced with the threat of shrinking landfill space, the demand for recycled paper products is expected to increase dramatically in the next five years. According to the American Paper Institute, U.S. paper manufacturers plan to invest billions of dollars in plants and equipment to recover clean, high-quality wastepaper. The institute has set a national goal to recycle 40% of all paper production by 1995.

Paper manufacturers that plan to build new recycling facilities or use existing plants for the process of recycling paper should be aware of Environmental Protection Agency (EPA) regulations for volatile organic compounds (VOCs). Standards of performance for new stationary sources are established under Section 111 of the Clean Air Act (42 U.S.C. 7411) as amended. The standards apply to any new stationary source of air pollution that "causes, or contributes significantly to, air pollution which may reasonably be anticipated to endanger public health or welfare."

Under the act, control technology guidelines (CTGs) have been issued for many industry groups. The guidelines are designed to reflect the degree of emission reduction achievable through the application of best reasonably available control technology (RACT), taking into consideration the cost of achieving such emission reduction, any non-air-quality health and environmental impacts, and energy requirements.

RACT regulations are a major component of the strategies by which states can achieve VOC emission reductions through effective implementation of the State Implementation Plan (SIP). EPA normally requires states to impose RACT on VOC sources that can potentially emit more than 100 tpy but do not fall into a CTG category. This 100-tpy cutoff is intended to apply to the entire

plant, not just the individual non-CTG emission units.

Under the definition of 100-tpy non-CTG source, the non-CTG source cannot merely apply less than RACT controls to avoid applicability. Further, EPA can restrict hours of operation by legally and federally enforceable permit conditions to limit emissions below 100 tpy. If emissions are found to be above the cutoff, then the state must apply RACT thereafter. The standards of performance are evaluated on a case-by-case basis.

PAPER MILL VOCs. Paper mills using primarily recycled paper normally clean the paper machine felts and screens frequently to remove stickies that can accumulate during the papermaking process. Recycled paper, in particular, contains residues that can eventually blind the felts and wire on the paper machine and cause imperfections in the final product.

A solvent wash is used on an as-needed basis to remove stickies when paper quality becomes unacceptable. The time between successive solvent cleanings varies and can range from several hours to several days depending on the quality of the recycled fiber and the amount of impurities it contains.

The cleaning solution consists of a caustic solvent solution made up in batches as needed. The solution is normally pumped from a batch tank to a spray boom, where it is applied to the felt or wire with spray nozzles. It usually takes about five to ten min to apply the solvent wash to the felt or screen.

Water from the paper machine felts is normally recycled to the whitewater system. However, during the solvent cleaning cycle, this water is usually directed to the wastewater sewer. Also, exhaust stacks over the paper machines operate continuously to remove warm, moist air from above the paper machines. These are the two possible points of VOC emissions.

ONE MILL'S EXAMPLE. Under the terms of an agreement with a state regulatory agency, a paper mill triggered RACT requirements by emitting more than 100 tpy

---

Mr. Inyard is vice president, Eder Associates, Locust Valley, N.Y.

of VOCs. The mill uses 100% secondary fiber to produce tissue paper. The recycled fiber (mostly ledger paper, register paper, and coated book paper) is trucked into the receiving yard, where the paper is weighed, inspected, and stored by grade.

Under RACT, three areas of modifications are evaluated: product substitution, process changes, and add-on controls. The mill had already installed various types of screens, cleaners, and flotation devices upstream of the paper machines to minimize the amount of stickies, and a non-VOC cleaning solution was unavailable. Therefore, the mill was forced to research various types of add-on control technologies.

The mill undertook an in-depth program to demonstrate the quantity and characteristics of VOC emissions that resulted from its papermaking operations. The program included evaluating VOC emissions that result from the removal of stickies and implementing a sampling program to quantify both air and wastewater emissions.

Sampling of the paper machine was conducted at the two exhaust stacks and at three wastewater discharge points (Figure 1). Only one of the mill's paper machines was sampled since the results were believed to be representative of all machines at the mill. The mass of the solvent exhausted by each of the two stacks was determined by EPA Method 25-Byron version. Method 25 results are reported on a carbon-mass basis. These results were then used to calculate the mass of solvent exhausted from the paper machine.

The sampling program quantified the fate of VOC emissions that resulted from the solvent cleaning operations. VOC emissions in wastewater and air were verified using mass balance calculations. Field measurements and analytical data were used to calculate the following parameters:

- The mass of solvent used per solvent cleaning episode, expressed as pounds of carbon and pounds of VOC
- The mass of VOCs exhausted from each of two stacks, expressed as pounds of carbon and pounds of VOC per solvent cleaning episode
- The mass of VOCs discharged with wastewater, expressed as pounds of carbon and pounds of VOC per solvent cleaning episode.

Test results showed that almost 97% of the solvent applied to the paper machine felts was discharged with the wastewater. The remaining 3% was exhausted by the paper machine exhaust stacks to the atmosphere. With such a low percentage of VOCs being exhausted, the cost of add-on controls could not be justified for reducing VOC stack emissions.

It was originally anticipated that a much larger percentage of the VOCs would have been exhausted at the paper machine. However, when it was determined that almost all of the VOCs were discharged with the wastewater, a bench scale treatability study was undertaken to determine the fate of the VOCs in the effluent once discharged from the mill.

The bench scale treatability study indicated that approximately 84% of the solvent reaching the treatment plant is absorbed in the biological flow or is biodegraded, and 13% is emitted into the atmosphere. Considering the 3% VOC emission at the paper machine, this results in an overall 16% emission of VOCs to the atmosphere.

This study clearly demonstrates that at this particular mill—based on the total VOCs emitted, large air volumes, and low VOC concentrations—add-on controls to reduce or eliminate VOCs would be cost-prohibitive. ■

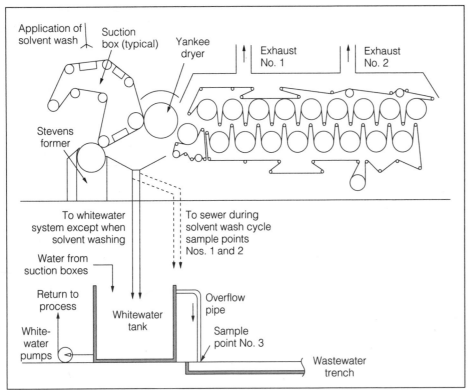

FIGURE 1: **To quantify air and water emissions of VOCs, the mill took samples from the two machine exhaust stacks and at three wastewater discharge points.**

Chapter 25

Continuous Drum Repulping System Features High-Consistency Stock

Newsprint, ledger paper, corrugated container, mixed waste recycling claims maximum strength with minimum degradation

By MOMDOUH A. BADAWI and DICK KOFFINKE

Several mills are repulping various grades of recycled furnishes, such as old newspapers (ONP) and magazines (OMG), ledger paper, old corrugated containers (OCC), and mixed waste, without using raggers, junkers, or auxiliary pulping devices necessary to produce a high-quality stock. In some cases, this has minimized downstream equipment.

These are the more than 50 mills worldwide using a Fiberflow drum repulping system from Ahlstrom-Kamyr, based on a new-generation pulper that combines the advantages of high-consistency pulping with continuous operation. This combination is most advantageous in large deinked newsprint operations.

One of the features of the system is its ability to process bales without removing the wires. This has been demonstrated in Europe as well as North America. Wires are cut but not removed and are passed instead through the drum pulper and discharged from the rejects opening.

In a recent installation in a North American newsprint mill, the pulper processes approximately 250 short tpd of 100% magazine furnish for blending with a separate newsprint furnish in a full deinking application. Although there were some initial problems with handling

Mr. Badawi is stock preparation manager, Ahlstrom C&V Inc., Largo, Fla. Mr. Koffinke is affiliated with Kamyr Inc., E. Walpole, Mass.

the massive amounts of wire found on large compressed magazine bales, the mill reports that the installation is now producing an essentially flake-free stock with a lower contaminant level than that found in the newsprint furnish.

Other systems currently under construction include a 600-metric-tpd newsprint deinking application as well as a 400-short-tpd installation. Both were selected after review of several similar installations in Europe and Japan, which highlighted the contaminant removal and deflaking characteristics of the Fiberflow system.

DESIGN. The Fiberflow drum pulper consists of a rotating drum that has both a defiberizing and a screening section (Figure 1). In both sections, a series of baffles and lifters combine to reduce the baled or loose furnish to a fiber and water stock.

The drum is slightly inclined to move the furnish axially from the deflaking section to the screening section. The length and angle are designed to provide a nominal 20-min retention time for defiberizing.

A patented device transfers the deflaked stock into the perforated screening compartment where a shower system reduces the consistency to a level suitable for pumping and high-consistency cleaning of heavies. The accept vat, which receives the stock from the perforated section, is agitated both for good fiber distribution and preparation for the discharge pump and is level controlled.

The overall design is similar to kiln construction and uses standard drive components, such as a parallel gear reducer used with a girth-and-pinion gear set to drive the drum at a predetermined rotational speed. This, when combined with an automatic lube system, results in a low-maintenance unit with a high uptime rating.

Some other features, such

FIGURE 1: Incoming paper is wetted to approximately 15% consistency in the first zone of the rotating drum, then reduced to a 3% to 4% consistency in the screening zone.

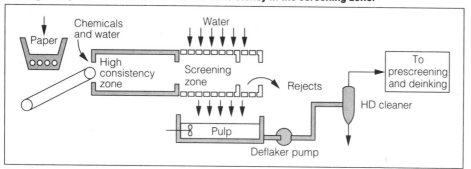

as continuous washed rejects discharge, fully automatic feed and dilution ability that can be programmed into a distributed control system, and constant retention time for repulping regardless of the feed rate, make the Fiber-flow drum pulper advantageous for all types of repulping from ONP to old corrugated stock.

PRINCIPLE. The basic principle of the system is relatively simple. The furnish is chemically wetted (typically caustic and water) in both the inlet chute and the deflaking section to a consistency of approximately 15%. Through the combination of rotation and the lifters, it is dropped a predetermined number of times while traveling through the deflaking section.

This action, at the high consistency, results in a gentle but effective shearing force that defiberizes the paper with minimum disintegration of contaminants or degradation of fiber properties. This is most important in processing recycled fibers that have already had sufficient work done on them initially. Adding to the continuous high-consistency features is the fiber-to-fiber rubbing motion, which loosens ink, size, hotmelts, etc., from the fibers for subsequent removal in either the screening section or in downstream equipment.

Once deflaking is nearly complete, stock is transferred to the screening section, where it is screened at a consistency between 3% and 4% while being subjected to the gentle dropping action of the lifters. The contaminants, screened through 6-mm holes and only minimally degraded, are passed along to the reject opening, where they are suitable for compacting and landfill with essentially no fiber loss. This principle of continuous gentle defiberizing at high consistency results in a virtually fully deflaked, high-quality stock with a very low contaminant level and high physical fiber properties.

OPERATION. The pulper is basically a feed-driven system. In a fully instrumented installation, the feed rates are set by the pulper conveyor with dilution water and chemicals and then controlled based on this rate. A feedforward level control loop on the vat then delivers the required tonnage to the downstream system.

Dilution water is usually supplied by the system thickener along with whatever makeup water is necessary. Temperatures can be held in the 100°F to 110°F range, which not only is beneficial in keeping various types of stickies in a screenable state for optimum removal but also keeps heating costs to a minimum.

For practical purposes, the operational parameters are fiber loss and yield. Fiber losses for a typical deinking system are generally about 0.8% while the yield is typically 98%. This yield is based on inlet fiber tonnage. Any reduction in this yield is usually because of the amount of out-throws in the furnish.

Power consumption for all sizes of the pulper is normally 0.7 to 1.0 hp • day/ton depending on the furnish. Systems are sized based on capacities ranging from 100 to 650 oven-dry short tpd. ∎

Chapter 26

Contour Surface Cylinders Boost Wastepaper Screening Efficiency

A decade of improvements has increased capacity of pressure screens, but newest design improves cylinder wear life

By CHRISTOPHER M. VITORI and IRENEE J. PHILIPPE

The use of contour-surface, slotted-screen cylinders has increased in the paper industry in recent years. The cylinders' benefits include lower reject rates, reduced long fiber fractionation, smaller slot sizes, higher capacity, and reduced sensitivity to consistency and contaminant content variations.

However, high wear rates have been reported in some installations for these cylinders, particularly in applications with secondary fiber furnishes, which have a substantial abrasive material content. Screen cylinder suppliers have tested various materials and surface treatments, but, in general, hard-chrome plating has been most successful for extending wear life. But even with hard-chrome plating, some installations have worn the contour off in as little as a few weeks to a few months.

Before the development of the contour surface, slotted-screen cylinders consisted of smooth-surface plates with milled-through slots. A contour surface is normally produced by milling shallow, narrow grooves parallel to the through slots into the inlet surface of the screen plate. The groove walls may be parallel or at an angle to the through slot. The milled-through slot is located at or near the bottom plane of the groove. Thus, the through slot inlet is recessed into the plate surface.

Contour surface cylinders used in pressure screens were first introduced in the paper industry in the early 1980s. Because of the benefits over smooth-surface cylinders, contour-surface cylinders found widespread acceptance in the mid-1980s.[1,2] Currently, it is estimated that 90% of all slotted-screen cylinders are sold with some type of surface contour.[3]

BENEFITS OF THE CONTOUR. Increased turbulence induced by stock flowing over the contour results in remixing and fluidization of the pulp near the screen plate surface. Such fluidization reduces the apparent viscosity of the pulp slurry, therefore greatly reducing the tendency of the screen to blind over.

This fluidization effect produces numerous benefits in the screening process, the most important being the ability to process increased stock throughput, particularly at high consistencies. When feed consistency, pressure differential, and accept capacity are analyzed, it becomes clear that the contour-surface cylinder provides increased throughput capacity at much higher consistencies on an equal slot width basis. Although the capacity of the contour-surface cylinder is higher than for the smooth-surface cylinder of equal slot width, the contour-surface cylinder allows slightly more contaminants to be accepted due to the reduced level of contaminant alignment accompanying fluidization.[4] However, when

FIGURE 1: **50 X photomicrograph cross section of conventional-contour, slotted-screen plate showing typical wear pattern on leading edge of contour.**

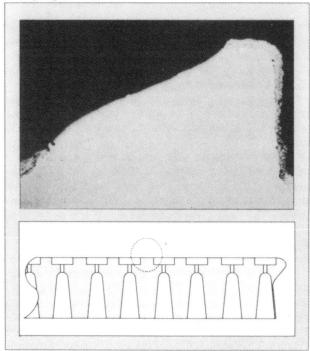

Mr. Vitori and Mr. Philippe are research engineers, Black Clawson Co., Middletown, Ohio.

compared on the basis of equal efficiency (smaller slots in the contour cylinder), the capacity of the contour-surface cylinder is still higher.

A reduction in the tendency to fractionate the long fiber into the reject stream generally allows pressure screens with contour-surface cylinders to be operated at a lower reject rate. Lower reject rates and reduced long fiber content in the reject stream from a primary screen reduce the required capacity for further screening in the secondary position. Therefore, less capital expenditure for reject screening is required.

Higher capacity allowed by contour cylinders at equal screening efficiency also requires less specific energy (kW hour/ton of pulp) than would be required for smooth-surface, slotted-screen cylinders.

REDUCED WEAR LIFE. In exchange for the substantial benefits, the contour-surface cylinder has a short wear life and will eventually lose its operating advantages due to contour surface erosion. Rotor peripheral speeds up to 26 m/sec combined with higher processing capacities result in accelerated velocities of the abrasive stock slurry at the plate surface and in the through slots.

The cross section of a contour-surface, slotted-screen plate in Figure 1 shows the typical wear pattern of the contour surface. The leading edge of the contour has been substantially eroded. In some cases, the contour surface on slotted cylinders has been worn away in as little as two weeks in extremely abrasive environments, such as minimally cleaned low-grade mixed waste or postconsumer old corrugated containers (OCC).

Heavy thicknesses of wear-resistant coatings, such as hard-chrome plating applied to the contour surfaces, have greatly increased screen cylinder wear life. In some cases, hard-chrome plating has extended wear life as much as 20 times normal. However, in many cases wear-resistant coated contour cylinders still wear substantially in as little as two to eight months. It is obvious that an improved wearing surface is needed, while the benefits of the contour-surface cylinder are maintained.

NEW DEVELOPMENTS. A new convex contour-surface cylinder design has been developed offering several advantages over the first contour-surface cylinder—greater capacities at higher consistencies, further reduction in fractionation of long fiber into the reject stream, and lower specific energy requirements. Furthermore, the contour surface of this new cylinder is less sensitive to erosion.

The convex cylinder technology consists of a conventional slotted-screen plate with vertical convex ridges made of a wear-resistant compound. This compound is fused to the land area between each slot. The entire inside surface of the cylinder then receives a heavy coating of hard-chrome plating to protect the areas not covered by the wear-resistant compound. The chrome plating also enhances the wear resistance of the contour ridges. The shape of the contour and the combination of

FIGURE 2: **Cross section of convex-contour surface, slotted-screen plate.**

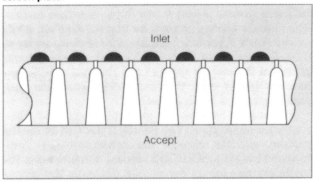

FIGURE 3: **50 x photomicrograph of cross section of hard chrome-plated, conventional contour-surface screen plate.**

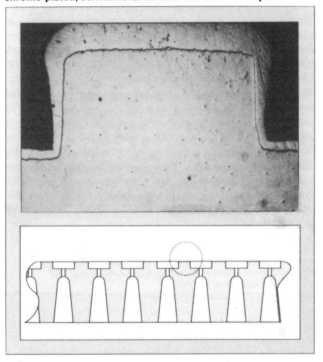

different materials provides a rugged wear-resistant contoured-cylinder surface.

Figure 2 shows the construction of this screen plate in cross section. The primary difference between this contour surface and contour surfaces produced by conventional machining is that the material is added to the surface rather than removed. This better preserves the structural integrity of the screen cylinder.

The extension of cylinder wear life is provided by taking advantage of the three very different characteristics of this technology:

- Contour height and shape
- Diverse metallurgical properties
- Reconstruction.

The convex silhouette, although slightly higher than conventional contour outlines, is less sharp. Therefore, it is less sensitive to erosion.

The lack of sharp edges also facilitates better distribution of chrome plating across the screen plate surface. The chrome plating process, by nature, does not apply an even thickness of metal to irregular or sharp surfaces. This is a result of electrical current densities being greater at the highest surfaces and sharpest outside corners and lowest at the recessed surfaces and inside corners of a surface being plated.[5]

Figure 3 is a cross section photomicrograph that illustrates this phenomena. The plating is thickest on the top surface, and the chrome has concentrated to form rounded bulges at the sharp corners. Furthermore, the thickness recedes as the plating descends the groove wall.[6] Excessive thicknesses are applied to the top surface of the contour so sufficient thicknesses reach the recess of the groove.

By taking advantage of the properties of the three different materials used to construct the cylinder, wear life can be further increased. The base material, 316L stainless steel, provides an economical corrosion-resistant and easily machined substrate. The compound used to produce the contour ridges has a hardness of 40 Rc. However, this material is quite ductile, providing not only hardness for wear resistance but also resistance to minute impacts. The chrome plating has a hardness of 70 Rc and is therefore extremely wear resistant.

The most unique feature of this technology is that the contour can be reconstructed. After the contour eventually wears away, the convex ridges can be reapplied directly over the existing worn ridges. However, the feasibility of this procedure must be determined on a case by

case basis by the overall condition of the screen cylinder. Extreme wear resulting in the widening of the trough slot or structural fatigue of the screen cylinder may render reconstruction impractical.

This technology can also be applied to some designs of conventional contour-screen cylinders if the contour is worn but the cylinder is in good condition. Existing smooth-surface cylinders can also be converted to contour-surface cylinders by adding the convex ridges and chrome plating.

OPERATING RESULTS. The new contour-surface cylinder, called PSB-90 by Black Clawson,[7] offers numerous operational advantages over conventional contour-surface cylinders. Laboratory tests of the new contour cylinder on screening newspaper, corrugated containers, and mixed waste furnishes, all at various consistencies, revealed the following trends:

- Increased capacity potential, especially at higher feed consistencies
- Higher consistencies practical for a given slot size
- Lower specific energy requirements
- Reduced fractionation of long fiber into the reject stream
- Improved runability (less sensitive to swings in operating conditions).

The potential screening capacity with the convex-contour cylinder is greater when operated at consistencies over 1.5% to 2.0% as illustrated in Figure 4. This graph compares accept capacity versus feed stock consistency for a given furnish with pressure differential held constant. Particularly when the feed consistency is above the 1.5% to 2.0% range, through put with the PSB-90 screen cylinder is dramatically higher than with the conventional-contour cylinder.

Energy consumption characteristics, illustrated in Figure 5, reveal that at consistencies above 1.5% to 2.0% the advantage lies with the convex-contour cylinder. This graph compares kilowatt hours per ton of pulp to feed consistency for a given furnish. As the feed consistency reaches the 1.5% to 2.0% range, the PSB-90 screen cylinder generally requires less specific energy to screen pulp.

The fractionation characteristics of the new contour cylinder are illustrated in Table 1 for each furnish at each consistency tested. The degree of fractionation was measured as the difference in Canadian Standard freeness (CSf) between reject and feed samples.

Table 1 also lists the change in CSf between feed and reject samples for both the new contour cylinder and the conventional contour-surface cylinder. In all cases, the use of the convex contour cylinder resulted in significantly less fractionation of the long fiber into the reject stream than the conventional contour cylinder at equal pulp reject rated. The new contour cylinder can be generally classified as nonfractionating on these furnishes. Therefore, screens can be operated at lower reject rates in many applications.

TABLE 1: **Difference in CSf values between reject and feed samples for conventional contour (PSL) and PSB contour slotted-screen cylinder on newsprint, mixed waste, and corrugated container furnishes.**

Feed consistency % fiber	Difference in CSf (refect CSf - feed CSf)					
	Newsprint		Mixed waste		Corrugated container	
	PSL	PSB	PSL	PSB	PSL	PSB
0.0	35	10	79	(-7)	119	8
1.5	50	10	69	(-20)	170	90
2.5	100	(-5)	155	26	230	104
3.5	85	25	191	80	226	34

TABLE 2: **Pressure differential between feed and accept for conventional contour (PSL) and PSB contour slotted screen cylinder on newsprint, mixed waste, and corrugated container furnishes.**

Feed consistency % fiber	Pressure differential at plugging (kPa) (Feed kPa-Accept kPa)					
	Newsprint		Mixed waste		Corrugated container	
	PSL	PSB	PSL	PSB	PSL	PSB
0.8	152	214	138	138	145	145
1.5	138	200	138	138	138	138
2.5	117	165	124	138	124	131
3.5	90	165	90	124	96	124

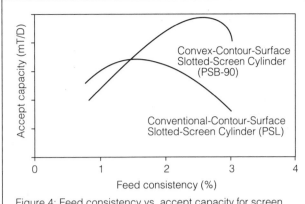

Figure 4: Feed consistency vs. accept capacity for screen cylinders with a conventional-contour surface and convex-contour surface. Clean corrugated clipping furnish, 0.25mm slots, and constant pressure drop.

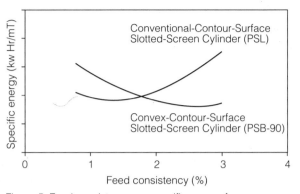

Figure 5: Feed consistency vs. specific energy for screen cylinders with a conventional-contour surface and convex-contour surface. Clean corrugated clipping furnish, 0.25mm slots, and constant pressure drop.

The runability of a screen cylinder within a given pressure screen is defined as its ability to absorb swings in operating conditions, such as feed flow rates and feed stock consistencies. No specific measurement for screen runability exists. However, a measurable indication of a particular screen cylinder's runability is the pressure differential at which the screen blinds over.

The screen would preferably be operated at a pressure differential of 40 to 80 kPa (6 to 12 psi) for hood efficiency. Table 2 illustrates the trend of the convex contour cylinder to resist blinding over at greater pressure differentials between feed and accept flows than the conventional contour cylinder. This indicates the new cylinders are more forgiving under irregular operating conditions, requiring less operator attention.

FIELD RESULTS. PSB-90 screen cylinders have been evaluated in several different field installations. In all cases, the PSB-90 screen cylinders have outperformed conventional contour-screen cylinders. At various installations in the Midwest and on the West Coast, the mills were able to reduce slot sizes from 0.45 mm to 0.35 mm, thereby improving cleanliness without sacrificing capacity.

Where four identical pressure screens were located in parallel at a mill in the South, a PSB-90 screen cylinder was installed in one of these screens. The mill reported that during swings in feed stock consistency, the new screen cylinder was always the last of the four screens to blind over and go into automatic purge cycle, if it blinded over at all.

In another West Coast mill, where thickening equipment limitations required higher pressure screen accept consistencies, a convex contour cylinder was installed.

The mill reported it no longer needed to operate limited thickening equipment, since the new screen cylinder allowed it to maintain production at higher consistencies than were possible with conventional contour-screen cylinders.

At two other installations, mills reported better runability, improved capacity, and a reduction in fractionation of long fiber into the reject stream. At one of these installations, the reduced fractionation was very beneficial because the mill was forced to operate at higher reject rates than desired prior to installation of the convex contour cylinder.

This mill also suffered from very short wear life of screen cylinders due to the high abrasives content of its furnish. The new screen lasted more than twice as long as previously installed conventional contour slotted-screen cylinders. ■

REFERENCES
1. Christopher McCarthy, "Various Factors Affect Pressure Screen Operation and Capacity," *Pulp & Paper 62*, no.9 (1988): 233-237.
2. Peter C. Boettcher, "Results From a New Design of Contoured Screen Plate," Proceedings, TAPPI Pulping Conference, Toronto, Ont., Oct. 1986.
3. J.L. Winkler, internal marketing report, The Black Clawson Co., March 1989.
4. T.H. Eck, M.J. Rawlings and P.A. Heller, "Slotted Pressure Screening at Southeast Paper Manufacturing," Proceedings, TAPPI Pulping Conference, Hollywood, Fla., Nov. 1985.
5. Metals Handbook, 8th ed., vol. 2, "Heat Treating, Cleaning, and Finishing," ASME Handbook Committee.
6. Bowser-Morner, Inc., Dayton, Ohio 45401, Laboratory Report No. T052826, "Plating Thickness Evaluation," May 1987.
7. D.E. Chupka, and C.C. Landegger, U.S. Pat. #4,795,560 (Jan. 3, 1989).

Chapter 27

Screening and Cleaning Systems Challenged by New Contaminants

Changes in wood handling techniques along with broad use of elastomers have led to some extreme stock preparation problems

By R.A. KOFFINKE

Because of the ever increasing contaminant loading in today's furnishes, whether they are virgin fiber or recycled fiber, the demands upon screening and cleaning equipment have increased tremendously. It has been said that we live in a plastic world. That plastic is finding its way into every facet of papermaking. To help combat this influx of contraries, screening and cleaning equipment is constantly being improved, systems are being subjected to more thorough analysis, and strategies of contaminant removal are being reevaluated.

Many years ago, virtually all screening was done through slotted plate screens of either the rotary or flat type. At the time, it was felt that this was the best method for both deflocculation and removal of the types of contaminants present in those early years. To keep the screen plates clean, vibration was the accepted practice. However, since tonnage and flow rates were limited in these machines, impetus was provided for the development of the pressure screen. Along with this development, screening through holes became the normal procedure. Again, the nature of the contaminants present was such that this type of screening was satisfactory.

In today's environment this is not the case. A full circle seems to have been achieved, and more and more applications are requiring slotted plate screens and high efficiency cleaners to remove the various bits and pieces of plastics, adhesives, coatings, etc., that are cropping up everywhere.

CONTAMINANTS. In a purely virgin furnish, the types of contaminants present are fairly well defined. They are shives, bark specs, strings, fiber bundles, etc. As mentioned, these appear to be satisfactorily removed with perforated screening and conventional cleaning. In fact, it was quite a common practice to send the rejects

Mr. Koffinke is vice president, Thermo Electron Web Systems, Auburn, Mass. This article is based on a presentation to TAPPI's engineering conference, New Orleans, La., Sept. 14-17, 1986.

from these systems back for further refining without actually performing any removal.

Today, probably the most widely experienced problem may be characterized by the word "stickies." These are contaminants of the synthetic type that become soft and tacky at elevated temperatures. They are especially detrimental in the lightweight coated and printing and writing grades. Some of the more common examples are as follows: hot melts, polystyrene foam, dense plastic chips (polystyrene, etc.), wet strength resins, latex, pressure sensitive adhesives, waxes, asphalt, and vegetable and synthetic fibers.[1]

To categorize these contaminants it is necessary to look at such characteristics as their specific gravity, their shape, tackiness, etc., in order to determine what methods will be effective in removing them. There is a tendency to place all stickies in the lightweight reject category, which has been shown in several studies not to be true. Analyses have shown that in some cases, as much as 75% of the contaminant loading in a process was stickies with the specific gravity equal to or greater than one. There is the tendency for some lightweight, tacky materials to agglomerate with other heavier filler particles, which changes their specific gravity. These characteristics must be taken into account when determining the removal equipment to be used in a process.

The problems generated by these contaminants are varied. Depending on the amounts present they can fill machine clothing causing runability problems, generate picks in lightweight coating applications, build up on dryer cans and doctors, cause breaks in rewinders, and generate appearance problems due to specs, etc., in the final sheet. Any one of these machine-related problems could be sufficient reason for reexamining the screening and cleaning portion of the process. This includes not only the machine approach systems but also back through the stock preparation area including pulping.

REMOVAL TECHNIQUES. One of the fields where considerable development work has been done in recent years is centrifugal cleaning. The conventional heavyweight or forward-type cleaner has been augmented by the lightweight removal device or reverse cleaner. These

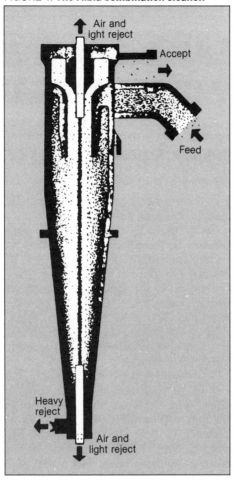

units still use centrifugal force separation techniques but tap the lightweight portion of the flow within a cleaner. Further developments have brought about the through-flow cleaner, which essentially accomplishes the same purpose as a reverse cleaner but with reduced reject rates, and consequently smaller secondary and tertiary systems can be utilized.

Because of the wide variance in contaminant specific gravities, the combination cleaner can be a viable economic solution to the problem. This equipment taps both the central core of the cleaner for the lightweight fraction as well as the outer portion of the mass flow to recover the heavyweights. This results in a minimum number of cleaners performing two functions as well as a corresponding decrease in pumping power, piping, etc. While there is a slight reduction in the removal of lightweights with this type of cleaner, the overall stickies removal efficiency is enhanced because it covers the broad spectrum of specific gravity.

Changes have also been made in the screening field, particularly with regard to the use of slots for stickies removal. After so many years of perforated screen plates

with holes being predominant, there are now literally thousands of slotted screen plate applications. This trend started off with slots in the 0.20-in. range and up, but slots have continually been reduced so that now 0.008-in. and 0.01-in. slots are very common, especially in the lightweight coated as well as other printing and writing grades. The 0.006-in. slots have been run, and testing is now proceeding on slots as small as 0.004 in. This trend has been brought about because of the size and shape of the contaminants that appear to be most bothersome   that is, the small cubicle stickies that can easily pass through a hole. Holes continue to be used for removing shives and long stringy types of contraries.

There are some caveats to be observed when using slots. First, it must be realized that there is considerably less open area in a slotted basket. The main reason for this is that slot length is limited by strength considerations. The number of unslotted bands required for this therefore reduces the area to at least half of a normal perforated plate. The pitch of the slots is also important relative to both the strength and the possibility of stapling of the fibers across the slots.

The result of this is that a new look must be taken at the capacity of a given screen plate basket. In most cases, the apparent difficulty of running a slotted screen in a stable condition has been due to attempting to pass too high a flow rate through the basket. An analysis of the actual flow velocity through the slot becomes valuable in determining capacity limits as well as efficiencies. Flow velocities in the range of 1 to 2 meters/sec are common in today's equipment, with the final selection of velocity based on fiber length, types of contaminants, and experience in handling similar furnishes.

The question of efficiency, especially in the high quality lightweight coated grades, becomes paramount. In a typical pressure screen, the two most important parameters affecting efficiency are the rotor speed and the flow velocity through the slots. In general, the efficiency is inversely proportional to the flow velocity through the slot and directly proportional to the rotor speed. This leads to a rather simple statement. When looking for maximum efficiency, keep the flow rate through the pressure screen as low as possible. While the screen may operate at higher flow rates without plugging, efficiency is definitely being affected adversely.

One of the far reaching developments in recent years that increases both the capacity and efficiency of screening is the profiled screen plate. Specially contoured surfaces are cut into the screen plate, which greatly influence the actual screening zone at the slot or perforation. This results in increased capacities of as much as 50%, while still keeping efficiencies within satisfactory tolerances. Because of the ability of the profiled plate to handle increased consistencies, for any given slot size and tonnage, the flow velocity through the slot can be decreased considerably. As mentioned above, this results in increased efficiencies. In general, the profiled screen plate coupled with the higher speed rotors found in to-day's pressure screens have opened up a wide range of screening possibilities which were previously felt to be unobtainable.

APPLICATION. To achieve the optimum operating conditions for a pressure screen, certain parameters should be established and adhered to. One of these is the capacity as mentioned above. The optimum capacity can be determined by both testing and experience. If tests are run, procedures for determining contaminant levels can be very complex, especially when trying to analyze the small particles that can affect high quality printing and writing grades.

A further consideration is the reject rate. As mentioned earlier, a simple retreatment of rejects was satisfactory in the past, but today these rejects must be removed from the system. The effect of the primary screen reject rate therefore becomes extremely important in determining the overall system efficiency. The general behavior of most pressure screens indicates that reject rates up to 20% by weight are satisfactory in achieving optimum efficiencies. Beyond that, the incremental increase in efficiency becomes rather small when compared with economic considerations. Higher reject rates have been utilized, but more for stability of operation than anything else.

Another facet of individual screen operation that is quite often overlooked is control. In order to keep a pressure screen within its optimum operating range, it is necessary to know the operating conditions. This involves flow rates, pressures, and consistencies. Instrumentation is available for these measurements and should be used if a high-quality output system is desired. Too often, pressure screens are installed, operating conditions ignored, and the resulting mediocre performance lived with.

A further important consideration in high-quality output from a process is the placement of the cleaning and screening systems. In general, two locations in the typical system should be analyzed. First is that area between the pulper and the thickener in the stock preparation portion of the circuit. This is the most beneficial location from the contaminant removal aspect since it screens out the contraries prior to refining. Refining is destructive to the general range of contaminants, reducing them to sizes that make their removal much more difficult in later stages. This should be of prime consideration in selecting cleaning and screening equipment location.

The major drawback to this particular location is a need for thickening equipment since most high-efficiency screening and cleaning is done at consistencies of 2% and lower. Since refining requires upwards of 3.5%, this dictates water removal somewhere in the process. However, development is continuing in the higher consistency screening and cleaning areas, and it looks promising.

Another location for this equipment is in the paper machine approach system. As mentioned, this provides a lower consistency environment but does mean a higher tonnage application since the recycle through the wire or mold cloth must be processed through any screens or cleaners used. Since this location is the final barrier before making the sheet, and since the contaminants are in their smallest possible state at this location, more and more applications have turned to slots. This seems to have been true more in Europe and the Far East than here in North America. This is probably true because of the large size of fourdrinier paper machines here and the corresponding increase in capital expense to install slots. The board industry has taken the lead in this area with a considerable number of cylinder molds equipped with slots of 0.01-in. width.

As a further aid in determining system makeup and equipment location, computers have become more common. There are several analysis programs available that are being used not only to balance systems but to determine efficiency effects due to equipment placement. Further study is being done on the commonly accepted full recycle system that may result in different flow routings, which can then enhance the overall system performance.

SUMMARY. In general, improvements in operating efficiencies of screening and cleaning equipment due to lightweight removal with cleaners and the ability to run finer and finer slots have opened up the possibilities of using secondary fiber to a greater extent, even in the lightweight high quality printing grades. Enhanced equipment capabilities coupled with effective system analysis and control can result in the high contaminant removal efficiency necessary for these grades. ∎

REFERENCES

1. "Removal of Sticky Contaminant from Recycled Fiber," Institute of Paper Chemistry Study, 1979.

FIGURE 2: **A profiled screen plate.**

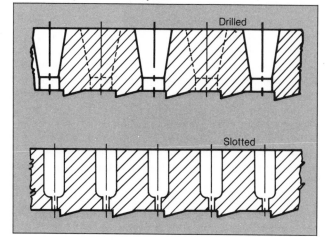

Chapter 28

Chemically Induced Drainage Boosts Recycled Board Mill Output by 50%

Other benefits include reduced sewer losses, lower furnish costs, fewer number of blows in dryer section, and improved sheet printability

By MADELYNN T. WILHARM

Increased production in secondary-fiber board mills has been an elusive goal for many years. The increased use of newsprint and other short fibers in these furnishes has made this objective even more difficult to achieve. Although the use of chemicals to increase speed has traditionally been unsuccessful due to over-flocculation of the sheets, new polymers specifically engineered for improved drainage have shown excellent activity in field testing and encouraging results in field trials.

MILL SURVEY. Normally, the first step in solving a recycled board mill's production-related problems is to conduct a mill survey. When conducted by Nalco Chemical, for example, this generally consists of a tour of the mill to find out what additives are used, their dosages, and application points. Chemical and physical characteristics are noted. Finally, but most importantly, interviews are done with various crew members to get their perspectives on the problem and to learn how they compensate to keep the machine running. This information, in conjunction with laboratory testing, is used to formulate a recommendation.

A Nalco survey at one secondary-fiber board mill revealed several areas that could be improved. For example, fines and fillers were not being retained well and were depositing on the rolls and presses. This resulted in wet end breaks and sheet defects. The sheet defects had an adverse effect on the printability of the board. In addition, sheet formation was inadequate, causing uneven drying in the layers and resulting in blows in the dryer. As a result, machine speed had to be slowed substantially (the chemical analysis and furnish character-

Ms. Wilharm is product manager, Nalco Chemical Co., Naperville, Ill. This article is based on a presentation given at the 1990 TAPPI Papermakers Conference, Atlanta, Ga.

istics of the machine are given in Table 1).

LABORATORY EVALUATIONS. A common problem encountered when trying to evaluate stock drainage is to find an accurate, reproducible test that is relatively easy to perform. Most tests used today focus on free drainage, or water removal, on the table of a paper machine. Past experience has shown that a dryer sheet at the couch does not necessarily result in a dryer sheet at the reel.

The tests used in laboratory evaluations for the board mill focused on free drainage (Figure 1). Attempts were made to account for other factors that influence water removal, such as turbulence, stock temperature, and mat formation. Because the mill was not using any chemical programs on the machine, headbox stock could be used in the screening. Temperature was maintained by placing the stock in a metal bucket on a hot plate and slowly agitating it. Because of the high-soluble

TABLE 1: **One of the first steps in a mill survey is the machine chemical and furnish analysis, such as these conditions established for the studied secondary board mill.**

Mill conditions

Furnish:

    Bottom liner — saturated kraft, newsprint
    Filler — OCC, chip, newsprint
    Top liner — envelope clippings

pH: 6.5
Stock temperature: 115°F
Fines content: 65 to 75%
Headbox
Soluble chrge in headbox: 0.8 neg.

Water conditions

Total hardness: 150 ppm
pH: 6.5
Cl: trace
Fe_3O_2: 7 ppm

iron content and the pH of the system, anionic polymers were eliminated from testing. Soluble iron severely impacts anionic performance (Figure 2). When the pH is raised above 8, iron is oxidized and no longer presents a problem. It was not viable to raise the pH in this system.

Table 2 lists the cationic polymers that were evaluated, including their charge and molecular weight. Both coagulants and flocculants were included in the evaluation.

Coagulants are defined as materials that have low

TABLE 2: **Several cationic polymers were evaluated, both coagulants and flocculants, for chemical-induced drainage tests and secondary board mill.**

Coagulants	Charge	Molecular weight
A	50	50,000
B	70	100,000
C	30	150,000
D	10	200,000
E	10	3,000,000
F	20	7,000,000
G	30	10,000,000

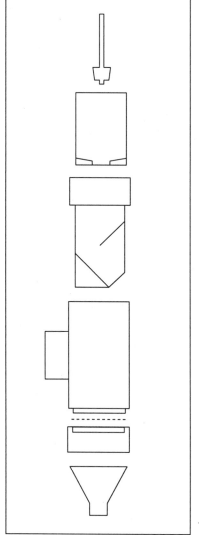

FIGURE 1: **Testing apparatus used for secondary board mill was designed to focus on free drainage, with attempts to account for other factors that influence water removal, such as turbulence, stock temperature, and mat formation.**

molecular weight and are cationic and in solution form. Because of their high charge density and low molecular weight, these types of polymers collapse the anionic cloud that surrounds colloidal particles. As the cloud shrinks, the molecules can move closer together. This creates conditions that allow flocculation to occur.

Flocculants can be defined as materials that have

Procedure for drainage tester

The following laboratory test can be used to simulate drainage, retention, and fines dewatering of a paper machine stock:

PRETEST PROCEDURES
• Prepare and dilute polymer solutions.
• Calculate polymer dosages on a lb/ton basis for comparison.
• Determine stock consistency and adjust pH.
• Assemble drainage testing apparatus in stand.

METHOD
• Take 500-ml sample of headbox stock (headbox consistency should be adjusted to give at least a 100-ml drainage volume in 5 sec)
• Mix stock for 10 sec (i.e., mix in a Britt Jar at the speed equivalent to machine shear), add polymer treatment, and continue to mix for an additional 10 to 20 sec.
• Pour treated sample into reservoir.
• Note appearance of flock formed (flock formation may indicate activity of polymer treatment—if large flock is formed, dosage may be too high).
• Remove plug and collect liquid for 5 sec.
• Measure volume (D), and record.
• Take 50 ml of above filtrate and pour through Buchner funnel-filter apparatus at constant rate of vacuum (vacuum should be set to constant pressure throughout the test).
• Record time required to drain (S).
• Use additional 10 to 25 ml of filtrate to measure turbidity of solution (T).

CALCULATIONS
D = drainage rate (ml/5 sec)
S = fines dewatering rate (sec/50 ml)

$$R = \frac{T_{Blank} = T_{Sample}}{T_{Blank}} \times 100 = \% \text{ first pass retention improvement}$$

COMMENTS. To approximate mill conditions, it may be necessary to vary the following:
• Mixing speed (shear)
• Polymer contact time/dosage
• Stock consistency.
For laboratory evaluations, 22-psi vacuum, 800- to 1,000-rpm mixing, and 1 to 3 lb/ton latex polymer dosages were typically used.

INTERPRETATION. Look for improvements in both retention and/or drainage—unlike the Britt Jar, this test will give information on the latter. The suction time results with various polymers should be compared with the blank. An increase in suction time over the blank indicates that the fines might be difficult to dewater and that sheet wetness at the couch and higher steam usage could result.

high molecular weight, are in emulsion form, and can be either cationic or anionic. As discussed, only cationic products were tested. All the materials evaluated were in liquid form, although flocculants are available as both liquid and dry.

Each product was evaluated according to the protocol in the sidebox item on page 216. The two coagulants and two flocculants that gave the best performance were then tested in various combinations. The final selection, coagulant B and flocculant G, were then tested under various conditions. Different pHs, temperatures, soluble charge levels, and higher amounts of recycled fibers in the furnish were all examined. This was done to understand how the program would react if these conditions would be encountered during a machine trial.

TRIALS RESULTS. Because the fines content of the furnish was high, caution had to be exercised when adding chemicals to the paper machine. If too many fines were retained too quickly, the sheet would get too wet, causing wet end breaks and blows in the dryers. Coagulant B was added at low dosages at the inlet side of the stuffbox pump. Addition at this point provided good mixing of the chemical in the stock. Fines content in the headbox, tray solids, headbox total, and soluble charge were monitored. Dosage was increased slowly to 5 lb/ton. After the machine stabilized over a period of five days, flocculant G was added to the vat in each cylinder.

The flocculant was prepared using a Nalco 500 Series automatic polymer feeder attached to a day tank to provide continuous product supply. A complete makeup system is shown in Figure 3. A distribution system was used to feed chemical to each cylinder. Feed rates could be adjusted for each cylinder as required. As with coagulant B, dosage was raised slowly until 4 lb/ton was reached.

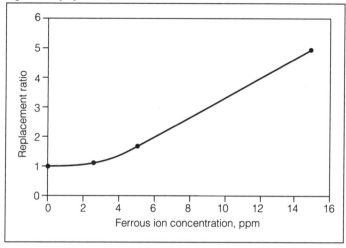

FIGURE 2: **Anionic flocculant solution performance is affected significantly by makeup water-soluble iron levels.**

After the first 24 hours of flocculant addition, tray solids dropped dramatically and then continued to fall until the system reached equilibrium. The soluble charge moved closer to neutral as the fines content decreased. Sheet defects and wet end breaks dropped. As a result, production increased by 50 tpd.

After the program ran for several months, other benefits became evident, such as reduced sewer loss and lower furnish costs because more newspaper could be used. Because the outside plies of the sheet could be drained faster than inside plies, water in the filler layers could escape in the dryers. The number of blows in the dryers was reduced.

In summary, the chemical program returned $4 to the mill for each $1 spent. It also allowed the mill to take advantage of less expensive furnish components and improve printability of the sheet. ■

FIGURE 3: **A typical emulsion polymer batch solution makeup system has a mix tank that is followed by an aging tank as well as an inline static mixer.**

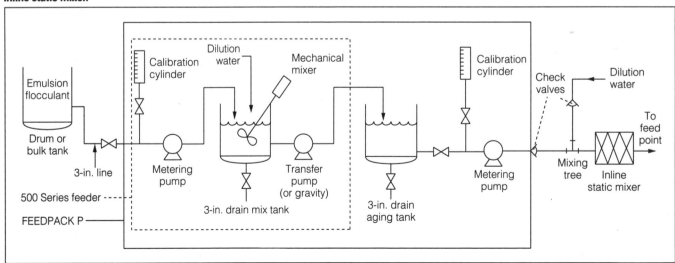

Deinking Technology

Most recycling-related research and development efforts of the past decade have been focused on the deinking process. Deinking is the heart of a modern recycling operation and, understandably, is one of the mill's most sensitive and protected operations.

As ink trends have changed, washing techniques for deinking common in most North American recycling mills only a few years ago, are now being augmented or completely replaced by flotation deinking methods used principally in European mills. Radically new deinking approaches are also being tried, along with newly developed chemicals and chemical formulations, with mixed results.

The 10 articles in this section report on mill experiences with various deinking systems. A review of basic deinking chemistry is complemented by several mill "guides" to proper deinking and bleaching. Environmental concerns related to the deinking process are also addressed.

Chapter 29

Mills Considering New Deinking Line Must Answer Environmental Questions

Physical and chemical properties of various wastepaper grades have to be analyzed before mills can permit and handle process wastes

By ROBERT C. CARROLL and THOMAS P. GAJDA

Deinking wastepaper for tissue and newsprint manufacture continues to grow rapidly, and newfound interest in using deinked pulp in fine paper and paperboard is developing. While these developments are primarily fueled by legislative pressures and operating advantages, deinking is attractive since it also provides global environmental benefits, such as extending landfill life and preserving forest resources[1] (see sidebox, "Environmental benefits").

To derive the benefits of deinking, however, questions must be answered and problems must be solved at the mill level. As more deinking plants are planned and environmental regulations are tightened, environmental specialists are increasingly called on to answer questions about permitting and waste handling strategies:

- How are the characteristics of deinking sludge different from virgin pulp sludge, and how can a mill dispose of sludge safely?
- How do effluent loadings and permit allowances change when deinked pulp production replaces virgin pulp production?
- What sources must be considered in air permitting?

WASTEPAPER GRADES—A PRIMARY ELEMENT. One major element in the environmental design and permitting of a deinking mill is to know which grades of wastepaper will be used. Each wastepaper grade has unique physical and chemical properties and contaminants that make permitting and mill design grade-specific.

For example, a mill planning to use file stock will have to consider that it may contain polychlorinated biphenyls (PCBs). A mill planning to use heavily coated grades will need the capability to handle and dispose of

Mr. Carroll is senior staff engineer, environmental, and Mr. Gajda is a staff specialist-technical writer, Simons-Eastern Consultants Inc., Decatur, Ga.

large quantities of sludge. The generation of biochemical oxygen demand (BOD_5) varies significantly depending on wastepaper grade.

To emphasize the grade-specific nature of deinking mill design, consider some of the wastepaper grades that are now recycled or deinked: waxed cups, poly-coated diaper stock, foil coated, wet-strength, computer printout, soft whites, white envelope cuttings, old newspapers, magazine, book, and ledger.[2]

SOLID WASTE CHARACTERIZATION AND HANDLING. Four varieties of solid waste are generated by deinking systems:
- Miscellaneous wastes
- Rejected wastepaper
- Screen tailings
- Sludge.

To obtain a disposal permit for these solid wastes, each waste stream must be characterized (Figure 1). This can be done by obtaining wastepaper samples and running laboratory trials. In some instances, data from similar installations or from wastepaper suppliers can be used. However, the most reliable data are mill-generated. The methods a mill uses to handle the wastes must also be determined before applying for a permit. Characterizing and handling diverse wastes, wastepaper rejects, and screen tailings are relatively simple, whereas characterizing and handling sludge can be complicated.

Miscellaneous solid wastes. Solid wastes generated in the wastepaper receiving and handling areas can include baling wire, pallets, and boxes. Baling wire can be chopped or baled and sold for scrap. Wastepaper shipped on pallets can pose a pallet storage and disposal problem. Pallets can be shredded and burned or can be given or sold to a pallet reclamation business. Boxes used to ship wastepaper can be pulped if the mill makes unbleached products, or the boxes can be sold or landfilled. The scope of a deinking mill project must address the various options for handling these wastes and include money for handling equipment.

Rejected wastepaper. In most mills, wastepaper is inspected and graded as it is received, and some of the paper is rejected. Rejected wastepaper consists of unusable paper or contaminated paper. The rejected paper can be sold if sufficient quantities and markets are available. It can also be landfilled, but if the paper is rejected due to contamination, the landfill must have a permit to receive the contaminants as well as the paper.

Food waste is a problem because it is putrescible (capable of rapidly decomposing), and many industrial landfills do not have permits for putrescible wastes. Putrescible waste landfills are expensive to operate and must be covered daily with soil. Therefore, bales contaminated with food may need to be disposed off-site in municipal landfills that are permitted for putrescible wastes. Such contaminants could be found in unsorted office waste or blends of postconsumer wastepaper.

Screen tailings. Depending on the wastepaper grade, screen tailings (rejects) can consist of fiber and water, plastic, glue, staples, rubber bands, paper clips, and other debris. The tailings will need to be drained or dewatered for transportation to a landfill or burning. Tailings are most often landfilled because they are usually nonhazardous and nonputrescible and are composed of small amounts of fiber. A possible option to landfilling is to burn the tailings in a boiler to recover heat and to conserve landfill volume.

CHARACTERISTICS, HANDLING OF SLUDGE.
Deinking sludge is the most expensive of the solid wastes to handle because it is generated in large quantities. Sludge from magazine deinking usually contains fiber, ink, and large amounts of clay and titanium dioxide (TiO_2). Sludge from newspaper deinking usually consists of fiber and ink and is lower in ash since newsprint grades contain little fillers and clay. The characteristics and the volume of sludge will change from day to day depending on the grades of wastepaper a mill uses. Deinking sludges are generally nonhazardous,[3] although each operation must verify this.

Sludge handling and disposal can be managed in four ways:

Burning sludge. This is an appealing method of disposal, allowing a mill to recover heat and reduce landfill volume. The heat recovered by burning sludge at 40% to 50% solids ranges from 0 to 3,000 Btu/lb, depending on its inorganic content. The landfill volume required for ash disposal is about 20% to 30% of that required for sludge. Still, sludge burning presents two environmental problems: air toxics and ash disposal.

Ash disposal. If a mill is planning to burn and landfill its sludge, the boiler ash must be characterized to determine if it is hazardous. The main concern is the leachability of the heavy metals in the ash. There are limits on leachable forms of metals, such as mercury, arsenic, and chromium. Ash is considered hazardous if it fails the Toxicity Characteristic Leaching Procedure (TCLP),[4] a test that simulates heavy metals leaching in a landfill (see sidebox, "Determining if a waste is hazardous"). It would be rare for a mill's ash to fail this test, but the permitting agency will usually require a mill to demonstrate that the ash is not hazardous. Some states require annual certification that the ash is not hazardous.

To determine if the ash from a proposed mill will be hazardous, a mill may use data from an existing similar mill. If either the proposed process or wastepaper supply is unique, the mill's environmental specialists can gather sludge during developmental deinking trials or produce sludge in the laboratory from representative samples of the wastepaper. The sludge should be analyzed for heavy metals. By assuming that all the metals in the sludge will end up in the ash and be leachable, this test becomes a conservative indicator of whether a mill's ash will be hazardous.

If testing demonstrates the ash is nonhazardous, it can be disposed in an industrial or municipal landfill. It can also be employed for beneficial uses, such as an additive in cement, concrete, and road-building materials. If the TCLP indicates the ash is hazardous, then a mill would have to dispose of it, at considerable cost, in a specially permitted hazardous waste landfill.

Landfilling sludge. Landfilling dewatered sludge is often the least expensive disposal method in terms of capital costs, although large land areas are required. A 250-tpd deinking mill operating at 75% yield generates about 70 tpd of sludge. That sludge, when dewatered to 40% solids, consumes about 175 yd³ of landfill/day, or about 2 acres (20 ft deep) of land/year.

Most states now require sludge landfills to have liners, leachate collection systems, and groundwater monitoring systems. Obtaining a permit can take six months

FIGURE 1: To obtain a disposal permit, each waste stream must be analyzed, which also enables a mill to determine handling methods.

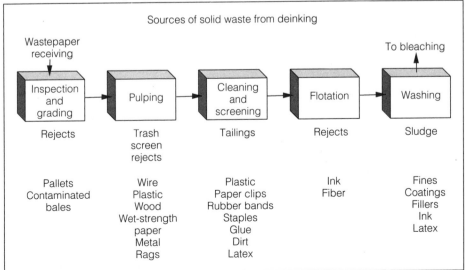

Sources of solid waste from deinking

Wastepaper receiving → Inspection and grading → Pulping → Cleaning and screening → Flotation → Washing → To bleaching

Rejects	Trash screen rejects	Tailings	Rejects	Sludge
Pallets Contaminated bales	Wire Plastic Wood Wet-strength paper Metal Rags	Plastic Paper clips Rubber bands Staples Glue Dirt Latex	Ink Fiber	Fines Coatings Fillers Ink Latex

to two years or more, depending on the level of public interest and the workload of the permitting agency.

Beneficial reuse. Many researchers have strived to find uses for waste sludge or ways to recover useful materials from it, but the economics have not been promising.[5] Some waste paperboard mills, however, do reuse sludge as part of their furnish,[6] and a deinking mill in Wisconsin announced an interesting use for sludge: dried sludge pellets will be used as a medium for the slow release of pesticides in agricultural applications.

The reuse of boiler ash in cement and concrete manufacturing and as a road-building material is an established practice. Ash used for manufacturing cement and concrete requires a low concentration of unburned carbon, and the cost of transporting the ash to the cement manufacturing location must not be prohibitive. Ash is also used as a fertilizer, and this market is growing.

Landfarming. Some sludge is currently applied to farmlands as a soil supplement (hence the name "landfarming") and to mill-owned land for biodegradation (called "land application"). There are few successful examples of land application for three reasons: 1) large land areas are required, 2) fine clays and fillers can lead to poor drainage, and 3) future liability due to the potential accumulation of PCBs or heavy metals is a concern. However, some facilities successfully landfarm, particularly where sandy soils are amended by the sludge.

CHARACTERISTICS OF DEINKING EFFLUENT. Effluent wastewater from deinking mills differs from virgin pulp mill effluent in several ways. Deinking effluent contains fewer color bodies and higher concentrations of heavy metals and TSS and may contain PCBs.

Biochemical oxygen demand. Five-day biochemical oxygen demand (BOD_5) loading from deinked pulp may be higher or lower than that from virgin pulp depending on the wastepaper grade used. One comparison indicates that by replacing groundwood with deinked newspapers for newsprint manufacture, BOD_5 loading would drop from 43.7 lb/ton to 31.7 lb/ton.[7] Conversely, BOD_5 loadings from a deinked tissue mill would be higher than its virgin pulp counterpart, due largely to high levels of starch and fines in the wastepaper.

Total suspended solids. The TSS from a deinking mill consist of fines, fillers, coatings, inks, and trace amounts of glues and plastics. The fillers are mostly clay, titanium dioxide, and calcium carbonate. The TSS from magazine deinking are about half organic and half inorganic. The organics include fiber fines, and the inorganics primarily include aluminum, silicon, calcium, and titanium. The TSS normally settle well, and primary clarification can be accomplished without coagulation aids, such as alum and polymer.

Deinking mill TSS loadings are almost always higher than virgin pulp mill loadings because of the low yields characteristic of deinking operations. Yields from deinking mills range from 60% to 85%, with coated grades exhibiting yields on the lower side and newsprint grades

exhibiting yields on the higher side.

Effluent toxicity. Properly treated deinking effluents typically will not exhibit toxicity problems, although specific toxic compounds may become a problem as regulations tighten. For example, chloroform has been found in the effluent of mills using sodium hypochlorite bleaching. Heavy metals from inks can be present in effluent, but concentrations should decrease as ink manufacturers use more organic pigments.

Dioxin and cyanide are other specific compounds that, at some point in time, may become a concern. While advanced bleaching technology has greatly reduced dioxin formation in bleached paper, dioxins continue to be present in bleached wastepaper. A paper presented by C. Rappe et al. at the 1989 Dioxin Conference reported detectable amounts of dioxins and furans in effluent and sludge from recycled fiber mills.[8] Currently, with dioxins at the forefront of environmental debates, research in this area will no doubt continue.

Cyanide levels in deinking sludge are usually below 100 ppb, yet problems with effluent toxicity have been reported. Toxicity due to the synergism of different compounds is always a potential threat and can be difficult to troubleshoot.

PCBs were a major component of carbonless copy ink until the early 1970s.[9] PCBs are present in some postconsumer wastepaper, such as office and hospital files (file stock grades). PCBs are no longer used in inks, so eventually all PCB-contaminated wastepaper will be consumed or landfilled. Nevertheless, PCBs are present in the wastepaper, treated effluent (low ppb), and sludge (low ppm) of mills using file stock grades.

PCBs have an affinity for suspended solids, hence most PCBs will be removed during primary clarification. A removal efficiency of more than 90% has been report-

TABLE 1: **New source performance standards from Federal Regulation 40CFR 430 represent actual permit limits that could be expected if there are no special water-quality restrictions.**

Grade	BOD₅ 30-day average (lb/ton)	TSS 30-day average (lb/ton)
Unbleached kraft (linerboard)	3.6	6.0
Unbleached kraft (bag)	5.4	9.6
Bleached kraft (board, course, tissue)	9.2	15.2
Groundwood (TMP)	5.0	9.2
Groundwood (course, molded, newsprint)	5.0	7.6
Groundwood (fine paper)	3.8	6.0
Deinked (fine paper)	6.2	9.2
Deinked (tissue)	10.4	13.6
Deinked (newsprint)	6.4	12.6
Paperboard from wastepaper	2.8	3.6

ed.[3] Sludge containing small amounts of PCBs is currently landfilled, although it could be burned if furnace conditions are adequate to assure PCB destruction. If a mill's removal of suspended solids from the treated effluent is efficient, minimal amounts of PCBs will be discharged. Concentrations of PCBs in treated effluent can trigger a periodic monitoring requirement and possibly an effluent limit. If the concentration in treated effluent is unacceptable, a mill must consider tertiary treatment, such as chemically assisted clarification and filtration.

TREATING DEINKING EFFLUENT. Deinking mill effluents can usually be treated by conventional biological systems, such as aerated stabilization basins or activated sludge. The effluent BOD₅ concentration will affect the choice of treatment options. The optimum BOD₅ concentration range is 150 to 350 mg/l for activated sludge, 100 to 500 mg/l for aerated stabilization basins, and 1,000 to 30,000 mg/l for anaerobic treatment. The low sulfur content of deinking effluent makes anaerobic treatment a possibility.

One significant factor influencing the design of treatment facilities is the amount of BOD₅ removed in primary clarification. For virgin pulp effluents, 10% to 30% BOD₅ removal is normal, whereas 50% is common for deinked pulp effluent. Also, larger than normal sludge handling equipment must be specified.

PERMIT ALLOWANCES. Assuming that the receiving stream is not water-quality limited, permit allowances will change, and a mill will need to modify its effluent permit when a deinking operation is added. For example, a mill producing 500 tpd of newsprint from thermomechanical pulp (TMP) would have a 30-day BOD₅ limit of 500 tpd × 5.0 lb/ton, or 2,500 lb/day.

If that mill converts half its production to deinking grades, the new BOD₅ limit would be 250 tpd × 5.0 lb/ton + 250 tpd × 6.4 lb/ton, or a total of 2,850 lb/day. A 14% increase in BOD₅ would be allowed.

The calculations are based on new source performance standards from Federal Regulation 40CFR 430 (Table 1). These new source performance standards represent actual permit limits that could be expected if there are no special water quality restrictions.

AIR QUALITY PERMITTING. Air quality permitting can involve toxics, criteria air pollutants, fugitive dust, and odor. Criteria air pollutants include particulates, volatile organic compounds (VOCs), sulfur dioxide, and nitrogen oxides.

Except for a relatively few federally regulated air pollutants, hazardous and toxic air emissions are regulated by the states. State-regulated toxic emissions include metal oxides from boilers, organics from process vents, and bleach plant emissions. Currently, there is a particular emphasis on bleach plant emissions of chlorine, chlorine dioxide, and chloroform.[10] While requirements in each state vary, limits are based on workplace threshold limit values (TLVs) established by the Occupational Safety & Health Admn. (OSHA) or the American Conference of Government Industrial Hygienists (ACGIH).

VOCs contribute to ozone formation. Some sources of VOCs are paper machine wire cleaning solvents, deinking solvents, and boiler fluegases. In some cases, mathematical modeling is necessary to predict ground level concentrations of air pollutants, such as VOCs or air tox-

Determining if a waste is hazardous

There are two ways to determine if a waste is hazardous:
- It can be compared with an EPA list that identifies hazardous wastes and processes.
- It can be tested to determine if it exhibits any of the four hazardous characteristics.

Deinking wastes are not "listed" wastes. The "hazardous characteristics" are used to determine if unlisted wastes, such as deinking sludge or boiler ash, are hazardous. The four hazardous characteristics are toxicity, ignitability, reactivity, and corrosivity.

EPA has recently changed the test that determines if a waste is toxic. The new test, published on Mar. 29, 1990, is called the Toxicity Characteristic Leaching Procedure (TCLP). It replaces the Extraction Procedure (EP), which had been used since 1980. The TCLP is designed to simulate the leaching of metals and pesticides that might occur in a landfill and is described in the Code of Federal Regulations, 40 CFR 261, Appendix II.

In the TCLP, a solid waste sample and an acetic extraction fluid are placed in an extraction vessel and agitated for 18 hours. The extract is analyzed for 31 organic chemicals (including pesticides) and eight metals. The EP required analysis of six pesticides and eight metals.

Although the TCLP is easier to run than the EP, laboratory costs will be higher because the analysis includes additional compounds. The cost to analyze a single waste sample will be about $1,100.

ics. Many complex factors exist, beyond the scope of this article, to determine whether modeling is necessary and which models to use.

Fugitive dust. Particulate emissions from open, non-point sources, such as storage piles and roads, are termed fugitive dust. Fugitive dust will not increase as a direct result of the deinking process but may increase from associated activities, such as construction, road use, and coal storage. Fugitive emissions can be controlled by paving, vegetation, and enclosing conveyors and storage piles. Off-site, over-the-road transport of fly ash or screen tailings, which can blow out of trucks, will require covering truck trailers.

Deinking processes produce less odor than chemical pulping, but potential problem areas exist. There is a sufficient quantity of sulfur in wastepaper to produce reduced sulfur compounds, which can produce offensive odors. Odors can be minimized by eliminating areas in the process where the pulp can stagnate and decay and by using oxidizing agents, such as hydrogen peroxide or sodium hypochlorite, in the pulper. Adjusting the process's pH may decrease the formation of some odorous organic acids.

Odor also becomes a concern when sludge is landfilled. The sludge should be kept as dry as practical to avoid anaerobic conditions that produce odors. A properly designed leachate collection system and proper sloping will help keep the sludge dry. Another method of reducing sludge odor is to minimize air contact by re-ducing the exposed "working face" in the landfill. More expensive control techniques include regulating pH and using oxidants, such as permanganate or hypochlorite, to discourage reduced sulfur formation. It is easier to anticipate these problems in the design of the plant than it is to solve them after the facility has been constructed. ■

REFERENCES

1. L.A. Broeren, "New Technology, Economic Benefits Give Boost to Secondary Fiber Use," *Pulp & Paper* 11 (1989): p. 69.
2. Circular PS-88, "Paper Stock Standards and Practices," Paper Stock Institute of America, January 1988.
3. NCASI Technical Bulletin No. 587, "Response of Selected Pulp and Paper Industry Solid Wastes to the RCRA Toxicity Characteristic Leaching Procedure (TCLP)," May 1990.
4. Code of Federal Regulations, 40 CFR 261, Appendix II, Mar. 29, 1990.
5. H. Edde, *Environmental Controls for Pulp and Paper Mills,* Noyes Publications, 1984.
6. A.M. Springer, *Industrial Environmental Control-Pulp and Paper Industry,* Wiley & Son, 1986.
7. J.D. Denit, R.W. Dellinger, and W.D. Smith, "Development Document for Effluent Limitations Guidelines and Standards for the Pulp and Paper, and Paperboard Source Category," EPA 440/1-82/025, October 1982.
8. C. Rappe, B. Glas, L.O. Kjeller, and S.E. Kulp, "Levels of PCDDs and PCDFs in Swedish Paper Industry Products," presented at the Dioxin Conference, Toronto, Ont. September 1989.
9. R. Derra, "PCB Problem and Its Importance for the Paper Industry," Allg. Papier-Rundschau, May 1973, pp. 670-688.
10. R.A. Flick, "Recent Experiences in Air Permitting," Presented at the NCASI Southern Regional Meeting, June 1990.

Chapter 30

Deinking of Secondary Fiber Gains Acceptance as Technology Evolves

More mills are considering deinking lines as process and equipment knowledge grows, but an analysis of options is necessary

By LAWRENCE A. BROEREN

The recent explosion of secondary fiber use in paper products has been driven by economic and legislative forces. This trend is expected to continue, with the most significant growth in deinked secondary fiber.

In the U.S., wastepaper use increased from 12 million tons in 1970 to about 15 million tons in 1979 (Figure 1). It remained at about 15 million tons for the next four years, but, in 1984, use began increasing again, reaching a high of 20 million tons in 1989.

The use of deinked secondary fiber in newsprint, tissue, and fine paper is expected to increase by 5.8 million tons in the next ten years (Figure 2). Most of the new supply of deinked secondary fiber—3.2 million tons —will be used in newsprint. That increase is based on a

Mr. Broeren is corporate consultant, Simons-Eastern Consultants Inc., Decatur, Ga.

25% utilization rate forecast for the year 2000. However, if the Environmental Protection Agency's goal of a 40% utilization rate is attained, an additional 1.4 million tons of deinked secondary fiber will be used in newsprint in the future.

Tissue manufacturers are expected to use 1.8 million tons of the new supply of deinked secondary fiber, and fine paper manufacturers are expected to use 0.8 million tons.

SECONDARY FIBER ECONOMICS, LEGISLATION. Economics is one force driving the use of secondary fiber. The operating cost of producing deinked secondary fiber can be lower than producing virgin fiber. For example, an efficient deinking mill that has an economical supply of wastepaper can produce deinked fiber for fine paper at a cost of $300 to $400/ton (Table 1). The operating cost to produce virgin kraft fiber is about $300 to $500/ton, while the market price for kraft pulp can be up to $700/ton.

FIGURE 1: **Annual U.S. utilization of wastepaper consisting of mixed paper, newspaper, corrugated, pulp substitutes, and deinking grades has continually increased.**

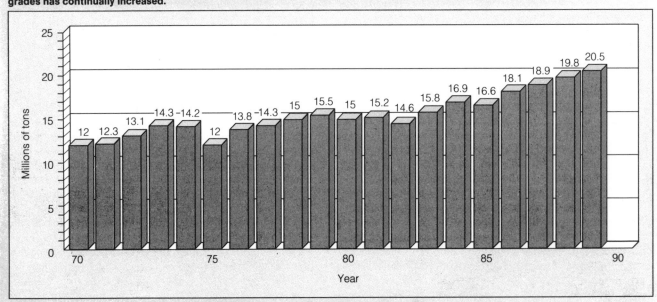

TABLE 1: **Typical operating costs to produce secondary fiber.**

	$/ton
Newsprint	140 to 170
Tissue	275 to 375
Fine paper	300 to 400

TABLE 2: **Typical capital costs (200-tpd system—in million dollars).**

	Newsprint	Tissue	Fine paper
Major equipment	8	7	11
Total direct costs	30	28	41
Total capital costs	39	36	53
Unit costs ($/daily ton)	195,000	180,000	265,000

TABLE 3: **In ten years, half of the newsprint used in California must contain at least 40% postconsumer wastepaper.**

Date of compliance	Percentage of newsprint that must contain at least 40% wastepaper
Jan. 1, 1991	25%
Jan. 1, 1994	30%
Jan. 1, 1996	35%
Jan. 1, 1998	40%
Jan. 1, 2000	50%

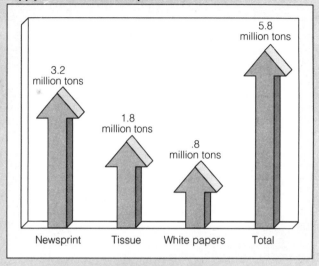

FIGURE 2: **The use of deinked secondary fiber is expected to increase by 5.8 million tons in the next ten years. Most of the new supply will be used in newsprint.**

The unit capital costs for a deinked secondary fiber facility are also less than for a virgin fiber facility. Unit cost is the capital cost divided by the daily production rate. Table 2 shows typical capital and unit costs for three types of deinking mills.

The unit capital cost for a deinked fiber facility for fine paper is $265,000/daily ton and is significantly lower than the unit cost of $500,000/daily ton for a virgin fiber facility. From an operating and capital cost viewpoint, it is clear why economics is driving the increased use of deinking secondary fiber.

In addition to the economic forces, however, legislative forces are also present. The goal of legislators is to encourage or require secondary fiber use to conserve forest resources and reduce the flow of waste to landfills. Federal legislation has established recycling goals and requirements for finished products. Paper towels purchased by the U.S. government, for example, must contain a specified amount of secondary fiber.

Current state legislation focuses on using secondary fiber in newsprint. States considering recycled newsprint legislation include Illinois, New Jersey, New York, and Wisconsin. In the meantime, Louisiana, Massachusetts, Nebraska, Oregon, Pennsylvania, Rhode Island, and Virginia have legislation pending. Florida, Connecticut, as well as California have already passed legislation.

In Florida, publishers pay a 10¢/ton tax on newsprint. The tax is refunded if the newsprint contains at least 50% recycled fiber. In 1992, the tax increases to 50¢/ton.

Connecticut requires newsprint to contain 20% recycled fiber by 1993 and 90% recycled fiber by 1998.

The California legislation, passed on September 29, 1989, is significant because California is a large newsprint-consuming state, and its environmental policies often influence the formation of environmental policies throughout the country.

In California, recycle-content newsprint is defined as newsprint containing at least 40% wastepaper (postconsumer). Publishers must use increasing amounts of recycle-content newsprint over the next ten years. In 1991, for example, 25% of the newsprint used by publishers must contain 40% postconsumer wastepaper. In 1994, 30% of the newsprint must contain 40% wastepaper. Table 3 shows the usage schedule required by the California legislation.

TECHNOLOGY. The quality of deinked pulp has been improved by technological improvements in deinking equipment and chemicals, even when low-quality wastepaper is processed. Significant improvements in technology have occurred in pulping, screening and cleaning, lightweight contaminant removal, flotation, and postdeinking fiber treatment.

• *Pulping.* High-consistency pulping decreases contaminant breakdown, which enhances contaminant removal. Wastepaper can be pulped at high consistency in batch and drum pulpers.

• *Screening and cleaning.* Low-reject-rate screens and cleaners have reduced the number of stages required for efficient screening and cleaning.

• *Lightweight contaminant removal.* Lightweight contaminant removal has historically been accomplished at relatively low efficiencies. The new flowthrough centrifugal cleaners have higher lightweight contaminant removal efficiencies. A new mechanical lightweight contaminant removal device operates at an even higher efficiency than centrifugal cleaners but is also more expensive.

• *Flotation.* Single-stage flotation systems are available. One design is pressurized, and another is atmospheric. In the pressurized system, the foam collapses as it leaves the pressure vessel. In the atmospheric system, the foam is removed from the flotation cell by vacuum and then is collapsed.

• *Postdeinking fiber treatment.* Several postdeinking fiber treatments are available. Dispersion, the most common, can be followed by flotation and/or washing. The use of postdeinking fiber treatment has been limited due to the high capital and operating costs, but it is expected to increase during the 1990s.

WASTEPAPER GRADES. The grades of wastepaper are defined in *Circular PS-83, Paper Stock Standards and Practices,* published by The Paper Stock Institute of America. Wastepaper is categorized as follows:
• Pulp substitutes
• Deinking grades
• Newspapers
• Mixed paper
• Corrugated.

Wastepaper in each category is processed differently and used in specific products (Table 4). Deinked fiber is used primarily in three finished products—tissue, newsprint, and fine paper. Deinked fiber is widely used in tissue products, and its use is growing. Many tissue products are made from 100% deinked fiber, while most newsprint does not contain it. However, because of the recycled newsprint legislation, manufacturers and publishers are showing a significant interest in deinking. Currently, nine newsprint mills in North America use deinked fiber. Of these mills, four use 100% deinked pulp.

Some manufacturers of fine paper use deinked pulp. Due to this success, favorable economics, and environmental considerations, interest is emerging in manufacturing fine paper from deinked pulp. Table 5 lists some mills using deinked pulp in tissue, newsprint, and white paper.

DEINKING PROCESSES. Manufacturers must consider three main processing parameters as they approach the design of a deinking facility:
• Which ink removal method to use
• How many chemical loops to use
• If postdeinking fiber treatment should be incorporated, and if so, what type of treatment to use.

Ink removal can be obtained by flotation, washing, or a combination of the two. A deinking system can have one chemical loop (alkaline) or two chemical loops (alkaline and acid). Postdeinking fiber treatment, if incorporated, can include dispersion or dispersion followed by flotation and/or washing.

TABLE 4: **Wastepaper in each category is processed differently and used in specific products.**

Wastepaper category	Process	Finished product
Pulp substitutes	Pulping	Fine paper Tissue
Deinking	Fine Paper Deinking	Tissue
Newspaper	Deinking	Newsprint Folding cartons
Mixed paper	Pulping Screening Cleaning	Packing Packaging Molded products
Corrugated	Pulping Screening Cleaning	Corrugated medium Linerboard Kraft towels

TABLE 5: **Tissue, newsprint, and white paper mills throughout North America are using deinked pulp as part or all of their furnish.**

Tissue mills
• Erving Paper Mills, Erving, Mass.
• Fort Howard Corp., Green Bay, Wis.
• Fort Howard Corp., Rincon, Ga.
• Wisconsin Tissue Mills, Menasha, Wis.
• James River Corp., Glens Falls, N.Y.
• James River Corp., Green Bay, Wis.
• Kimberly-Clark Corp., various locations
• Pope & Talbot Inc., Eau Claire, Wis.
• Pope and Talbot Inc., Ransom , Pa.
• Scott Paper Co., Winslow, Maine
• Tagsons Papers Inc, Mechanicville, N.Y.
• Wisconsin Tissue Mills, Menasha, Wis.

Newsprint mills
• FSC Paper Co., Alsip, Ill.
• Garden State Paper, Carfield, N.J.
• Golden State Paper, Pomona, Calif.
• Manistique Papers, Manistique, Mich.
• Quebec & Ontario Paper, Thorold, Ont.
• Smurfit Newsprint, Oregon City, Ore.
• Smurfit Newsprint, Newburg, Ore.
• Southeast Paper Manufacturing, Dublin, Ga.
• Stone Container, Snowflake, Ariz.

White paper mills
• Appleton Papers, West Carrollton, Ohio
• Fraser, Thornold, Ont.
• Boise Cascade, Vancouver, Wash.
• P.H. Glatfeiter, Neenah, Wis.
• Georgia-Pacific, Kalamazoo, Mich.
• Miami Paper, West Carrollton, Ohio
• Simpson Paper, Pomona, Calif.
• Sorg Paper, Middletown, Ohio

The preferred ink removal method is flotation, followed by washing. A one-loop alkaline chemical loop is best for tissue and white paper. For newsprint, a one-loop system is used with washing, and a one- or two-loop system can be used with flotation.

Postdeinking fiber treatment enhances the quality of deinked pulp and is often incorporated to reach the highest quality level or to allow the use of lower-quality wastepaper. The postdeinking treatment systems are relatively expensive in both capital and operating costs.

DEINKING CHEMICALS AND EQUIPMENT. The deinking process involves both mechanical and chemical systems. Both are equally important. The following chemicals typically used are for deinking and bleaching:

TABLE 6: **Some of the major deinking equipment suppliers and the equipment they manufacture.**

Suppliers	Equipment
Ahlstrom	Drum pulpers, screens
Arus Andritz	Belt presses
Celleco	Cleaners, disc thickeners
Dorr-Oliver	Washers, disc thickeners
Finckh	Drum pulpers, screens
Hooper	Gravity deckers, screens
Hymac (Thune)	Screw presses, gravity deckers
Krofta	Clarifiers

Deinking chemicals
- Caustic
- Sodium silicate
- Hydrogen peroxide
- Calcium chloride
- Soap

Bleaching chemicals
- Hydrogen peroxide
- Hydrosulfite.

Five major equipment suppliers can provide a complete or nearly complete deinking system: Beloit Jones, Black Clawson, Bird Escher Wyss, FiberPrep (Lamort), and Voith. These companies can supply information, assist in arranging deinking mill visits, and conduct deinking trials. Table 6 shows some of the major deinking equipment suppliers and the equipment they manufacture.

The optimum deinking system is a multi-supplier, "mix and match" system, where the most suitable equipment is selected for each process step. The capital cost is also usually lower with a mix-and-match system because the most cost-effective equipment can be selected.

Figures 3, 4, 5, and 6 show typical system designs for two newsprint deinking systems (a one-loop and a two-loop system), a tissue system, as well as a fine paper system.

FIGURE 3: **A block flow for a one-chemical-loop newsprint deinking system.**

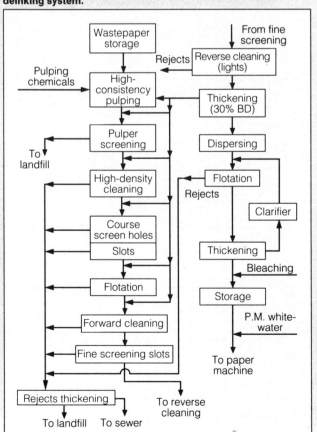

FIGURE 4: **A block flow for a two-chemical-loop newsprint deinking system.**

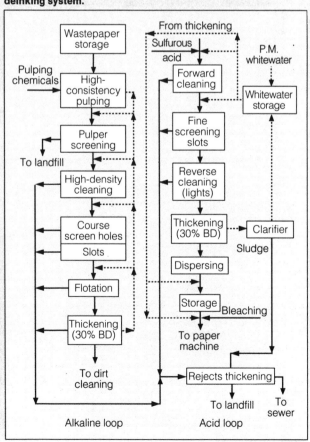

THE ELEMENTS OF A DEINKING PROGRAM. The four major elements of a deinking program include wastepaper procurement, finished product requirements (defined by end use requirements), the deinking process (both mechanical and chemical systems), and management involvement, including support for R&D.

Procurement, including wastepaper testing, downgrading, and rejection, is the foundation of a successful deinking program. One step in developing a deinking program is a study of wastepaper availability and quality. Considerations include price, quantities, location, and shipping.

Another step is visiting several deinking facilities. Most North American deinking facilities are closed to visits, but European facilities are more accommodating. Equipment supplier presentations can also provide an opportunity to find out what equipment and processes are available.

Deinking program leaders need to bring together the people within their organization that have expertise in a variety of areas, including research, operations, management, and engineering. Engineering consultants can also be helpful.

Deinking trials should be run, but there are limitations to such trials. For example, whitewater is not recycled during a trial, and trials are usually too short to optimize chemical usage.

R&D should be part of a deinking program to assist in defining the process and finding solutions to deinking problems and operation. For example, one current problem in newsprint deinking is removing letterpress printing ink from the washing filtrate. The ink is readily removed from the fiber but is difficult to remove from the filtrate during clarification. Hence, it is recirculated back into the deinking process. As the use of letterpress printing increases, a way to get the letterpress ink out of the system will have to be developed.

Likewise, nonimpact inks are difficult to remove and, further, can show up in the finished product as ink specks. As new inks, binders, and printing processes are developed, there will be no shortage of problems that will need to be solved. It is important, therefore, for management to support R&D so it can meet the challenges deinking provides.

A list of the critical factors in developing a successful deinking program includes the following:

- Acceptance
- Research
- Development
- Investigation
- Reasonable facility
- Procurement.

Finding the right combination of deinking equipment and processes is like trying to solve Rubic's Cube. There are numerous ways to solve the puzzle, and, at first, the myriad of combinations and interrelationships of moves can be overwhelming. As time goes on, however, the patterns and results of moves become clearer. ∎

FIGURE 5: **A block flow for a tissue deinking system.**

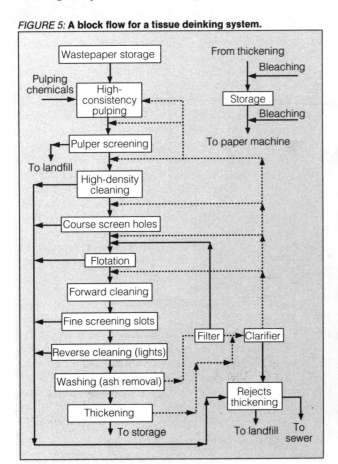

FIGURE 6: **A block flow for a fine paper deinking system.**

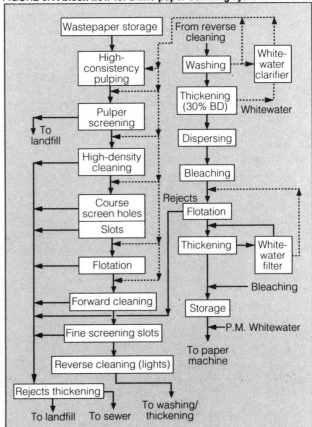

Chapter 31

Mill Chemistry Must Be Considered Before Making Deink Line Decision

Understanding the complex relationship between the various chemical additives can help optimize performance in a deink mill

By KENNETH E. SCHRIVER

Modern deinking systems are designed to remove a variety of contaminants. In addition to foreign material that enters the system with the furnish, the system must also remove coatings (clays, waxes, latexes,), adhesives, and the most common contaminant, printing inks.

Designing a system to accomplish this efficiently is difficult enough. In addition, the extent to which deinking systems are "closed" has increased as restrictions on mill effluent and solid waste disposal throughout North America have increased.

This increases the potential problems from chemical buildup and interaction within the system. In designing new deinking systems or when seeking ways to optimize existing systems, it is necessary to consider not only the unique mechanical and chemical requirements of a given furnish but also the impact that a specific chemical treatment may have on other aspects of the mill. It is important to consider the "total chemistry" within a deinking system or within an entire pulp and paper mill.

There are basically two techniques for removing suspended ink from a pulp slurry: washing and froth flotation. For many years, washing has been the most common process in North American mills, especially for newsprint deinking. In groundwood-free deinking mills, new types of inks have entered the furnish—specifically, polymeric and nonimpact inks, such as laser, UV radiation-cured, and heat-set.

These inks are almost impossible to remove by washing because of the difficulty in dispersing the polymeric materials comprising them. For this reason, the number of mills using froth flotation in the deinking process has increased. The most versatile deinking processes use both washing and flotation stages in "combination" or "hybrid" deinking systems.

To better understand the unique chemical requirements of these systems and the impact of a given chemistry on the overall system, the various steps of the deinking process are reviewed in this article for the simplified combination system illustrated in Figure 1.

PULPING STAGE. The first stage in the deinking plant is the most common point of chemical addition. Chemicals added to the pulper may include, but are not limited to, the following: caustic soda, sodium silicate, a surfactant, hydrogen peroxide, and a chelant. The pulper is usually an ideal point of addition because the chemicals can be applied at a relatively high concentration, and the mechanical action helps mix them into the pulp for maximum effectiveness.

Also, as the ink is removed by the action of the fibers rubbing against each other, the presence of a surfactant helps stabilize the ink particle in solution and reduces reattachment. The type of surfactant used will depend on the stage that follows—flotation, washing, or both.

Caustic soda is often added to the pulper to raise the pH to effect swelling of the fiber, which also aids in the physical removal of the ink, much like a coat of paint will crack and peel off a balloon when it is inflated. Many of the binders found in inks break down more readily at higher pH also.

With groundwood-containing furnish, if the pH is raised much above 10, the pulp will yellow unless hydrogen peroxide is present. To prevent decomposition of the peroxide by metal ions, sodium silicate and organic chelants are often added. The peroxide also appears to help lift the ink from the fiber and will accomplish some bleaching of colored material and lignins. The sodium silicate acts as an alkaline buffer and a detergency builder. It is also a moderate dispersant and, as such, can reduce the ink particle size, making flotation more difficult if too much is used.

If freshwater is used for the makeup in the pulper, then the effective chemical concentrations are determined entirely by the chemical addition rates and the pulp consistency. There may be, however, a return loop from a washer, thickener, or clarifier in the deinking mill that provides part of the water going to the pulper. In this case, there may be some equilibrium concentration of chemicals, ink, and fines that exist within the

Mr. Schriver is technical manager, Lion Industries Inc., Vancouver, Wash.

loop. A change in the type of chemistry going into the pulper will often be accompanied by a need for change in chemistry elsewhere in the loop.

FLOTATION. Deinking that is accomplished by froth flotation is most effective on inks not amenable to dispersing, such as the polymeric inks previously mentioned. Froth flotation cells utilize primarily dispersed air and some dissolved air, as compared with dissolved air clarifiers, which are used in effluent clarification. Ink is removed by attachment to a small gas bubble, which is introduced into a dilute pulp slurry, typically 0.8% to 1.2% consistency.

The foam formed at the top of the flotation cell is removed from the slurry, and these rejects are usually further concentrated prior to disposal. The dilution water is normally derived from the thickening or washing stages that follow flotation.

Particle size is an important aspect in froth flotation.[3,4] The particles must be large enough so that a collision with a gas bubble is ensured yet small enough that the resultant bubble-particle agglomerate survives the ascent to the flotation cell surface.

The optimum size for effective ink flotation is gener-

The successful performance of a deinking system is . . . .dependent on having a general understanding of the chemical composition of the various makeup and dilution streams within the system.

ally in the range of 30 to 60 microns. The larger particles, generally contaminants other than ink, are removed by screens and cleaners. Particles smaller than 30 microns must be removed by washing, and this stage is placed after the flotation stage when possible. Removal of the larger particles early in a flotation stage leaves less total ink to be removed in the washing stage, which therefore increases the overall efficiency of the system.

In froth flotation, ink must be stabilized as insoluble, hydrophobic particles. As will be discussed, washing surfactants are designed to disperse the ink particles into small, hydrophilic colloids. Washing surfactants may produce a substantial foam in a flotation cell, but preferential removal of the ink rather than the fiber is not achieved. Instead, froth flotation has traditionally been accomplished using a "collector," a type of surfactant that acts by gathering the ink particles into large aggregates and rendering them hydrophobic.

The collectors used in flotation systems in Europe for years are fatty acid soaps (Table 1). The soap may be added as a dry material directly to the pulper at additions of roughly 0.7% to 1.0% of pulp weight. The soap is soluble as added but is made insoluble by the addition

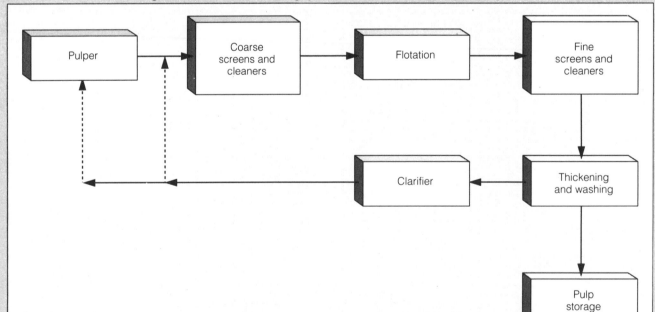

FIGURE 1: **Basic schematic diagram of a combination deinking system with flotation followed by washing.**

TABLE 1: **General chemical structure of several classes of surfactants commonly used in deinking systems. The alkylphenol ethoxylates and linear alcohol ethoxylates are traditional washing surfactants, the fatty acid soap is a collector, and the fatty acid ethoxylate is one type of combination surfactant or displector.**

$$CH_3(CH_2)_n(C_6H_4)(OCH_2CH_2)_m\text{-}OH$$

Alkylphenol Ethoxylate

$$CH_3(CH_2)_n\text{-}(OCH_2CH_2)_m\text{-}OH$$

Linear Alcohol Ethoxylate

$$CH_3(CH_2)_nC(O)O^-/Na^+$$

Fatty Acid Soap

$$CH_3(CH_2)_n\text{-}C(O)\text{-}(OCH_2CH_2)_m\text{-}OH$$

Fatty Acid Ethoxylate

of calcium ions, usually from calcium chloride, prior to the flotation stage.

The resultant insoluble aggregates of collector and ink collect preferentially at the gas bubble solution interface and are floated to the top of the flotation cell and mechanically removed. This type of chemistry can have a very significant impact elsewhere in the system. The addition of the metal ions to precipitate out the soap may create undesirable scaling problems. If the soap is allowed to carry forward with the fiber, deposits can form in the paper machine system. Interference with sizing operations, acid formation, and corrosion have also been observed in some systems.

Perhaps the least understood aspect of froth flotation is the apparent requirement of high ash content in the pulp feeding the flotation cell. There is a linear relationship between the amount of clay added and the ink removed in a flotation stage, as measured using image analysis[6] and pulp brightness.

A typical working target for optimum flotation is to have an ash content in the pulp feeding the flotation cell of at least 8% to 10%, preferably 12% to 14%. Approximately 25% to 30% of the added clay is removed with the flotation cell rejects.

Depending on the types of washing stages, a substantial fraction of the remainder can be carried forward with pulp to the paper machine. The clay addition is usually accomplished by blending a certain amount of coated waste with the furnish going into the pulper. However, this method has several disadvantages, including the following:

• The degree and type of coating varies considerably between bales of waste.

• There is only a limited supply of coated waste available.

• Magazines, a common source of coated furnish, often contains inks that are more difficult to deink than the majority of furnish and may contain metals that are

of concern in solid waste disposal.

An alternative is to add a commercial clay directly into the system prior to the flotation stage. The clay then becomes another "chemical" variable, although it is one that is relatively easy to monitor and control. Not all clays give equal performance, however. Characterization of the various types of clays and testing their impact on flotation deinking has been carried out in the lab.[7]

WASHING. Washing, loosely defined, involves preferential rinsing of undesirable particulates from the pulp. In deinking, washing involves the process of dispersing the ink particles to a size small enough that they can be removed by rinsing through the fiber mat.

The process is distinguished from thickening in that with the latter, nothing is removed from the system.[1] Washing also requires that the particulate in the effluent be removed in an additional stage, usually clarification. To maximize yield and minimize clarification costs, a side stream containing only part of the effluent may be clarified.

There is usually an equilibrium concentration of fiber, ink, and chemicals within a washing loop, and reduced volume should be balanced carefully so that ink removal efficiency and pulp quality do not suffer. Shifts in that equilibrium can also be realized by changing the washing surfactant or by changing the clarification chemistry.

In most washing, ink is removed as colloidal particles, which are smaller than 30 microns. Low-foaming nonionic surfactant is usually used as the dispersant. This washing surfactant stabilizes the ink particle in solution, making it hydrophilic. A popular class of surfactants for this application has been ethoxylated alkylphenals, although in some applications ethoxylated linear alcohols have been used. The difference between the two classes of surfactant can be seen in Table 1.

Often, proprietary blends of different surfactants are used, depending on the type of furnish and the mechanical restrictions of a given system. These surfactants are typically 100% active liquids applied in the pulper at 0.5% to 0.75% of pulp weight, although additional surfactant may also be used prior to a washing stage.

The traditional collectors, fatty acid soaps, are very poor dispersants, and, therefore, poor washing surfactants. This may not be of much concern in systems using only flotation, but in the increasingly prevalent combination or hybrid systems, the lack of dispersing chemistry leads to unsatisfactory performance in the washing stages following flotation.

Unfortunately, it is usually not possible to simply add a traditional dispersant-type washing surfactant into the system with the fatty acid soap. The strong dispersing action in the pulper by these surfactants drives the ink particle size below 30 microns, where they are no longer effectively floated.

Even if the washing surfactant is added at a different point in the system, such as just prior to the deckers or presses, the recirculation of the effluent back to any stage prior to flotation can cause the dispersant concentration to build up, causing a reduction in the flotation efficiency.

To obtain the maximum benefits of the combination froth flotation/washing systems now installed and being installed, products have been designed specifically for use in these systems. Some common names for these products are "dispersant-collectors," "displectors," and "combination surfactants."[8] They are usually proprietary formulations of alkoxylated fatty acid derivatives. Hence, they share some of the physical properties of both dispersants and fatty acid collectors.

For instance, Lion Industries, formerly Lion Chemicals, has developed five distinct lines of products in this class. Variations within each product line can also be made according to the specific application. These products have several unique advantages in combination systems over the more traditional soap chemistry.

They are 100% active liquids, like the washing surfactants, but they are only mild dispersants. They may contain a fatty acid derivative, but they require no added calcium since they are not precipitated out of solution like the fatty acid soaps. Additionally, they do not result in deposit formation elsewhere in the mill.

CLARIFICATION. Following a washing stage, all or part of the effluent containing surfactant and ink is sent to the clarifier, where it is removed from the system by the addition of flocculants. Essentially, one must undo what has just been accomplished, in that the finely dispersed ink must now be reagglomerated so that it can be separated from the recycled water.

As discussed, effective washing requires dispersing the ink. However, the cost of clarifying the effluent increases with the degree to which it is dispersed. Usually, the cost of clarification in a combination system will be less than in a washing-only system because the surfactants used are weaker dispersants. This is possible, in turn, because the majority of the ink is removed as larger particles in the flotation step.

The flocculants work in a reverse manner to the dispersants. The foreign material in the effluent is collected until a floc forms of sufficient mass that it can be removed either by settling or by floating in a dissolved air clarifier. Since washing effluent contains some fiber, clarification lowers overall yield and increases disposal costs. Therefore, a balance must be achieved so enough clarification is accomplished to remove the dispersed ink and maintain product quality, but not so much as to reduce the yield intolerably.

The choice of clarifier chemistry will thus be a function of the amount of clarification to be achieved, the type of surfactant of other dispersants present in the effluent, and the concentrations of the ink, ash, and fiber.

Often two chemical treatments are required to clarify a given effluent stream effectively. The primary flocculant is generally a low-molecular-weight cationic liquid polymer or papermaker's alum to neutralize the system charge and build "pin floc." This fine suspension is then further treated with a secondary flocculant, such as a high-molecular-weight anionic polymer or possibly a weakly charged cationic.

The molecular weight, charge, and dosage rates of these polymers are dependent on the deinking system and the chemistry used in the flotation and washing stages. The flocculant characteristics may also depend on the furnish, in that the type of ink being removed will put different demands on the clarification system. For instance, flexo inks, which are water soluble, contain a strong dispersant as part of the ink formulation and typically require higher dosages of flocculant.

The successful performance of a deinking system is critically dependent on having a general understanding of the chemical composition of the various makeup and dilution streams within the system. This is because the chemistry at a given point in the system is determined by not only the added process chemicals mentioned previously but also the characteristics of the freshwater, such as hardness, and the residual chemicals brought back from other mill processes.

For example, a common source of makeup is to bring back water from the paper machine. If alum is being used on a newsprint machine, however, the same aluminum hydroxide gel that aids the papermaker in retaining fines at the machine can also act to strongly bind the ink particles to the fiber within the deinking mill. Therefore, it is necessary to reduce the aluminum ion concentration by neutralization or clarification prior to introducing this water into the deinking process.

Other paper machine additives—e.g., felt cleaning products, defoamers, or solvents used for stickies control—can interfere with deinking chemistry and effectiveness if sufficient concentrations are present in the makeup water or if compatible products are not used. ■

REFERENCES
1. R.G. Horacek, "Deinking By Washing," TAPPI Monograph Series.
2. D.R. Crow and R.F. Secor, *TAPPI Journal* 70, no. 7 (1978): 101.
3. L. Marchildon, M. LaPointe, and B. Chabot, *Pulp & Paper Canada* 90, no. 4 (1988): 90.
4. A. Larsson, P. Stenius, and L. Odberg, *Svensk Papperstid.* 87, no. 18 (1984): r158 no. 3 (1985): r2.
5. J.M. Zabala and M.A. McCool, *TAPPI Journal* 71, no. 8 (1988): 62.
6. M.A. McCool and C.J. Taylor, *TAPPI Journal* 66, no. 8 (1983): 69.
7. K.E. Schriver and S. Bingham, paper to be presented at 1990 TAPPI Pulping Conference.
8. R.B Horacek and B. Jarrehult, *Pulp & Paper* 63, no. 3 (1989): 97.

Chapter 32

Deinking Equipment Demand Increases as More Mills Study Wastepaper Use

Major suppliers worldwide discuss their process equipment developments for improving pulp cleanliness and brightness

By JOHN PEARSON, International Editor

Wastepaper looks set to become an increasingly important part of the papermaking furnish during the 1990s. Currently, worldwide wastepaper consumption is about 31% of total paper and board production. By the end of the decade, that figure could pass 40%. Pressures leading to the increased utilization rate are numerous and include environmental concerns among both consumers and governments and tight virgin fiber supplies in some countries.

Legislative changes may put a burden on papermakers to raise the wastepaper content of their furnishes. But, at the same time, consumers will continue to demand high-quality paper grades. For this reason, all major suppliers of deinking equipment are developing systems to improve cleanliness and brightness. Improved dispersion and combined flotation deinking and washing systems are among the latest developments.

BDS FORMS THE BUILDING BLOCK. Voith, of Fed. Rep. Germany, has designed a new elliptical deinking cell, said to allow better air flow to a larger surface area. Apart from this, other design aspects, such as plugging-proof injectors and self-priming air intake, remain as in previous models. To meet demands for larger systems, the company now offers a module that can handle 320 tpd of accept in one line.

Process development from Voith involves the use of dispersing machines, bleaching during dispersion, flotation after dispersion, and combined washing and flotation systems. One such system, for producing a 100% deinked furnish for newsprint, starts with what Voith calls the standard BDS sequence (pulping, prescreening at medium consistency, flotation deinking, cleaning, low-consistency screening, and dewatering). This is followed by combined dispersing and peroxide bleaching, followed by hydrosulfite bleaching. The final product has a brightness of 65 to 68 ISO.

Voith says the highest achievable results have been reached with a system consisting of a BDS sequence followed by dispersing with peroxide bleaching, flotation,

thickening, and hydrosulfite bleaching. Process waters from the BDS and flotation and thickening stages are collected, treated, and recycled. The resulting pulp has a brightness of 70 to 72° and can be used in fine paper or super-newsprint grades.

For tissue production, Voith recommends BDS, followed by washing/thickening (initial brightness 65 to 70°), dispersing, hydrosulfite bleaching, and washing/thickening. Final stock brightness of greater than 80° can be reached. Process waters are clarified and ash and fillers removed. A similar system could also be used in the case of wastepaper containing a high proportion of flexo inks. Washing and clarification are said to take care of the unfloatable inks.

SPLIT FLOTATION GAINS ACCEPTANCE. Explaining its strategy, Sulzer Wyss (SEW) of Ravensburg, Fed. Rep. Germany, says it developed the concept of "split flotation" some years ago and that this idea has since found wide acceptance.

Secondary fiber used by papermakers today contains a number of printing inks, coatings, and other components that disturb the traditional deinking system. SEW says these printing inks can be divided into two groups: soft and greasy, and brittle and hard. Soft, greasy inks must be treated gently, with low energy density. If the energy density is too high, these types of inks are wiped onto the fibers, leading to greyness in the stock. For this reason, soft, greasy particles are removed before dispersion by screening, cleaning, preflotation, and washing and/or partial washing.

Hard, brittle inks are reduced to a grain size by dispersion (intensive fiber treatment). These can then be washed and floated off. Further flotation and washing can be used if necessary. SEW says this split-flotation method leads to a very clean half stuff with a high brightness. Washing out of fibers on the paper machine is also minimized by this method, says the company.

FINAL ASH CONTENT OF 2% ACHIEVED. Black Clawson Internationl, U.K., makes similar points. The trend. says the company, is to use three basic elements in the deinking process: flotation, washing, and disper-

TABLE 1: Some recent and planned flotation deinking installations. (Table 1 continues on next page.)

Country	Company name	Mill location	Startup date	Capacity (000 tpy)	Wastepaper grade	End use	Supplier
Austria	Steyrermühl	Steyrermühl	1989	84	Np, Mag	Newsprint	Voith
Brazil	Clinton Pessoa	Santa Therezinha	1988	42	Mag, Wf waste	Tissue	Sulzer Escher Wyss
Brazil	Scott Copa	Cruzeiro	1988	30	Mag, List	Tissue	Voith
Canada	Atlantic Packaging Corp.	Scarborough, Ont.	1988	60	Ctd, Unctd	Tissue	Voith
Canada	Atlantic Packaging Corp.	Scarborough, Ont.	1988	150	Np, Mag	Newsprint	Voith
Canada	Cascades Inc.[1]	Kingsey Falls, Que.	1990	64	Led	Tissue	Beloit
Canada	Cascades Inc.	East Angus	1990	21	Ctd bk, List, Mag	White board	Lamort-Fiberprep
Canada	Kruger Inc.	Bromptonville	1990	63	Np, Mag	Newsprint	Lamort-Fiberprep
Chile	CMPC	Puente Alto	1991	53	Mixed waste, Np, Mag	Tissue	Lamort
China	Yingkou[1]	—	1990	10	Np	Linerboard	Black Clawson Int
Colombia	Familia	Medellin	1991	21	Off. waste	Tissue	Lamort
Colombia	Papeles Nacionales	Pereira	1990	18	Wt	Tissue	Lamort
Costa Rica	Tissue producer	—	1989	7	Mag, Led, Ctd	Tissue	Sulzer Escher Wyss
Czechoslovakia	Steti	Steti	1991	35	Np, Mag	Newsprint	Lamort
Denmark	Brodrene Hartmann	Tondem	1989	18	Np, Mag	Egg trays	Sulzer Escher Wyss
Denmark	De Forenede Papir	Copenhagen	1991	42	Wf sorted paper	Tissue	Sulzer Escher Wyss
Ecuador	Technopapel	Quito	1990	9	Np, Mag	Tissue	Lamort
Finland	Tampella	Tampere	1991	25	Np, Mag	FBB	Sulzer Escher Wyss
Finland	United Paper Mills	Kaipola	1989	135	Np, Mag	Newsprint	Voith
Finland	United Paper Mills	Kaipola	1989	120	Np, Mag	Newsprint	Voith
France	Matussière-et-Forest	Turckheim	1988	42	Mag, Prom	Pr/wr	Voith
France	Matussière-et-Forest	St. Girons	1989	21	Mag	—	Voith
France	Papeteries du Bourray	St. Mars-la-Brière	1988	28	Prom, pr trim, List	Pr/wr	Lamort
France	Papeteries d'Essones	Corbeil-Essones	1989	42	Mag, Np, bk, lacq	Pr/wr	Lamort
Germany, Fed. Rep.	Euler	Bensheim	1988	16	NCR broke	File board	Lamort
Germany, Fed. Rep.	Friedrich Erfurt	Wuppertal	1990	28	Wf paper	Wallpaper base	Voith
Germany, Fed. Rep.	Gruber-Weber	Gernsbach	1990	53	Wdcntng, wf	Topliner	Sulzer Escher Wyss
Germany, Fed. Rep.	Haindl Papier	Schongau	1989	265	Np, Mag	Newsprint	Voith
Germany, Fed. Rep.	Hermes	Düsseldorf	1990	44	Sorted waste	Pr/wr	Sulzer Escher Wyss
Germany, Fed. Rep.	Niederauer Mühle	Düren	1989	28	Mixed waste	Board	Voith
Germany, Fed. Rep.	Not disclosed	—	1989	77	Wdcntng, wf	Tissue	Sulzer Escher Wyss
Germany, Fed. Rep.	Strepp	Kreuzau	1989	50	Wdcntng pr/wr	Tissue	Voith
Germany, Fed. Rep.	Peter Temming	Glückstadt	1990	53	Np, mag	Pr/wr	Lamort
Germany, Fed. Rep.	Peter Temming	Glückstadt	1990	35	Np, mag	Pr/wr	Lamort
Germany, Fed. Rep.	Peter Temming	Glückstadt	1990	21	Np, mag	Pr/wr	Lamort
Germany, Fed. Rep.	Not disclosed	—	1989	42	Sorted waste	Tissue	Sulzer Escher Wyss
Germany, Fed. Rep.	Not disclosed	—	1989	44	Sorted waste	Tissue	Sulzer Escher Wyss
Honduras	Tissue producer	—	1989	4	Ctd paper, Led	Tissue	Sulzer Escher Wyss
Indonesia	Fajar Surya	—	1990	25	Col. led	White board	Lamort-Aikawa
Indonesia	PT Pakerin	Surabaya	1990	28	Sorted Waste, List	Tissue	Sulzer Escher Wyss
Indonesia	PT Pakerin[1]	—	1990	8	Led	Board	Black Clawson Int
Indonesia	Surya Kertas	—	1988	21	Col. led	Pr/wr	Lamort-Aikawa
Indonesia	Surya Kertas	—	1991	21	Np	White board	Lamort-Aikawa
Italy	Cartiera Lucchese	Porcari	1990	70	Wt	MG papers	Lamort
Japan	Daini Paper	—	1988	18	Np	Printings	Lamort-Aikawa
Japan	Iyo Paper	—	1988	12	Col. leg	Tissue	Lamort-Aikawa
Japan	Hyogo Seishi	—	1989	20	—	Newsprint	Voith
Japan	Nihonkako Paper	Takahagi	1989	21	Ctd wf book	Ctd paper	Lamort-Aikawa
Japan	Nihonkako Paper	Takahagi	1989	21	Ctd wf book	Ctd paper	Lamort-Aikawa
Japan	Nihonkako Paper	Takahagi	1990	21	Ctd wf book	Ctd paper	Lamort-Aikawa
Japan	Nihonkako Paper	Takahagi	1990	21	Ctd wf book	Ctd paper	Lamort-Aikawa

1. Flotation/washing system. Abbreviations: Ctd = coated; Unctd = uncoated; FBB = folding boxboard; Np = newspaper; Mag = magazines; Prom = promotional material; Led = ledgers; List = computer listings; Pr/wr = printings/writings; Wdcntng = woodcontaining paper; Wf = woodfree paper, HPBK = heavily printed bleached kraft.

sion. Treatment of the clarified water loop to remove residual inks (particularly flexo inks) is seen as a growing trend.

For the preparation of wastepaper stock for tissue production, BCI has introduced its new DNT Washer. It is said to be highly effective in removing inks and ash. Final ash contents of less than 2% are achieved using a ledger furnish containing over 25% ash.

TABLE 1, continued: **Some recent and planned flotation deinking installations.**

Country	Company name	Mill location	Startup date	Capacity (000 tpy)	Wastepaper grade	End use	Supplier
Japan	Taio	Iyomishima	1989	45	Np	Pr/wr	Voith
Japan	Taio	Kawanoe	1989	60	Mag	Newsprint	Voith
Japan	Taio	Mishima	1989	110	—	Newsprint	Voith
Japan	Takao Paper	—	1989	35	Np, List	Comic book	Lamort-Aikawa
Japan	Tamagawa Paper	—	1990	28	Np, List	Comic book	Lamort-Aikawa
Japan	Tokai Pulp	Shimada	1989	46	Np	Copier paper	Lamort-Aikawa
Kenya	Panafrican Paper Mills	Webuye	1991	26	Wf	Pr/wr	Lamort
Rep. Korea	Mitto Paper	Seoul	1990	53	Wf waste	Pr/wr	Sulzer Escher Wyss
Malaysia	Not disclosed	—	1989	18	Led, List	Tissue	Sulzer Escher Wyss
Mexico	Inpamex (Copamex)	Uruapan	1989	35	List, white led	Pr/wr, tissue	Lamort-Licar
Mexico	Kimberly-Clark Corp.	Bajio	1991	210	Mag, List	Tissue	Sulzer Escher Wyss
Mexico	Papeleras Higienicos	Monterrey	1989	25	Mag, office waste	Tissue	Sulzer Escher Wyss
Netherlands	Celtona BV	Cuyck	1991	26	Ctd wf board	Tissue	Lamort
Netherlands	Celtona BV	Cyuck	1990	53	Ctd wf board	Tissue	Lamort
Netherlands	Van Houtum BV	Swaimen	1990	28	Np, Mag	Tissue	Lamort
Pakistan	Packages	Lahore	1988	7	Wdcntng, Wf	Tissue, MG	Sulzer Escher Wyss
Romania	Piatra Neamt	—	1990	20	Mixed waste	White liner	Beloit
Spain	Echezarreta SA	Legorreta	1988	30	List	Printings	Lamort-Licar
Spain	Papelera d'Orpi SA	Carme	1988	5	Office waste, Np	Tissue	Lamort-Licar
Spain	Romani Esteve SA	Barcelona	1990	28	Led, News, White bd	White liner	Beloit
Sweden	Hyite Bruk[1]	Hyite	1989	175	Np, Mag	Newsprint	Voith
Taiwan	Ban Yu[1]	—	1989	60	Np	Board	Black Clawson Intl.
Taiwan	Ban Yu[1]	—	1989	60	Np	Board	Black Clawson Intl.
Taiwan	Cheng Loong	Taipei	1990	25	Mag, Wf, List	Pr/wr	Sulzer Escher Wyss
Taiwan	YFYu[1]	—	1990	30	Led	Board	Black Clawson Int
Thailand	Hiang Seng	Bangkok	1990	18	FBB, Wf waste	Liner, pr/wr	Sulzer Escher Wyss
Thailand	Patcharavit	Bangkok	1989	9	Sorted waste	Tissue	Sulzer Escher Wyss
Thailand	Not disclosed	—	1989	14	Led, List	Tissue	Sulzer Escher Wyss
U.K.	Kimberly-Clark Ltd.	Coleshill	1991	26	Wf	Tissue	Lamort
U.K.	Shotton Paper Co.	Shotton	1989	165	Np, Mag	Newsprint	Voith
U.S.	Atlas Tissue Mills[1]	Hialeah, Fla.	1990	25	Led	Tissue	Beloit
U.S.	Erving Paper Mills[1]	Erving, Mass.	1989	32	Led	Tissue	Beloit
U.S.	F.S.C. Paper Co.	Alsip, Ill.	1990	81	Led, List, Mag	Tissue	Sulzer Escher Wyss
U.S.	James River Corp.	Ashland, Wis.	1988	37	Ctd pr/wr	Tissue	Voith
U.S.	James River Corp.	Green Bay, Wis.	1989	85	Led	Tissue	Voith
U.S.	Miami Paper	W. Carrollton, Fla.	1988	55	Led	Pr/wr	Sulzer Escher Wyss
U.S.	Miami Paper	W. Carrollton, Fla.	1988	55	Led	Pr/wr	Sulzer Escher Wyss
U.S.	Putney Paper Co.	Putney, Vt.	1989	9	Led, cup stock	Tissue	Sulzer Escher Wyss
U.S.	Smurfit Newsprint Corp.[1]	Oregon City, Ore.	1989	130	Np, Mag	Newsprint	Beloit
U.S.	Sorg Paper Corp.	Middletown, Ohio	1989	44	Book, Led, cup stock	Tissue, pr/wr	Sulzer Escher Wyss
U.S.	Stone Container Corp.[1]	Snowflake, Ariz.	1988	110	Np, Mag	Newsprint	Beloit
U.S.	Stone Container Corp.[1]	Snowflake, Ariz.	1989	125	Np, Mag	Newsprint	Beloit
U.S.	Tagsons Papers Inc.[1]	Mechanicville, N.Y.	1990	16	Np, Mag	Tissue	Beloit
U.S.	Tissue producer	—	1990	65	Ctd paper, Led	Tissue	Sulzer Excher Wyss
U.S.	Tissue producer	—	1989	23	HPBK	Tissue, pulp	Sulzer Escher Wyss
U.S.	Not disclosed[1]	—	1989	80	Led	Tissue	Beloit
U.S.	Not disclosed	—	1990	80	Np, Mag	Newsprint	Beloit
U.S.	Not disclosed	—	1990	160	Np	Newsprint	Beloit
U.S.	Not disclosed	—	1989	70	Mag	Newsprint	Voith
Venezuela	Maracay	Maracay	1990	32	Led	Tissue	Beloit
Yugoslavia	Krsko	Krsko	1990	48	Np, Mag, Led	Pr/wr, Newspr	Beloit

1. Flotation/washing system. Abbreviations: Ctd = coated; Unctd = uncoated; FBB = folding boxboard; Np = newspaper; Mag = magazines; Prom = promotional material; Led = ledgers; List = computer listings; Pr/wr = printings/writings; Wdcntng = woodcontaining paper; Wf = woodfree paper, HPBK = heavily printed bleached kraft.

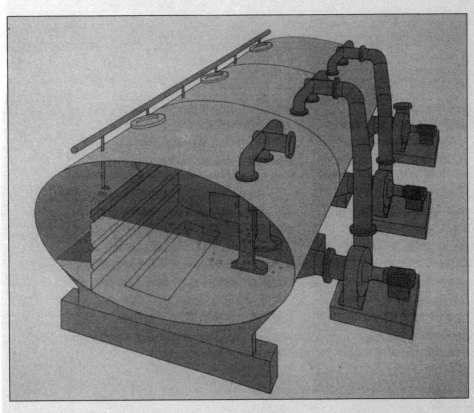

HYLTE SHOWS THE WAY. This year's reference list from Beloit also shows an increasing use of combined flotation-washing deinking systems. One 500-tpd line is at Hylte Bruk in Sweden. It uses Beloit's Pressurized Deinking Modules (PDMs) for the deinking process. Immediately after these, stock is treated in the forward cleaners and is then thickened and diluted four times in Hedemora disc filters and Thune screw presses. An after-flotation stage, with two more PDM units, is used to remove residual ink.

DEINKING STARTS WITH THE PULPER. Reviewing developments in deinked pulp for tissue making, French group Lamort says that new printing inks, lacquers and contaminants, present in increasing quantities, have required changes to the traditional washing-hot dispersion line. The company says it believes deinking starts with the repulping equipment. Its Helico Pulper is designed to achieve ink detachment and ink calibration adapted to washing or flotation deinking. Industrial studies using laser inks have shown that the dot count is reduced by at least 50% when changing from a low consistency to a Helipoire system, adds the company.

Flotation deinking is now commonly used in tissue systems for removing ink specks that would not otherwise be washed out. Plug-free MT injectors and the ability to operate with double or single aeration are features of the group's Verticel flotation deinking cell. The company says the Verticel achieved a market share of 35%

in new deinking lines for tissue production in 1989, up from 25% in 1988.

Lamort's opinion on stickies and varnishes is that hot dispersion is not sufficient. Removal is the only cure. The T version of its Gyroclean is said to develop an efficiency of 95 to 99%, compared with 70 to 75% for conventional reverse cyclones in a single stage or lower with two or three stages. The new unit, which has a capacity of up to 520 m³/hour at 1.6% consistency, can be placed before or after flotation. For removing varnish and lacquer specks, Lamort has introduced the ELP 136, 3-in. cleaner. It is said to develop efficiencies of 85 to 95%.

Turning to newsprint production, Lamort says the deinking line put on the pulping equipment should integrate flotation deinking and washing, depending on grammage and the percentage of deinked pulp used. Again, stress is put on the deinking equipment, which should allow efficient ink detachment. For removing stickies, Lamort quotes a trial using a Gyroclean T at a European newsprint mill. The mill used the unit to clean 45% to 50% of the deinked pulp flow to its twin-wire paper machine. As a result, any unplanned downtime for wire cleaning has been eliminated, says Lamort.

Finally, on printings/writings, Lamort says that a major development is selective flotation of washer filtrate. The combined high-yield, washing-flotation system is said to result in high brightnesses. ∎

Chapter 33

Chemical Application Expands in Washing/Flotation Deinking Systems

Synthetic, active liquids called displectors provide good adhesion
and superior results in combination washing/flotation systems

By ROBERT G. HORACEK and BENGT JARREHULT

Deinking in North America was once performed almost completely by multiple-stage washing systems. This technology relied on the use of dispersants to diffuse ink into colloidal particles below 30 microns. This was possible with conventional printing processes, but is not possible with the use of heavily coated, highly polymerized, or nonimpact inks, such as ultraviolet, heat-set, Xerox, laser and ink jet. The explosion of the computer age has had the biggest single effect on deinking system design due to the proliferation of nonimpact inks and the related difficulty and high cost of obtaining wastepaper containing fully dispersible inks. This has caused many North American deinking mills to add froth flotation modules.

Dilution washing is the mechanical process of rinsing dispersed ink particles from pulp. Ink-laden washing effluent is clarified to concentrate ink for economical treatment and disposal, and recycling of second- or third- washer effluent is a typical way of minimizing water consumption. Froth flotation, or dispersed air flotation, is the chemimechanical process of selectively floating ink particles from dilute pulp. As much as 20 to 25% air (by volume) is injected or drawn into pulp to provide bubbles to pick up the particles. The concentrated foam is removed from the surface for further treatment and disposal.

In almost every modified system, washing equipment has been retained to remove dispersible inks and ash, and the modified systems are referred to as combination or hybrid washing/flotation systems. Chemically, this creates a substantial problem. This is because effective washing depends on rendering ink particles hydrophilic (attracted to water) so they are removed with washing effluent, while flotation requires particles to be hydrophobic (repels from water) for proper collection and attachment to bubbles.

Mr. Horacek, formerly with Berol Chemicals Inc., is now eastern regional manager, Lion Industries Inc., and Mr. Jarrehult is with Eka Nobel Inc., Paper Chemicals Division.

CHEMICAL MECHANISMS. A typical surfactant is illustrated in Figure 3, with the hydrophobic part to the left and the hydrophilic part to the right. The hydrophobic part may consist of fatty alcohols, alkylphenols or other oil-soluble substances. The hydrophilic part consists of cationic, nonionic or anionic molecules. When a surfactant is drawn like this it is usually an anionic surfactant with a part consisting of a glycol chain.

A primary requirement for effective washing is fine ink dispersion so that particles can pass through the fiber network and screen of a washing device. Conventional washing dispersants lower the surface tension to improve penetration of the area where the ink is in contact with the fiber, and by hydrophobic interaction they attach their hydrophobic chain to the ink particle. Thereby, the hydrophilic part is directed toward the water phase. The particles covered with a hydrophilic layer are commonly called mycelles and will not adhere to other surfaces in the solution.

As in washing, flotation starts with the removing and washing of particles, but the same degree of dispersion is not required. A collector is added to agglomerate ink into larger particles and attach them to the air bubbles. Collectors are required for effective flotation and are usually anionic molecules or micron-size particles covered with anionic molecules (fatty acid). Fatty acid collectors are precipitated with calcium or aluminum ions to form larger, insoluble aggregates from ink particles and collector particles. With injection of air in the flotation cells, the agglomerated ink particles adhere to the bubbles, rise to the surface and are skimmed from the system.

Because of the importance of ink particle size in relation to removal efficiency by various types of equipment, it is always important to have a clear idea of the waste furnish and inks to be encountered. Optimum flotation, just as in washing, requires ink particles to be in a certain size range. If they are too small, the collision with a rising air bubble will not occur. When they are too big, they are more likely to be knocked off a bubble before it reaches the surface. Particles must also be sufficiently hydrophobic to be accepted by the air bubble.

When they are too hydrophilic, they will be repelled, which is the primary reason washing dispersants are not effective for flotation.

DEVELOPMENT OF SYSTEM TECHNOLOGY. As previously discussed, the wide particle size distribution commonly encountered in many waste furnishes has led to installation of flotation and washing equipment in the same systems. Berol, now part of Nobel Industries Paper Chemical (NIPC) group, saw the need for more effective products for combination systems and several years ago developed a series of dispersant/collector systems as well as a unique series of single-product "displector" (DISP-ersant/col-LECTOR) formulations.

Displectors are synthetic, 100%-active liquids and have become particularly popular in North America due to their simplicity and effectiveness. They provide good adhesion to air bubbles in flotation and are so hydrophilic that fine particles do not reprecipitate onto the fi-

ber surface. The collecting action does not work on the principle of calcium bridging and, therefore, is not as pronounced as with the fatty acid/calcium chloride approach. Displectors make possible the removal of ink with washing equipment, which does not occur with flotation collectors.

The benefits of displector application in combination systems are illustrated by comparing results with newsprint/magazine wastepaper (Figure 4). In the flotation module, the use of a dispersant results in a large amount of foam, but it does not carry much ink and increased brightness is marginal. In the washing section, however, a pronounced increase in brightness is achieved because of the finely dispersed ink. Using the fatty acid/calcium chloride collector system, a very good flotation effect is indicated with the flotation module, but washing devices provide virtually no ink removal.

Since the displector is necessarily a compromise, results are not always quite as good as with the collector

FIGURE 1: **Washing.**

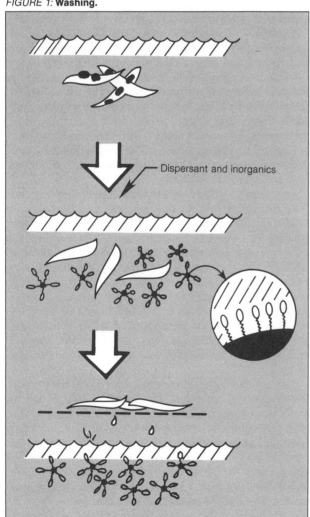

FIGURE 2: **Flotation.**

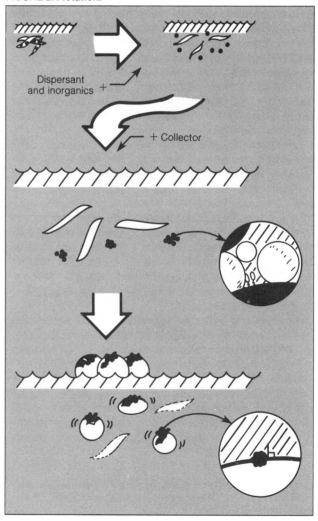

in flotation, but there can be significant removal in washing. The combined effect is, therefore, almost always superior to either a dispersant or a collector. Whenever a waste furnish containing a wide variety of ink particle sizes is used, the combination system and displector chemistry will provide superior results.

In addition to superior results in combination washing/flotation systems, displectors also offer additional process advantages over the conventional fatty acid/calcium chloride approach:

- They are 100%-active liquids, easy to handle and store.
- They require no makeup or dilution before use.
- They require no calcium chloride addition or hardness monitoring/adjustment (especially important in areas having soft water).
- They are stable and do not depend on balance of hardness and soaps for effectiveness.
- They will not result in or contribute to scaling on equipment in any part of the system.
- They result in very low carryover from the deinking system, causing virtually no impact on other paper mill operations, including the yankee coating or sizing, and will not cause organic buildup on tissue machine wires and felts.
- They result in no acid formation or in any related damage.
- They result in lower fiber losses.

COMMERCIAL APPLICATION. Currently, there are ten combination washing/flotation deinking installations in North America that use Berol displectors. These systems cover the widest variety of applications, including waste furnishes such as newsprint/magazine, various mixtures of groundwood-free grades and high proportions of Xerox, laser, and ink-jet print. The washing/flotation systems range from the very simple to the most technically up-to-date and sophisticated systems. The flotation module is located in several different system locations.

Berol has developed related displectors to meet specific mill conditions or needs in several instances. After flotation startups, several mills continued to add the solvent-based dispersant used previously for washing, in addition to the displector. However, subsequent testing confirmed that results were as good or better using the displector alone, and the dispersants were eliminated. This significantly reduced their chemical costs in addition to improving product quality.

With use of the displector and combination washing/flotation technology, these systems have been able to achieve many of their objectives:

- Downgrading waste furnishes to cheaper grades
- Achieving sufficient quality to displace expensive bleached market pulp
- Achieving effective ink removal with high concentrations of laser and other nonimpact inks

- Reducing or eliminating use of bleach or optical brighteners while maintaining desired brightness
- Reducing chemical addition and overall costs vs washing dispersants
- Improving quality and process stability and eliminating process buildups that previously occurred with the use of fatty acid/calcium chloride
- Operating at changing temperatures and process conditions.

Quality in these mills has reached 60 to 62 brightness (GE) with newsprint/magazine furnishes and 81 to 82 with groundwood-free furnishes. Berol has also been able to help pinpoint mechanical and process deficiencies in several cases during optimization work, which helped improve the overall system effectiveness. ■

FIGURE 3: **Elementary surface chemistry.**

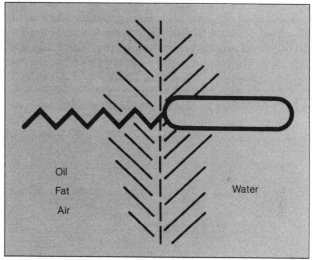

FIGURE 4: **Brightness raise with flotation/wash.**

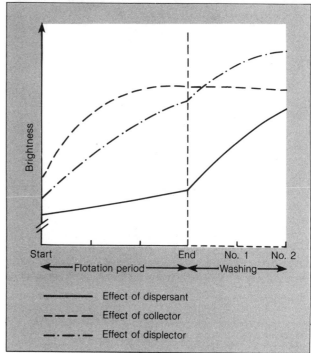

Chapter 34

Fiber Substitution with Pulper Deinking Reduces Furnish Costs

Inks are either removed from the fibers without further mechanical treatment or dispersed well enough not to cause operating problems

By T.W. WOODWARD

Conventional deinking involves mechanical treatment following repulping for separating ink particles from fiber. Pulper deinking is an alternative method in which the inks are solubilized, dispersed, or otherwise rendered innocuous in the pulper without further mechanical treatment.

Pulper deinking allows mills with no deinking facilities that are using uninked or lightly inked waste as furnish to downgrade their furnish to printed or heavily printed material without sacrificing product quality. As a result, cost savings to mills of $20 to $25/ton can be achieved.

Many paper and board mills using virgin pulp, unprinted pulp substitute, or lightly printed secondary fiber can considerably reduce furnish costs by utilizing more heavily printed waste. Conventional deinking facilities allow this substitution by removing the ink from the fiber and subjecting the fiber/ink suspensions to a mechanical treatment (e.g., washing and/or flotation), which separates the ink from the fiber.

In pulper deinking, inks are removed from the fibers and rendered innocuous in the pulper without further mechanical treatment. This is accomplished by carefully adjusting the chemistry of the pulper to achieve maximum ink breakup, emulsification, peptization, and dispersion. The objective is for most of the ink to be removed from the pulp during the papermaking process and the remainder to be retained in the final sheet without adversely affecting sheet quality. The main advantage to the mill is a significant reduction in furnish costs without the addition of capital-intensive deinking equipment and systems.

For pulper deinking to be viable, inks must be broken up and dispersed into small enough particle sizes (less than 0.10 microns) so that ink particles remaining with the sheet do not affect the quality of the finished product. This can be accomplished by carefully prescreening

Mr. Woodward is manager-specialty chemicals, Betz Paperchem Inc., Jacksonville, Fla.

the furnish, using appropriate deinking chemicals, and carefully controlling pulping conditions. All are equally important in achieving the objective.

PULPER DEINKING CHEMISTRY. The functions of pulper deinking chemicals are similar to the functions of chemicals in a washing deinking system, the main difference being the degree of chemical action. Deinking chemicals must be chosen very carefully relative to furnish type, pulping parameters, paper forming equipment, and final sheet characteristics.

Both positive and negative effects of residual deinking chemicals on system operation and sheet quality must be anticipated, and proper steps must be taken to compensate for them. Printed wastepaper containing inks that cannot be rendered innocuous in the pulper must be removed by prescreening.

LABORATORY TESTING. Many questions concerning the viability of pulper deinking can be answered with a thorough laboratory investigation. The following factors should be determined in the laboratory:
- Types of furnish that are candidates for substitution
- Levels of deinking furnish that can be tolerated
- Necessary pulping parameters
- Chemicals and addition levels required
- Impact on sheet quality (including optical and physical properties).

This preliminary laboratory work is mandatory for all potential pulper deinking applications. Once this information is obtained, a systematic program approach can be developed for each mill situation.

PRESCREENING. As mentioned previously, pulper deinking programs are designed for specific wastepaper grades. Therefore, an effective prescreening procedure is critical to the success of the program. A unique spot test has been developed for use on coated paper and paperboard waste. If incoming secondary fiber passes the spot test, it is certain that inks and coatings will be properly processed in the mill system. Careful prescreening with the spot test eliminates the possibility of costly contamination and assures optimum sheet quality.

In applications utilizing ledger and computer printout (CPO) waste, microscopic techniques can be used to identify laser-printed material. If uncertainty still exists about using any waste fiber, the laboratory pulper can provide a clear picture of how the furnish will deink by simulating actual operating parameters and chemical additions.

TOTAL SYSTEM APPROACH. Pulper deinking is viable only when all factors affecting the outcome are considered. Addition of deinking chemicals to the pulper represents just a small portion of the overall effort required to make the program successful.

Pulping parameters, such as pH, temperature, time, consistency, mechanical action, and chemical addition, have a major impact on deinking efficiency in the pulper. Each of these must be controlled and optimized to ensure the success of a pulper deinking program.

The potential impact of new furnish and deinking chemicals on machine operation and sheet quality must be addressed. Pulper deinking can have a residual chemical effect in the following areas of papermaking: refining, fiber bonding, drainage, sizing, forming, retention, deposit control, and pressing and drying. The relative importance of each of these factors will vary from mill to mill. They do point out, however, the importance of implementing a carefully planned deinking program that encompasses many parameters and considerations other than a specific deinking product selection. For fiber substitution by pulper deinking to be successful, it is extremely important that each application be studied from this total systems approach so that problems are anticipated and addressed prior to the initiation of a program.

PULPER DEINKING OPPORTUNITIES. Replacing expensive white or lightly printed furnish via deinking, without major capital expenditures, and by a less costly inked furnish is the primary objective of pulper deinking. The following examples demonstrate cost-saving opportunities available through pulper deinking. All prices are based on wastepaper costs quoted for second-quarter 1988.

Coated boxboard. Pulper deinking allows use of lower-cost substitutes for market pulp and/or the unprinted or lightly printed grades currently used in top liner, underliner, or bottom liner. In the following case, the top liner furnish consists of 75% lightly printed bleached sulfate (LPBS) and 25% forms ledger:

75% LPBS @ $230/ton	$172.50
25% white ledger @ $230/ton	57.50
Costs ($/ton)	$230.00

Since the mill produces coated board, ink needs only to be dispersed finely enough so as not to show through the coating. Pulper deinking allowed the use of 100% heav-

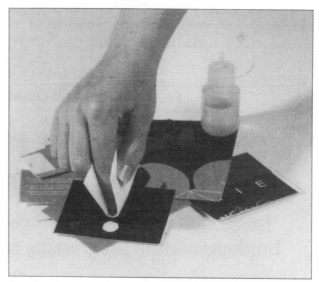

A spot test prescreens coated paper and paperboard waste.

ily printed bleached sulfate (HPBS) at a treatment cost of $35/ton, which includes the cost of caustic for pH control. The savings for the mill are as follows:

Previous topliner furnish cost	$230.00
100% HPBS @ $170/ton	−170.00
Deinking cost	− 35.00
Savings of topliner furnish ($/ton)	$25.00

If this was an uncoated boxboard mill, a recommendation might include substitution of LPBS at $230/ton for the pulp substitutes currently being used, which might frequently be hard-whites or envelope cuttings ($420/ton).

Tissue and toweling. In the tissue and towel industry, pulper deinking can be an effective means of reducing costs by a partial or total substitution of a lightly or heavily printed bleached board into furnishes that contain 100% envelope cuttings or 100% unprinted solid bleached sulfate.

The following scenario is for a 50% furnish substitution of LPBS with a pulper deinking treatment cost of $30/ton (this includes the cost of caustic for pH control):

	Envelope	**Unprinted**
Previous furnish cost	$420.00	$500.00
New furnish:		
50% of above	−210.00	−250.00
50% LPBS @ $230/ton	−115.00	−115.00
Deinking cost	− 15.00	− 15.00
Savings ($/ton)	$ 80.00	$120.00

SUMMARY. The traditional deinking process uses mechanical systems to provide suitable furnish from printed waste stocks. Pulper deinking is an alternative method that allows many secondary fiber mills pulping high-quality white pulp substitutes to use more heavily printed wastes. The mills achieve a quality finish without additional equipment. A pulper deinking program is complex, and many factors other than merely adding deinking chemicals to a pulper must be carefully considered to make the program work. ∎

Chapter 35

Flotation Deinking Is Critical in Unit Process Method of Deinking

Integral unit processes are required for making a flotation operation a viable system for removing inks from usable fiber

By ANDY HARRISON, Technical Editor

Deinking is the process of removing the ink from usable paper fiber. Improved deinking technology in the past few years has allowed more recycled fiber use in the papermaking process while maintaining and improving quality of the final product. This has been achieved due to better understanding of deinking technology (see sidebar), improved equipment, and more efficient chemicals for ink removal. The most prominent deinking process today is the flotation system. This process removes the largest range of ink particles found in wastepaper and, when used in combination with various other deinking processes and specific chemical additives, can remove virtually all types of ink particles.

The deinking process of separating ink particles from usable fibers is done by submitting printed wastepaper to a number of component systems. The individual systems can be used in combinations or singularly depending on type of furnish used and quality of finished product required.

Different ink particle sizes require various types of equipment for effective removal. Figure 1 shows the comparison of removal efficiencies vs particle size. The diagram shows that washing efficiency is best at a range between 1 and 10 microns. Flotation efficiency is high through the next range of 10 to 150 microns. Cleaning equipment works best at 100 to 1,000 microns and screening at 1,000 microns and above.

Figure 1 also indicates other factors of ink particle properties that relate to the efficiency of each deinking process. In the washing process, where water is separated from the fiber, particles that are hydrophilic (attracted to water) tend to go along with the water as the fiber solution is dewatered. In the flotation process, where air and chemicals are added to the solution, particles that are hydrophobic (repel water) tend to attach themselves to the air/chemical additives, hence separating from the fiber. Cleaning systems work on differences in specific gravity and tend to remove ink particles that are relatively large. Screening technology is an effective remover of large, stiff particles. Ink particles, though some-

times large, are shaped like plates, are not stiff, and tend to pass through screen slots and larger perforations.

THE DEINKING SYSTEM. Deinking systems are integral processes made up of separate unit operations. Many systems use only some of these unit operations. The mechanisms of removal are based on different principles of operation. Ultimately, the design must be patterned after the type of furnish used and the finished pulp required.

Though ink particles are typically in the range where flotation is most efficient, other contaminants are normally found in wastepaper containing ink. Other types of removal equipment, such as cleaners and screens, are found in deinking processes because contaminants like stickies and plastics are removed as well. In addition, cleaners and screens remove the inks that flotation systems have difficulty handling. In combination, the various systems work together to remove many varieties of contaminants and the widest range of ink particles.

The following are brief descriptions and operating parameters of some of the processes used in the deinking system.

Pulper. Pulping, which is usually performed on a batch basis, is where the wastepaper and chemicals are added. Separation of the ink particles from the fiber begins as fiber-to-fiber action, and chemical reaction with the ink vehicle causes dispersion of the ink particles. Deinking plants use higher-consistency pulpers, up to 15% consistency, with helical impellers to achieve the best rubbing action between fibers.

Alkaline-based chemicals are also added to disintegrate wastepaper into an ink-pulp solution. Ink separation from the fiber can then be achieved in the subsequent process.

Screening. The screening system consists of slotted or perforated pressure screens and tailing screens. These screens are used to remove plastics, Styrofoam, and stickies. Separation of contaminants from fiber occurs due to the variance in size and stiffness. Ink particles are shaped like plates and are pliable. Therefore, they are more apt to align themselves with the paper fiber and pass through the screen slot. This phenomenon makes screening very poor for removing ink. However, screening is the most efficient way of removing stickies typically found in most printed paper waste furnishes.

Cleaning. Cleaners can be broken down into two groups: light cleaners and heavy cleaners. The premise of cleaning technology is based on specific gravity. Light cleaners, or through-flow cleaners (reverse cleaning), separate contaminants that are less than the specific gravity of water or density of 1. Heavy cleaners, or forward cleaners, separate contaminants greater than 1. Cleaners remove specks most efficiently and ink particles in the 100-to-1,000-micron range.

Flotation. The flotation system consists of a flotation cell or combination of cells that are injected with a waste fiber solution. Tiny air bubbles and chemicals are mixed with the waste fiber solution. Chemical addition helps separate ink from the fibers. After separation occurs, the air bubbles attach to the ink particles and rise to the top of the cell where a foam is produced. The ink-laden foam is then taken off by skimmers or vacuum.

Flotation is the most effective method of ink removal, especially in the 10 to 150 micron range, where the majority of ink particles are found. Below 10 microns, flotation is not as effective.

Washing. Types of washers include gravity deckers, sidehill screens, dewatering screws, and twin-wire machines (Figure 2). The method of removal is simply to dewater the fiber and take along the ink particles with the water. Small particles, typically below 10 microns, are more likely to be removed by washing. As the size gets larger, the particles tend to be trapped in the fiber matrix, making removal more difficult. Washing efficiency begins to decrease as particle size dips below 1 micron because the particles adhere to the fiber surface.

Dispersion. This method of treatment breaks the ink down into small fragments that are undetectable by

FIGURE 1: **Removal efficiency of varying unit operations depends on particle size of the contaminant and other properties.**

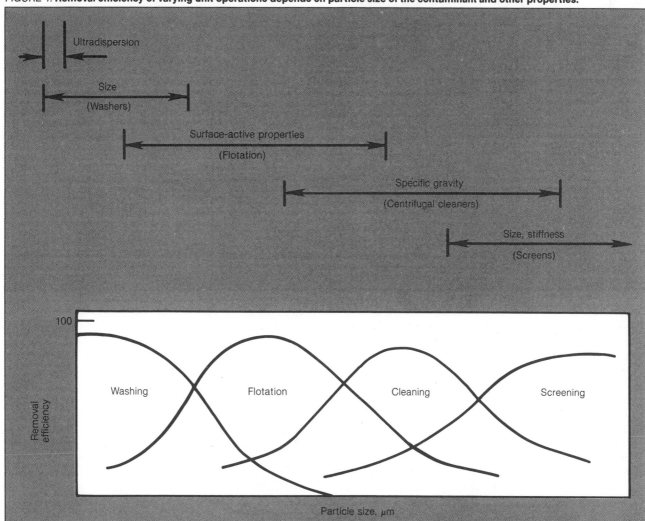

the naked eye. The ink particles are not actually removed but dispersed into the fiber. Dispersion can be accomplished by chemical addition, steam injection, or mechanical mixing units. Though dispersion hides detectable ink particles from sight, the side effect is a darker pulp. To counter this problem, many mills add bleach to give whiteness to the pulp, although this does not always work.

FLOTATION DEINKING. The flotation process has emerged as the dominant deinking method. The separation process requires specific chemical conditions, which are created by adding chemicals to the system prior to the flotation cells. Typical chemicals used are described in Table 1. The equipment, design, and theory of flotation deinking of various vendors are examined in the following examples.

Beloit. The Beloit deinking flotation cell is a selective flotation process in which ink particles are attached to air bubbles that rise to the surface of the pulp, producing inky foam that is then removed. The Lineacell, introduced in 1983 (Figure 3), and the Pressure Deinking Module (PDM), introduced in 1987, are Beloit first- and second-generation deinking cells. The mechanism of

FIGURE 2: **BEW's Vario split washer effectively removes small particles.**

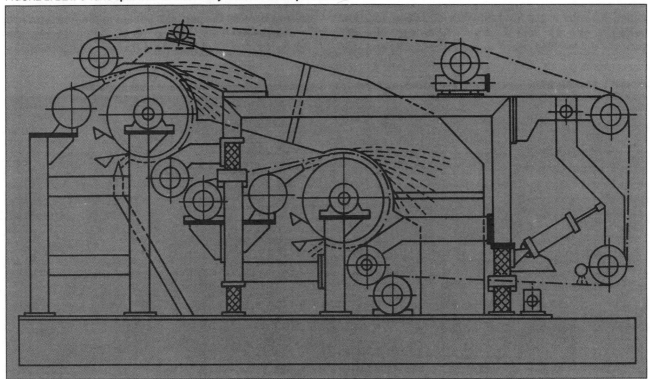

FIGURE 3: **Beloit's flotation deink cell removes ink particles with virtually no fiber loss.**

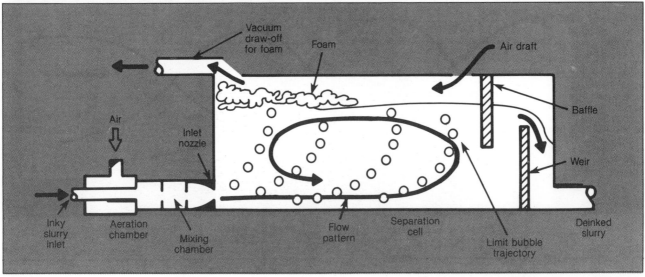

Deinking Technology

flotation of these units can be divided into three stages.

1. Aeration of the ink suspension by controlling the exact amount of air into the stock and breaking this up into controlled bubble size
2. Mixing and attachment of the ink particles and air bubbles, forming an ink bubble complex or foam
3. Separation of foam from the fiber solution.

In the aeration zone, air is added with accurate control into the flow stock. Many tiny bubbles are produced at approximately five times the ink particle size to obtain maximum ink particle removal. These bubbles are generated hydraulically in the aeration and mixing zones. Ideal sizing of the bubbles is achieved by adding chemicals, such as surfactant to reduce bubble size, and optimizing the geometry of the aeration zone.

The mixing zone improves the attachment of ink particles to air bubbles by increasing the intensity and frequency of collisions. By using micro-turbulence, this process is optimized, increasing ink removal efficiency. PDM makes use of high pressure to increase the ink-to-air mixing action by further controlling the size and amount of air bubbles. The mixing zone is the most critical stage in the process since attachment of ink particles to air bubbles is crucial to the success of flotation deinking.

The separation zone brings the foam to the surface of the stock where the foam is then taken off with a minimum of fiber removal. The Lineacell uses a vacuum system designed to remove only the foam and not the fiber stock. PDM uses internal pressure to expel the foam rejects directly to the rejects handling unit.

Voith. The Voith flotation unit is the Multi-Injector-Cell. The object of the Multi-Injector-Cell is the complete separation of the inks from the fibers. Optimal efficiency is achieved by developing the relevant parameters of the flotation machine, which include the specific air load, the energy applied for dispersing the air into fine bubbles, and the injector design.

The phenomena in Voith's flotation cell can be broken down into the following single actions:

- Pumping the pulp from cell to cell
- Air intake by the injector
- Dispersing air into fine bubbles
- Collecting the ink particles on the air bubbles
- Separating air from the cleaned pulp
- Separating the ink-laden froth.

Air intake, air dispersion, and collection of the ink particles on the air bubbles take place in the injector itself.

The injector works according to the venturi principle, without any external blowers or compressors. The high turbulence in the pulse exchange pipe ensures frequent contact of air bubbles and ink particles, resulting in good ink collection. Those ink-laden air bubbles then rise to the surface of the deinking cell, forming a black froth that overflows into the foam trough.

The basic design and main dimensions of the injector determine the specific air intake related to pulp flow, whereas the available energy mainly controls air dispersion. For the efficiency of the injector, the most important parameters are specific airflow, specific energy, and throughput through the single injector. Provided the air bubble diameter is regarded as constant, the efficiency of an injector increases with increasing airflow simply because higher airflow rates mean a larger surface area for ink particle collection. There is a limitation beyond a certain specific airflow rate. Further improvement of efficiency does not occur when the injector design no longer allows complete dispersion of the high amount of air.

Each injector design has its own specific air-intake characteristic. Voith multi-injectors have optimum airflow rates of approximately 50% of the pulp flow pumped from cell to cell. High energy input improves flotation efficiency by better dispersing the air into fine bubbles.

All injector designs have optimum throughput. Any deviation from that optimum reduces the efficiency remarkably. Consequently, each injector flotation system should always be operated at that optimum flow rate. To overcome throughput variation, Voith developed tubular flotation cells that are connected to each other by large openings in the sidewalls. These openings permit a balance of flows in case the actual throughput is less than the nominal flow. This important feature allows the injectors to always operate at their optimum, despite the actual production rate. Even a reduction to 50% of

TABLE 1: **Major chemicals used in the flotation process.**

Chemical	Dosage (kg/ton)	Function
Sodium hydroxide	10 to 20	Creates alkalinity and releases ink to the suspension.
Sodium silicate	15 to 25	Acts as a dispersant for released ink. Stabilizes alkalinity.
Sequestrant	1 to 2	Stabilizes hydrogen peroxide by the complex binding of heavy metal ions.
Hydrogen peroxides	10 to 15	Gives higher brightness to the pulp by suppressing the yellowing action caused by the alkaline on mechanical pulp.
Soap	10 to 15	Is a collector chemical in combination with calcium in the flotation cells.
Calcium salt	—	Interacts with soap, making insoluble sticky particles that precipitate on the surface of ink. These water-repellent particles have a strong tendency to attach themselves to air bubbles.

the designed capacity is possible without any intervention of the operator.

Other important features of the Voith flotation cells are the large diameter of the injector nozzles, to prevent any plugging by coarser impurities, and the closed tubular design, to avoid any ink-laden vapors.

Fiberprep. New printing processes, new types of ink, and varying impressions require careful consideration when designing a system for deinking all grades of paper. Considerations are based on raw materials, end use, quality requirement of the final paper product, and operating cost.

The flotation process is designed to remove all free inks from the pulp slurry (Figure 4). Air is injected in volumes of approximately 30% relative to stock flow through injectors that are designed to efficiently mix the air (in bubble form) with the inlet stock stream. The air bubbles trap the ink particles and carry them to the top of the cell for removal.

Design of the injectors is critical. The incoming pulp must be passed at the correct velocities to effect proper shear forces, and the air must be introduced at the exact point of pressure transition to ensure bubble formation at the size proper for trapping and conveying the inks.

Based on mill experience, four air-stock sequences are required to achieve 100% removal of the free, floatable ink. In the Verticel system, 4.6 such contacts occur.

Flotation is performed at consistencies up to 1.3% through two Fiberprep/Lamort Verticel Deink Cells installed in series. These are double-aeration units with 100% recirculation in each cell. Air introduction is accomplished with venturi-type injectors, without requiring external compressed air. This air is mixed in the injectors with the incoming stock, ensuring complete mixing and availability of sufficient air for entrapment of ink particles over the full system to provide a means of floating the ink from the system. These injectors are designed with large orifices for trouble-free operation.

The stock circulates upward and then overflows downward toward the accept of the cell. A portion of accept stock from each cell is recirculated and reaerated to provide a final polishing effect before its discharge.

The Verticel system requires no secondary cells for fiber recovery. The positive removal of foam is done through a vacuum system, resulting in system fiber losses of less than 2%.

Black Clawson. Flotation deinking has become much more common in removing today's difficult-to-remove inks, such as laser printing and copier printing. The Black Clawson flotation machine is the Ultra Cell, a multistage unit that can be operated with a single pump. Consistency of 1% stock is pumped into the upper cell and then gravity-fed to the remaining cells. Air is introduced into the furnish by a variable-speed diffuser,

FIGURE 4: **Fiberprep flotation deinking loop.**

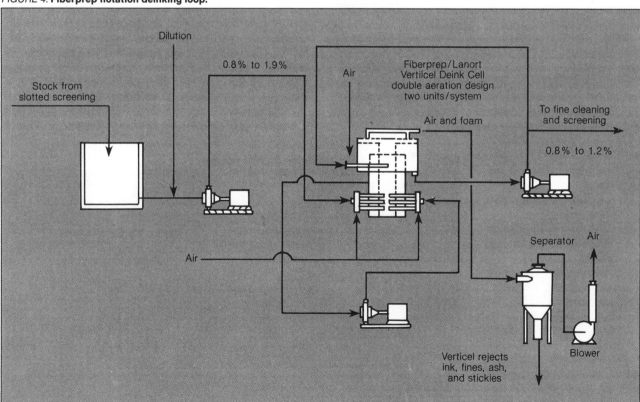

which provides precise bubble size control. Additional diffusers may be used at each individual cell location for multiple introduction of air. As the ink-laden froth rises to the surface, self-adjusting floating skimmers remove the contaminants. The process is repeated in each cell until all of the accepts and rejects are discharged from the bottom of the unit.

Black Clawson's philosophy toward flotation deinking is to interact the flotation cell process with other deinking processes. For example, chemical addition in the pulper provides better mixing and allows the use of a simplified chemical addition in the flotation cell. High clay content and removal in the flotation cell enhances flotation efficiency but also reduces washer load and improves washer efficiency.

Bird Escher Wyss. The CF Deinking Cell, the flotation unit by BEW, uses a unique aeration principle to acquire proper dispersion and separation of ink particles at low operating costs. Air bubbles are introduced into the flotation cell by a step diffuser. The self-suction effect of the step diffuser creates efficient aeration without the use of compressed air. Air and gray stock are first mixed in the narrow portion of the diffuser. Then, they flow through the larger-diameter section of the diffuser where the flow of the suspension is reduced, resulting in low flow speeds and low flotation tank turbulence. As the suspension enters the cell, foam floats to the top and spirals toward the center. The foam discharges by gravity, feeding into a centrally located collecting pipe. The accepts flow out the bottom, where level control is below the fluid line. The accepts can go through another deinking cell to ensure absolute ink removal. A typical flotation system has four flotation cells in series, depending on throughput and deinking requirements.

BEW believes that flotation will continue to be an important technique in the future. As the types of contamination increase and become more complicated, the technology to separate ink from fiber, improve overall brightness, and reduce fine contents will also improve. Environmental compatibility will improve as well. ■

REFERENCES
John Mattingley, "Chemical Use and Cost in Flotation Deinking," *Pulp & Paper International* 20, no. 6 (1978): 64.
Lothar Pfalzar, "Deinking Technology and its Application in Waste Paper Recycling" (Voith Inc.).
W.H. Siewert, *Future Stock Preparation Development Trends.*
Michael A. McCool and Luigi Silveri, "Removal of specks and nondispersed ink from a deinking furnish," *Tappi Journal* 70, no. 11 (1987): 75.
Jaakko Pöyry Oy, "Today We Know More about the Deinking Process" (Sulzer Escher Wyss Inc.).
Michael A. McCool and C.J. Taylor, "Image analysis techniques in recycled fiber," *Tappi Journal* 66, no. 8 (1983): 69.
Peter E. DeBlanc and Michael A. McCool, "Recycling and separation Technology" (Beloit Corp.).

Image analysis

A unique method of analyzing contaminants, specifically ink particles and stickies, is the automatic image analysis system. Image analysis is used to determine removal efficiencies of screening, cleaning, and deinking systems. This is accomplished by quantifying the removal efficiencies of the units, determining the major parameters that control the efficiency of contaminant removal, and then developing more effective units by optimizing these controlling parameters.

The image analysis system consists of four parts:
- A powerful microscope to magnify the sample
- A high-resolution camera to transmit the image to an image processor
- A processor that stores the information and allows an operator to prepare the data for analysis
- A black and white monitor screen for display of the image.

A sample is prepared on a milli-pore filter so that all the ink in the sample is captured and a single layer of ink particles and fibers can be evenly distributed without any consequential overlapping. This sampling method allows for high contrast between ink particles and the fibers, with low contrast between the fiber in the background. An image magnified and transmitted to the processor is then displayed on the monitor in the form of picture points or pixels. The light intensity of each pixel is measured by the processor and given a numerical value called a gray level.

An ink particle would have a dark gray level and would be easily identified from the lighter-level fiber. Area and length of the ink particle also can be distinguished by the gray level.

Automatic image analysis has become a valuable tool for measuring specks and the brightness of paper and for developing deinking and recycling equipment.

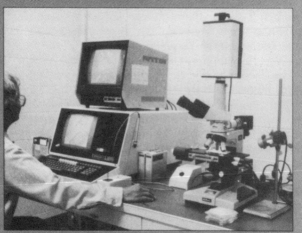

Image analysis is an effective way to determine removal efficiencies of screening, cleaning, and deinking systems.

Chapter 36

Proper Deinking Chemistry, Bleaching Technique Crucial to Pulp Brightness

Bleaching trials of deinked groundwood grades show that understanding residual ink's impact on brightness will help improve pulp quality

By MICHAEL DODSON and LOWELL DEAN

The U.S. paper industry has historically recycled about one-fourth of its total production, except during World War II. This rate is approximately half that of countries with limited natural resources, such as Great Britain, Holland, or Japan. The U.S. recycling rate peaked during the war years at 35% due to the need for conservation of raw materials. After the war, legislation was passed to stimulate the development of natural resources, which gave the production of finished goods from virgin materials a distinct economic advantage.

Although newspaper was recycled during the war, afterwards, until the mid-1970s, recycling back into newsprint was practiced by only one corporation, Garden State Paper. In the mid-70s, three mills in the U.S. began recycling newspaper because of wood supply limitations. Before that, most deinking was conducted with wood-free wastepaper, mainly for tissue production and to a lesser degree printing and writing paper.

Wood-free grades have become less available, forcing major wastepaper consumers to evaluate groundwood wastepaper grades. Also, over the next decade more high-quality mechanical fiber will be used in traditional wood-free grades, with the increased acceptance of bleached chemi-thermomechanical pulp (BCTMP). As the use of groundwood grades increases, so will the need for upgrading quality through bleaching technology.

Why should there be an interest in recycling groundwood grades? Table 1 lists the U.S. production of all grades of paper and paperboard. As the table shows, groundwood grades (newsprint, uncoated groundwood, coated groundwood) account for a significant portion of total paper production. In fact, the 11.7 million tons account for 31% of 1989's paper production and, if tissue is excluded (much being unrecyclable), these grades ac-

Mr. Dodson is southeast regional manager, and Mr. Dean is manager-chemical sales, Lion Industries, Vancouver, Wash.

count for 36% of the total. When Canadian production is included, more than 20 million tpy could potentially be recycled in North America.

WASTEPAPER QUALITY. A readily available supply of wastepaper is not enough. The resulting pulp must have adequate quality for its final end use at competitive manufacturing costs. The key pulp quality issues are strength at a reasonable drainage rate and good optical properties (brightness, opacity, and cleanliness). This article deals with the brightness quality spectrum that can be expected from peroxide and hydrosulfite bleaching of deinked groundwood content pulps.

Various key factors determine the brightness of deinked pulp. They include the following:
- Type of wastepaper
- Pulping/deinking chemistry
- Efficiency of ink removal by washing or flotation equipment
- Amount and efficiency of water clarification
- Bleaching method.

Meeting quality expectations requires good performance in all areas. Furthermore, since many of these factors are interrelated, there may be compromises between them. This places a great importance on field op-

TABLE 1: Groundwood grades (newsprint, uncoated groundwood, coated groundwood) account for a significant portion of paper production, making those grades major candidates for recycling.

	1989 annualized[1]
Newsprint	6,088
Uncoated groundwood	1,754
Coated groundwood	3,894
Coated free-sheet[2]	3,300
Uncoated free-sheet	11,043
Other printing/writing	1,494
Packaging and other paper	4,925
Tissue	5,636
Total paper	**38,133**
Total paperboard	**38,492**
Total paper and paperboard	**76,625**

1. American Paper Institute.
2. *Pulp & Paper* estimate.

timization of deinking chemistry, water clarification, and bleaching conditions.

The type and quality of the paper furnish is probably the major factor in determining ultimate brightness development of deinked pulps. The proper wastepaper grade should be selected based on the final product with respect to strength and optical property needs. Both the proper grade and the age and homogeneity of the furnish are important.

Lower-quality grades can contaminate wastepaper and must be avoided. Adherence to guidelines such as the paperstock standards and practices of the Paper Stock Institute of America are effective in minimizing contamination. Age of the wastepaper is also important, especially in groundwood grades, which are more susceptible to yellowing from light than wood-free grades. Even short periods (less than six months) of aging can result in the loss of one or two brightness points. Severe aging or yellowing from sunlight will result in even lower brightness and ink removal problems.

In general, newsprint brightness varies depending on the region where it was manufactured. West Coast newsprint produced from darker wood species is normally about 55 brightness, while southern newsprint is approximately 57 and eastern Canadian and northeastern U.S. newsprints are normally 59 and higher. Since newsprint sales tend to be regionalized, it can be anticipated that deinked pulp brightness will be dependent on the region in which the wastepaper is collected.

The majority of coated groundwood paper is No. 5 grade, although there is also production in the higher-quality No. 4 grade. Much of this production has low basis weight and is used in magazines. The basesheet brightness for No. 5 paper is typically 64 to 70 brightness depending on individual mill quality specifications, coating coverage, and coating brightness.

The uncoated groundwood grades have the widest range of brightness levels. Upgraded or specialty newsprint is on the low end of the spectrum at 61 to 65 brightness, while some supercalendered grades can be as high as 74 to 76 brightness. These grades are probably the most difficult to segregate as postconsumer waste since much ends up as inserts in newspapers.

BLEACHING OF DEINKED PULPS. Groundwood deinked and wood-free pulps are bleached by different chemicals. Traditionally, wood-free pulps have been bleached to 76 to 80 with chlorine-based oxidants. Single-stage hypochlorite bleaching is most common. Both CEH and CH bleach sequences are used when wastepaper quality is lower and brightness standards higher.

Delignifying bleaches, such as chlorine or hypochlorite, are not appropriate for groundwood due to the high loss in yield. Traditionally, sodium hydrosulfite and hydrogen peroxide have been used to bleach deinked groundwood pulps.

The following discussion endeavors to define the brightness development of deinked pulps made from

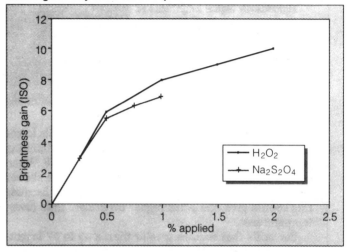

FIGURE 1: **Good brightness can be obtained through application of peroxide up to 1%. However, increasing the application level further gives only incremental improvement.**

100% newsprint, 60% newsprint/40% coated magazine, and 100% coated magazine. The information on 100% newsprint is a compilation of data accumulated during 16 years of bleaching of commercially generated deinked pulps. This is supplemented by recent work on a commercial pulp made from a 60% newsprint/40% magazine furnish and a lab pulp made by simulating a flotation/washing system from 100% magazine stock.

100% NEWSPRINT BLEACHING. Deinked pulps do not respond as well to bleaching as virgin pulps.[1] For instance, in peroxide bleaching of mechanical pulps, six to eight point increases can be expected from 1%, 12 to 15 points from 2%, and 17 to 18 points from 3%. These numbers can be contrasted with the curve in Figure 1. Good response is obtained with up to 1% peroxide applied. However, increasing the application level further gives only incremental improvement.

Residual ink and metal contamination critically affect the response. In fact, some deinked pulps with high metals and residual ink give only limited response—two to four point increases with 1% peroxide. High residual ink and metals can be the result of a system closure that is too tight, especially with respect to fines removal. The metals and ink have a tendency to travel with the fines, so it is important to establish the proper balance between yield and good bleach response in addition to using chelants for metal control.

Interestingly, hydrosulfite bleaching also seems to be affected by residual ink, although to a lesser degree than peroxide bleaching. This effect may be more a masking of residual ink than hydrosulfite decomposition from iron, although the variation in response is not well understood. In mill operations brightness response on 100% newsprint varies from five to eight point increases, with six to seven point increases being normal. When only a six or seven point increase is required, hydrosul-

	100% newsprint		60%/40%		100% coated	
	Brightness	Bleach response	Brightness	Bleach response	Brightness	Bleach response
Deinked pulp	47 to 50	—	54 to 56	—	62 to 67	—
Single-stage hydrosulfite[1]	53 to 57	6 to 7	60 to 63	6 to 7	68 to 74	6 to 8
Single-stage peroxide[2]	53 to 58	6 to 8	60 to 64	6 to 8	71 to 77	9 to 10
Two-stage peroxide/hydro[3]	57 to 62	10 to 12	63 to 67	9 to 11	74 to 80	12 to 13

1. 1.0% sodium hydrosulfite applied.
2. 1.0% hydrogen peroxide applied at high consistency.
3. 1.0% hydrogen peroxide/1.0% sodium hydrosulfite applied.

TABLE 2: **Mechanical pulp in coated groundwood has a higher brightness than in newsprint, resulting in a significantly higher brightness vs 100% newsprint.**

fite bleaching is preferred over peroxide due to its lower chemical and capital costs. Groundwood paper deinking is conducted at low temperatures, 110° F to 120° F. When hydrosulfite bleaching is installed, consideration should be given to heating the pulp to 135° F to 150° F because this should give one point higher brightness than lower temperatures.

For mills that require greater than a 55 to 57 brightness with a 100% newsprint furnish, serious consideration should be given to two-stage bleaching. The peroxide stage can be moderate or high consistency. High-consistency bleaching requires higher capital but has lower chemical costs.

60% NEWSPRINT/40% MAGAZINE BLEACHING. Until a year ago, two Canadian operations were the only mills in North America using a mix of newsprint and coated paper. Currently, there are two in operation in the U.S. and three new systems have been approved. The systems being installed are combination flotation/washing deinking plants. Thus, there is not much information on bleaching response of these pulps in U.S. and Canadian wastepaper furnishes.

Care must be used in drawing direct conclusions from European data. For example, their furnishes include not only newsprint and magazines but also printing and writing paper. There is little segregation of wood-free wastepaper for wood-free deinking as in North America, and this can affect the base brightness and bleachability.

FIGURE 2: **In bleaching of both 100% newsprint and a 60%/40% newsprint/magazine blend with hydrosulfite, similar responses were obtained, except that responses leveled off at lower dosages for the blend.**

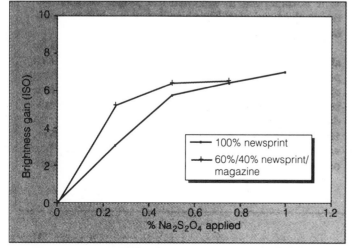

As magazine is added to newsprint, pulp characteristics change in three ways. Strength properties increase since coated groundwood has a much higher kraft content. The mechanical pulp in a coated groundwood sheet has a higher brightness—typically 64 to 70—than in a newsprint sheet. This difference results in a significantly higher brightness (six to seven points) vs 100% newsprint (Table 2). Slightly higher brightness can be expected if either high-quality newsprint is used or if the newsprint is sourced from eastern Canada or the northeastern U.S.

As magazine addition is increased, ash content also increases. For good flotation performance, a minimum amount of ash is required. Unfortunately, ash can be detrimental to peroxide bleaching.[2] The ash carries high levels of metals, even to the degree that the effectiveness of a chelating agent can be overwhelmed. Thus, it is important to have adequate washing if peroxide bleaching is a part of the process.

A laboratory study was conducted on pulp produced in a combination deinking system with minimal washing. The ash content was high (about 9%). The purpose of the study was not only to check the response to peroxide bleaching but also to compare Lionsperse 855, a proprietary chelant, with DTPA. This initial study indicates that more severe conditions (longer retention, higher temperature) should be used than when bleaching pulp from 100% newsprint.

Using pulp of 53.6 initial brightness, a five-point increase was obtained with 1% peroxide by bleaching for two hours at 10% consistency. Another half-point increase was obtained using 1.5% peroxide. Improved results were obtained since 30% to 40% residual peroxide remained and high-consistency conditions were not used. Either 0.2% DTPA or Lionsperse 855 as a pretreatment gave similar results. With Lionsperse 855 as the chelant, 58.9 brightness was obtained with a peroxide residual of 32% vs 58.7 and 37% residual with DTPA.

A different sample from the same system was tested for hydrosulfite bleach response. Comparing 60%/40% blend with 100% newsprint produced similar bleach responses, except that the response leveled off at lower dosages for the blend (Figure 2). This difference could be explained by the lower amounts of mechanical fiber available for bleaching reactions in the blend. Single-stage hydrosulfite bleaching gives adequate brightness for standard newsprint and low brightness (low 60s) for specialty grades. For higher-brightness grades, a two-stage bleach plant could be necessary.

100% COATED BLEACHING. Deinking of 100% coated wastepaper has the greatest potential for use in higher-brightness grades of paper, such as coated and uncoated groundwood, as well as tissue. Currently, only two mills in the U.S. use this furnish.

To round out this study, a sample of magazine stock was deinked in the Lion research laboratory. The paper was deinked using flotation followed by two wash stages with a 60 mesh screen. A typical deinking formulation was used with 0.1% Lionsperse 855, 1% sodium silicate, 0.5% H_2O_2, 0.5% Lionsurf FA-709, and 0.5% NaOH.

After deinking, the pulp with 62 brightness was used for subsequent peroxide bleaching. Chelant pretreatment on this pulp did not improve the bleach response, indicating that ash removal was effective with the laboratory washing techniques. However, this indication does not imply that chelants will not be necessary in a commercial installation where higher residual ink and ash levels can be expected than in lab pulps.

Bleaching with 1% peroxide for two hours at 10% consistency gave a 9.5% lift to 71.6 brightness. Using 1.5% peroxide resulted in an additional increase of 0.5 to one point. More severe bleaching conditions should be used on this pulp than on the 60%/40% blend. Even at a bleaching temperature of 150°F (vs 135°F for the 60%/40% blend), there was 46% residual peroxide with

1% applied and in excess of 50% residual with 1.5% applied. Further optimization (including longer retention and higher consistency) should improve the results of this study.

Lionsperse 855 was evaluated to determine the feasibility of reducing costs by partially replacing silicate in the peroxide bleach liquor. With 0.2% chelant, the silicate level could be reduced from 3% to 1% at an equal brightness of 71.6. The residual peroxide level was slightly lower without silicate, 48% vs 44%. At this replacement ratio, savings should be more than $1/ton.

Although hydrosulfite bleaching was not conducted on this sample, previous lab work and mill experiences indicate that a slightly better bleach response can be obtained with coated groundwood. This response may be the result of lower residual ink levels since magazines have a lower ink content initially than newspaper. Also, ink removal from coated paper is easier since the ink is on the coating and has not penetrated into the fiber.

The deinking and bleaching of 100% coated paper produces the highest-brightness pulp. This pulp could be used in higher-quality grades since a properly designed deinking and bleaching system could produce 74 to 80 brightness (Table 2). ∎

REFERENCES
1. G. Galland, E. Bernard, and Y. Verac, "Achieving a deinked pulp with high brightness," *Paper Technology*, Dec. 1989, p. 28.
2. D. Ring, "Deinking of Coated Groundwood Papers Using Hydrogen Peroxide," PITA Symposium Proceedings, March 1990.

Chapter 37

Appropriate Chemical Additives Are Key to Improved Deinking Operations

Process chemistry should be studied to find the most effective way to deink secondary fiber prior to selecting a chemical additive program

By T.W. WOODWARD

Modern deinking technology has made possible the production of high-quality paper from printed secondary fiber. This technology consists of a careful matching of deinking equipment and chemistry. The performance of deinking systems, whether washing or flotation, is greatly dependent upon the type and concentration of the deinking chemicals.

Another equally important consideration in the selection of deinking chemicals is the fiber furnish. Deinking processing aids are chosen carefully, relative to the type of printed secondary fiber, system type, end product, and percentage of deinked stock in the final product. With proper use of deinking process aids in conjunction with modern deinking facilities, it is possible to achieve brightness and dirt levels equivalent to or better than those of the unprinted secondary fiber.

Given a deinking system type and furnish, there remains a myriad of potential chemical programs suitable for producing the desired grade. Careful laboratory work designed to simulate the system should provide sufficient information to allow trials in the plant, where further changes can be made until optimization is achieved. Knowledge of the function of deinking chemicals will allow blending in order to maximize results.

PRINTING INKS. The classification of printing inks is not rigorous and is based on application, chemical type, drying method, and special properties. These cate-

Mr. Woodward is a group leader, New Market Research, Betz PaperChem Inc., Jacksonville, Fla.

gories are obviously interrelated, with the chemical type being the most important factor when considering the chemistry of ink removal.

Basically, printing inks consist of pigments, providing color and contrast to the ink, incorporated into a vehicle that carries the pigment and binds it to the sheet. Other additives (modifiers) may be used to provide the ink with special properties. Modifiers are usually added in small amounts. The pigment is not soluble in the vehicle and must be mechanically dispersed. With respect to deinking chemistry, it is the vehicle that determines the ease with which inks may be removed from the fibers. Ink vehicles commonly consist of a resin (either natural or synthetic) and a solvent. There are many types of vehicles, their composition depending mainly upon the method by which the ink is dried.

The ink industry is rapidly developing new ink vehicle systems. Unfortunately, the trend appears to be toward vehicles that are increasingly resistant to conventional deinking chemicals. Food & Drug Administration and Environmental Protection Agency regulations tend to inhibit the development of novel chemicals for deinking these chemically resistant inks and varnishes. The thrust in deinking over the last decade has been in development of new technology for mechanical removal of ink particles.

DEINKING PROCESS. Deinking of secondary fiber involves repulping or defibering, during which the ink is removed from the fibers; cleaning and screening; separating ink contaminants from fiber stock; and if necessary, bleaching.

Pulping may be batch or continuous, although the batch method is more commonly used as it provides better control of the process. Some mills prefer continuous pulping as it provides more production for a unit of given size. Chemicals are normally added to the pulper just prior to the addition of furnish. Consistencies are usually in the range of 4% to 6%, although there seems to be a trend toward higher-consistency (12% to 15%) defibering with the objective of saving chemicals, heat, and operating manhours.

Where high brightness is necessary, bleaching is required. When high groundwood wastepapers are being deinked, bleaching can be accomplished with peroxides and/or hydrosulfite added to the pulper, although a more efficient utilization of chemicals will be realized if bleaching takes place following screening and washing.[1,2]. Wood-free pulps are usually bleached in a single-stage hypochlorite process, although some mills use an initial chlorination stage followed by hypochlorite. If percentage of groundwood is less than 5%, brightness values of around 80 GE can be achieved.

CHEMISTRY OF DEINKING.

The most important determinant of the type and concentration of deinking chemicals is the raw material to be deinked. Next in importance is the design and efficiency of the system. For a given deinking system, changes in furnish type will call for an adjustment in the chemistry of the system. For this article, an efficient cleaning and screening system will be assumed, and the chemistries will be differentiated for low and high groundwood content furnishes.

Removal of ink from paper fibers is accomplished primarily in the pulper and is basically a laundering operation. Water and a large amount of mechanical action are sufficient to remove and disperse most inks, but the level of mechanical energy that is necessary cannot be achieved in a conventional pulper. Chemical energy is thus used in place of some of the mechanical energy.

CAUSTIC SODA.

Sodium hydroxide is one of the most important deinking chemicals for woodfree secondary fiber and may be used, with caution, for deinking high groundwood content grades, such as newsprint and coated publication papers. High concentrations of alkali (pH 11.5 to 12.0) can saponify and/or hydrolyze some ink vehicles and will swell fibers to aid in breaking up inks and coatings. The alkali also helps prevent the aggregation of small ink particles into larger ones that are difficult to wash out. The inks on woodfree ledger, computer printout, book, and lightly printed board grades may be effectively removed and dispersed (with the use of other chemicals) at pH values in the range of 10 to 11. Heavily printed and/or varnish-overcoated grades may require a pH of 11.5 or higher.

It is unfortunate that dosages of caustic soda are expressed as a percentage of oven-dried fiber. It is the amount of hydroxide ion that is critical for deinking performance, and the dosage required to achieve a given pH will vary. Sufficient caustic soda should be added to each batch to attain the desired pH. The efficiency of many deinking plants could be increased substantially by better control of sodium hydroxide.

SODA ASH, SILICATES.

Sodium carbonate is sometimes used in conjunction with sodium hydroxide. It is said to cook less harshly and produce slightly brighter pulp than caustic soda alone. It is uncommon for soda

TABLE 1: Deinking processing aids.

Deinking chemical	Structure formula	Function	Furnish type	Dosage (% of fiber)
Sodium hydroxide	NaOH	Fiber swelling-ink breakup, saponification, ink dispersion	Wood-free grades	3.0-5.0%
Sodium silicates	Na_2SiO_3 (hydrated)	Wetting, peptization, ink dispersion, alkalinity and buffering, peroxide stabilization	Groundwood grades Lightly inked ledger	2.0-6.0
Sodium carbonate	Na_2CO_3	Alkalinity, buffering, water softening	Groundwood grades Lightly inked ledger	2.0-5.0
Sodium or potassium phosphates	$(NaPO_3)_n$, n = 15 Hexametaphosphate $Na_5P_3O_{10}$ Tripolyphosphate Tetrasodium pyrophosphate	Metal ion sequestrant Ink dispersion Alkalinity Buffering Detergency, peptization	All grades	0.2-1.0
Nonionic surfactants	$CH_3(CH_2)_nCH_2$-$O(CH_2CH_2O)_xH$ Ethoxylated linear alcohol Ethoxylated alkyl phenols	Ink removal, ink dispersion Wetting, emulsification Solubilizing	All grades	0.2-2.0
Solvents	C_1-C_{14} aliphatic saturated hydrocarbons	Ink softening, solvation	Wood-free grades	0.5-2.0
Hydrophilic polymers	$CH_2CHC=OOH(Na)_n$ Polyacrylate	Ink dispersion Antiredeposition	All grades	0.1-0.5
Fatty acid	$CH_3(CH_2)_{16}COOH$ Stearic acid	Ink flotation aid	All grades	0.5-3.0

ash to be used alone due to slower cooking time, but it does provide required alkalinity and buffers at a slightly higher pH than sodium silicate.

Silicates have been used since the turn of the century for deinking wastepaper. Compared with soda ash or caustic alone, silicates provide better ink removal and brighter pulps with less fiber damage.[3] Silicates are complex solutions of polymeric silicate anions. These surface active (detergent) anions are responsible for many of the silicate's deinking functions, such as emulsification and suspension of dispersed ink. This allows deinking to occur at a lower pH, which is effective in high groundwood furnishes, tending to cause less yellowing of the pulp. Silicates seem to work better with small amounts of nonionic surfactants to aid in wetting. The sodium metasilicates are most commonly used. Sodium silicate is a good stabilizing agent in hydrogen peroxide bleaching. Peroxides tend to decompose when they are in the presence of various metal ions. Silicates apparently deactivate these metal ion catalysts and thus control peroxide decomposition.

POLYPHOSPHATES, SURFACTANTS, SOLVENTS.
Sodium tripolyphosphate ($Na_5P_3O_{10}$) and sodium pyrophosphate ($Na_4P_2O_7$) are very effective at low concentrations in sequestering calcium and magnesium ions and forming uncolored complexes with cations such as iron.[4] These polyphosphates are also fairly good buffering agents and ink dispersants, and they have detergent properties.

Nonionic surfactants contain an organic part that has an affinity for oils (hydrophobe) and another part that has an affinity for the water phase (hydrophile). The hydrophobic group is usually a long-chained hydrocarbon residue, while the hydrophilic group is an ionic or highly polar group. These surfactants function in deinking systems by lowering the surface tension of water to enable it to "wet" more effectively, absorbing onto surfaces to aid in ink removal and dispersion, and by solubilization and emulsification.[5]

Two of the most common nonionic surfactants used for deinking are the ethoxylated alkyl phenols and ethoxylated linear alcohols. The hydrophilic portion of these surfactants is formed by a polyoxyethylene chain with the degree of hydrophilicity controlled by the number of ethylene oxide units. There appears to be little difference in deinking performance between the two groups of surfactants, although there is evidence that the ethoxylated alcohols perform slightly better on newsprint.[6] Optimum brightness of deinked ledger occurs with nine ethylene oxide units.[7]

Solvents are available for dissolving most inks and varnishes. Unfortunately, the cost of the majority of these prohibits their use in most deinking programs. Also, in order to function properly in the pulper, a solvent must be insoluble in water at rather low concentrations (less than 1,000 ppm). Many good ink solvents are soluble in water at this concentration and, therefore, solvent-water emulsions cannot be formed. This decreases the solvating power of the solvent. Environmental concerns also limit the use of many effective solvents, such as the chlorinated hydrocarbons. These factors have resulted in aliphatic hydrocarbons being the most common solvents used in deinking systems. Aromatic hydrocarbons are better solvents for most inks, but their higher water solubility negates their greater solvent action. Their use is also limited due to environmental concerns. A surfactant with good oil in water emulsifying properties should be included when using a solvent to ensure good emulsification of the solvent in the pulper.

Although many binders used in inks and varnishes are not soluble in the solvents that are practical for deinking, many of these binders are softened in the presence of a solvent. This allows easier breakup and dispersion by the mechanical action of the pulper and surfactants and dispersing agents that are added with the solvent.

POLYMERS, SOAPS.
Hydrophilic polymers are not widely used in deinking programs. Proponents of hydrophilic polymers claim they assist other deinking chemicals in performing detergent functions. Hydrophilic polymers are water soluble, multifunctional organic polyelectrolytes that aid in the dispersion of ink particles and build up electrostatic cleaning forces between ink particles and fiber surfaces. They function similarly to antiredeposition aids in laundry formulation.

Laboratory studies should be performed prior to mill

FIGURE 1: **Washing deinking.**

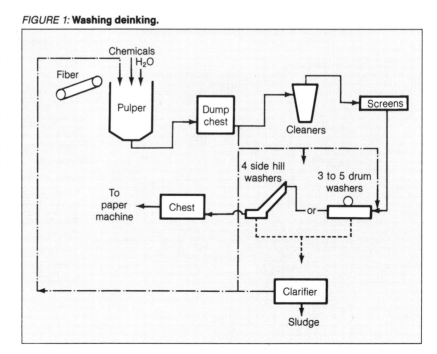

use of these costly materials. Optimum dosage depends on the chemical environment of the deinking system, and overdosing can have a negative effect on ink removal and dispersion. Two common types of hydrophilic polymers are polyacrylates and carboxymethylcellulose.

Fatty acid soaps function as collector chemicals in flotation deinking systems. Calcium soaps formed from these fatty acids and calcium ions are the most widely used flotation collectors. Flotation collector chemicals destabilize the ink dispersion and extract the ink particles from the ink-fiber suspension. These destabilized ink particles are attracted to air bubbles in the flotation cell and carried to the surface for removal. Calcium chloride is often added to provide sufficient calcium ion to convert all the fatty acid to insoluble soap.

Newer, more effective flotation collector chemicals (modified polyester resins) have been developed. They are more expensive but are effective at much lower dosage levels. They tend to act as foaming collectors, give more rapid flotation, and do not require hardness ions. The usual dosage is 0.1% to 0.3%.

WASHING AND FLOTATION CHEMISTRY.
There are some significant differences in the chemistry of washing and flotation systems. In the washing system, attempts are made to reduce ink particle size to less than 5 microns and to emulsify, dissolve, and disperse as much ink as possible. This results in optimum washing. In flotation systems, reduction of particle size to this level and emulsification of ink are undesirable, as they lead to poor separation in the cells. In combined washing and flotation systems, dispersants should not be added to the pulper but added before washing to aid in the removal of very finely dispersed ink not removed by flotation.

In the flotation system, it is also essential that all collector chemical (fatty acid or soap) be converted to insoluble calcium soap and that all of this chemical is removed by flotation in secondary cells to avoid concentration buildups in process water that would lead to lower efficiencies and machine performance problems.

FIGURE 2: **Flotation deinking.**

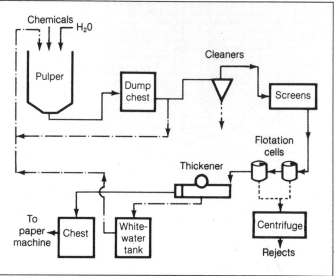

EVALUATION OF DEINKING PERFORMANCE.
Handsheet or pulp pad brightness and an estimate of dirt or specks are the methods most commonly used in evaluating deinking performance. Other sheet properties that may be important are color and ash content.

For proper evaluation of deinking performance, the objectives of the deinking program must be well specified. It is important that the test methods used in the evaluation adequately reflect the performance of the deinking operation. Brightness and dirt measurements are relatively easy to make, but both require making handsheets or pulp pads. Handsheet making is, in effect, a high dilution washing stage. The loss of fines and ink during sheet preparation may obliterate any quantitative analysis of the particular step being evaluated. Cruea recommends making pulp after dilution to 1% consistency or vacuum draining the pulp—at testing consistency without further dilution—on a 60-mesh screen.[8] These procedures provide close approximations of the condition of the pulp at a particular stage in the deinking operation. TAPPI Standard T213 os-77 ("dirt in pulp") is an adequate method for quantifying ink specks remaining in the pulp. The size (area) of a dirt speck on a sample is determined by comparing it with standard reference specks on TAPPI's dirt estimation chart. Dirt is reported as square millimeters of equivalent black area per square meter of surface examined (ppm).

Another method is to count the number of specks (ink particles) on both sides of the sample and divide by the weight of the sample. Results are reported as specks per gram of fiber. A measure of both TAPPI dirt and specks per gram may be used as a measure of degree of ink dispersion.

The dispersion in a laboratory pulper may be measured by adding small pieces (1×0.5 in.) of polyethylene to the pulp shortly before the end of the cook.[9] A clean and ink-free plastic sheet will indicate good ink dispersion, while an ink-coated plastic sheet will indicate poor ink dispersion.

RESIDUAL CHEMICAL EFFECTS.
Deinking chemicals have a number of potential negative effects, both within the deinking plant and as a result of carryover into the paper machine.

Foaming may be a problem when surfactants are used as deinking aids. In general, the most effective surfactants for deinking also have the greatest tendency to foam. Proper blending of surfactants will minimize the foam problem while maintaining deinking efficiency. In most systems, this type of foam may be controlled with small amounts of defoamer, and many mills currently using defoamer exhibit no foam problem. Defoamer should not be added to the pulper along with deinking chemicals.

These same surfactants, if carried over to the paper machine, could have a negative effect on sizing, which may cause problems with increased starch and/or coating penetration. This problem may be alleviated by isolation of the system or by adding size or increasing the level of size addition.

Calcium ion—entering the system as water hardness, as a flotation aid, or in the secondary fiber—may cause deposition on side hill screens and auxiliary equipment. Treatment for calcium carbonate deposition involves the addition of a suitable precipitation inhibitor.

Excess hydrosulfite from groundwood bleaching may hydrolyze to form thiosulfates. Thiosulfates may cause severe corrosion problems. Careful control of hydrosulfite levels or replacement of some hydrosulfite with peroxide should reduce the severity of the problem.

Dispersants and flocculants must be chosen to minimize negative interactions. Dispersant carryover to the clarifiers may reduce their performance, and carryover to the paper machine may cause problems in retention and drainage. Likewise, flocculants in whitewater from the clarifiers could interfere with ink dispersion if carried over to the deinking pulper.

Careful control of flotation collector chemistry is critical; 30% to 60% of the fatty acids added will remain in the pulp and may cause deposition problems downstream. Addition of calcium chloride to provide sufficient calcium ion for formation of the insoluble soap must be carefully controlled. Excess calcium ion may lead to carbonate scaling or be carried downstream to form insoluble calcium soaps with resin acids in pulp.

Excess chloride ion may increase corrosion, especially if there is also chloride carryover from bleaching. ∎

REFERENCES

1. J.P. Casey, ed., *Pulp and Paper Chemistry and Chemical Technology*, 3rd ed. (New York: Wiley-Interscience), vol. 1, chap. 4.
2. R.R. Kindron and J. DeCeuster, "Hydrogen Peroxide Use Benefits Washing-Deinking Systems," *Pulp and Paper* 55, no. 7 (July 1981): 176-80.
3. J.S. Falcone and R.W. Spencer, Silicates Expand Role in Waste Treatment, Bleaching, Deinking, *Pulp and Paper* 49, no. 14 (December 1975): 114-17.
4. "Phosphates for Industry," Monsanto Industrial Chemical Co., technical bulletin.
5. M.J. Rosen, *Surfactants and Interfacial Phenomena* (New York: Wiley-Interscience, 1978).
6. D.L. Wood, "Alcohol Ethoxylates and Other Anionics as Surfactants in the Deinking of Waste Paper," TAPPI pulping conference proceedings, Toronto (1982).
7. D.W. Suwala, "A Study of the Deinking Efficiency of Nonionic Surfactants," TAPPI pulping conference proceedings, Houston (1983).
8. R.P. Cruea, "Deinking: Laboratory Evaluations and Total System Concepts," *TAPPI* 61, no. 6 (June 1978): 27-30.
9. T. Mah, "Deinking of Waste Newspaper," *TAPPI* 66, no. 10 (October 1983): 81-3.
10. "The Continuing Development of Deinking," *Paper*, (Aug. 4, 1980).
11. E.C. Korte, "Use of Chemicals in Deinking," TAPPI pulping conference proceedings, New Orleans (1978).
12. "Hydrogen Peroxide for Deinking," FMC Corp., Technical Bulletin 133.
13. E. Sjostrom, *Wood Chemistry—Fundamentals and Applications* (New York, Academic Press, 1981).

Chapter 38

Cold Dispersion Unit Boosts Deinking Efficiency at Japanese Tissue Mills

Flotation and washing, combined with dispersion units, reduces number and size of ink particles and increases strength properties

By M. GILKEY, H. SHINOHARA, and H. YOSHIDA

Studies at several mills have shown that cold (non-pressurized) dispersion of deink furnishes in conjunction with flotation and washing is an effective method of ink removal. Dispersion units have been successfully installed in front of flotation and washing stages processing nonimpact-printed material as well as ultraviolet inks and xerographic CPO (computer print-out) inks. These studies have shown a reduction in the size and number of ink particles and an increase in strength properties.

Flotation also appears to be very effective for laser-printed ink removal. Laboratory work on newsprint-to-newsprint furnishes indicates dispersion is effective in reducing ink particle size for a variety of newsprint furnishes at different points in a mill's system.

To address the problem of using recycled deink stock for the production of tissue, newsprint, and other fine paper grades, approaches to deinking applications are divided into two general categories. The first category is ledger-to-tissue applications, where an increasing amount of nonimpact (laser)-printed material is being used in the starting furnish. The second category is newsprint-to-newsprint, specifically for offset-printed newspapers.

LEDGER-TO-TISSUE DEINKING. The amount of laser-printed CPO is increasing rapidly in Japan and the U.S. In response to the growing challenges these new inks present, both laboratory and mill test work have been performed to overcome deinking problems. The effective means of treating nonimpact-printed material are high-consistency, fiber-to-fiber treatment to produce good separation of ink from the fibers and flotation to remove the ink particles, which tend to remain large due to the type of ink binders used.

High-consistency pulping is an effective method of

Mr. Gilkey is with Black Clawson, Middletown, Ohio; Mr. Shinohara is with Mendori Paper Co., Kanawoe, Japan; and Mr. Yoshida is with IIM Co. Ltd., Tokyo, Japan.

imparting fiber-to-fiber contact for the treatment of non-impact printed material. High-consistency pulping takes place at approximately 15% to 18% consistency vs 6% to 8% consistency for standard- or low-consistency pulping. Based on recent laboratory studies treating two identical batches of 100% laser-printed material, high-consistency pulping at approximately 18% consistency produced much better ink separation from the fibers than did low-consistency pulping.

The observation sheets used in these studies show ink removal is much improved by the reduction of ink particles in high-consistency observation sheets compared with low-consistency observation sheets. This reduction appears to result from the rubbing action of fibers with one another under high-consistency pulping conditions, separating the ink more completely from the fibers so it can be removed more effectively by washing and/or flotation.

Examining ink particles under 30× magnification shows both the number and size of the ink particles were reduced on the high-consistency pulping observation sheets compared with the low-consistency pulping observation sheets. Using a total area of 1 cm² examined under 30x magnification on identical, 100% laser-printed starting material, the felt side of the low-consistency observation sheets had approximately four times the ink area compared with the felt side of the high-consistency observation sheets. Similar results were observed for the wire side. Results are summarized in Table 1.

In addition, the high-consistency observation sheets had not only a smaller total area of ink but also a smaller average size of these particles than did low-consistency sheets. Test work in the laboratory showed ink particle average diameter decreased from 41 microns for low-consistency pulping to 23 microns for high-consistency pulping. These results indicate that the ink is being

TABLE 1: **Flotation results on 100% laser-printed material.**

	Total number of ink particles/ 0.25 cm² area	Total ink particle area (mm²)/ 0.25 cm²
Flotation feed	735	0.132 mm²
Flotation—one stage	101	0.0032 mm²
Flotation—two stages	94	0.0029 mm²
Flotation—four stages	62	0.0019 mm²

Ink particles examined under 30x magnification.

separated from the fiber and broken down to be removed by washing more efficiently under high-consistency treatment.

U.S. MILL EXPERIENCE. A high-consistency pulper was recently installed at a U.S. mill on a ledger-to-tissue system processing a certain percentage of nonimpact-printed material. Significant improvement of sheet appearance and reduction of ink particles were apparent shortly after the startup of the high-consistency pulper.

Additional laboratory test work indicated that flotation is an effective method of removing ink particles from laser-printed material after treatment with high-consistency pulping.

Due to the nature of laser inks and their binders, a significant number of ink particles created by defibering tend to remain relatively large (about 30 microns or larger in diameter) and do not wash out readily due to their size. Flotation is more effective in removing these large ink particles. The furnish for the trials was 100% laser-printed material, which had been pulped under high-consistency conditions.

Examining flotation observation sheets under 30× magnification for a 0.25 cm² area produced the results summarized in Table 1. It can be determined that the majority of ink particles were removed after one stage of flotation and that subsequent stages reduced the number of ink particles but were not as effective as the first stage. Also, the average size of particles remaining in the flotation accepts decreased compared with the feed, indicating the larger particles were selectively removed.

JAPANESE MILL EXPERIENCE. Another method of achieving a fiber-to-fiber rubbing/rolling action is to use a continuous high-shear dispersion device (Figure 1). This device consists of a single, high-speed rotor with a series of feeding and retarding bars, which impart a high-shear mixing action to the fiber. A series of bars is also on the stator, with a relatively large clearance between the rotor and stator. This clearance minimizes fiber length degradation and freeness drop. By using a high-speed rotor, the dispenser is able to strike the fibers numerous times to knock ink loose.

One of these dispersion devices was installed, in conjunction with flotation cells and washing equipment, at Mendori Paper Co. in Japan. The mill makes toweling and facial tissue from ledger, which includes a certain percentage of nonimpact CPO and Xerox CPO. The basic system is shown in Figure 2, with the disperser located ahead of flotation and washing. Various configurations were tried before settling on the final system.

The initial system did not involve dispersion or flotation, instead only washing with a decker for ink removal. The first modification added a dispersion unit after soaking but before a vibrating screen. This was followed by washing with a decker.

To improve ink removal, a two-stage flotation cell was added near the front of the system after pulping, soaking, and screening with a vibrating screen. The dispersion was added near the end of the system for dispersing any remaining ink particles. The problem with this approach was that high-power input was required (4.5 kW-day/ton) to disperse the remaining ink particles. Since no washing stage followed dispersion, the dispersed inks remained in the stock, lowering brightness and causing ink buildup in the paper machine whitewater loop.

A third modification was implemented. It substituted

FIGURE 1: **Dispersion unit.**

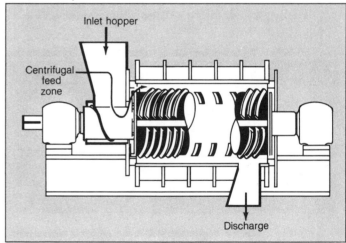

FIGURE 2: **Basic deinking system at Medori Paper Co., Japan.**

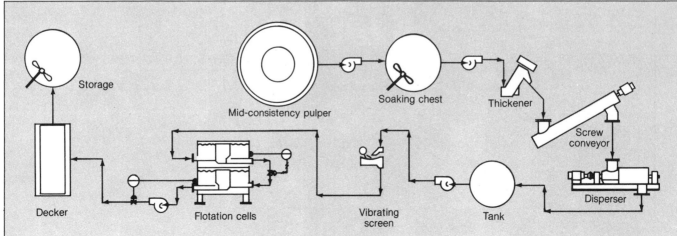

mid-consistency pulping for low-consistency pulping but kept the rest of the system the same.

The fourth configuration was tried by placing the dispersion near the front of the system, after pulping and soaking but before flotation, washing, and screening. This arrangement was the most effective. The dispersion step efficiently separated the ink from the fiber at 20% consistency with approximately 3 kW-day/ton. Temperature conditions were about 28°C in and 34°C out. The temperature increase resulted from the mechanical action of the disperser. After dispersion, the stock goes through a two-stage flotation. A collector is added in the disperser for thorough mixing with the furnish prior to flotation. After flotation, the next step is washing with a decker, followed by pressure screening and storage.

To benefit from the high-shear method of dispersion, a higher-consistency pulping system was needed. Low-consistency pulping was replaced by mid-consistency pulping. The mid-consistency pulper defibers stock into individual fibers with ink attached to the fiber as well as being in suspension. Binders are softened by soaking for periods of 6 to 12 hours. The next step is dispersion, which separates the ink from the fiber. Flotation removes the larger ink particles while washing removes smaller particles.

Since the dispersion action is more of a fiber-to-fiber rubbing action than a cutting action, freeness drop and fiber-length degradation is minimal. In addition, increases in breaking length and tear index of approximately 5% from dispersion were noted at Mendori.

A dispersion unit was also installed at a second Japanese mill, Goda Paper. This mill produces tissue from ledger. A typical starting furnish in the pulper is 80% impact CPO and 20% nonimpact CPO. This mill's dispersion system is also installed ahead of flotation and replaces a conventional refiner. The mill originally had a pulper followed by a conventional refiner to improve the sheet appearance.

To improve sheet quality, flotation cells were added to remove ink particles. Although the sheet quality improved, some ink particles remained in the observation sheets. As a final improvement, a dispersion unit was installed to replace the refiner ahead of the flotation cells. The result was a sheet virtually free of ink particles and a large improvement in sheet appearance. This improvement was reached with the power consumption remaining the same (approximately 3.5 kw-day/ton).

NEWSPRINT-TO-NEWSPRINT DEINKING. Cold dispersion application on recycled newsprint used for production of newsprint has also been tested at the Mendori and Goda mills. Several different furnishes were investigated in laboratory work. Cold dispersion proved to be an effective method of ink particle removal for newsprint-to-newsprint application.

FIGURE 3: **Typical newsprint-to-newsprint deinking system used in Japan.**

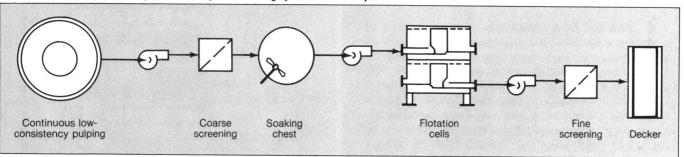

| Continuous low-consistency pulping | Coarse screening | Soaking chest | Flotation cells | Fine screening | Decker |

TABLE 2: **Effect of dispersion at different points in newsprint-to-newsprint system.**

Mill	Chemical addition	Sample point	Consistency	Without dispersion ink particles (%)	With dispersion ink particles (%)	% reduction due to dispersion
No. 1	2% NaOH	BS	15.2	0.09	0.05	45
(low-consistency		BS	20.7	0.08	0.04	50
pulping)		AW	19.1	0.05	0.04	20
	1% NaOH	BS	13.6	0.07	0.06	14
		BS	23.2	0.08	0.05	29
		AS	13.6	0.07	0.05	38
		AS	19.5	0.08	0.05	38
No. 2	1.5% NaOH	AW	19.8	0.07	0.06	14
(low-consistency	0.5% H$_2$O$_2$	AW	22.1	0.06	0.05	17
pulping)						
No. 3	1.7% NaOH	AW	17.6	0.09	0.06	33
(low-consistency	0.2% H$_2$O$_2$	AW	19.1	0.10	0.06	40
pulping)						

BS = Before soaking
AW = After washing
AS = After soaking

Chapter 39

Augusta Newsprint Brings Recycled ONP/OMG Retrofit System Online

Goal of 250-metric tpd recycled fiber is about to be reached as groundwood mill is replaced and TMP kraft use is reduced

By JIM YOUNG, Technical Editor

In late 1990, less than a year after corporate approval, the first roll of recycled paper was shipped from Augusta Newsprint Co. in Augusta, Ga. This is the first recycled fiber retrofit of a newsprint mill in the eastern U.S., and according to general manager John Weaver, the key to the fast-track startup was on-time delivery by equipment suppliers. Delivery for the $27-million project was so on time, in fact, that some equipment was being installed before the engineering was 100% complete.

The new recycled fiber line replaces a stone groundwood operation and shifts the newsprint furnish from the 75% thermomechanical pulp (TMP), 11% groundwood pulp, and 14% purchased kraft pulp used before the conversion toward a planned 65% TMP, 25% secondary fiber, and 10% kraft. Currently, the mill has been

able to run with 8% to 9% kraft. Jim Herrmann, recycled newsprint plant manager, observes that production for the new line has passed 220 metric tpd and is about to reach the goal of 250 metric tpd. The preliminary engineering study was done by Simons-Eastern; procurement and construction was handled by Fluor Daniel.

FIBER LINE. Water heated to 120°F to 140°F in a head tank is floated into a Black Clawson Hi-Con batch pulper where old newspapers (ONP) and old magazines (OMG) are repulped separately at a capacity close to 10 tons (Figure 1). From initial water fill-up to total extraction, cycle time is about 26 min for ONP and 40 min for OMG. A Hydrapurge III detrashing sytem extracts the stock from the pulper, entrapping and concentrating contaminants as the stock continues through Liquid Cyclone centrifugal cleaners that remove additional high- and medium-specific-gravity contaminants.

The ONP and OMG stocks are mixed in a blend chest ahead of the coarse screens at approximately a 70:30 ratio. This balance is critical because while the magazine stock enhances brightness, it also generates additional sludge.

The blended stock passes through the Ultra-V coarse screens at a 2.5% consistency before entering a series of four Beloit Jones PDM-6000 pressurized flotation deinking modules. Deinked at 1% consistency, the next step is reverse cleaning through a bank of Uniflow cleaners to remove lightweight contaminants. After thickening and washing in an existing 12-ft Dorr-Oliver disc filter from the groundwood mill, followed by passing through two parallel Sprout-Bauer screw presses, the stock is at 25% to 30% consistency. Effluent from the thickening process moves through a spray-filter scalping device that reclaims fiber and returns it to the process from water that is then recycled through a Krofta clarifier.

The fiber line continues past a water lock, where clarified water from the following loop joins water from the paper mill to bring stock consistency down to 0.07%. Forward cleaning in Beloit Jones Posiflow cleaners removes small-size, heavyweight particles ahead of Black Clawson Ultra-V fine screens. Two existing 9-ft disc fil-

FIGURE 1: **Augusta Newsprint's recycled fiber line.**

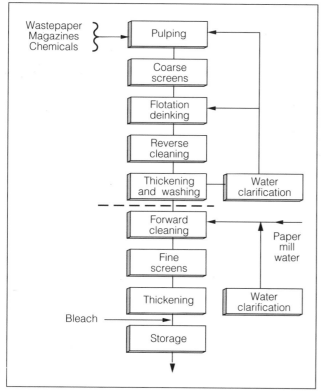

- Wastepaper / Magazines / Chemicals → Pulping
- Pulping → Coarse screens
- Coarse screens → Flotation deinking
- Flotation deinking → Reverse cleaning
- Reverse cleaning → Thickening and washing
- Water clarification
- Forward cleaning
- Fine screens
- Thickening ← Water clarification
- Bleach
- Storage
- Paper mill water

ters, also from the ground-wood mill, bring the stock to a 4.5% consistency.

The bleaching is accomplished in two stages, with hydrogen peroxide added in the pulper and sodium hydrosulfite added in the suction side of the pump that sends stock to the storage chest. Final pulp brightness is between values of 59 and 60.

Reviewing the rapid pace of the installation and start-up, Weaver and Hermann

Jim Herrmann (left) and John Weaver walk past a bank of pressurized flotation deinking modules in the new recycled fiber line.

find little they would do differently. One consideration would be having a larger selection of variously designed baskets for the coarse screen system on hand prior to startup to come up to desired capacity more quickly.

Also, Weaver recommends allowing ample time for reviewing the distributed control system (DCS) with the vendor because paper mill people traditionally aren't used to thinking in computer logic. While the Measurex DCS is working well, what was thought to be in sequence at startup sometimes wasn't. Recalling an experience

with the automated pulper, Weaver explains, "We added soap early in the process and made a giant washing machine with foam all over the place."

COLLECTION PROCESS. ONP is primarily collected from Georgia, the Carolinas, and northern Florida. Most of it comes from stock dealers affiliated with Sonoco or from municipalities that are serviced by Browning-Ferris Industries. OMG has been more difficult to collect, but it is being done through brokers and printing facilities. Some magazine suppliers may generate only one truckload a month, so numerous locations extending farther north are used. Trucks are doing a lot of backhauling, while backhauling by rail is limited thus far. Market price runs around $40/short ton, with freight costs adding $10 to $20/ton, depending on the distance hauled. On the distribution end for the recycled newsprint, sales remain primarily within the mill's original customer base. ■

Chapter 40

Recycled Paperboard Inc. Restarts Idled Mill With $14-Million Overhaul

Former Whippany paperboard mill in Clifton, N.J., producing chip board after extensive refurbishment of equipment and facilities

By ANDY HARRISON, Technical Editor

Recycled Paperboard Inc., a recycling operation established by V. Ponte & Sons Inc., started up a refurbished recycled paper mill on July 23, 1990, in Clifton, N.J. The 106,000-ft^2 facility, located on an eight-acre site that straddles the Clifton-Passaic borderline on the outskirts of Newark, was formerly operated by Whippany Paperboard, which went bankrupt in 1980. Ponte, a New York-based hauling and recycling firm, purchased the mill in 1987.

The mill will be capable of producing 300 tpd of chip board used for packaging and cardboard. The raw material for the operation will be wastepaper obtained from local companies, municipal recycling operations, commercial paper recycling operations, and individuals.

The $14-million project was funded by $10 million in low-interest financing provided through the New Jersey Economic Development Authority, a $700,000 Urban Development Action Grant (UDAG) provided through the city of Passaic by the U.S. Department of Housing & Urban Development, and the remainder provided by Recycled Paperboard.

Robert Silvestri, general manager, spearheaded the design and installation of the $14-million project.

"The cities of Clifton and Passaic played an instrumental role in turning our plans into reality," said Vincent M. Ponte, president of Recycled Paperboard. "The work of Senator Bill Bradley (D-N.J.) and his staff in guiding us through UDAG financing was particularly important. Without the UDAG, which triggered funding from the state economic agency, this project would not have moved forward."

After completion of the financing arrangements, the renovation of the mill began in late 1988. The project consisted of refurbishing the production equipment, installing new heating and ventilation systems, installing a new electrical system, and rebuilding an adjacent office building.

MILL BACKGROUND. "When Whippany Paperboard was in operation, we were their main supplier," said Ponte. "When they went bankrupt, they owed us money. One thing led to another, and we began negotiating with them and eventually purchased the mill."

The Ponte family continues to operate its recycling and hauling firm. Wastepaper is collected and sorted for the Clifton mill and other nearby mills, including Garden State Paper Co., Ft. Howard Corp., and Marcal Paper Mills Inc. Ponte's wastepaper facilities are located at Jersey City, N.J. Clifton and other surrounding towns are the primary sources.

Wastepaper is trucked into the Jersey City operation, dumped on the floor, and sorted. Sorting is done by hand for the mills. Plastic bags and Styrofoam are removed from the lower grades.

A REBUILT MACHINE. When the Whippany mill was closed, it was almost completely intact. "Nothing had been pirated from the mill," according to Bill Brand, plant manager at Recycled Paperboard. "There were even some wool felts still on the machine when the renovation began."

The beater room, the beginning of the recycling process, is primarily a Black Clawson design. The Black Clawson Hydrapurge II and Selectpurge II system replaced a bucket-style junker, making the system more efficient, more maintenance-free, and easier to operate.

Updated beater room equipment improves operator efficiency in the mill as well as quality of the finished sheet.

The 20-ft pulper was in nearly new condition when the mill was shut down. The mill, still in the process of bringing the beater room up to date, has also added Black Clawson V-300 screens, cyclone cleaners, and vibrating screens.

Four separate stock systems are capable of feeding the mill's two machines. Three stock systems are designated for the cylinder machine, with one system for the fourdrinier machine. Each of the stock systems can be operated independently, but they are all connected in such a way that one can support another. They are separate but interchangeable. Two new 1,000-hp Beloit Jones double disc refiners have been installed in the filler system and three smaller Sprout Waldron refiners for the liner system. Those pipes are also interchangeable.

All of the spills of the rejects in the mill are collected and pumped to a Beloit Jones poly-disc filter. Fiber is removed and sent back into the filler systems, and the water is reused.

The existing 136-in.-trim cylinder machine is from Beloit, consisting of 48-in.-dia counterflow vats with a conventional long top fabric arrangement. New Albany Engineered Systems showering equipment was installed for the fabrics and the cylinders. A completely upgraded vacuum system was installed, consisting of Nash 9004 vacuum pumps with accompanying separators and piping systems.

The machine has three suction presses, a suction drum, a plain primary, main, second, and third press. The press section is a reverse press with two smooth roles, each applied to the bottom and top of the sheet respectively. This gives the mill more flexibility in allowing for smoothness on each side of the sheet. A conventional headbox arrangement has typical chemical and dye addition points so color can be added to any part of any vat.

A new Liquiflow lubrication system with new bearings was added to the 170 stacked dryer section. The existing dryers were tested and reused.

The cylinder machine produces a full range of uncoated grades in calipers 0.02 through 0.075, single ply. The mill uses a slightly higher-grade paper in the outside plys. The filler plys for the most part are lower-grade wastepaper. Variations to the wastepaper input depend on the finished product produced. High volume commodities in white and colored stock will be produced along with the high-density, high-strength grades and some specialty grades.

The startup of No. 1 machine, a fourdrinier with 114-in. trim, is planned for mid-1991. This machine will produce a caliper range from 0.009 through 0.035.

A Measurex process control system was obtained through a closed mill in Maine. The eight-month-old system had not started up, leaving it virtually new. As a result, the mill now has basis-weight control on the wet end and dry end of the machine for a third of the cost that a new system would have commanded.

The winder, originally a Cameron, was rebuilt by A&F. The rebuilt winder is capable of making 76-in.-dia paper rolls. The winder also includes new slitters, a new Mount Hope roll, and a new drive system. The role winder drums were turned and plasma coated.

TABLE 1: **Suppliers for the Clifton recycling operation.**

A & F Corp.	Machine winders
Albany Engineered Systems	Purgable showers
Allen Bradley	PLCs
Beloit Jones	Refiners
Bird Johnson	Vibratory screens
Black Clawson	Trash removal system, cyclone high-density cleaners, Hydra-purge II, Selectpurge II, V-300 high-consistency screen, two-valve junker
Brookbridge	Development construction management
Cleaver Brooks	Package boiler
Cutler Hammer	PLCs
DeZurik	Consistency control system
Eastern Energy	Energy consultants
Foxboro	Smart controllers
Gould Pumps	Fan pumps
Liquiflow	Lubrication system
Measurex	Process control system
Michaels Electric	Electrical contractor
Nash	Vacuum system
Nissan	Forklift trucks
North Jersey Mechanical Contractors & Arlo	Mechanical contractors
Passaic Rubber	Press rolls
Spinella & Spinella	Architects
Sprout Bauer	Hydrasieves
Sprout Waldron	Refiners
Stamm	Dryer drainage system
Stowe-Woodward	Dri-Press rolls

An antiquated electrical system was brought up to date with full 5,000-kVA service. The 50-year-old electrical distribution was replaced with a combination of new and used equipment. A great deal of work has gone into the building renovation area, including roof repairs, replacements, and painting.

FAST-TRACKED JOB. The ownership objective was to be operating as quickly as possible. A construction management team was created and headed by Robert Silvestri, general manager of Recycled Paperboard.

"It would normally have taken four to six months to do proper engineering and two years to do the job," said Silvestri. "Bearing that in mind, we basically did everything ourselves on the fly."

Expertise came from numerous sources, including in-house experience, manufacturers, local and state officials, and the power companies. Though much of the equipment was already in place, antiquated equipment had to be replaced, the deteriorating building needed repair, and code violations had to be addressed.

The in-house experience came from those who had previously worked for the Whippany mill and Silvestri, with background mostly from high-rise construction. Art Lockwood, an in-house paper expert with 30 years' experience, was originally with Whippany and was performing outside consulting after the mill shut down. He went to work with Recycled Paperboard when the mill reopened.

Many of the people hired for construction of the project were kept on as mill operators. This tactic, in part, deals with the difficulty of competing for personnel in a metropolitan area because there are other paper mills in the area and other trades where people can find jobs.

Suppliers were given the mill's objectives and then bid competitively to supply the equipment. In this process, those vendors also supplied valuable proposals and engineering assistance to the mill.

At construction meetings, held weekly with in-house personnel, the objectives were reviewed, with a set agenda for the whole job. The mill also met every week with the unions to discuss how the job would run. As many as 47 to 60 union electricians and 40 union steamfitters were on the job at one time. "We really needed a good working relationship with the union to do the job this fast," Silvestri explained. "They wanted the work, and so they worked very closely with us."

Pictured are Vincent J. Ponte (left) and Vincent M. Ponte, secretary and president, respectively, of Recycled Paperboard Inc.

Code violations, including OSHA, steam, and electrical violations, had to be cleared before operation began. Officials from Clifton and the state of New Jersey were called to the mill to provide proposals for proper operating procedures and guidelines. Proposals prepared by government officials and the insurance company were used in bid specs for equipment and construction.

"I hired a local mechanical engineer with paper experience and picked his brain," Silvestri said. "We know that this job did not receive the full engineering attention that such a job normally gets, but we are also operating a year and a half early. It is much easier to correct things out of cash flow."

The largest void at the mill was electrical. Records were not available. Nameplates of each piece of equipment were listed. Equipment was then graded as to whether or not it was going to be reused, based on what grades the mill was going to make.

When construction began, only 200-amp service was at the mill. When the Whippany mill shut down, the public service company bypassed power to the mill. Portable generators had to be brought in for construction until permanent power could be installed.

"The power company offered to supply a temporary 2,000-amp service to the mill," Silvestri explained. "But I did not want to get into the position where temporary wiring was being installed, then removed, and then permanent wiring installed. We would end up doing the same work twice, and typically what happens when you put up temporary wiring is that the temporary becomes permanent."

The electrical equipment, therefore, had a critical delivery schedule. All the starters, distribution panels, layouts, and drawings were coordinated and supplied by Cutler Hammer and arrived on the mill site in five weeks. Used switchgear was located with the power companies' help. One 3,000-kVA switchgear unit was located in New Jersey.

"We went from 200 amps to 5,000-amp service rating in a matter of months," Silvestri explained. "Normal delivery time for most electrical items is 20 to 30 weeks. Finding the switchgear at this electrical supply company right in our backyard was very fortunate. We could not have made our construction schedule without the availability of these electrical items." Electricity to the mill allowed the start-up of the new package boiler, followed by steam power being supplied to the mill. ■

Chapter 41

Wisconsin Tissue Expands Recycled Capacity with $160-Million Upgrade

Menasha, Wis., mill project features expanded deinking plant and new paper machine, wastewater treatment operation, and converting facilities

The Eagle II expansion at Wisconsin Tissue will increase overall production by 70%.

By ANDY HARRISON, Technical Editor

The startup of the No. 4 paper machine on June 24, 1990, six months ahead of schedule, was the crowning achievement of a $160-million expansion project at Wisconsin Tissue Mills' Menasha, Wis., mill. Within 24 hours of startup, paper from the machine was processed through the converting operation and shipped.

The expansion, called Eagle II, included the new paper machine, an additional water plant, an expanded deinking facility, a wastewater treatment facility, an additional warehouse area, more converting machines, and expanded computerized storage and shipping facilities to support the new tissue production capacity. Eagle II adds 80,000 tpy of production, increasing capacity at the mill by 70%.

Wisconsin Tissue has achieved a market niche in the commercial "away from home" sector of the tissue business, producing more than 2,500 tissue products, including napkins, facial tissue, toilet tissue, toweling, place mats, tray covers, table covers, and wipers. The new No. 4 machine will produce mainly high-quality natural and white towels and napkin stock.

Currently, all these products are produced from 100% recoverable paperstock, following a tradition of recycling at Wisconsin Tissue that dates from 1927. The mill recycles a broad range of recycled paper using more than 120 suppliers to secure wastepaper for the manufacture of all its products.

"We have had a very successful startup mainly because of our team approach to the project," said Bill New, executive vice president. "Wisconsin Tissue now has some of the finest equipment made for the production and converting of tissue products from 100% recoverable paperstock. Moreover, our people were directly involved in the design, installation, implementation, operation, and maintenance of this equipment from the very beginning."

MILL HISTORY. When the Asmuth family sold Wisconsin Tissue to Philip Morris in 1977, the business began an aggressive expansion approach, introducing a new product line with the backing of a new paper machine (No. 3), a new deinking facility, and a new automated storage and retrieval system (AS/RS). That product line consisted of toilet tissue and towels, which were made by Wisconsin Tissue in the 1940s and 1950s, but the line was discontinued.

The success of the installation and marketing of new products to an existing customer base prompted a proposal in 1984 for an additional expansion, which became known as the Eagle Project. However, Philip Morris had other plans, and the project was put on hold when Wisconsin Tissue was sold to Chesapeake Corp. in 1985.

Chesapeake bought Wisconsin Tissue because of the modern facilities, the excellent customer relationship, and the solid management team that had carried over from the days when the mill was family owned. In 1988, Eagle II was resurrected, and Wisconsin Tissue's aggressive expansion continued.

THE NEW NO. 4. The featured component and culmination of Eagle II is a Beloit paper machine, consisting of a C-wrap, twin-wire former with a Concept III headbox, yankee dryer, and afterdryers. The 210-in.-trim machine is capable of running at 6,000 fpm.

Experience with the startup of No. 3 machine in 1982

The 210-in.-trim Beloit paper machine is capable of speeds up to 6,000 fpm.

gave Wisconsin Tissue a guidepost to plan for production and quality expectations. After only six months of operation, No. 4 machine is operating at 100% of projected capacity. Because No. 4 produces many of the same products as No. 3, both machines can run longer, with less downtime due to changeovers. The productivity of No. 3 has improved significantly since No. 4 started up.

"We are a year ahead of the projected ramp of where Eagle II was expected to be at this point," said Sal Cianciola, president of Wisconsin Tissue and group vice president of Tissue Products for Chesapeake Corp. "And we are probably going to increase production by 90,000 tons rather than 80,000 tpy."

The Beloit C-Wrap machine consists of an 18-ft-dia yankee dryer, with a single-felt, double pressure roll arrangement. The main difference between the new No. 4 and No. 3 lies in the afterdryers on the new machine. The Beloit afterdryer section consists of nine 6-ft-dia dryers. When dry crepe paper is produced, the sheet is wound up at the reel. However, to run wet crepe paper, the sheet from the yankee dryer is transferred over a bridge to the afterdryers.

The transfer bridge, a collaboration between Beloit and Wisconsin Tissue, allows the machine to operate at maximum efficiency whether running dry or wet crepe paper. Rather than slowing down the machine to run wet crepe paper, as is done on No. 3, the sheet on No. 4 is dried by the yankee dryer to a 15% to 20% moisture level before going on to the afterdryers.

As part of air environmental requirements on the machine, a carbon absorption unit built by Amcec was installed to

The mill produces a broad range of tissue products, all from 100% recoverable paperstock.

Effluent from the mill goes through primary, secondary, and tertiary stages of water clarification before going out to the lake.

handle volatile organic compound (VOC) emissions on Nos. 3 and 4 machines. VOCs occur when solvents are used to clean stickies that accumulate on machine wires and fabrics.

Since solvents are used only on a periodic basis, the carbon absorption unit was designed to handle only one paper machine at a time. Interlocks exclusively allow solvent to be applied to either No. 3 or No. 4 at any given time.

The twin-wire former has an exhaust fan that blows air to the atmosphere. Vacuum pump exhaust from the machine also goes to the atmosphere. When solvent is required on the machine, the VOC system is manually activated. Dampers change so that emissions are diverted to the carbon absorption system. Solvents are applied to the machine, and the air laden with VOCs passes through three large chambers filled with activated carbon, before being blown out to the atmosphere by a large fan.

Air monitors keep the VOC system operating until VOC levels drop below a minimum. Calculations are done to determine the efficiency of the carbon bed, which the mill reports to the state regularly.

Steam for the new paper mill operation is supplied by a Babcock & Wilcox 60,000-lb gas-fired boiler. Electrical power is purchased from a power company at 34,500 v and stepped down by two 50-mVA GE transformers to 4,160 v. Motors above 200 hp use 4,160 v, and smaller motors use 480 v from Westinghouse 1,500- and 2,000-kVA substations.

DEINKING PLANT EXPANSION. During the past 11

years, Wisconsin Tissue has committed more than $68 million to its deinking facilities, including a $33-million expansion that was part of the Eagle II project. The new investment has enabled the mill to increase its use of postconsumer wastepaper and other lower grades of waste significantly.

The basic design of the deinking plant involves pulping, screening, cleaning, flotation, and bleaching sequences that remove contaminants from the various recoverable fibers used in the process. Major pieces of equipment include pulpers from Black Clawson and Lodding/Aikawa, pressure screens from Bird and Black Clawson, cleaners from Bird, Noss, and Beloit Jones Div., and a flotation system from Krofta.

Major pieces of equipment in the bleach plant include a Dorr-Oliver chlorine washer, Kamyr medium-consistency pumps, an Aris Andritz press with a medium-consistency headbox, SHW towers that are built with unique nonbridging devices, and Kajaani sensors that detect brightness, residual peroxide, and residual chlorine.

WATER AND EFFLUENT TREATMENT. The mill can treat up to 6 million gal/day of water. The new wastewater treatment plant, a three-stage system, including primary, secondary, and tertiary clarification, treats all water and effluent before the water is returned to the lake.

"Water taken from Little Lake Butte des Morts is used in the papermaking process, cleaned, and then sent back out," according to Bernie Kopp, project manager and plant engineer. "The water is usually cleaner going out of the effluent plant than when it is pumped into the mill," he said.

The surface water treatment plant and effluent water treatment plant are computerized on a Honeywell TDC 3000 system. The system is part of a large overall network that also controls the automation of No. 4 paper machine and the deinking plant. Operators from the various individual plants not only have control over their areas but also have access to displays throughout the control network.

CONVERTING OPERATIONS. The first phase of Eagle II began taking shape on Apr. 15, 1989, with the startup of the automatic guided vehicles (AGVs) and the AS/RS expansion. Four more storage cranes, 15 automated guided vehicles, and 17 shipping doors were added to the existing AS/RS system. Since the AS/RS system expansion startup, more than 40 converting machines, (mostly Bretting and Perini) have been installed.

The 115,000-ft^2 facility is controlled automatically by an IBM AS/400 Model B60 computer. This computerized distribution center handles customer service, order entry, shipping, sales, and administration. It also pilots the AGVs, cranes, and inventory control. Real-time inventory and up-to-the-minute production data allow for speedy distribution.

The computer-controlled storage-retrieval cranes are able to handle 5.9 million ft^3. Pallet loads of finished goods are delivered and positioned in the warehouse, product location is recorded, and then the product is retrieved for shipment at a future date. Many products are untouched from the time they are produced until they are loaded for shipment. A two-story distribution building, adjacent to the AS/RS, includes 24 docks and inside facilities to load eight railroad cars.

TEAM DESIGN. "We set up a project team at the design phase," said Kopp. "The team that was set up consisted of a number of individuals that work for me (electrical and mechanical engineers) and personnel from each department in the project," he continued.

Dan Waselchuck, vice president-engineering/technology, served as overall project manager. Jim Haeffele, No. 4 paper machine manager, represented production on the paper mill end. Steve Smith from the deinking plant and Gene Koeppel from the water treatment plant also served. This group formed a team with engineers from Simons-Eastern, which handled the process and design of the paper mill and deinking plant. CPR & Associates oversaw civil, structural, and architectural work. Team members met monthly with Simons-Eastern in Atlanta, Ga., to go over drawings, flow diagrams, water balances, piping arrangements, and equipment layouts.

Reviews were also made weekly with top management. Throughout the entire project, Wisconsin Tissue maintenance, production, engineering, and purchasing personnel were involved. When equipment selection was considered, vendors came to the mill and made

their presentations to the design team as well as to the mill personnel that had a stake in the process.

Startup of the new paper mill required breaking down the project into smaller, manageable systems. Specific areas of the deinking plant, paper mill, or treatment plant were designated and highlighted on P&ID drawings for the contractors. Meetings were held with maintenance and engineering personnel as well as contractors to define which equipment, what instrumentation loops, and what motors were to be ready.

When the contractor finished a system, static and dynamic tests were performed by the mill. Static tests included visually inspecting the system, stroking valves, turning motors, etc. Dynamic testing involved actually operating a system with material.

"We wanted to make sure each system was operational before we attempted to make paper," said Kopp. For example, the startup of the paper machine broke system required filling the broke pulper, pumping water through piping, and working automatic valves.

"We had to install some bypass piping in the system to keep the material from flowing into other areas," Kopp said. "However, as it turns out, the bypass piping comes in handy in certain situations in the operation of the paper machine." ∎

TABLE 1: **Suppliers for the Eagle II Project.**

Aikawa	Scavenger detrashing units
Albany International	Showers
Allen Bradley	MCCs, variable-speed a.c. drives
Allen Bradley Stromberg	d.c. drives
Amcec	Carbon absorption system
Babcock & Wilcox	Boiler
Beloit	Paper machine
Beloit Jones	Saveall, refiner, headbox screen, cleaners
Bird Escher Wyss	Pressure screens
Black Clawson	Deflaker, machine pulpers, vibrating screen, repulper, Selectifier screens
Boldt Construction	General contractor
CPR & Associates	Civil, structural, and architectural work
Donohue & Associates	Engineering, treatment plant
Dorr-Oliver	Washers
EIMCO	Primary clarifiers and secondary clarifiers
EM	Vacuum pumps, motor, 2,000 hp
Falk	Gearboxes
Flakt Ross	Yankee hood
General Electric	Transformers, d.c. motors
Gould Pumps	Centrifugal pumps, fan pump
Honeywell	TDC 3000 DCS system, PLCs
Kamyr	Medium-consistency pumps
Krofta Engineering	Sandfloat clarifier, spray filter, Super Cell air flotation unit
Lodding	High-consistency pulpers
Marathon	Motors, 200 hp and below
Measurex	Basis weight and moisture control
Nash	Vacuum pumps
Noss	Cleaners
Siemens	Switchgear, motors, 250 hp and above
Simons-Eastern Consultants	Engineering for deinking plant, paper mill
Valmet Enerdry	Afterdryers hood, trim system
Westinghouse	Unit substations

Chapter 42

MacMillan Bloedel Pine Hill Expansion is Quality Driven

Greater linerboard sheet strength and smoothness is the goal as freight regulations shift emphasis, recycling concerns increase

By JIM YOUNG, Technical Editor

The expansion program at MacMillan Bloedel Inc.'s (MBI) containerboard mill in Pine Hill, Ala., has a dual focus of quality enhancement and increased capacity, with the former driving the latter. Installations improving quality call for additional pulp, which in turn opens the door to using more secondary fiber.

In 1990, PM No. 1, the mill's linerboard machine, received a new Beloit dual-flow primary headbox and top-wire forming unit, followed by a new Valmet winder. A fractionation system, including Beloit's Bel Bond washers and fractionation screens supplied by Bird Escher Wyss, was installed in the pulp mill to fractionate a short, clean fiber for the top liner furnish.

PM No. 1 will continue to improve sheet strength and smoothness when it brings online a new secondary headbox, another top-wire forming unit installed on the basesheet ahead of the secondary headbox, a rebuilt press section with a Beloit Extended Nip Press, and additional dryer cylinders replacing a breaker stack. "Compression strength is the name of the game in the '90s, and we have to do something about it," says Van McCamish, manager-operations and manufacturing. These modifications will allow the 1,250-tpd machine to produce a three-ply sheet, while at the same time adding 200-tpd capacity.

McCamish notes that the pulp mill and the original old corrugated container (OCC) plant are supplying all of the pulp that they can produce, so, in lieu of adding another pulp mill, recovery boiler, and lime kiln, MBI opted for an additional secondary fiber plant. The older OCC system produces 300 tpd of machine-ready secondary fiber, and the recent startup of a new OCC system is adding an additional 350-tpd capacity. The mill runs 24 hours/day, seven days/week.

PM No. 1 had been running in the neighborhood of

From left, Brooks Donald, Van McCamish, and Trenton Agee observe the new OCC line.

8% to 10% secondary fiber before last year's upgrade advanced the range from 12% to 14%. When the revised wet end and press section come online in June 1991, the target is 25%, all of which will go to the middle ply in a mixture with broke. The bottom ply will be virgin kraft pulp, and the top ply will be fractionated pulp. The remaining fiber from the new OCC line will be added to PM No. 2, the corrugated medium machine, to bring its secondary fiber content up to a 30% to 35% range from the current 18% to 20%.

Engineering for the $66-million upgrade was provided by BE&K. Total optimization of both machines, including a new drive to take PM No. 1 past 2,100 fpm, is estimated to carry to 1994.

OCC COLLECTION. Quality likewise is the overriding concern in OCC collection. Hotmelt adhesives and wax-coated boxes cause most recycling problems, followed by plastics, such as those found in shrink-wrap packaging. Edward Harvey, corporate director-transportation and recycled fiber, believes that it may be possible to reduce these contaminants through the influence that OCC collectors have with the recipients of packaged goods, continuing back to their shippers. He cites an example where this was successfully done several years ago to solve OCC recycling problems caused by asphalt-laminated tape.

To avoid short-term market whims in meeting the Pine Hill mill's doubled OCC supply requirements, Harvey has established long-term contracts in the Deep South with grocery stores and packing house collectors that gather OCC from both large trash-hauling operations and small bailers. He is pleased with the freight logistics in southwest Alabama, where several mills ship paper,

FIGURE 1: **OCC flow diagram.**

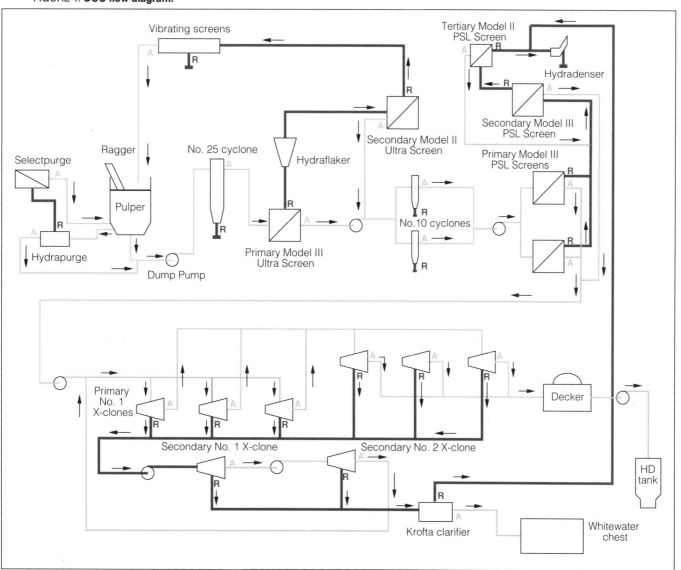

leaving an excess of both truck and rail backhauling capacity available.

Harvey lends his voice to the chorus of those who believe that recycling should be driven by economics rather than legislation. "If you can make it attractive enough, you can do it," he says, adding, "It's an exciting time for recycling, particularly in the southern kraft mills."

NEW OCC FIBER LINE. The new OCC line basically mirrors the older line. It starts with a Black Clawson Model 9D continuous Hydrapulper with a 500-hp motor driving a 63-in. rotor at 200 rpm. It is currently pulping at a consistency between 2.3% and 2.5% (Figure 1).

Accepts pass through ⅝-in. holes to the cleaning and screening line. Reject material that can be further refined passes through a Hydrapurge II and Selectpurge loop; other material is discharged to a trash well with a clamshell hoist.

Stock leaves the pulper at a 439.7-tpd rate at about 2.7% consistency. This figures to be a flow rate of approximately 2,705 gpm. It continues through a single No. 25 Liquid Cyclone cleaner, where heavy contaminants are removed before a Worthington pump advances it to a 50,000-gal dump chest, from where it is pumped to a primary Model III Ultra Screen. Brooks Donald, project engineer, estimates about two-thirds of the stock coming into the primary screens will be accepted, and the one-third reject stock circulates through a Hydraflaker refiner and a secondary Model II Ultra Screen.

Accepts from the secondary screen, an estimated 99 tpd of the 142 tpd being recycled in this loop, return to the primary screen. The remaining stock passes over a vibrating screen that removes heavy contaminants, and accepts return to the pulper to start over in the process.

No. 10 Liquid Cyclones and primary Model III PSL screens, two each in parallel, constitute the next stage with rejects circulating through secondary and tertiary PSL screens. Final rejects from this loop, at a 1.65% consistency, are sent to a Hydradenser, where they are trapped in a set of screens, compressed, and discharged from the system. Returning accepts from the secondary and tertiary PSL screens join the initial accepts from the primary screen to yield a 386-tpd flow rate to the X-Clone feed tank.

The X-Clone feed tank supplies stock to six banks of primary X-Clone cleaners and two banks of secondary

Ralph Michaels (left) and Ed Harvey, responsible for MBI containerboard marketing and OCC collection, respectively, agree that these are interesting times for the corrugated container industry.

X-Clone cleaners. At the completion of the X-Clone cleaning stage, accepts move on to an Ingersoll-Rand vacuum decker, where consistency is raised to approximately 12% to 14% before an Ahlstrom MC 22 pump sends the stock to a 300-tpd storage tank. Rejects are passed on to a Krofta feed tank supplying a clarifier of the same make. Clarifier rejects go to the Hydradenser, and whitewater is refiltered into a whitewater tank for reuse in the process.

MARKETING. The recent startup of the new OCC line and the linerboard machine upgrade coming online this summer coincide with changes in the corrugated container regulations of the railroad's Rule 41 and the trucking industry's Item 222. The changes shift priority from bursting strength to compression strength. Ralph Michaels, MBI vice president-marketing, echoes Ed Harvey's sentiments that these are interesting times for the corrugated container industry. "We should have the capabilities of producing a higher ring-crush sheet that is going to have a decent percentage of recycled material in it," he predicts, "so I think we are going to answer two questions at the same time."

These answers will be determined after the modified stock has been on the market for a while, meeting the demands of the end user. Michaels believes the revisions at Pine Hill place his company in a position to answer a lot of questions that customers are asking. "We all have a lot to learn in a short time," he says. ■

TABLE 1: **Major suppliers of the MBI expansion.**

Beloit	Wet end rebuild, press section
Valmet	Winder
Black Clawson	Old corrugated container line
Worthington	Pumps
Ahlstrom	Pumps
Ingersoll-Rand	Decker
Krofta	Clarifier

Chapter 43

Mobile Paperboard's Recycled Board Cylinder Machine First in 15 Years

With a second "new" machine online, the Newark Group mill at Mobile, Ala., can now produce up to 400 tpd of various recycled boxboard grades

By KEN L. PATRICK, Editor in Chief

In early 1990, Mobile Paperboard Corp., a part of the Newark Group, started up a "resurrected" cylinder machine at its Mobile, Ala., facility, currently the oldest operating paper mill in the state of Alabama. Including a new beater room to provide furnish for No. 2 machine, the expansion cost approximately $10 million and doubled the mill's capacity to more than 120,000 tpy of recycled grades.

Mobile Paperboard's products are used in the manufacture of a wide variety of converted and semiconverted products. These include cereal boxes, detergent boxes, shoe boxes, cones, cores, tubes, produce shipping boxes, board for book covers, three-ring binders, game boards, and furniture molding.

COMPANY BACKGROUND. The salvaged No. 2 machine was purchased from Scott Paper Co.'s mill in Mobile and was heavily rebuilt by Mobile Paperboard.

Cylinders on wet end of No. 2 machine are run on a closed pressure loop rather than a standard gravity headbox.

When in operation at Scott, the machine won the Army/Navy "E" award for exceptional performance on the industrial front during World War II. The wet end (cylinder) section has been almost completely rebuilt, new presses have been installed along with additional drying capacity, and the latest process controls are being used.

The Mobile mill began operations in 1918 as Gulf Paper Mills Corp., which was destroyed by fire in 1923. It was rebuilt as Mobile Paper Mills Inc. at the present site and operated under that name until 1952 when it was sold to Stone Container Corp. Stone subsequently sold the mill to the Newark Group in 1984.

Currently, the mill employs about 200 people, with some 60 being new employees brought on for the No. 2 machine expansion. In addition to receiving 24,000 tpy of recyclable old newspapers, corrugated boxes, office waste, and other mixed wastepaper onsite, Mobile Paperboard also accepts 50,000 lb of aluminum cans and 40,000 lb of beverage glass/year, which are sent to specialized recyclers of these materials in the area.

The Newark Group operates 11 recycled paper mills nationwide, with a total of 16 paper machines producing more than 875,000 tpy and consuming more than 1 million tons of wastepaper annually. In addition, the company operates nine commercial wastepaper packing plants and regional sales offices, handling about 2 million tpy of wastepaper for sale in domestic and export markets.

The Newark Group's converting and semiconverting operations include BCI (Book Covers Inc.), which manufactures (at four locations) a variety of laminated paperboards for use primarily in cover and binder applications; SFP (Southern Foam Products) in Dalton, Ga., which manufactures foam and board combinations for the book, album, and protective packaging industries; Growers Packaging Co. in Fresno Calif., which makes grape and tree fruit packaging from Fiberwrap, a special laminated board developed by BCI; Cedartown/Misco, which manufactures cores and tubes at six southeastern

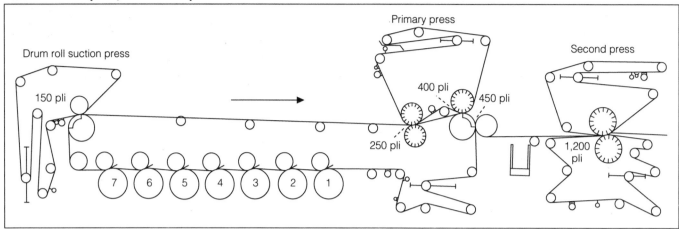

locations; and Freeport Paper Products Inc., which supplies custom printed pizza boxes out of Freeport, Long Island.

ALABAMA RECYCLING GOALS. Like most states in the U.S., Alabama has recently set some definitive recycling goals. Several recycling programs have been launched in state government, and private business and industry are being urged to participate. State Law Act 89-824, passed in 1989, calls on separate county governments to develop immediately a comprehensive waste management plan and establishes a statewide recycling target of 25%.

In dedicating the Mobile Paperboard expansion, Governor Guy Hunt pointed out that "for every ton of wastepaper recycled at the mill, 3.3 yd³ of landfill space is not needed." Based on the mill's current capacity with No. 2 machine online, this represents approximately 400,000 yd³ of landfill space each year.

Edward Mullen, chairman of the board for the Newark Group, was at the mill's dedication, along with Fred Von Zuben, president. According to Mullen, the company decided to expand the Mobile operation "because of its proximity to an existing and growing customer base and easy access to the deep water port of Mobile."

WASTEPAPER FURNISH. Brian Canty, assistant mill superintendent, explained that No. 1 machine has nine cylinders. The first and last cylinders (Nos. 1 and 9) are used for applying top and bottom liners of higher-quality fibers, e.g., from double lined kraft (DLK). The middle filler sheet is made of a broad mix of wastepaper, including all local "off the street" collections that come in loose. The community collections are "a pretty good mix," according to Canty. Daily collections vary from about 80 to 120 to 130 tons, which is approaching 50% of the furnish for No. 1 machine. The caliper of heavier grades made on this machine ranges between 20 and 60 points.

No. 2 machine currently has only seven cylinders and does not yet apply top and bottom liners. In the near future, however, it will also be fitted with Nos. 1 and 9 cylinders for applying higher-quality surface plies. In the meantime, furnish for the new machine is comprised of old corrugated containers (OCC), core tube waste from the Cedartown/Misco operations, chip-box cuttings, and mixed paper acquired through the Newark Group's own wastepaper packing plants.

About 75% of the lighter-weight paperboard from No. 2 machine, with caliper ranging between about 16 and 40 points, is sold "back" to the parent company's core and tube converting operations as well as other independent converters. However, these sales are not necessarily "captive." The company's converting plants can buy board from any manufacturer; likewise, the com-

The press section has a rebuilt primary press and a completely new second press with a nip loading up to 1,200 pli.

Dryer section has 68 4-ft-dia dryers in five drive sections, followed by two calender stacks.

After the calender stacks, the reel, with a dry end trim of 110 in., is sent to a winder for slitting to customer sizes.

pany's board mills can and do sell their products to other converters. The remaining production from No. 2 machine is mainly chipboard-type grades for manufacture of industrial boxes and assorted containers.

Very little old newsprint (ONP) is currently used on No. 2 machine, but No. 1 machine, which has a three-stock system, does use considerable amounts of this fiber in its center filler sheet, Canty explained. When lining cylinders have been installed on No. 2 machine, its filler sheet furnish will also contain increased amounts of ONP and off-the-street mixed wastepaper. All of the mill's outside wastepaper bales are being shipped in by truck.

BEATER ROOM. The stock preparation system for No. 2 machine consists basically of a 20-ft-dia Black Clawson Hydrapulper, followed by Black Clawson primary, secondary, and tertiary screening and six C-E Bauer sidehill screens for thickening. A Voith Contaminex unit and a Black Clawson Selectpurge screen are used on the junker for trash removal. No deinking is done at this mill.

Stock from the pulper passes through a dilution tank before being pumped to the Ultra Screen III primary screen, which has 0.014-in. slots, as do the secondary and tertiary screens. Primary accepts are sent to the sidehill screens. Rejects pass through a primary rejects tank to one of two secondary Selectifier screens. Secondary screen accepts are sent to the sidehill screens along with primary screen accepts, while rejects are collected in a rejects tank and sent to the tertiary Selectifier screen. Tertiary accepts can be sent to the primary rejects tank or to the sidehill screens. Final tertiary screen rejects pass over a Black Clawson tailing screen prior to disposal.

Stock from the sidehill screens is collected in a filler dump chest and sent to the refiners at 4% consistency. Two of the three refiners are Black Clawson 34-in. double disc units, each with 1,000-hp motors. The tickle refiner is a 26-in. Pilao triple disc unit with a 450-hp motor. Refined stock goes to a filler loop chest before being sent to the machine at about 3.5% consistency.

NO. 2 CYLINDER MACHINE. No. 2 board machine cylinders are rebuilt versions of those that were used on the original Scott Paper machine, but the stainless steel vats were fabricated locally. All seven cylinders are 48 in. in dia with a 124-in. face. Canty pointed out that operation of the cylinders is rather unique in that they are run on a closed pressure loop rather than a gravity headbox.

Currently, the seven cylinders are all counterflow types. But plans are for the new Nos. 1 and 9 outside lining cylinders to be of uniflow design. Canty explained that uniflow cylinders generally produce a smoother, lighter ply than the counterflow units, which will be producing a filler ply after the lining cylinders are added, possibly later this year. Furnish for the lining plies will be primarily from clean DLK clipping, according to Canty.

The formed sheet goes through a rebuilt Escher Wyss drum roll suction press, loaded up to 150 pli, then changes direction and goes back down the machine to the rebuilt primary press, which contains a Beloit Compress unit and has consecutive nips of 250 pli, 400 pli, and 450 pli (Figure 1). The second press is a brand new Miami Machine unit with rubber-covered, blind-drilled rolls and a nip loading up to 1,200 pli.

The first section of 13 Moore & White dryers is from the original Scott Paper machine, as is the rewinder. Altogether, the machine has 68 48-in. dryers in five drive sections. The dryers in sections two through five—Black

Clawson units followed by Lukenwelds—were acquired from various sources.

Two calender stacks follow the dryers. The first is a wet stack where a moderate finish can be applied to both sides, primarily water and starch—no calender stain or color is being added at this time. The calendered sheet is then wound on a horizontal pope reel before going to the completely renovated Cameron winder. Dry end trim is 110 in.

Slitters on the winder, which operates at speeds up to 3,000 fpm, can be positioned from a minimum of 4 in. to 50, 60, or 70 in. wide. Finished rolls from the rewinder go through an upender, are put on skids, and are then "sent down" by towmotor to the warehouse. All finished shipments are by truck.

The machine's new a.c. line shaft drive was supplied by Louis Allis. Process control for the beater room (stock consistency, chest levels, etc.) and board machine is provided by new Moore Products digital controllers.

No. 2 machine speed, depending on specific grade, currently ranges from about 250 to 450 fpm. It produces 7.5 to 8.5 ton/hour of board, or approximately 160 tpd. The near-future target for No. 2 machine is up to 200 tpd, Canty emphasized. No. 1 machine production averages between 180 and 200 tpd.

WATER RECYCLING. The mill has two aerated lagoons, into which anything not recycled is transferred. The first acts as a "settling" pond. Water having passed through this stage is then stored in the lower lagoon, from which it is pumped back into the mill for reuse in the process.

Before being sent to the lagoons, water from No. 1 machine goes through a Black Clawson flotation saveall unit. No. 2 machine has a more complicated system for cleaning up its waste stream before it goes to the lagoons, including a clarifier unit. Canty pointed out that altogether, the mill uses very little makeup water, most of the time recycling almost all that it uses. All fresh-water comes from deep water wells.

EMPLOYEE TRAINING. Many of the 60 new positions for No. 2 machine were filled by relatively inexperienced employees previously assigned to No. 1 machine. The vacated slots on No. 1 machine as well as some positions for the new machine were then filled from the outside.

"Help-wise, we basically started from scratch," Canty said. "We had very little experience to work with, particularly as machine tenders, back tenders, etc." Training for the new machine startup was done in-house.

"All used equipment was rebuilt here at the mill," Canty added. "We used our own in-place maintenance people and a temporary crew brought on just for this purpose. We installed and aligned the cylinder vats and some other equipment and did a little work in the beater room, but almost everything else—the wet end setting, press trains, press rolls, etc.—was contracted out." ∎

Chapter 44

Cascade's Deinking Plant Producing High-Grade Market Pulp from Waste

Sixteenth mill of the dynamic Canadian company is now in full operation at Breakeyville, Que., utilizing flotation technology

By JOHN C.W. EVANS, Consulting Editor

The only market pulp mill in Canada that utilizes deinked wastepaper is now in full and successful operation at Breakeyville, Que. The mill, located near Quebec City, is operated as a subsidiary of Cascades Inc., with the name Desencrage Cascades Inc. ("Desencrage" translates as "deinking.") Nominal capacity is 100 tpd of a 56 to 60 brightness pulp produced from magazine and newspaper waste. A second grade is made from printed kraft waste with a 75 to 83 brightness.

The mill is located on the site of a former market groundwood pulp plant. Very little of the equipment from the groundwood mill has been utilized in the new operation. A major exception to this is in the sheet forming, cutting, and baling operation.

Wastepaper is delivered by the trucks of Cascades' wastepaper collection system. In the province of Quebec, six Cascades' paper mills are based on wastepaper furnish. The wastepaper is delivered to Breakeyville loose or baled from Cascades' numerous collection stations. A fork truck moves the wastepaper onto the first conveyor. Here the bales are opened. This conveyor elevates the paper to a 40-ft-long horizontal conveyor from which corrugated waste is removed by hand for shipment to a Cascades mill using this grade of waste. Large contaminants are dropped to a bin below for disposal. When the conveyor holds the approximate weight of paper desired, it is weighed and delivered to a pulper. The pulper is a Beloit-Jones Shark batch unit equipped with a standard rotor.

Chemicals used are sodium hydroxide, hydrogen peroxide, chelating agents, surfactants, and sodium silicate. The required quantity of chemicals for the weight of paper is determined by the control system and is automatically added to the pulper. Pulping is carried out at 4% to 6% consistency.

FIRST INK REMOVAL. The first step in ink removal involves dilution of the screened stock from the pulper and then dewatering of this stock up to a consistency of 8% to 10% in a Beloit-Jones CDC (Controlled Drainage Cycle) thickener. This new CDC thickener gives economical dewatering from a minimum inlet consistency of 0.5% to a maximum discharge consistency of 12%.

The design allows the amount of dewatering to be controlled to constant discharge consistency even as throughput, inlet consistency, freeness, and temperature vary. Pressure filtration is the principle behind the operation of the CDC. The pulp is pumped to the interior of a cylindrical screen basket and conveyed through the basket, where a close-fitting screw wipes the screen clean. Back pressure is provided by the head of a discharge chute. The effluent chamber of the CDC thickener is maintained under pressure by throttling the effluent valves on the outside of the chamber. Thus the pressure differential and subsequent flow rate through the screen basket can be controlled. The fiber mat, which forms on the inside of the screen basket, is wiped by a rotating double-flight screw. The clearance between the screw flights and the screen is maintained at a minimum for effective wiping.

The controlled discharge consistency from the CDC means a greater uniformity in removal of the "free" ink at this stage and controlled consistency in the feed to the air flotation stage of ink removal.

The pulp from the CDC stage is diluted to a 3.2% consistency, then passed through a deflaker and screened in a Beloit-Jones S-series high-consistency screen. The

Headers and air injectors for Lineacell flotation units aid the process of ink removal.

rotor/profiled screen combination creates a fluidized boundary layer that extends well ahead of the rotor. This means that the screening operation continues at consistencies as high as 3%. The screen at Breakeyville is equipped with 0.010-in. slotted plates. Rejects at present are purged on a time basis, and accepts are delivered to the feed chest of the flotation system.

FLOTATION STAGE. The flotation cells used in ink removal are the new Beloit-Jones flotation units named Lineacell. The system uses a series of stages, usually one mounted above the other. At the Breakeyville mill, five stages are stacked vertically, with 5 ft between units for maintenance.

The Lineacell has separate aeration, mixing, and foam-separation chambers. Air is fed into the stock and dispersed in the aeration chamber. The stock then moves to a separation cell where carefully controlled patterns of stock and minute air bubbles maintain the fibers in suspension while the ink containing foam forms at the surface and is drawn off by vacuum. Fiber loss is slight here.

The Lineacell is unusual in that it has no moving parts and therefore requires minimal maintenance.

FINAL CLEANING. The deinked stock from the Lineacells is pumped to a Beloit-Jones two-stage Uniflow centrifugal cleaner system. These cleaners are a new design for improved removal of lightweight contaminants. Stock enters tangentially at the top of the unit, creating a fast spinning motion. As the flow continues to spin in the cleaner body, it passes through an area of maximum centrifugal force near the bottom of the cone, ensuring separation of the slower-moving, lighter-weight material from the bulk of the stock. Both rejects and accepts are removed (separately) at the bottom of the cone.

The lightweight particles move inward in a spiral flow toward a single, central rejects outlet at the base of the cleaner. Air is removed at the same time with the contaminants. The accepted stock is discharged from the cleaner through a tangential outlet located at the base of the unit, thus eliminating the possibility of stock recontamination due to flow reversal, leakage, or short-circuiting.

Following the removal of lightweight contaminants by the Uniflow cleaners, heavy material is removed through use of the Bauer standard Centricleaners remaining from the groundwood operation.

HIGHLY AUTOMATED OPERATION. The wastepaper processing system at Breakeyville is completely controlled by a Honeywell computer system. All phases of the process are monitored and controlled by a Honeywell TDC distributed control system located in the center of the operation. For example, the process begins with the conveyor delivering a weighed amount of wastepaper to the pulper. The amount of required chemicals is determined automatically and added along with a predetermined volume of water. Two operator consoles serve as windows into the heart of the various stages in the processes.

Use of graphics and integrated real-time data displays provide the operators with constantly updated process status data. The entire process, beginning with the batch pulping operation, is logically broken down into multiple graphic displays that allow the operators to examine the operating conditions in a specific area of the mill.

Process overviews are provided, which allow monitoring of the entire process with rapid access to specific

Ink containing foam floating on top of stock in a Lineacell is drawn off by vacuum.

FIGURE 1: **Flow sheet showing the basic components of the Desencrage deinking system.**

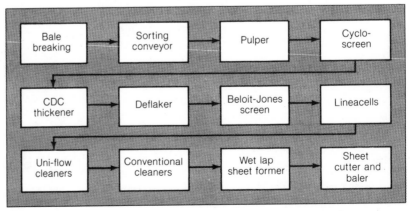

areas when necessary. The control room also has a data logger for recording alarm conditions.

SHEETING AND BALING. An existing wet machine from the groundwood pulp operation is used to form sheets of pulp from the deinked stock, which has been thickened to 4% consistency on gravity deckers. The wet machine sheets at 55% to 60% air-dried consistency are cut, stacked, and baled for shipment. A pulp flash-drying system is also available at the mill.

WATER RECYCLING AND EFFLUENT TREATMENT. Effluent from the CDC thickener goes to an existing Krofta dissolved air flotation clarifier. Clarified water is used back at the pulper, thus reusing residual chemical and heat. The water for the pulper is raised to the desired temperature by a gas heater. Rejects from the scavenger at the pulper, the coarse screen following the pulper, and the vibrating screen are sent to local landfill. Sludge from the Krofta clarifier, inky foam from the Lineacell units, and rejects from the third stage Bauer centrifugal cleaners following the Lineacell units are collected in a sludge tank. This sludge goes to a reconditioned belt press for thickening and then to the landfill. Effluent from the belt press goes back to the Krofta clarifier.

Uniflow centrifugal cleaners have improved designs for removal of lightweight contaminants.

Clarifier water not used in the mill processes goes to two settling ponds and then to an aerated lagoon before release to the Chaudière River. Filtrate from the gravity deckers and excess water from the machine that forms the wet pulp laps is used where dilution is required in the process following the CDC. ■

Chapter 45

Seminole Kraft Advances Recycling of Newspapers with "Good News" Bag

Grocery bags containing a minimum of 20% ONP are claimed equal to 100% virgin kraft bags in tear, burst, and tensile strength

By JIM YOUNG, Technical Editor

A Florida grocery chain recently filmed a television commercial at Stone Container Corp.'s Retail Bag Div. plant in Yulee, Fla., promoting the chain's use of the "Good News" grocery bag that incorporates recycled newspaper fiber.

Larry Stanley, general manager of Stone's Seminole Kraft mill in nearby Jacksonville, where the bag paper is made, notes that in the past 12 to 14 months the public has responded to the need to recycle in a way that hasn't been seen since World War II.

Ivey Crump, production manager at the Yulee plant, adds that many of his customers are ordering only bags containing recycled fiber, and most of the rest are asking about them.

Larry Stanley, Seminole Kraft general manager (left), and Ivey Crump, production manager of Stone Container's Yulee bag plant, discuss the next paper shipment for the Good News bag.

Seminole Kraft began production of grocery bag paper incorporating old newspapers (ONP) in May 1990. The Good News bag has a minimum of 20% recycled fiber and according to Ken Johnson, Seminole's operations manager, it meets the tear, burst, and tensile strength specifications of a 100% virgin fiber bag. The recycled fiber gives it a somewhat softer texture and a slightly lighter shade that enhances printability.

RECYCLING CHEMISTRY. Testing of the mixed stock began in February with a reapplication of existing equipment and a revised approach to recycling chemistry. The mill worked closely with Jacksonville-based Betz PaperChem in developing the chemistry for additives. Mark Manning, Betz process specialist, says the first concern addressed was the strength of the bags, which was aided by adding starch and cationic polymers for fiber retention (Figure 1).

A second concern was newsprint ink getting into the whitewater and contaminating machine wires and clothing. Detackification additives keep the inks from conglomerating, and ink particles, smaller than the eye can see, are locked in the sheet.

Drainage and retention aids successfully maintain the running speed of the machine, but machine deposition has increased. These deposits can be cleaned during the machine's normal 30-day production schedule and have not limited production. Doctor blades are being considered to remove buildup on the first section of dryers.

"We're still in a quality partnership mode here," Manning says. "We've come a long way, but we're still in a learning curve, especially with deposit problems."

MINIMAL EQUIPMENT MODIFICATION. Depending on the grade produced, 80 to 100 tpd of ONP are repulped in a 20-ft-dia Black Clawson Hydrapulper driven by a 400-hp motor. The mill has been adding 2 to 3 tpd of telephone books to the ONP with no ill effect from the adhesives. Much of the ONP arrives stuffed in kraft grocery bags that also join the repulping process. The pulper alternates ONP with 95 to 100 tpd of double-lined kraft (DLK) clippings pulped for Seminole's linerboard machine every 4 hours, with each stock sent to its respective high-density storage chest. The total system has a combined capacity of approximately 260 tpd.

No adjustment is made at the Hydrapulper as the stock alternates from ONP to DLK and back, but as it leaves the pulper at 4% consistency, the ONP is not as free-draining as DLK and requires three sidehill screens as compared with two for DLK pulp. The screens running ONP also require more cleaning.

The stock is pumped from the storage chest to a blend chest to a beater chest, where it joins virgin kraft fiber coming from a decker at 6% to 7% consistency. The combined pulp is reduced to about 3.5% consistency before it passes through a 54-in. Beloit Jones refiner. Stock flow continues through a machine chest, stuffbox, fan pump, screen, and into the PM No. 1 headbox.

The fourdrinier bag machine receives approximately 17 tons/hour of pulp slurry—4 tons originating as ONP and 13 tons of virgin kraft fiber—and runs at 1,400 fpm for 70-lb grade production. No major modification was required to convert to a mixed virgin-kraft/ONP stock. Adjusting foil blades to create activity on the table for improved sheet formation was about all that was required. The previously mentioned chemical changes

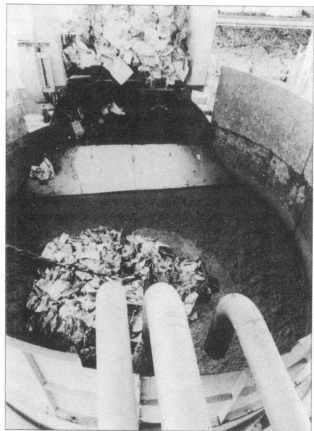

Seminole's Hydrapulper alternates between pulping ONP for inclusion in the Good News bag and double-lined kraft clippings for linerboard production.

FIGURE 1: **PM No. 1 "Good News" stock flow.**

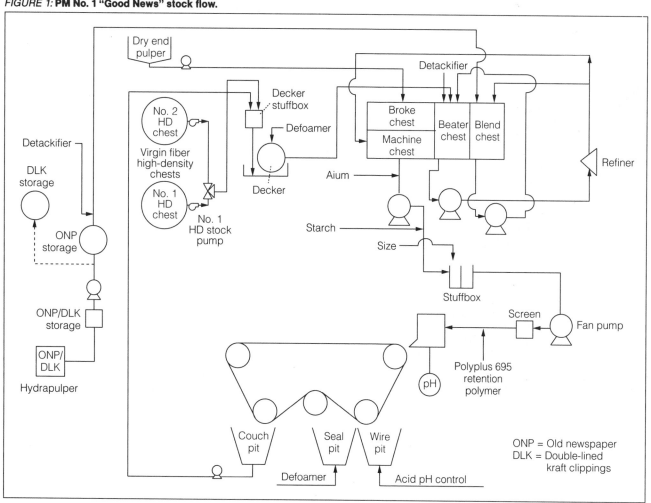

Andrew Puckett, PM No. 1 crew leader (left), and Ken Johnson, operations manager, observe a 1,400-fpm run that includes more than 20% ONP.

maintain a stock consistency of 23% coming off of the couch roll, the same as virgin fiber.

Seminole's PM No. 1 has been refurbished since Stone purchased the shut-down mill in 1986, most recently with upgrades in the wet end and felt-run changes in the three-nip tandem press section. These changes were incidental to the addition of 20%-plus ONP, as was the upgrading of the stock prep area to add additional refining capacity, but they all contributed to the successful trials.

PM No. 1 was originally installed in 1952 with a size press that hasn't run in several years. The size press rolls and drive were reconditioned, and the unit was reinstalled to improve caliper without affecting sheet properties the way calendering would. Caliper for a 70-lb sheet is 7.0 mils. Depending on grade mix, machine output is 325 to 350 tpd of paper for the Good News bag.

The mill gets quick feedback on product quality from the bag plant in Yulee 15 miles to the west. Purchased by Stone Container in 1988, the 400,000-ft² plant averages 250 tpd production from 25 machines, three to nine of them running the Good News bag. The plant purchases paper from at least five suppliers, producing small 30-lb to 40-lb bags and grocery checkout bags from 50 lb to 80 lb. The 70-lb bag is currently in greatest demand. Seminole Kraft supplies at least 30% of the paper stock, and Crump figures that percentage will go higher as demand increases for the Good News bag.

Stone Container is sharing knowledge gained from this startup with other paper bag producers in the belief that information that can help solve America's growing solid waste problem is too important to remain proprietary. Stanley reports that several representatives from other firms have already toured the mill. ∎

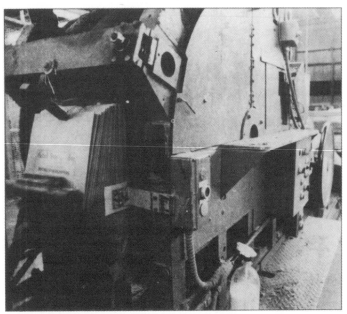

Many grocery chains are ordering and promoting exclusively bags containing recycled newspapers.

Chapter 46

Miami Paper Uses Washing, Flotation at Recycled Fine Paper Mill in Ohio

Company combines latest technology with unique operating approach to produce a quality recycled sheet that competes head-on with virgin fiber

By ANDY HARRISON, Technical Editor

Jobe Morrison, president of Miami Paper Corp., talks with *Pulp & Paper* about deinking technology and contaminant removal, legislation, and definitions that will effect printing and writing grades in the near future. He also discusses the basic philosophy behind Miami Paper's success in making quality paper products from recycled fiber.

Miami Paper is a subsidiary of Cross Pointe Paper Corp., which is part of the Pentair Organization. Over the years, the company has diligently explored new developments in recycling technology, incorporating many of them into its own papermaking process at the Miami, Ohio, mill. A combination of washing and flotation technology is currently used in the 150-tpd deinking process, which provides paperstock for such grades as book paper, commercial printing, technical specialties, and text and cover.

P&P: Miami Paper has been recycling for many years. How has your company adapted to the changing needs of the recycling business during this period?

Morrison: We have been recycling since 1915. In the old days deinking was not a very complicated process. The inks and binders were simple since very few synthetic latexes and coatings were used. From 1915 to 1975, we used the same recycling technology to successfully manufacture book paper. As the graphic arts world changed—using more heatset inks and ultraviolet set inks—that 1915 technology became less effective in handling the wastepaper stream.

In 1975 we put in a new plant, which included displacement washing, cleaning, and bleaching. That technology lasted until about 1985. As the graphic arts world continued to change relative to xerography, laser printing, etc., processing the wastepaper coming through the system became progressively more difficult. In 1985 we added European-type flotation capability to our washing

operation and effectively tied both processes together. Now we have the best of both worlds.

P&P: Don't the washing and flotation technologies have opposing chemistries that can cause problems in the overall operation of the deinking plant?

Morrison: We had problems at first but were soon able to make the two systems work together. By supplementing our existing system with new technology, we were locked into certain designs that we would not have used if we were to build a brand new system from scratch.

Just about any piece of equipment currently on the market will get the job done to some degree. The trick is to put it together in sequence and manage that process. This determines how successful an operation is going to be. For us, that expertise has come from in-house more than anywhere else. However, our project team has recently been examining new German technology.

Even though technology is changing fast, it takes three years for a project to take shape—involving first the decision to do it, then designing a system, buying the equipment, installing the equipment, and, finally, starting up the operation. Three years from now we are going

Jobe Morrison, president of Miami Paper Corp.

to be in the same position we were in back in 1975 and 1985, i.e., calling for new technology to handle the changing wastepaper stream.

In addition to the recycling facility, you need to learn how to make paper out of secondary fiber. Part of the learning curve is changing the machine's wet end around.

P&P: What is your basic philosophy on deinking and contaminant removal technology?
Morrison: Deinking is the dispersion and the separation

of the printed substrate from the fiber substrate—simple to define but difficult to do. We disperse in the pulper, and everything afterwards is a separation process. To get that separation process to work properly, the ink particle must be dispersed to a size that the separation units can handle. In displacement washing, that size is 35 microns, which is right at the threshold of visibility. Anything less than that can be taken out in the washing operation. Flotation technology can handle particle sizes in the 35 to 125 micron range.

A problem with xerography and laser printing is try-

Miami Paper Corp.'s advanced recycling operation

The Miami Paper deinking facility was rebuilt in 1975 with the addition of displacement washing, cleaning, and bleaching systems. Since then, the mill has been in a continuous mode of upgrading with improvements to the bleach plant, new stock contaminant removal equipment, and the latest technology in flotation deinking cells. The following is a description of the mill's deinking operation.

At the beginning of the process, a conveyor is loaded with 10,000 lb of recycled paper for the furnish charge into the pulper. The mill can run through inventory of raw material in a day and a half.

PULPING. The SEW pulper is a high-consistency (HC) tub-type pulper with a large screw or helical center rotor. The defibering zone is from the tip of the screw to the bottom of the tub. This design will vortex a 15% consistency stock slurry. At high consistencies, the defibering is accomplished by intense fiber-to-fiber contact and less by mechanical rotor action. This principle has several advantages: reduced energy consumption, less thermal energy needed, reduced chemicals usage,

"In 1985 we instituted a project using the European flotation technology, which added the flotation to our washing operation and tied both processes together," Morrison said.

contaminants remaining in larger pieces, and reduced pulping time.

The HC pulper with ¾-in. extraction-plate holes will defiber normal waste very efficiently but leave certain dirt in larger particle sizes. The wastepaper slurry is defibered for 20 min, then diluted to 7% to 8% consistency before being pumped out to the dump chest. Pulping longer than the set pulping time results in unnecessary energy consumption and reduction of contaminant size. Continued defibering and dirt separation will take place in the SEW Fibersorter.

SCREENING AND CLEANING. From the dump chest, the slurry goes to an intermediate chest where the stock is diluted. From here the stock goes through the Fibersorter. The Fibersorter is a combination high-density pressure screen working at 3% to 5% consistencies and a deflaker, with respect to the action at the rotor and screen plate. It is like a small conical-shaped pulper on its side, with the screen plate and rotor at one end and a cover with a hole in the center for overflow rejects at the other end.

Because of the rotor and conical shape of the unit, heavy contraries follow along the inside wall and are removed at an outlet near the largest dia of the unit housing. Lighter contraries or rejects that will not travel through the screen plate flow to the middle of the unit end cover and through the center outlet. Stock lumps and fiber chips that concentrate on the screen plate will be deflaked by the impact blocks at the circumference along with the rotor action. Accepted stock will pass through the screen plate's 0.093-in. perforations.

Since the Fibersorter operates continuously, it is controlled by the relationship between concentration of materials around the screen plate and rotor with respect to the motor load. Motor load control regulates the unit by automatically adjusting the accept valve. Stock going to the Fibersorter must be regulated to a uniform 4.2% consistency. Changes in consistency will affect the motor load control on the unit, resulting in poor performance. Two additional units tail the Fibersorter reject system—the SEW high-density cleaner for heavy rejects and the SEW Rejectsorter for the light paper chips and contaminants.

The large vertical-cone-shaped high-density cleaner works by having heavy impurities thrown against the outside wall, where the gravity effect and the downward spiral path of the stock result in heavy material settling into a tank below the stock reversal zone. The stock fibers are

---

ing to break their ink binders down. Xerography printing is really a piece of plastic. Consequently, it takes a great deal of energy to break that particle size down. For the particles bigger than 125 microns, if the specific gravity is greater than one, then centrifugal cleaners can take out the particles. The particle sizes between 125 and 200 microns are tough to handle, which are where the xerographic contaminants fall.

The basic deinking principle for grades we produce is the application of energy. There are three forms of energy—mechanical, chemical, and thermal—which provide a matrix to obtain optimum performance. Excess chemical usage wastes caustic and increases problems in the separation process due to excess alkalinity. There are, however, some adjunct chemicals, such as dispersants to help wet the ink particles for the dispersion process. There are limits on thermal energy because of synthetic binders. We try to stay down below 140°F in our pulpers. Above 140°F, synthetic binders found in the waste stream start solubalizing. Problems never show up in the deinking operation but will show up in the paper machine. When stickies start accumulating in the

prevented from entering the collecting tank by adding seal water. The clean fiber rises in the middle to the top of the unit, passing through the rotor and back to the dump chest standpipe.

The Rejectsorter is a trough-shaped screen with 0.093-in. perforations. A rotor is located above the screen that provides action to separate and move impurities down along the screen trough toward the outlet. Above the rotor is a turbulence zone, which provides for a continuous loosening of contaminates. Accepted fibers pass through the screen and are combined with the Fibersorter accepts in the intermediate chest ahead of the screen extractors and bleach tower.

BLEACHING. The basic units in the bleach plant are the 9-in. water extractors or the Morden Model 9 inclined screw presses. Each machine has an internal screw with 0.062-in. perforations that thicken 4% brownstock from the intermediate chest up to 11% to 12%. Before the thickened stock is dropped into the mixing screws, bleach or sodium hypochlorate is added. The bleach fibers are mixed in the mixing screw just prior to the bleach tower. The bleach reaction takes place in the plug-flow retention tower (95% of the reaction takes place in the first 5 min). A dilution zone at the bottom of the tower dilutes the stock to a pumpable consistency. The stock, now at 4% consistency, is then pumped from the bleach tower to the dilution tank.

Hot water leaving the extractor flows by gravity to a level control tank. This tank is pumped to an SEW flotation cell to clean light contaminants and ink from the water. The water is bled from this water line to a settling tank, where some of the ash is removed at the bottom. Water from the settling tank flows to the hot water tank and is then returned to the pulper. This process saves both heat and chemicals.

FLOTATION, WASHING. Stock leaving the bleach tower is diluted to 1.5% and pumped through Black Clawson 24 PH Selectifier screens. The slotted pressure screens have 0.008-in. cuts. From the pressure screens, the stock goes over the first-stage sidehill screen, where the stock is diluted again before going through the second-stage sidehill screen. Accepts are pumped over to the flotation conditioning chest, then through four SEW flotation cells.

The stock is diluted to 0.8% consistency in the cleaner dilution tank before being pumped through the Bauer forward cleaners. Accepts then go through the Beloit Uniflow cleaners. Accepts from the cleaners are thickened to a 4% consistency in the SEW Vario-Split thickener and washer. From here the stock goes to a blend system, which

Stock diluted down to 0.8% consistency is pumped through the Bauer forward cleaners and Beloit Uniflow cleaners.

is part of the stock preparation system, and then forward to the paper machine.

In the displacement washing section of the deinking process, foaming agents cannot be used because of the low consistency of the sidehills. Dispersing agents are used to enhance the sidehill efficiency. The flotation chemicals used to enhance foam production in the flotation cells are injected into the flotation conditioning chest just after the sidehills. Restrictions exist as to how much foam can be created in the flotation cells because too much foam can cause pressure drops in the cleaners. Defoamer is added in the cleaner dilution tank after the flotation cells and before the Bauer cleaners. Here again, careful amounts of defoamer must be added because that water comes back to the flotation cells after going through the Vario-Split thickener and washer.

PROCESS CONTROL. All of the hydraulic process parameters in the deinking plant are monitored and controlled by a Rosemount System 3 process control system. Automation of the process is a critical part of the system due to the varying consistencies and chemistries required of the different pieces of equipment in the deinking plant.

paper machine, it is usually because the pulpers have been cooking too long or too hot.

So, in reality, the only variable left is the mechanical method. This is why we have gone with the high-consistency pulper from a dispersion standpoint. Because we are putting more of the horsepower into the dispersion process and less of it into moving the water around, we are running 15% consistency on our big pulper.

Contaminant removal is difficult and an ever changing technology. Obviously, the first step is to minimize the amount of contaminants introduced through the waste material stream. We do this by inspecting every bale of wastepaper received during the unloading process and again when the bales are broken at the pulper belt. Our rejection rate at the door is running only 1%, but this didn't just happen. We have done a considerable amount of work with our suppliers in defining what is acceptable and what isn't. Our relationship with our suppliers is a key factor in this program.

Also, we recognize that all the various unit processes associated with the separation system have efficiency factors—nothing is 100%. We use this efficiency factor, plus our quality standards for finished stock, to determine what is acceptable from the pulpers. If the pulper stock doesn't meet our standards, then we either process it longer or divert it to a bad batch system for further processing. It is this type of operating philosophy, plus the skills of our team members, that produces the consistent quality stock required for printing and writing products.

P&P: In addition to all the changing technology, what are some of the other problems Miami Paper faces in the recycling business?

Morrison: One of the problems from our end of the business is that people still think recycling might be a marketing fad. Companies might do things to satisfy a specific marketing demand but not make the commitment to build a secondary fiber facility. A 200-tpd deinking plant can cost up to $40 million.

One of the biggest problems we are running into now is definitions. What is postconsumer and what is preconsumer? I think that issue is going to separate itself out. One of the most active groups that will define what our industry has to do to meet the various demands is the National Assn. of State Purchasing Officials. They have formed an advisory committee, which I serve on, under the auspices of ASTM. Also, The National Recycling Coalition is a group concerned with how the federal government will handle definitions and legislation. So there will be some legitimate, and, hopefully, meaningful definitions developed in the near future.

P&P: How are the various definitions going to effect your business?

Morrison: What we are afraid of, and are trying to resist, is the attempt to develop another grade of fine paper called recycled. By de facto, this classification will re-

sult in mills offering a lower-quality product. Because of the limitations and types of processing being used, it is going to be dirtier, have lower brightness, and some colors may vary. What will happen is that a mill will offer the customer a lower-quality recycled paper, and, if the customer does not like it, then the mill will offer their better-quality virgin product. The graphic arts world will not accept lower quality just to have recycled.

We have been competing against the virgin mills for a long time. We don't believe it is in our best interest to have recycled paper classified as an inferior product. Looking at it from a printability standpoint, there should not be any difference between a recycled sheet and a virgin fiber sheet. If a customer has a graphic arts problem and the printer blames it on recycled fiber content, the customer should not accept that. Problems occur for customers when paper is not made properly on the paper machine. Our goal is to make recycled paper comparable to a virgin paper. The customer should not see any problems or defects associated with the product just because it has been recycled.

P&P: How are you able to achieve the high quality standards that must be obtained to match that of virgin fiber?

Morrison: We stress quality continuously since we are working with an unknown raw material. We run some postconsumer furnish called laser printed and nonlaser printed (green bar CPO). Every once in a while some of the laser-printed CPO will get mixed in with the green bar. When laser-printed CPO gets into the deinking operation, it starts showing up as little specs. Our finished deinked stock, then, does not meet our paper mill quality standards. We grade from 1 to 3 for dirt specs. If there are one or two visible dirt specs, then it is rated a 2. If there are too many dirt specs, the pulp is recirculated through the operation, where the efficiencies of the various process units can take out the contaminants. Recirculation is a fact of life and an important operating parameter in this business.

We have done lab work in Europe and in the U.S. Although the U.S. is starting to catch up to European technology, part of the problem in Europe is that their finished paper quality requirements are a lot different from ours. They accept more dirt, more specs, and lower brightness in their finished product for printing and writing grades than we do.

P&P: With America's present environmental awareness, how are your customers reacting to Miami Paper's recycling efforts?

Morrison: McDonald's Corp. came to one of our merchants and requested that their annual reports and other promotional material be manufactured out of 100% recycled fiber collected from their printing operation. The merchant came to us with this project. This is what our people call Fun Projects.

We also make the paper for the Esprit De Corp Spring Catalog, which features young people dressed in clothing apparel in environmental scenes but no prices. Why then, I asked, put out a catalog? What they are trying to do is create an image and market that image to a culture that is very concerned about our environment. The clothing might be at an Esprit store, or it might not. That is why in the first few pages there is an article about the magazine being on recycled paper and the impact that this is having on the environment.

Another interesting publication that we are currently working on is *Step by Step*, a how-to book on the graphics arts world. The publisher of the magazine wants to include a recycled paper pullout section of the new fall Esprit Catalogue and then talk to the various printers and graphics arts people involved and show them that a quality job can be printed on recycled paper.

We did provide Esprit with extra paper because it is a promotional campaign for us. We are trying to make sure the industry understands that quality graphic arts can be attained with secondary fiber. It has to be approached that way.

P&P: Your mill must be getting quite a few calls from customers asking for recycled paper.

Morrison: Our business is very good at this time. However, our marketing position is not that we are selling recycled paper but that we are marketing a premium printing and writing grade that is made from secondary fiber. We are meeting a demand, a demand not generated by us but from the end of the marketplace—the consumers, who are requesting that their printers use recycled paper. The printer doesn't know what to do because of his stereotype image that recycled paper is off-quality.

P&P: Recycling has not always been a national concern like it has been for the past few years. How has a recycled papermill, like Miami Paper, been able to compete with virgin fiber mills in the printing and writing grades over the long term?

Morrison: What do you do with a 130-year-old mill? First, you change your culture. We did just that in 1985 in regards to our people. Basically, we are a team concept mill—very involved in participative management. And it has paid off for us from the standpoint of our productivity, quality, and all of the aspects that go along with involvement of the people. If you take care of your people, they will take of you. We've eliminated our middle management group and are now nonunion. We now have a very flat organization, which has replaced our old functional organization consisting of the president, the vice president, and production superintendents. We have four teams with a team leader each, except for our research and support groups, which still have some functional organization. We have a director of manufacturing, and I still have responsibilities for the staff's functions.

The most important thing in involving your people in your business is to reward them. We have a very successful gain-sharing program where everyone shares

"We inspect every bale of wastepaper received during the unloading process and again when the bales are broken at the pulper belt." Morrison said.

equally, except for the amount of overtime worked. People who work more overtime get a bigger share of the pie. The person sweeping the floor and the highest associates in the mill all share equally.

The second thing to do is find a niche in the marketplace. Although Miami was successful primarily as a book publishing mill, it is a cyclical business. We needed to balance out our product line and move more into commercial printing, technical specialties, and text and cover grades.

Historically, text and cover have always been manufactured from virgin fiber. We discovered that, using secondary fiber, we can very effectively manufacture quality text and cover grades equal to, or better than, virgin fiber. That gave us a significant margin and a significant market. We were able to go into the market, sell at a good value, increase our share of the market, and still make money.

The third thing you have to do is add margins to the operation. We did this with our deinking operation. By adding 50 tons in our deinking capacity, we need 50 tons less of virgin fiber, which is a great payback for us. Since we are a class II semi-integrated operation, we still purchase some virgin fiber but much less than we used to buy.

The forth thing you do is run the mill efficiently. Even though we are a specialty mill, we run our operation like a commodities mill. This involves a lot of planning, including how we run orders and how we take our maintenance downs.

Miami has been very successful in putting these four concepts together. In addition, our Chicago distribution and converting operation has really helped us in the text and cover business. Now, with the ability to sell one or two cartons instead of truckloads only, we have added a high-value business that keeps

The ink particle must be dispersed to a size that the separation units can handle. Anything less than 35 microns can be taken out in the washing operation.

an older facility like ours competitive.

P&P: Aren't there only a certain amount of times that paper fibers can be effectively recycled?

Morrison: One of the myths associated with recycling is that a fiber can only be recycled one or two times before it is degraded to the point that it can't be used. That is not quite true because we look at the complex and dynamic system of recycling and do not look at individual fibers. We recognize that the separation process associated with deinking involves separating out the unusable portion of the fibers. Surprisingly, there is a very uniform and consistent fiber supply going to the paper machine as a result of this separation process. If the fiber is really degraded, our shrinkage might increase. We average about 21% to 22% loss; of this loss, half is filler and half is fiber. Looking at the fiber morphology of virgin fiber and recycled fiber strictly from a commercial standpoint, the only difference is the degree of development. The trick in the papermaking end of the process is to understand that degree of development and know how to adjust your machines to compensate for it.

The recycled fiber may have similar strength characteristics to a virgin fiber at comparable development levels. It is a mixture of hardwoods and softwoods. Usually about 65% hardwood and 35% softwood is the average from the waste material we buy. You can't look at secondary fiber and a virgin fiber and say one is virgin and one is secondary, other than the degree of development. The fact that people say recycling can only be done one or two times is not quite true because it is a dynamic, complex system that corrects itself.

We also recognize that because some fiber will always go into landfill, there is always going to be a need to bring in a fresh supply of virgin fiber. That is why I believe a 50% range will be the overall limit of our nation's recycling rate. ∎

Chapter 47

Atlas Starts Second Tissue Machine That Runs on Recycled Wastepaper

Hialeah, Fla., mill to double production with machine rebuild, second machine, expanded deinking line, and added converting line

By JIM YOUNG, Technical Editor

Atlas Paper Mills is a privately owned tissue mill where internal engineering and innovation substitute for a large corporate budget. The Hialeah, Fla., facility is doubling its 25-tpd production and adding towels to its bathroom tissue line in a $6-million expansion.

The added 25- to 30-tpd capacity will be provided by a 1956-model 120-in. trim Beloit fourdrinier and yankee dryer unit purchased from the Cascades Inc. mill (formerly Nitec) in Niagara Falls, N.Y. Remberto Bastanzuri, Atlas president, observes that while the machine needed reconditioning, its potential and that of the dryer in particular were evident.

With PM No. 2 now running, PM No. 1 will be shut down for upgrading. The deinking line is being expanded, and a second converting line is being added to accommodate the running of both machines in 1991. PM No. 2 will produce bathroom tissue exclusively, while No. 1 will produce towels and additional tissue. Towels will be produced on the older machine because it has an afterdryer following the yankee dryer. Bathroom tissue, the mainline product, will take advantage of PM No. 2's faster speed of 3,000 fpm.

Seventy-five percent of the bathroom tissue is purchased by the commercial/industrial market and the remainder by the retail market. The industrial market is in the continental U.S.; the retail market serves the Caribbean, primarily from Puerto Rico. Towels will be manufactured for the retail market.

PULPING, DEINKING, CLEANING. White ledger paper is supplied by Flores Recycling in Florida and Ponte & Sons in New York and New Jersey. The current pulper is Black Clawson's first Hi-Con model, 10 ft in dia, and the new unit joining it is similar but 12 ft in dia. Both will be pulping at 16% consistency. Bastanzuri says the installed equipment, including flotation devices and reverse-flow cleaners, is the best available for removing laser, UV radiation-cured, and heat-set inks.

Beloit cleaners running at 3.0% to 3.5% consistency are followed by Black Clawson's slotted Ultra Screens. Atlas is again building its own two-stage belt washer, an updated version to add to its current patented washer. The new washer will include an option for a third stage. New Dorr-Oliver disc filters will be installed along with Beloit centrifugal cleaners, and a new bank of Albia cleaners has been added ahead of the second machine.

Since much of the water is recycled, freshwater makeup from the city of Hialeah for the current production line never exceeds 100 gpm. Sludge is reduced in a dewatering press to a 40% solids content, continues to compactors, and then goes to a landfill. In keeping with its in-house engineering approach, Atlas is designing its own dryer for drying sludge.

Remberto Bastanzuri, Atlas president, exhibits new case-packing equipment ready for installation.

The Hurricane I tissue machine, newly decked out in Univ. of Miami colors, will be running bathroom tissue at 3,000 fpm.

OPERATION/INSTALLATION EXPERIENCE. The expansion features a cross-fertilization of a decade's operating experience with PM No. 1 applied to the installation of PM No. 2 and the installation experience of the newer machine utilized in the rebuild of the 1929-model PM No. 1. Both machines bear the nicknames of area sports teams: PM No. 1 is designated Dolphin I after Miami's N.F.L. Dolphins, and PM No. 2 is designated Hurricane I after the Univ. of Miami Hurricanes.

Pulp enters the headbox of Hurricane I at a consistency between 0.25% and 0.35%. As the sheet passes the blind-drilled roll against the 12-ft-dia yankee dryer, it has a 39.5% dryness. The yankee dryer was cleaned by grinding and metalized with stainless steel and molybdenum. Originally designed for 125-psig steam pressure when new, it is now operating at 85 to 90 psig. The machine is running with clothing that was supplied by Huyck, Albany International, and Niagara Lockport. Its d.c. drives are from Banshaw, and the d.c. motors are from General Electric. Jumbo rolls are sent to the converting plant where the rewinder and the unwind stands are located.

No major rebuilding is scheduled for the upgrade of Dolphin I. A cantilever adjustment in the fourdrinier will match the new Hurricane I machine, and some metal parts will be replaced and the felt run changed in the press section. The electrical system will remain basically the same, with a few parts replaced by later-model components. Machine speed is expected to increase from 1,500 fpm to an 1,800 to 1,900+ fpm range.

ADDING A SECOND CONVERTING LINE. The international nature of papermaking is demonstrated in the converting plant with new equipment from the U.S, Canada, and Italy. The added line at Atlas will include a second Perini rewinder, three additional Valley Tissue wrappers, a second Edson case packer and Bemis case sealer, as well as Valley Tissue diverters and conveyors. What is new to the converting area is a polybonder machine from Cassoli that will augment the corrugated container shipments with polyethylene-wrapped shipments. ∎

Eversoft tissue is one of the 100%-recycled products in the Hialeah mill's current 25-tpd production.

Chapter 48

Ponderosa Fibres Expands to Meet Demands for Recycled Market Pulp

Growing market interest prompts addition of pulp dryer at Augusta, Ga., mill and consideration of expansion at its other mills

By KELLY H. FERGUSON, Project Editor

As the major player in secondary fiber market pulp, Ponderosa Fibres of America Inc. is experiencing increasing demand for its product, leaving the company only one enviable alternative—improve and expand. Ponderosa's four market pulp mills—Santa Ana, Calif.; Oshkosh, Wis.; Memphis, Tenn.; and Augusta, Ga.— have a combined production of about 700 tpd. But with current corporate and public demand for products made with recycled fiber, the 27-year-old company is spending much of its time modernizing and expanding (see sidebox).

Until recently, Ponderosa's mills were shipping 100% wet lap pulp, which, because of shipping costs, limited the amount and distance that could be shipped to cus-

Ponderosa has about 80,000 ft² of warehouse space to hold shipments of its colored ledger, white ledger, and poly-coated board wastepaper.

tomers, especially overseas buyers. However, the recent addition of a pulp dryer at the Augusta mill has enabled the mill to cut shipping costs by about 40%, with pulp that will be shipped at about 80% to 90% air dry.

Three grades make up the majority of secondary fiber at all of Ponderosa's mills: colored ledger, white ledger, and poly-coated board. Ponderosa deinked market pulp is recycled from 100% bleached chemical pulp fibers, with no groundwood, mechanical, or unbleached fiber included.

Fiber is purchased from wastepaper dealers, major manufacturers, and end users and shipped—baled and loose—to the mills by train and truck. The mills also have back hauling arrangements with many of their major carriers.

AUGUSTA'S OPERATION. The Augusta mill produces about 150 tpd currently, with 45 employees, but expects to increase production within 18 months, according to Jerome Goodman, executive vice president of Ponderosa. Once the dryer operation is optimized, output should reach about 220 tpd, and the mill is considering other process improvements to increase production and quality.

The mill has about 80,000 ft² of warehouse space, from which wastepaper is metered and dumped into two high-consistency Black Clawson Hydrapulpers. Caustic and other chemicals are added in the pulper, which operates at 100°F to 150°F and 10.5 pH for approximately 60 min. The fiber is pulped at about 12% consistency.

From the pulper, the slurry is screened and sent through high-consistency cleaners. The pulp is then deinked (washing) and thickened using sidehill screens. "We are investigating flotation. However, at this time, we don't know whether flotation is the best way for us to go," Goodman said.

Although pulp brightness ranges from 76 to 78 GE, Goodman says very little actual bleaching occurs. "We don't really bleach, as such, which would be delignifying the fiber. We use no chlorine. Sodium hypochlorite is added near the end of the process to strip dyes and other color materials out of the pulp. Currently, we are investigating different methods of bleaching with no chlorine compounds at all. Our tissue customers, especially in Europe, are requesting a product with no chlorine compounds, so depending on the success of our trials, we'll be implementing new bleaching technology fairly rapidly."

The mill is also experimenting with a prototype thickener/washer developed by Fields & Boyd of Lakewood, Colo. According to Neil Clarke, vice president of Ponderosa, "This is a belt type washer, where a moving sheet is washed between two wires, exiting at about 12% to 13% consistency. The unit operates at fairly high speeds—2,000 to 3,000 fpm. We expect to send the sheet in at about 0.9% consistency and exit at about 12%. Although small, the washer should handle about 300 tpd."

After the sidehill screens, the pulp is screened once more and sent to the pulp press. This press has a pressurized headbox and a twin-wire forming section. The mill still has the option of making wet lap, or it can send the sheet through the new dryer section.

The press section was custom built by Fields & Boyd. "Three of our mills use this type of press, and we just bought two more," Goodman said. "We plan to change two out and use the two older machines to build a third machine that will be installed at the another mill, instead of taking machines down for extensive rebuilds.

"The dryer is, again, our own design. We basically took old dryer cans and designed our own conventional dryer." Out of the dryer, the sheet is cut, baled, and loaded onto truck or rail.

The mill currently landfills its solid waste. "We're doing some trials at a couple of our mills on drying the solid waste. We might be able to make a product with it after it's dried—maybe as cattle bedding or for use in concrete," Goodman explained. Effluent is sent through primary clarification and then into lagoons, where the water is discharged into the city's sewer system.

Ponderosa's Hydrapulper has a helical-type rotor for pulping ledger grades and poly-coated board at about 12% consistency.

Conveyors are used to dump wastepaper into Ponderosa's two high-consistency Hydrapulpers.

The sheet leaves the dryer at about 80% to 90% air dry, where it is then cut, baled, and loaded onto truck or rail.

Recycling Mill Expansions and Modernizations

SATISFYING THE CUSTOMER. Because Ponderosa's product is used in a number of grades, quality and run-ability have always been major factors. These factors have become even more important now that more mills are considering using secondary fiber in their products.

Goodman said the company is considering various technological options at all its mills. "We're looking at drum pulping, dispersion, and flotation deinking. We have excellent control over stickies and have had no problems running our materials on conventional flat paper fourdrinier machines. We certainly have no problems running on tissue machines.

"There's nothing a mill has to do to use our pulp—just take it out of the truck and put it in the pulper. A mill can also start with very low inclusion rates—2.5% or 5%—and raise the level slowly to see how the pulp acts on their machine. For some, its an opportunity—even if they plan to install their own operation—to develop knowledge of how secondary fiber pulp is going to operate on their machine and allow their employees to become familiar with the difference in the operation and the finished sheet. Also, some mills don't want to bother with the cost, environmental problems, and technical problems associated with adding a deink line.

"Because of the variation in systems at mills we sell to, we try to use the least amount of chemicals possible. Therefore, most of our process is mechanical, rather than relying on chemicals to clean the pulp. This avoids problems when the material is put into a mill's system. Some mills we sell to run an alkaline furnish, some run acid—and they all use different types of polymers. It's possible we could use a polymer in our system that would work against a polymer in a customer's system, which might cause problems. ∎

Meeting a growing demand

In only five or six years, Ponderosa Fibres' status in the paper industry has changed dramatically. Executive vice president Jerome Goodman said mills no longer "hide" the fact that they use secondary fiber in their products.

Ponderosa began operation in 1963 as B.J. Fibres (Santa Ana, Calif.) to supply secondary fiber market pulp to a major tissue manufacturer. The original mill, still in operation, produced approximately 10 to 20 tpd and was started with the idea of taking materials away from the landfills, mostly poly-coated board.

At the request of this customer, another mill was constructed in Augusta, Ga., then two others were added—Oshkosh, Wis., and Memphis, Tenn. Business grew rapidly with the customer, but eventually Ponderosa began to branch out to other customers. "We were shipping primarily to tissue manufacturers because they were the big users of secondary fiber," Goodman said. "And in fact, currently tissue makers use anywhere from 53% to 54% recycled fiber. However, a major part of that is going into commercial products rather than consumer."

Ponderosa's main customer base has changed, though, in the last few years, mirroring a change in the industry. "It once was a rarity for us to supply printing and writing grade manufacturers with pulp," Goodman said. "Until two years ago, there were mills that used high-grade, direct-entry materials but no postconsumer materials. Those mills would never buy from us."

Now, printing and writing mills make up about 50% of Ponderosa's business, and that percentage continues to grow. The reason, Goodman said, is that those companies are trying to comply with various state and federal guidelines in using secondary fiber.

The other 50% of Ponderosa's business is divided among such grades as tissue, mottled white corrugated, and other specialty products. In the tissue market, most of Ponderosa's market pulp is used to make consumer tissue products.

Ponderosa bills itself as the largest supplier of secondary fiber market pulp in the world. Competition comes from two mills in North America and a few small mills in Europe, but at 700 tpd from four mills, Ponderosa remains the largest. "We pretty much dominate this market for now because it's almost prohibitively expensive to put up a deinking market pulp mill. We estimate the price to be about $50 million for a 200-tpd mill."

DEALING WITH DECLINING QUALITY. Besides increasing production and quality at its mills, Ponderosa is working to increase its use of postconsumer waste. "Our next big push will have to be in the office waste area," Goodman said. "We think there's probably about 6 million tons of office waste that can be used."

Vice president Neil Clarke said, "You don't really need a crystal ball to know that as more and more printing and writing and specialty grade manufacturers begin using more secondary fiber, they're going to demand quality pulp. But as you dig deeper and deeper into the pile of recycled waste, quality will decline. Therefore, we have to produce a better product, but we must do it with lower-quality material. That involves a great deal of research and evaluation of new equipment and technologies."

Goodman added, "We use a certain amount of postconsumer waste, as much as the system can tolerate, and we would like to use more. That means we have to upgrade our system. Customers don't want to give up quality with the inclusion of secondary fiber."

MARKETS OUTSIDE NORTH AMERICA. Prior to 1987, Ponderosa shipped no pulp to Europe. And Goodman said that even though demand for hardwood market pulp is weaker than it was a year ago, demand for secondary fiber market pulp is higher than ever and continues to grow worldwide.

"We have found great interest in our product in Europe. Of course, until we added the dryer, we were shipping about 50% wet lap, which meant high shipping costs. However, much of the current demand is coming from the northeast U.S. and eastern Canada. While we'll continue to ship to Europe, I don't know how much we'll be able to ship to Europe because of heavy demand here."

Chapter 49

Stone-Snowflake Boosts Newsprint Quality with Deink System Upgrade

Old newspaper, magazines provide more than half of stock requirements, aid mill in reducing dependence on virgin fiber sources

By TIM DOWNS, Technical Editor

Stone Container Corp.'s Snowflake, Ariz., mill, one of the most remote paper mills in the U.S., has turned its geographic disadvantage into an opportunity to help in reducing the looming landfill problems in the U.S. Located some 450 miles from the nearest cluster of paper mills in Los Angeles, Calif., and in the sparsely forested desert Southwest, the mill has also lessened its dependence on virgin fiber by using recycled newspapers and magazines as a viable fiber source.

Not a newcomer to the recycling scene, the Snowflake mill was actually ahead of its time in realizing the potential of recycled fiber. G. Merlin Hancock, general pulping manager at Snowflake, explained that almost two decades ago the mill began a study that would reduce its dependence on virgin raw materials, primarily the residual chips and trimmings from local sawmills

The new cleaner system has helped greatly to improve deinked pulp quality.

and small trimmed logs from local forests.

In 1972, as a result of this study, the mill started up a conventional washing system, using 200 tpd of old newspapers (ONP). Further progress was made in 1981, when the mill purchased a new 400-tpd conventional wash deinking system. Then in late 1988, the mill began its third stage of recycled fiber use by upgrading No. 1 deinking system to include new screening, cleaning, and pressurized flotation deinking technology. This upgrade increased capacity by 300 tpd, bringing Snowflake's total deinking capacity to 700 tpd.

The new No. 1 deinking system, in operation since May 1989, includes a continuous pulper, coarse (0.050-in. perforations) and fine (0.010-in. slots with special bell wave baskets) primary screens, secondary screens on both coarse and fine screens, Beloit pressurized flotation deinking modules (see sidebar) and a series of forward and reverse cleaners.

EXPEDIENT PROJECT. Once the mill decided to upgrade the No. 1 deinking system, it quickly moved to investigate available technology and to get the project completed. The pressurized flotation deinking technology was initially tested in No. 2 deinking system with a trial unit. Based on results from that study, the mill then purchased four additional units (which are run in a series) for the No. 1 system upgrade.

"This project moved quickly, I'd say six to eight months from the inception of the idea to project approval," Hancock said. Then, within nine months from the time the equipment was ordered, the revamped No. 1 deinking system was installed and started up in May 1989—on time and on budget.

Once started, it took the mill only one week to reach full capacity. "We did some optimization later to get the brightness levels we wanted, but for the most part, startup was extremely efficient," Hancock added. He credits others as key to turning the project over quickly and efficiently. Errol Larson, deink superintendent, and Bob Ferry, mill engineer and project leader, were the two key people. Larry Stanley, coproject leader with Ferry (until being named mill manager of the Jacksonville, Fla., mill in mid-project) was also cited.

INCREASED FLEXIBILITY. In addition to increasing capacity and producing a cleaner, higher-quality fiber, the new system has also allowed the mill to expand its recycled fiber use to include old magazines (OMG), which currently comprise 20% to 30% of No. 1 deinking system capacity. Although somewhat more difficult to

PDM improves ink removal

Flotation deinking is a process by which ink (and other contaminants) is separated from recoverable fiber by the introduction of air into the pulp slurry, attachment of ink particles to the air bubbles, and subsequent removal of the ink/air agglomerations after they have floated to the surface of the pulp slurry. The ink removal process is characterized by three distinct actions: collision (of the air bubbles and contaminants), attachment (of contaminants to the bubbles), and separation (of air/contaminant foam from the air/water interface).

Conventional flotation deinking cells operate under atmospheric conditions and achieve ink removal by gravitational and mechanical forces as the pulp slurry overflows a weir at the air/water interface. Beloit's Pressurized Deinking Module (PDM) is a flotation deinking cell that operates under controlled pressure. Unlike its conventional predecessor, PDM uses pressure in an enclosed cell (module) with a reject pipe (or port), instead of a weir design, to enhance the deinking process by minimizing the limitations inherent in open-air flotation cells, namely fiber loss and ink removal efficiency.

FIBER LOSS REDUCTION. PDM allows control of the stock level in the flotation cell *just below* the reject port. Thus, it can significantly reduce the amount of usable fiber that enters the reject stream. Instead of using overflow design principles, ink removal is achieved by the controlled and continuous movement of the pulp within the cell past the opening (port) above the air/water interface.

INK REMOVAL EFFICIENCY. PDM has three distinct operation zones, which coincide with the three steps of ink removal. A key to the efficiency of PDM technology is that the three zones—aeration, mixing, and separation—have each been designed to operate separately and may be optimized independently.

In the aeration zone, controlled, pressurized air injection has replaced venturi-type devices found in conventional systems. With a venturi device, air intake is generally controlled and limited by the flow velocity of the pulp stream and may exhibit plugging tendencies. The pressurized air system allows independent adjustments to meet the requirements of a variety of pulp characteristics.

The mixing zone is designed to create high turbulent flow to increase the number of air/ink particle collisions. The design also produces a large spectrum of air bubble sizes to match the wide range of ink particle sizes typically found in ink-laden pulp slurries. Studies by Beloit have shown that ink removal efficiency with the flotation process is dependent on this correlation.

In the separation zone, the cell widens (slows pulp flow) to allow the air/ink agglomerations to rise to the surface. The air cushion found in this area is controlled much like that of an air-padded (pressurized) headbox. This design allows improved control of the pulp level within the cell, which in turn controls both fiber loss and ink removal as described previously.

First introduced in 1987, PDM technology is currently in use or under construction in 12 paper mills located throughout the world, producing newsprint, tissue, and fine paper.

The PDM is one of four installed on No. 1 deinking line at Snowflake.

Old magazines are hand sorted to keep contaminants out of the deinking system.

process, the use of OMG has increased the mill's flexibility in procuring supply. The downside to using OMG is that the quality of the raw material varies greatly and sometimes contains contaminants, which can cause severe operating restrictions.

Hancock explained, "The variability of the raw materials is a big factor. The raw material changes so much that the deinking system needs to be designed to handle the worst situation. With ONP, high alum content or low freeness fiber (high short-fiber content) generally are a lot tougher to handle. With OMG, there are special coatings (on covers and inserts) and glues in the binding that can turn a system upside-down. And in our system, we don't have separate pulpers for ONP and OMG, so we really rely on the screening and cleaning operations."

To help dilute the impact of OMG contaminants, the OMG stock is fed at a constant and controlled rate (interspersed with the ONP) into the continuous pulper in No. 1 system. In addition and to further reduce upsets, the mill has implemented a hand-sorting quality control operation to identify the amount of outthrows (unusable contaminants found in purchased bales of fiber).

Hancock points out that while this is a time-consuming process, it is relatively inexpensive compared with machine downtime or downgraded paper. He also believes that recyclers must continue to maintain quality, particularly in the face of mandated recycling. "The contamination problems could get worse," he added, "because the average person is not geared to thinking about how their recycling methods are going to affect the reuse of the recycled material. A lot of education needs to be done."

The precautionary measures taken, along with a greatly improved cleaner system, have allowed the mill to produce high-quality finished products. Hancock said that other than the occasional upset due to OMG contam-

inants or low-quality ONP, "we generally are able to run No. 1 and No. 2 news consistently."

CONSUMPTION AND SUPPLY. The mill currently uses approximately 665 tpd of ONP (245 tons in No. 1 deinking system and 420 tons in No. 2 deinking system) and about 105 tpd of OMG. The recycled fiber comprises about 65% of the total furnish for the mill's newsprint production. Semibleached kraft (from the chips) and stone groundwood (from the logs) constitute the other 35% of the mills total furnish.

To handle the demand of both deinking systems, the mill keeps about a 16-day supply in inventory, of which about 40% comes in by truck and 60% by rail. The fiber supply to support this use comes from as far north as Minneapolis and as far east as the Dallas/Ft. Worth area. However, most of the ONP comes from western cities such as Denver, Albuquerque, Tucson, and Phoenix. Some paper is bought in California when available, but much of the paper collected on the West Coast goes to export markets on the Pacific Rim.

Hancock said that the mill also gets "quite a bit of loose newsprint" collected from Sun City, Ariz., a retirement community. In an effort to secure fiber supplies on a more consistent and permanent basis, Stone Container recently announced a new partnership with Waste Management of North America. Stone will purchase all of its recycled fiber from the newly formed company, an equally held joint venture.

The mill's newsprint is sold to many major U.S. newspapers (including companies in Phoenix, Denver, Albuquerque, and Los Angeles) and to some foreign markets, including Rep. Korea. ∎

G. Merlin Hancock inspects a bale of ONP prior to the continous pulper.

Index